MISCELLANEOUS WORKS
Of Mr. John Greaves,
Professor of Astronomy
IN THE
University of *Oxford*:

Many of which are now first Published.

I. PYRAMIDOGRAPHIA; or a Description of the PYRAMIDS in *Egypt*. With a great many ADDITIONS and ALTERATIONS, from a Copy corrected by the AUTHOR.

II. A DISCOURSE of the *Roman* Foot, and DENARIUS; from whence, as from two Principles, the Measures and Weights used by the ANCIENTS may be deduced.

III. TRACTS upon various *Subjects*. *Letters*, *Poems*, and *Observations* in his *Travels* in *Italy*, *Turky*, and *Egypt*.

IV. A Description of the Grand SEIGNOR'S SERAGLIO.

To which are added,

I. REFLECTIONS on the PYRAMIDOGRAPHIA, written by an anonymous AUTHOR, soon after the Publication of that BOOK.

II. A DISSERTATION upon the SACRED CUBIT of the *Jews*, and the CUBITS of the several Nations; in which, from the Dimensions of the greatest *Egyptian* PYRAMID, as taken by Mr. GREAVES, the antient *Cubit* of *Memphis* is determined.

Translated from the *Latin* of Sir ISAAC NEWTON, Not yet published.

Adorn'd with SCULPTURES.

To the whole is prefix'd,
An HISTORICAL and CRITICAL ACCOUNT of the LIFE and WRITINGS of the AUTHOR.

In TWO VOLUMES.

Published by THOMAS BIRCH, M.A. F.R.S. and MEMBER of the SOCIETY of ANTIQUARIES, LONDON.

LONDON:
Printed by J. HUGHS, near *Lincoln's-Inn-Fields*, For J. BRINDLEY, Bookseller to his Royal Highness the Prince of *Wales*, in *New-Bond-Street*; and C. CORBETT, over-against St. *Dunstan's* Church, *Fleet-street*. 1737.

TO THE

Right Reverend Father in GOD,

THOMAS,

Lord Bishop of DERRY.

My Lord,

THE established reputation of the Author of the following tracts will excuse me from those apologies, which would be very proper, if I were to

A 2 offer

The Dedication
offer your Lordship any composition of my own. To rescue the writings of great men from obscurity, and to make them an easy purchase, is a design, which may justly claim the patronage of the most eminent for a true taste in polite and useful learning, and an hearty zeal for the promotion of it.

To give the reasons of addressing this collection to your Lordship, would be superfluous; since the character of the the late Lord Chancellor *Talbot*'s Friend is as great an endearment of you to those,

who

The Dedication.

who have not the honour
of your acquaintance, as
your own personal merits
are to those who have. On
these accounts with the utmost satisfaction I embrace
this publick opportunity of
professing myself,

My Lord,

Your Lordship's most obliged,

and most obedient

humble Servant,

1737.

Thomas Birch.

My Lord,

They who have not the honour of your acquaintance, and are to think who have, (for this account with the utmost satisfaction I embrace this publick opportunity of professing myself,

My Lord,

Your Lordship's most obliged,

[illegible signature lines]

AN

HISTORICAL and CRITICAL

ACCOUNT

OF THE

Life and Writings

OF

Mr. JOHN GREAVES.

MR. JOHN GREAVES was eldest son of the reverend Mr. JOHN GREAVES, rector of *Colmore*, near *Ailresford* in *Hampshire* (*a*), and the most eminent schoolmaster of that county (*b*). He was born at *Colmore*

(*a*) Vita Joannis Gravii, scriptore Thoma Smitho, S. T. D. p. 3. *printed among* Vitæ quorundam eruditissimorum & illustrium Virorum, scriptore Thomâ Smitho, S. T. D. & ecclesiæ Anglicanæ presbytero. Edit. Lond. 1707. in 4to.

(*b*) Id. ibid. & Wood, Athen. Oxon. Vol. II. col. 196. Edit. 2. Lond. 1721.

more in the year 1602 (*c*), and, being well grounded in grammar-learning, was sent to the university of *Oxford* in 1617 (*d*). *July* 6. 1621. he took the degree of Batchelor of Arts (*e*); and in 1624, being of Master's standing, became a candidate for a fellowship of *Merton College*, and, on account of his uncommon skill in philosophy and polite literature, was the first of the five who were elected (*f*). *June* 25. 1628. he took the degree of Master of Arts (*g*).

Having now read over all the *Greek* and *Latin* writers with great attention, he applied himself to the study of natural philosophy and mathematicks; and having contracted an intimate friendship with Mr. *Henry Briggs*, professor of geometry in the university of *Oxford*, Dr. *John Bainbridge*, professor of astronomy there, and Mr. *Peter Turner*, a senior fellow of his college, who afterwards succeeded Mr. *Briggs* in the professorship of geometry at *Oxford*; he was animated by their example to prosecute the study of the mathematicks and astronomy with indefatigable industry. And not content

---

(*c*). Smith, *ubi supra*.
(*d*) Wood, *ubi supra*.
(*e*) Id. Fasti Oxon. Vol. I. col. 218.
(*f*) Smith, p. 4.
(*g*) Wood, Fasti Oxon. Vol. I. col. 240.

tent to have read over the writings of *Copernicus*, *Regiomontanus*, *Purbach*, *Tycho Brahe*, *Kepler*, and other celebrated astronomers of that and the preceding age, he made the ancient *Greek*, *Arabian*, and *Persian* authors in that science familiar to him, having before gained an accurate skill in the oriental languages (*b*).

His reputation begun now to be so considerable, that *Feb.* 22, 1630 he was chosen professor of geometry in *Gresham College* at *London*, upon the resignation of Mr. *Peter Turner*; and at the same time held his fellowship of *Merton College* (*i*). By means of Mr. *Turner* he was introduced into the acquaintance and favour of Dr. *William Laud*, archbishop of *Canterbury*, and chancellor of the university of *Oxford* (*k*). He had now form'd a resolution of travelling into foreign countries; and it appears, that about the year 1635, before his voyage to the East, he went to *Paris* and *Leyden*, where he contracted a friendship with the celebrated *James Golius*. Dr. *Smith* was at a loss to determine, whether our author went to *Paris* and *Leyden*, before or after his voyage to the East. But it is evident, that he was at

Paris

(*b*) Smith, p. 5.
(*i*) Smith, p. 6.
(*k*) Wood, Athen. Oxon. Vol. II. col. 157.

Paris in 1635, from a paſſage in M. *Hardy*'s letter dated in that city *Sept.* 1. 1641, where he ſays, *Dubium eſſe tibi potuiſſe non exiſtimo, quin de tuo reditu in Europam maximum perciperem gaudium, vir eruditiſſime, pro eo affectu quo te colui, cum apud nos degeres.--- Ante* ANNOS SEX *cognovi te ſtudioſiſſimum linguæ Perſicæ.* It was probably at this time, that he went into *Italy*; for it appears from an original letter of his to Mr. *Edward Pocock* dated at *Greſham College, Dec.* 23. 1636, in the poſſeſſion of the reverend and learned Mr. *Leonard Twells,* that he had been in that country before his voyage into the Eaſt; and this is confirm'd by a paſſage in a *Latin* letter written from *Italy* by Mr. *George Middleton* to Mr. *Thomas Greaves* brother of our author, dated *Jan,* 18. 1635. and now in the hands of the very learned Sir *Richard Ellys,* Bart. But his grand deſign was to viſit the eaſtern countries, which, by means of the archbiſhop, he was enabled to do. Mr. *Wood* obſerves (*l*), " That his " Grace ſent him to travel into the eaſtern " parts of the world, to obtain books of " the languages for him. " And Dr. *Smith* informs us (*m*), " That Mr. *Greaves* fur- " niſh'd himſelf with quadrants and other
" inſtru-

(*l*) Athen. Oxon. Vol. II. col. 157.
(*m*) Pag. 7.

Mr. JOHN GREAVES.

"instruments neceffary for taking the altitudes and diftances of the ftars, and the latitudes of cities, for meafuring the pyramids, and making obfervations of the eclipfes, at his own expence, having in vain applied for the patronage and affiftance of the magiftrates of the city of *London*, whofe honour and advantage he defign'd to confult in this voyage; but that he was very probably affifted by the archbifhop, who gave him letters of recommendation to Sir *Peter Wyche*, ambaffador from king *Charles* I. to the Port, and a full power to purchafe, at whatever price he thought proper, any manufcripts of value, efpecially in the *Arabic* language." Mr. *Greaves* likewife in his Letter dated at *Conftantinople, Aug.* 2. 1638. and probably written to Mr. *Peter Turner*, obferves, "That the city of *London* had failed him in his expectations of their contributions towards mathematical inftruments; and that he had been neceffitated to fell moft of his books, which he brought with him; but that the love and care of his brothers ftraining their own occafions to fupply his, had enabled him, in defpite of the city, to go on with his defigns." He embark'd in the river of *Thames* in 1637 for *Leghorn*, from whence he proceeded to *Rome*, where he accurately view'd the venerable remains of antiquity there; and it appears from his note-book, that he not only wrote down the inscriptions, but likewise measured the pillars and other monuments there, and took a draught of them, particularly *Cestius's Pyramid* and the *Pantheon*. He view'd likewise the Catacombs, and examined all the principal cabinets and Museums in that city. Here he became acquainted with *Lucas Holstenius*, keeper of the *Vatican* library, *Athanasius Kircher*, famous for his learned writings, and *Gaspar Bertius*, a celebrated astronomer, who inform'd him, that he had found by repeated observations with a large instrument of *Clavius's*, that the altitude of the pole at *Rome* was 41 degrees and 46 minutes. From *Rome* he went to *Padua*, where he was introduced to the acquaintance of *Francis Ursati*, *John Rhodius*, and *Andrew Moretti*, professors there. Hence he went to *Florence*, where he staid a few weeks, and afterwards to *Legborn*, whence he embark'd for *Constantinople*. He arriv'd there about *April* 1638, and was very kindly received by Sir *Peter Wyche*, the *English* ambassador (n). In this city he became acquainted with *Cyrill Lucaris*, patriarch of

Con-

(n) Smith, p. 8, 9, 10.

Constantinople, who assisted him in procuring of *Greek* manuscripts. But his friendship with that learned and pious prelate was soon interrupted by the unhappy fate of the patriarch, who, thro' the contrivance of the Jesuits, was put to death on the 27th of *June*, by express command from Sultan *Amurath* IV. on pretence that he had sent letters to the Czar of *Muscovy*, by means of which, about two years before the *Muscovites* had surpriz'd a town upon the Black Sea belonging to the *Turks* (*o*).

Mr. *Greaves*, during his stay at *Constantinople*, was assured by some of the *Greeks*, that the library, which belong'd formerly to the Christian Emperors, was still preserved in the Sultan's palace. But as no Christian is allow'd access thither, he could not examine into the truth of that account (*p*); and Dr. *Smith* observes (*q*), "That there never "has been any opportunity since that time "of doing it; and that very little regard is "to be paid to the *Greeks*, who, out of va- "nity or a desire of pleasing, exaggerate "things extreamly, and invent stories with- "out the least colour of truth.

a 4 How-

(*o*) See Mr. *Greaves's* Letter dated from *Constantinople Aug.* 2, 1638; and Dr. *Thomas Smith's Miscellanies* printed at *London* 1686, in 8vo.

(*p*) Smith, Vita Joann. Gravii, p. 10.

(*q*) Ibid.

However, it appears from Mr. *Greaves*'s Letter from *Constantinople* dated *August* 2, 1638, that he believ'd there was a treasure of *Greek* and *Latin* authors in the Seraglio; for having obferv'd, that amongft other manufcripts he had procur'd *Ptolemy*'s *Almageft*, the faireft book he had ever feen, ftolen by a Spahy from thence, he writes thus: "Whereby you fee there is a poffibility of having alfo thofe *Greek* and *Latin* authors, which I mentioned in my former Letters to be buried in the Seraglio, if the * were handfomely followed by an ambaffador."

Mr. *Greaves* had a defign to have gone to *Mount Athos*, which is about four days journey by fea from *Constantinople*, whither he fhould have been recommended by the patriarch, and have had liberty of entering into all libraries in that place, in order to collect a catalogue of fuch books as either were not printed, or elfe by the help of fome there might have been more correctly publifh'd. Thefe the patriarch propos'd (by difpenfing with the anathema's, which his predeceffors had laid upon all *Greek* libraries, to fecure the books from the *Latins*) to have prefented to archbifhop *Laud*, for the better profecution of his Grace's defigns in the edition

---

* The word here is quite effac'd in the original Letter.

Mr. JOHN GREAVES.

tion of *Greek* authors. But the patriarch's death prevented Mr. *Greaves* from this journey (r). In his Letter from *Constantinople* dated *Aug.* 2. he observes, that he was in that month to depart for *Egypt*; but Dr. *Smith* tells us (s), that he embark'd for that country in the beginning of *September*; but being oblig'd to put in at *Rhodes*, he went ashore, and taking with him a brass astrolabe of *Gemma Frisius*, because he durst not make use of any larger instrument, for fear of giving suspicion to the *Turks*, he found the elevation of the pole there to be 37 degrees and 50 minutes (t).

At last he arrived at *Alexandria*, where he stay'd four or five months, and made a great number of useful observations. Hence he went twice (u) to *Grand Cairo*, to measure the Pyramids, carrying with him a Radius of ten foot most accurately divided into 10,000 parts, besides some other instruments, for the fuller discovery of the truth (w). While he was there, he made the measure of the foot observed by all nations,

(r) See Mr. *Greaves*'s Letter from *Constantinople* Aug. 2, 1638.
(s) Vita Joannis Gravii, p. 11.
(t) See his account of the Latitude of *Constantinople* and *Rhodes*.
(u) In 1638, and 1639.
(w) See his Preface to his *Pyramidographia*.

tions, in one of the rooms under the said Pyramids, with his name *John Gravius* under it (*x*). Having made a curious collection of *Greek*, *Arabic*, and *Persic* manuscripts, (a catalogue of which he afterwards sent to M. *Hardy* and *James Golius* at their request) with a great number of gems, coins, and other valuable antiquities, he returned to *Leghorn* about Midsummer 1639 (*y*). In a Letter to Mr. *Edward Pocock* dated there *June* $\frac{14}{24}$, he observes, that he had been near two months sailing thither from *Egypt*. From *Leghorn* he proceeded to *Florence*, where he was received with great civility by *Ferdinand* II. Grand Duke of *Tuscany*, to whom he inscrib'd a *Latin* Poem written by him at *Alexandria* in 1638, in which he exhorted that Prince to clear those seas from pirates, who extremely infested them. At *Florence* he contracted an intimacy with *Robert Dudley*, who was generally stil'd in *Italy* Duke of *Northumberland* (*z*), and was son of *Robert* Earl of *Leicester* by *Douglas Howard* daughter of *William* Lord *Howard* of *Effingham*, and widow of *John* Lord *Sheffield*. This gentleman endeavoured to prove his legitimacy in the beginning of the

reign

(*x*) Wood, Athen. Oxon. Vol. II. col. 157.
(*y*) Smith, p. 13.
(*z*) Id. ibid.

reign of King *James* I. in order to inherit the estate and titles of his father, and of his uncle *Ambrose* Earl of *Warwick*; but fail'd of his design thro' the endeavours of *Lettice* his father's widow, and therefore returned to *Florence*, where he had the title of Duke of *Northumberland* conferr'd upon him by *Ferdinand* II. Emperor of *Germany*, and became an excellent mathematician, physician, and navigator, and skill'd in all arts and sciences. He wrote *Arcano del Mare*, printed at *Florence* 1630 and 1646, in two Volumes in Folio (*a*). Mr. *Greaves* had frequent conversations with him upon subjects of learning, and was inform'd by him, that after a careful observation, and allowing for the refractions and parallax according to *Tycho Brahe*'s method, he found the elevation of the pole at *Florence* to be 43 degrees and 46 minutes (*b*). From *Florence* our author went to *Rome*, in order to repeat the observations which he had made there before, and to make new ones; and design'd to have staid there several months; but the desire of returning to his own country induc'd him to shorten his stay there; upon which he went to *Legborn*, where he took ship for *England*, and arrived there in the sum-

---

(*a*) Wood, Athen. Oxon. Vol. II. col. 126, 127.
(*b*) Smith, p. 13, 14.

summer of the year 1640 (*c*). *Nov.* 14. 1643 (*d*), upon the death of Dr. *John Bambridge*, which happened *Nov.* 3, he was chosen *Savilian* Professor of Astronomy in *Oxford*, and superior Reader of *Linacre*'s Lecture in *Merton College* (*e*), and had a dispensation from the King for holding his fellowship of that college, because the stipend belonging to his professorship was extremely lessen'd during the civil war (*f*). The the day following he was remov'd from his place of professorship at *Gresham College*, on account of his absence; and Mr. *Ralph Button* was chosen to succeed him. In 1645, he propos'd a method of reforming the Kalendar, by omitting the bissextile day for forty years to come (*g*). The paper which he drew up for this purpose was extremely approved of by the King and council; but the situation of public affairs at that time was such, that it was impossible to put it in execution (*h*).

In 1646 he publish'd his *Pyramidographia, or a Discourse of the Pyramids in Egypt. London* 1646, in 8vo.

Soon

(*c*) Id. ibid.
(*d*) Wood, Hist. & Antiq. Universit. Oxon. Lib. II. p. 42.
(*e*) Wood, Athen. Oxon. Vol. II. col. 157.
(*f*) Smith, p. 15.
(*g*) See his Tract upon the Reformation of the Kalendar.
(*h*) Smith, p. 16.

Soon after the publication of this discourse, some animadversions were written upon it by a gentleman of great learning, as Dr. *Smith* stiles him (*i*), tho' he does not name him; in which the animadverter endeavour'd to invalidate our author's observations, as if his instruments had been defective, or not well applied, thro' the neglect of some circumstances necessary to be observed in an accurate inquiry. Dr. *Smith* remarks (*k*), " That these animadversions
" did not want learning, but were ill-
" grounded and unjust, and that he should
" have wonder'd how the author would
" suffer them to fall from him, to the injury
" of his friend's reputation, which he had
" so justly acquir'd by his book, but that it
" appears from the history of those times,
" that he wrote the animadversions out of
" resentment to Mr. *Greaves*, who had re-
" fused him his interest for procuring a
" place, which he sollicited in vain.
Mr. *Greaves*, upon seeing these objections, applied himself with the utmost care to the revisal of his book, and upon repeated calculations found, that he had assign'd too small an height of the largest of the Pyramids, which he now discover'd to be 499 foot high,

instead

(*i*) Pag. 22.
(*k*) Ibid.

instead of 481, as he had affirm'd in his book, p. 69. l. 15. This correction he sent in a Letter to Dr. *Charles Scarborough*. He made a great number of alterations and additions in a copy of his book, which he presented to his brother Mr. *Thomas Greaves*, Fellow of *Corpus Christi College* in *Oxford*; agreeably to which improvements the present edition is publish'd. The *Pyramidographia* was translated into *French*, and printed in the first Volume of *Relations de divers Voyages* publish'd by M. *Thevenot*. Dr. *Smith* had some thoughts of translating this and the *Discourse of the Roman Foot and Denarius* into *Latin*, for the sake of Foreigners (*l*); but this design was never executed.

Dr. *Robert Hooke*, in his Discourse of Earthquakes (*m*), remarks some defects in our author's book. For having observ'd, with regard to the inquiry, "Whether the axis of
" the earth's rotation hath and doth conti-
" nually by a slow progression vary its
" position, with respect to the parts of the
" earth; and if so, how much, and which
" way, which must vary both the meridi-
" an lines of places, and also their particu-
" lar latitudes?" that *it had been very desirable, if from some monuments or records in an-*

(*l*) Smith, p. 22.
(*m*) Printed in his *Posthumous Works*, p. 355. Edit. Lond. 1705. in Fol.

antiquity, somewhat could have been discover-ed of certainty and exactness, that by com-paring that or them with accurate observa-tions now made or to be made, somewhat of certainty of information could have been pro-cur'd; he proceeds thus: "But I fear we "shall find them all insufficient in accurate-"ness to be any ways relied upon: how-"ever, if there can be found any thing cer-"tain and accurately done, either as to the "fixing of a meridian line on some build-"ing or structure now in being, or to the "positive or certain latitude of any known "place, tho' possibly these observations or "constructions were made without any re-"gard or notion of such an hypothesis; yet "some of them compared with the present "state of things, might give much light to "this inquiry. Upon this account I per-"us'd Mr. *Greaves*'s description of the "great Pyramid in *Egypt*, that being fabled "to have been built for an astronomical ob-"servation, as Mr. *Greaves* also takes notice: "I perus'd his book, I say, hoping I should "have found, among many other curious "observations he there gives us concerning "them, some observations perfectly made, to "find whether it stands east, west, north "and south, or whether it varies from that "respect of its sides to any other part or
"quarter

"quarter of the world; as likewise how
"much, and which way they now stand.
"But to my wonder, he being Astronomi-
"cal Professor, I do not find that he had
"any regard at all to the same, but seems
"to be wholly taken up with one inquiry,
"which was about the measure or bigness
"of the whole and its parts; and the other
"matters mention'd are only by the bye and
"accidental, which shews how useful theo-
"ries may be for the future to such as shall
"make observations; nay, tho' they should
"not be true, for that it will hint many in-
"quiries to be taken notice of, which would
"otherwise be not thought of at all, or at
"least but little regarded, and but superfi-
"cially and negligently taken notice of. I
"find indeed that he mentions the south and
"north sides thereof, but not as if he had
"taken any notice whether they were ex-
"actly facing the south or north, which he
"might easily have done. Nor do I find,
"that he hath taken the exact latitude of
"them; which methinks had been very
"proper to have been retained upon record
"with their other description. Here by the
"bye, because it agrees with a former con-
"jecture I here proposed, concerning those
"stupendous works, namely, that the core
"of them was probably some natural rock,
cut

"cut and shaped fit to be cased or cover'd
"with another sort of stone, which was at
"that time much contradicted by affirma-
"tions, that the whole country and place of
"their stations was nothing but sand. Give
"me leave to take notice, that Mr. *Greaves*
"doth affirm, that the great Pyramid is
"founded upon a natural rock, which riseth
"above the rest of the sand; and that the
"rooms about the second Pyramid are hew-
"en and shapen out of the natural rock;
"and I doubt not but that if they were all
"examin'd, they would be found to be so,
"and nothing else; which would much al-
"leviate the stupendous labour and work
"of men, that must otherwise have been
"suppofed to be made use of."

Upon this occasion we may observe, that M. *de Fontenelle* in his *Eloge de Monsieur de Chazelles* (n) tells us, that when that gentleman was in *Egypt*, he measur'd the *Pyramids*, and found, that the four sides of the largest of them were expos'd exactly to the four quarters of the world. Now as this accurate situation was in all probability designedly chosen by those, who rais'd that mass

———

(n) Histoire du Renouvellement de l'Academie Royale des Sciences en MDCXCIX. & les Eloges Historiques de tous les Academiciens morts depuis ce Renouvellement, Tom. II. p. 57, 58. Edit. Amst. 1720.

of stones above three thousand years ago; it follows, that during this long space of time there has been no alteration in the heavens in that respect, or, what amounts to the same, in the poles of the earth, or in the meridians.

In the *Miscellaneous Observations upon Authors ancient and modern*, Vol. I. (o) there are inserted some *Observations on the Dimensions of the greatest Egyptian Pyramid*, the author of which tells us, that upon reading the accounts of the measures of the great *Egyptian* Pyramid, as related in the *Universal History* (p), and remarking the great difference between the authors there mention'd, and especially concerning the perpendicular height in proportion to the base, he was desirous to see how these accounts would severally come out upon a true mathematical calculation, supposing the base to be a perfect square, upon which are placed four equilateral triangles, as is generally allow'd by authors; and to shew, if possible, how the differences of the ancient authors from one another might probably happen; and at the same time to offer a conjecture, in order to reconcile the dimensions given of this Pyramid by Mr. *Greaves* and Mr. *Chazelles*. As to

---

(o) Pag. 119. & seq. Edit. Lond. 1731. in 8vo.
(p) Pag. 186, 187, & 192.

to the proportion, which the perpendicular height bears to the base, Mr. *Greaves* tells us, that the altitude, if measured by its perpendicular, is 481 feet; but if taken as the Pyramid ascends, inclining, then is it equal, in respect of the lines subtending the several angles, to the latitude of the base.

Now to prove whether this height be justly calculated, according to the foregoing supposition, the following rule must be observed, *viz.* the perpendicular height of any equilateral Pyramid will be equal to the square root of half the square number of one of its sides. Mr. *Greaves* says, that the base of this Pyramid is 693 feet, which being squared, is 480249 feet, the half of which sum is 240124 1/5 feet, whose square root being extracted is 490 feet, which is the true perpendicular height, supposing it to end in a point. But as Mr. *Greaves* rightly observes, it does not end in a point, but only seems to do so to those, that stand below; which is owing to its great distance from the eye. Therefore the perpendicular height of the upper triangle, which is wanting, must be subtracted from the height already found, and the remainder will be the true height of the Pyramid. Now Mr. *Greaves* says, the flat stone, which terminates this Pyramid, is about 13 1/28 feet square, which number

being

being squared produces 176 | 3584 feet; the half of which is 88 | 1792 feet, whose square root is 9 | 39 feet; which subtracted from 490, the height already found, leaves 480 | 61 feet for the true height of the Pyramid; which shews, that Mr. *Greaves*'s height is exactly calculated in proportion to his base. *Straba* makes the height to exceed the breadth, and so consequently makes it an Isosceles triangle, whose sides must be much longer than the base. *Diodorus Siculus* makes the height something less, and so consequently nearer the truth. *Thevenot* says, the base is 682 feet, and its height 520 feet; but as these dimensions are given us in *French* measure, they must be reduced to *English*, that they may be more easily compared with Mr. *Greaves*'s. So then the base, according to *Thevenot*, will be 728 feet, and the height 555 feet; whereas it ought not to be more than 514 | 74 feet upon the foregoing supposition, and ending in a point, which is about 40 feet more than the true height in proportion to the base. *Gyllius*'s height, computed from his number and height of steps, is certainly a great deal too much, being no less than 937 | 5 feet, which is considerably more than the base; for he supposes 250 steps in all, of equal height, of about 3 feet 9 inches each; but it is much more probable,

ble, that they are not all of equal height, but rather diminish as the Pyramid. *Le Bruyn* makes his base 128 fathom, or about 704 feet, and its height 112 fathom, or 616 feet, which should not be above 498 feet; so that his height is too much by 118 feet in proportion to his base upon the foregoing supposition; except he means the perpendicular height of the triangle, and then it is not above 11 feet too high. This base of 704 feet exactly agrees with the number quoted from M. *Chazelles* by *Rollin* in his *History of the Egyptians*, but does not suit with the dimensions quoted from the same author (*Chazelles*) in the *Memoirs of the French Academy* for the years 1702 and 1708; for they make it 682 *French* feet, which correspond to 728 *English* feet; and the height of 77 ¹ toises, or 498 *English* feet, as *Rollin* quotes it, is the true height upon *Rollin*'s base of 704 feet; but by *Chazelles*'s base of 728 feet, as quoted by *Memoirs of the French Academy*, it ought to be 514 | 77 feet high to the point. The *Arabic* writers say, that the base is 460 cubits, and the height 317 cubits; which is but 8 cubits less than the true height in proportion to the base. Now by comparing the measures of the aforesaid authors together, we may easily observe which of them seems

seems to have taken the most care in measuring the Pyramid, and whose perpendicular height approaches the nearest in proportion to their bases. For instance, Mr. *Greaves*'s perpendicular is exactly in proportion to his base; and so is that of *Chazelles*. *Thevenot*'s is too much by about 40 feet; and the *Arabic* writers too little by only 8 cubits. The other authors, which are widely different, seem only to have guess'd at the height. But upon the whole, the author observes, that it may be safely concluded, that the base of this Pyramid is a square, or nearly so; and that the sides are equilateral triangles, whose dimensions are not less than Mr. *Greaves*'s, nor more than M. *Chazelles*'s; and this last author seems to be supported by several good authorities, agreeing with him in the same dimensions of the base, as will be seen in the sequel. As to the difference of the ancients in their measures of the base of this Pyramid, as between *Herodotus*, *Diodorus Siculus*, and *Strabo*, it might not happen thro' any neglect or carelesness of these authors in measuring, but from a difference in the length of the foot, and consequently of the *Stadia* or *Plethra*, which they make use of; for as the feet and miles are very different among the *Europeans*, so might they be among the *Grecians*,

ans, &c. And it is very probable, that if we could certainly know the true length of the aforesaid different measures, we should not see so considerable a difference in the base of the Pyramid, as at present appears. As to the quotation from *Wansleb* concerning one side's being a small matter longer than the other, there appears to be no difficulty in it. For, if this be true, yet in buildings of this prodigious bulk they must appear very near, if not exactly the same; and this may be the reason why Mr. *Greaves* differs 35 feet from the measure given us by M. *Chazelles, &c.* for they might measure different sides, and the sides appearing so near alike, they might take them for granted to be equal, and so not trouble themselves to measure any more than one; for this difference of 35 feet in 728 would scarce be perceptible, if it were laid down upon paper, tho' view'd upon a plane. And as to *Wansleb's* expression, that *the north side is longer than that which stretches from east to west,* it can mean no other, than that the line from north to south is longer than from east to west, thereby making the base of a parallelogram instead of a square.

 "But whether, continues the author of
" the *Observations,* this be the case or not,
" is uncertain; it is only hinted as a proba-
" ble

"ble conjecture, and may be a means of
"settling the difference between M. *Cha-*
"*zelles* and Mr. *Greaves,* the one a Mem-
"ber of the Royal Academy of Sciences,
"who went there on purpose in the year
"1693, to measure this Pyramid; and the
"other a person noted for his exactness in
"taking dimensions; so that without ima-
"gining some such method as this, one can-
"not avoid being surpriz'd at the difference
"between them, in measuring the same fi-
"gure, if they both measured the same side.
"Besides *Chazelles*'s measures are confirm'd
"by several other authors; as *Gemelli,* who
"made a voyage round the world in 1693,
"gives us the measures of this Pyramid as
"he received them from *Fulgentius* of *Tours,*
"a Capuchin mathematician, who found
"the breadth of the base of this Pyramid
"682 *French* feet, which answers to 728
"*English* feet, exactly the same as *Theve-*
"*not* found it in his voyage to the *Levant.*
"These measures also agree with those of
"M. *Jeaugeon* received from M. *de Noin-*
"*tel,* the *French* ambassador to the Port,
"which he communicated to the *French*
"academy. All these authors agreeing in
"the same measure, one cannot account
"for *Greaves*'s dimensions, except from the
"reason

"reason mentioned above, of the sides be-
"ing something different in length. Now
"supposing the base of the Pyramid to be a
"parallelogram, and that *Greaves* measured
"the shortest side, and the other authors the
"longest; I say, upon this supposition, the
"longest side will bring out 400 cubits, up-
"on *Greaves*'s length of a cubit, full as
"well as the shortest side, which he has sup-
"posed to be 380 cubits; and will agree
"with Dr. *Arbuthnot*'s round number of
"400 cubits, which he mentions in his book
"*of Weights and Measures*, as being the
"most probable number for an architect to
"choose in the setting out a great building:
"but it will not agree with his measure of a
"cubit, because he has divided 693 by 400,
"whereas upon this supposition it should be
"be 728 divided by 400."

In 1647, Mr. *Greaves* publish'd his *Discourse of the Roman Foot and Denarius: from whence, as from two principles, the measures and weights used by the ancients may be deduced*. Dr. *Edward Bernard*, professor of astronomy at *Oxford*, in his book, *de Mensuris & Ponderibus Antiquorum*, printed at *Oxford* in 1683, highly applauds this treatise of our author, whom he stiles *Justitiæ Romanæ diligentissimus Indagator*

Indagator (*q*), and in his manuscript lectures, cited by Dr. *Smith* (*r*), says, that his book is *aureus, imo supra aurum omne & metallorum Lucem pretiosus, luculentus*; and that he excell'd in diligence and learning *Agricola, Lucas Pætus, Villalpandus, Mersennus*, and others, who had written upon the same subject.

In a Letter to Mr. *Pocock*, dated *March* 25, 1647. Mr. *Greaves* writes thus: " I thank " God, I am thus far proceeded in my " troubles, that by the committee of Lords " and Commons I am pronounced innocent, " to the shame of my accusers, if they had " any. And now I am attending upon the " court of Aldermen, and the committee " at *Camden* house for restitution." And in another Letter to the same gentleman, dated *May* 17, 1648. he has the following passage: " I am now going into " *Kent*, to my good friend Mr. *Marsham* " (*s*) not far from *Rochester*, who hath " been very importunate, admitting of no " excuse, that I must make his house and " library, who hath a fair one, mine own. " It will be this fortnight e're I return, and, " it may be, shall afterward live with him, " if I see at my coming to *Oxford* the same
" confusion,

(*q*) Pag. 105.
(*r*) Vita Joan. Gravii, p. 37.
(*s*) Afterwards Sir *John Marsham*, author of the *Canon Chronicus*.

" confusion, which I hear, and which is like-
" ly in probability to continue."

The same year, he publish'd at *Oxford*, in 12mo, Dr. *John Bainbridge's Canicularia*, to which he added, *Demonstratio Ortus Sirii heliaci pro parallelo inferioris Ægypti, & Insigniorum aliquot Stellarum Longitudines & Latitudines ex Astronomicis Observationibus* Ulug Beigi, Tamerlanis magni Nepotis. Mr. *Greaves* dedicated this book to Dr. *George Ent*, fellow of the college of Physicians at *London*; and in the dedication observes, that Dr. *Bainbridge* wrote his *Canicularia*, at the request of Archbishop *Usher*. To which our author added, the *Demonstratio Ortus Sirii heliaci*, at the desire of that Prelate.

October 30, 1648. (*t*) he was ejected by the parliament visitors from his professorship of astronomy and fellowship of *Merton-College*, and oblig'd to quit the university, on pretence of his avoiding an answer to these articles alledg'd against him:
" 1. That he had betray'd the college, in
" discovering to the King's agents 400 *l.* in
" the treasury, which thereupon was taken
" away for the King's use. 2. That con-
" trary to his oath, he had convey'd away
" a

(*t*) Wood, Hist. & Antiq. Universit. Oxon. Lib. II. p. 42.

"a considerable part of the college goods,
"without the consent of the company, and
"thereby gratified courtiers with them in
"other houses. 3. That he feasted the
"Queen's confessors, and sent divers pre-
"sents to them, among which was an holy
"throne; and that he was more familiar
"with them, than any true Protestants use
"to be. 4. That he was the occasion of
"ejecting Sir *Nathaniel Brent* from his
"wardenship, for adhering to the parlia-
"ment, and bringing in Dr. *Harvey* (*u*)
"into his place. 5. That he was the occa-
"sion, why Mr. *Edward Corbet* and Mr.
"*Ralph Button* were turned out of their res-
"pective offices and chambers in the college,
"because they abode in the parliament's
"quarters, &c. 6. That he gave leave to
"father *Philips*, the Queen's confessor, and
"*Wyatt* *, one of her chaplains, to come
"into the college-library to study there;
"and that he put Mr. *John French*, a fellow,
"out of his chamber in *Merton*-college,
"and put them into it, &c. (*y*)." Among
our author's papers, I find that his brother,
Dr. *Thomas Greaves*, made the following
deposition

(*u*) Dr. *William Harvey*, the Physician, who discovered the circulation of the blood.
* *Veat*, a *Frenchman*.
(*y*) Wood, Athen. Oxon. Vol. II. col. 157.

deposition in his favour: "I, *Thomas* "*Greaves*, do testify, and will be ready to "depose, that Mr, *John Greaves*, fellow "of *Merton*-college, when the plate of "the said college was demanded by the "King, kept himself private in his cham- "ber for many days, that he might not "be present, nor give his consent: neither "did he go abroad till he had heard, "that the plate was already delivered."
Mr. *John Greaves* in a note upon this observes, that he had kept his chamber three weeks together at that time, under pretence of taking physic. His brother further depos'd, that "Mr. *John Greaves* left *Ox-* "*ford*, and lived privately in the country, "on purpose to avoid the delivering up of "such bonds, and other things, of Mr. "*Bainbridge*, deceased, which were in his "custody as executor, unto the commis- "sioners at *Oxford*."

Dr. *Walter Pope*, who erroneously calls our author *Edward* (*z*), observes (*a*), that he had been, *for a season, skreen'd against the fury of the visitation, by some powerful friends; yet finding 'twas impossible for him to keep his ground, he made it his business*

(*z*) Life of *Seth Ward*, Lord Bishop of *Salisbury*, Ch. IV. p. 18. Edit., *Lond.* 1697.
(*a*) Ibid.

to procure an able and worthy person to succeed him. Upon that design he took a journey to London, to advise with some knowing persons concerning that affair, and amongst the rest with Dr. Scarborough, who had then very great practice, and liv'd magnificently, his table being always accessible to all learned men, but more particularly to the distressed Royalists, and yet more particularly to the scholars ejected out of either of the universities for adhering to the King's cause.

"After mature consultation it was agreed
"upon by a general consent, that no person
"was so proper and fit for that employment,
"as Mr. *Ward*. Mr. *Greaves*, who had
"heard much of Mr. *Ward*, but had no
"acquaintance with him, readily consented
"to what they had concerted, and under-
"took to find Mr. *Ward* out, and make
"him the proffer; and accordingly he made
"a journey to *Oxford*. Mr. *Ward*, wholly
"ignorant of this design upon him, or ra-
"ther for him, rides casually from *Tame*
"*Park* in *Oxfordshire* (b), as he frequent-
"ly used to do, either to consult some
"books in the publick library, or to visit
"his friends and acquaintance. Just as he
"was

(b) A seat of the Lord *Wenman's*, who had invited Mr. *Ward* to his house.

"was entering the *Bear-Inn*, he luckily
"meets Mr. *Greaves* coming out of it, who,
"being inform'd who he was, accosted
"and courteously saluted him, testifying his
"great joy, by many kind expressions, for
"this fortunate and unexpected rencounter;
"after which taking him aside, he imparted
"his business, the design he had to have
"him for his successor, urging him with
"great importunity, not to deny him this
"favour. I remember, I heard the Bishop
"(c) say, that, among other arguments,
"Mr. *Greaves* told him, *If you refuse it,
"they will give it to some cobler of their
"party, who never heard of the name of
"Euclid, or the mathematicks, and yet will
"greedily snap at it for the salary's sake.*
"But Mr. *Greaves* was out in his divina-
"tion; for the other place, I mean the pro-
"fessor's of geometry, was fill'd by a very
"learned man in that science (d), as his ela-
"borate works have sufficiently manifested
"to the world. This address of Mr.
"*Greaves* did so surprise Mr. *Ward*, that
"it did at once assault his modesty, and
"perplex his counsel. After many thanks
"for so great and unexpected a favour, he
"objected the difficulty of effecting it; say-
  "ing

(c) *Ward.*
(d) Dr. *John Wallis.*

"ing, he could not with any reason expect to
"enjoy quietly a publick professor's place in
"*Oxford*, when 'twas notoriously known,
"that he was turn'd out of *Cambridge*, for
"refusing the covenant. Mr. *Greaves*
"replied, that he and his friends had con-
"sider'd that obstacle, and found out a way
"to remove it. And it was effectually re-
"moved a little while after, by means of
"Sir *John Trevor*, who, tho' of the par-
"liament party, was a great lover of learn-
"ing, and very obliging to several scholars,
"who had been turned out of the two uni-
"versities. Sir *John* had great interest in
"the committee, which dispos'd of the places
"of those, who were ejected; and by that
"brought Mr. *Ward* into the professor's
"chair, and preserv'd him in it, without
"taking the covenant, or engagement (*e*)".
Dr. *Pope* then observes (*f*), that when Mr.
Ward was settled in the professor's chair,
he procur'd for Mr. *Greaves* the full ar-
rears of his salary, amounting to five hundred pounds; for part, if not all the land
allotted to pay the Savilian professors, lies
in Kent, which county was in the power of
the parliament, who withheld the money;
and it had been difficult, if not impossible
for

(*e*) Life of *Seth Ward*, p. 18, 19, 20, 21.
(*f*) Ibid. p. 21.

for Mr. *Greaves, who was not rectus* in *Curia, ever to have recover'd it. And he* (g) *also design'd him a considerable part of his salary; but Mr.* Greaves *died soon after.* But Dr. *Pope* is mistaken in asserting, that our author died *soon after* he lost his professorship, since he surviv'd it about four years. Mr. *Greaves*, upon his ejectment, had his chests broken open by the soldiers, and his papers and manuscripts taken from him; part of which were lost, and the rest recovered by him, by means of his friend Mr. *Selden* (h). He then retir'd to *London*, where he married, and prosecuted his studies with great vigour.

In 1649 (i), he published at *London* in 4to, *Elementa Linguæ Persicæ*. In the Dedication to Mr. *Selden*, he observes, that he drew up this Grammar of the *Persian* language, at the request of that gentleman, who approved of it; and that he propos'd to have published it nine years before, but wanting types, and being diverted by other affairs, and particularly his journey into the east, he had been obliged to suspend the edition. To this he subjoins, *Anonymus Persa de Si-ghi*

(g) Mr. *Ward*.
(h) Smith, p. 33.
(i) Or rather 1648, the Printers usually anticipating part of the following year.

glis Arabum & Perfarum Aftronomicis, printed at *London* 1648, in 4*to.* In the Dedication to *Claudius Hardy,* dated at *London, July* 28, 1648. he obferves, that tho' many perfons had written of the *Siglæ* of the *Jews,* which occur every where among the *Rabbins*; yet no writer had publifh'd any account of thofe ufed by the *Arabians* and *Perfians,* efpecially in their aftronomical tables. Mr. *Greaves* having met, at *Conftantinople,* with this anonymous *Perfian* writer, who explains this fubject with great clearnefs and accuracy; thought it not improper to be join'd to his *Elementa Linguæ Perficæ,* which he had begun at *Paris,* at Monfieur *Hardy's* follicitation.

In a Letter to Mr. *Pocock,* dated at *London, Nov.* 15. 1649. he writes thus: " Mr. *Seaman* " and myfelf are both in hand with a *Turkifh* " Dictionary."

In 1650, our author publifhed at *London* in 4*to. Epochæ celebriores, Aftronomis, Hiftoricis, Chronologicis, Chataiorum, Syro-Græcorum, Arabum, Perfarum, Chorafmiorum, ufitatæ, ex traditione* Ulug Beigi, *Indiæ citra extraq; Gangem Principis. Eas primus publicavit, recenfuit, & Commentariis illuftravit* Johannes Gravius.

This is dedicated to the republic of *Venice,* to which he addreffes a compliment in elegant *Latin* verfe. In order to render

thefe

these *Epochæ*, which are of great importance for correcting a vast number of errors in our books of chronology, the more intelligible, Mr. *Greaves* has reduced them to the *Julian* Period, and the vulgar *Dionysian Æra* of Christ, and added a *Praxis* of the tables, with proper *Lemmata* and examples.

To this work he subjoin'd, *Chorasmiæ & Mawaralnahræ, hoc est, Regionum extra Fluvium Oxum Descriptio ex Tabulis Abulfedæ Ismaelis, Principis, Hamah:* London, 1650, in 4to. Dedicated to Archbishop *Usher*. In the *Preface* he observes, that he collated these *Tables* of *Abulfeda*, with five manuscripts; one which belong'd to *Erpenius*, and was transcribed from a manuscript in the Elector of *Palatine*'s library; another, which was the very manuscript, from which *Erpenius*'s copy was taken, and remov'd to the *Vatican* library; two others, in Mr. *Edward Pocock*'s library; and the fifth bought by Mr. *Greaves* at *Constantinople*. By the assistance of those he corrected a great many errors in each of the tables; but never made the least alteration, unless where the case evidently required it, or the greatest part of the manuscripts justified it.

Learned men had long wish'd for, or promised to publish the Tables of the celebrated *Abulfeda*.

Ramusius seems to have been the first, who cited them, and shewed the use of them. After this *Castaldus*, an eminent geographer, corrected a great many passages in them relating to *Asia*, which he had undertaken the description of, especially with regard to the longitudes and latitudes of places, which had been before corrupted. Next followed the learned and judicious *Ortelius*, who, in his *Thesaurus Geographicus*, frequently mentions them; not as having seen them himself, but upon the authority of *Castaldus*. *Erpenius* regretted, that the whole work of *Abulfeda* was not publish'd, and promised an edition of it; but, being prevented by death, left it to *William Schickard*, who, in his *Tarick seu Series Regum Persiæ* (k), gave the world, out of *Abulfeda*, a great many curious things, till then unknown to the *Europeans*, and illustrated the geography of the eastern countries, by means of the manuscript of *Vienna*, communicated by the noble *Tengnagelius*. But *Schickard*, in a Letter to Mr. *Greaves*, observ'd that this manuscript of *Vienna*, which he had made use of, was in a variety of places impossible to be read, and generally very doubtful in the numbers; so that no tables, or at least only very incorrect ones,

---

(k) Printed at *Tubingen* 1628, in 4to.

ones, could be form'd by it. Our author therefore undertook this work, in the midſt of his own private misfortunes and anxiety, and the publick calamities; and compleated it. He informs us, that *Abulfeda* ſucceeded his brother, as Prince of *Hamah* in *Syria*, in the year of the *Hejira* 743, or of the Chriſtian *Æra* 1342, and died in the year 746 of the *Hejira*; and for this he quotes the author of a book, intituled, *Al Sacerdan*. But the learned Mr. *George Sale* in the article of Abu'lfeda, in the *General Dictionary Hiſtorical and Critical* (*l*), has ſhewn, that the paſſage cited by our author from *Al Sacerdan*, (or rather *Al Sukkerdân*, which is a *Perſian* word, and ſignifies a *ſugar-diſh*) does not relate to our *Abulfeda*, but to another, who was a King of *Egypt*, and did not begin his reign till ten years after our *Abulfeda*'s death. Mr. *Gagnier* (*m*) had before diſcovered this miſtake of Mr. *Greaves*, but committed ſome inaccuracies in his examination of it, which are taken notice of by Mr. *Sale*. But to proceed to Mr. *Greaves*'s *Preface*, he obſerves, that the title of this work of *Abulfeda* in the *Arabick* ſignifies *Canon*, or rather *Rectificatio Terrarum*; and and that it is declared at the concluſion of

the

(*l*) Vol. I. p. 115. Edit. Lond. 1734. in Fol.
(*m*) In Præfat. ad Abulf. Vitam Moh. p. 4. & ſeq.

the work, that it was finished in the 721st year of the *Hejira*, or of the Christian *Æra* 1321. It appears to be compiled from the principal *Arabian* writers, about sixty of whom Mr. *Greaves* remarks to be cited in it.

With regard to the method of these tables, he observes, that *Ptolemy* and the rest of the *Greek* and *Latin* writers compute the longitude of places from the fortunate islands; and that the ancient *Arabians* follow the *Greeks* in that point. But *Abulfeda* and some others compute from the extreme promontory, which runs out into the *Atlantic* ocean. Hence appears the reason why, in some of the astronomical tables and geographical charts of the *Arabians, Alexandria* in *Egypt* is in fifty one degrees of longitude, in others in sixty one degrees; the former computing from the shore of the *Atlantic* ocean, the latter from the fortunate islands: But the *Indian* geographers and astronomers have a quite different method of computing the longitude; for they draw the first meridian in the east thro' *Caneador*, contrary to the *Greeks, Latins, Persians, Arabians*, and others, who fix it in the west; as appears from *Ali Kofhgi*, an eminent *Persian* astronomer, in his Institution of astronomy. With regard to the climates,

Abulfeda

Abulfeda takes a method very different from the common one. The ancient *Greek* writers reckon seven climates; in which number they are followed by the *Arabians* and *Persians*. But *Abulfeda*, besides these seven climates, which are real and κατὰ θέσιν, depending on the length of the days, assigns twenty eight others, καθ' ὑπόθεσιν. In his tables therefore he distinguishes between *Clima verum* and *Clima cognitum*; " the
" latter being, *says he*, any country or king-
" dom, which contains several provinces or
" tracts of land; as *Syria*, *al Erak*, and
" other countries. Sometimes *Clima cogni-*
" *tum* is part of one true climate, some-
" times of two; as *Syria* is partly in the
" third, and partly in the fourth climate.
" Sometimes *Clima cognitum* contains part
" of seven climates, as it is reported of *China*;
" the latitude of which is said to exceed the
" latitude." The reason why *Abulfeda* reckons *Arabia*, or, as he calls it, the *Peninsula of Arabia*, the first climate, was on account of the temple of God, and the sepulchre of *Mahomet*, which are seated there. Mr. *Greaves* then proceeds to explain the measures of the distances of places used by *Abulfeda*.

In the same year our author publish'd at *London* in 12mo, *A Description of the Grand Seignior's Seraglio, or the Turkish Emperor's Court,*

Court, written by Mr. *Robert Withers*, and dedicated by Mr. *Greaves* to his *honoured and truly noble friend*, GEORGE TOOKE, Esq; In the Dedication he observes, that this *is a piece of that exactness, as the like is not extant in any other language*; that he *assumes nothing to himself, either as author of the discourse, or as publisher of it*; that *it was freely presented him at* Constantinople; and that the name of the author being then unknown, upon enquiry he had since found it to be the work of Mr. *Robert Withers*, " who by the favour of the *English* ambas-
" sador, procuring him admittance into the
" Seraglio (a courtesy unusual) and by con-
" tinuance many years in those parts, had
" time and opportunity to perfect his ob-
" servations. To him therefore are solely
" due the thanks of his labour; to me it is
" sufficient, that I have faithfully dischar-
" ged my trust, in publishing, since the au-
" thor's death, the fruits of his travels, and
" in communicating to the reader the plea-
" sure and satisfaction of perusing a rela-
" tion full of truth and exactness". It appears, that Mr. *Greaves* did not know, that this piece was already printed (tho' very imperfectly, compar'd with his edition) in Mr. *Purchas's Pilgrims*, Part II. Lib. IX. c. 15. p. 1580, *& seqq.* Edit. *Lond*. 1625,

1625, in *Fol.* and in the *Preface* to it we have the following words: "It is a royal "present worth the receiving, to set thee "in possession, and make thee master of "the Grand Seignior's Seraglio; a sight "hitherto prohibited in a manner to Chri- "stian eyes.—These hath Mr. *Robert Wi- "thers* collected after his ten years observa- "tion at *Constantinople*, where he was edu- "cated by the care and cost of that late "honourable ambassador from his Majesty "Sir *Paul Pindar*, and well instructed by "*Turkish* schoolmasters in the language, and "admitted also to further sight of their un- "holy holies, than is usual.

In 1652 our author publish'd at *London*, in Quarto, *Astronomica quædam ex traditione* Shah Cholgii Persæ: *una cum Hypothesibus Planetarum: studio & operâ* Johannis Gravii *nunc primum publicata*. In the Dedication to *John Marsham*, Esq; afterwards Sir *John Marsham*, dated at *London, Oct.* 1. 1650, he observes, that it was upon his sollicitations that *Marsham* was induced to publish his *Diatriba Chronologica*, printed at *London*, 1649, in Quarto, and dedicated to Mr. *Greaves*; who, in the Preface to his *Astronomica quædam*, tells us, that it was very near four hundred years before, that *Gerardus Cremonensis*, a man excellently

skill'd

skill'd in the *Arabic* language, tho' not so well vers'd in astronomy, publish'd theories of the planets. His errors, which were every were received in the schools, and rashly adopted by the ignorant professors of the sciences, were first refuted by *Regiomontanus* (*l*); a little before whose time *George Purbach* (*m*), an eminent astronomer, and *Regiomontanus*'s master, seeing these studies neglected, because no person had laid down the elements of the science in a solid and perspicuous manner, wrote his book *de Theoricis Planetarum*, by which he facilitated the reading of *Ptolemy* and the ancient astronomers. Tho' this was done long before by *Ptolemy* himself in his old age, (not to mention a great number of *Arabian* and *Persian* writers after him, particularly *Albattani*, *Alfergan*, *Costa Ebn Luka*, *Nassir Eddin*, and *Kushgi*;) for *Ptolemy*, having finish'd his Μεγάλη Σύνταξις, subjoin'd to it his treatise *de* περὶ Ὑποθέσεων Πλανωμένων, i. e. *De Hypothesibus Planetarum*, with a view either to refresh his own memory, or to assist the youth. But this piece continued in obscu-

(*l*) He was born *June* 6, 1436. and died *July* 6, 1476. Vide *Petr. Gassendum in Vita Johann. Regiomontani*, p. 67, 92. Edit. Paris 1654. in 4to.

(*m*) He was born *May* 30, 1423. and died *April* 7, 1461. Vide *Gassendum in Vita Georgii Purbachii*, p. 58, 74.

obscurity, scarce known to the *Greeks*, much less to the *Latins*, till Dr. *John Bainbridge* publish'd it with *Proclus*'s *Sphæra* at *London* 1620 in 4to. *Purbach* is therefore highly to be commended for being the first after the restoration of learning in *Europe*, who wrote a short introduction into the more abstruse parts of the science.

Since his time there have been publish'd several treatises upon the elements of astronomy, or commentaries upon that writer. Amongst these the most eminent are *Erasmus Rheinhold* and *Michael Mæstlin*, the latter of whom is frequently recommended by *Tycho Brahe*. But Mr. *Greaves* observes, that it must be confess'd, that even these writers, tho' otherwise very valuable, have not explain'd every thing to such advantage, as an attentive reader could wish. For, to omit other defects, we meet in them a great number of barbarous terms unknown to the *Latin* language, but every where used in the writings of astronomers, the origin of which is requisite to be understood. For since the time that *Alphonsus*, King of *Castille*, had with immense cost, by the assistance of the *Jews*, *Moors*, and *Arabians*, whom he sent for from all parts, form'd the tables, which bear his name, this mass of exotic words overspread the *Latin* writers

ters upon astronomy. Hence came the words *Juzahar, Zenith, Nadir, Buth*, with a prodigious variety of others, either taken from the *Arabians*, or form'd in imitation of them. Mr. *Greaves* gives some instances of this, and remarks, that in the time of *al Mamon* (by whose direction the *Greek* writers were first translated into *Arabic* at *Babylon*) all the books of science, especially physic and mathematicks, came out of the *Arabian* schools; so that it is no wonder, if, even in this more enlighten'd and polite age, there are still retain'd some words, which discover their first origin. For it happens in science as in the names of countries and places, that what has once been commonly received, will scarce be obliterated by length of time. Mr. *Greaves* therefore thought it would not prove unacceptable to the republic of letters, to trace up these exotic words to their original, and for that purpose to fix upon some genuine and approv'd writer. But as it was of no importance whether this was a *Persian* or *Arabian* author, since both nations us'd the same technical expressions; he chose the short tract here publish'd, taken from the Commentaries of *Mahmud Shah Cholgi*. From this the reader will receive a double advantage; for those, who are conversant

in

in astronomy, will see the origin of several words without which the tables us'd, by the *Arabians* as well as the *Persians* and *Indians*, cannot be understood; and perceive that the celestial hypotheses of those nations are exactly conformable to those of *Ptolemy*; and have them succinctly and clearly explain'd here, and adapted to the motions of the planets from the accurate observations of *Nassir Eddin* in the city of *Maraga*. Those likewise, who study the oriental tongues, will be pleas'd to see a book publish'd in the genuine *Persian* language; since what has hitherto been publish'd in that tongue, and particularly the *Pentateuch* by *Tawush* the *Jew*, and *Xavier*'s *Historia Christi & Petri* publish'd by *Ludovicus de Dieu* at *Leyden* in 1639, are full of barbarisms and improprieties. Mr. *Greaves* concludes his Preface with remarking, that *Shah Cholgi* flourish'd in the year 866 of the *Hejira*, and 1461 of the Christian Æra; at which time he compos'd his Commentaries upon the Historical Tables dedicated by *Nassir Eddin* to *Hechan Tatar*. Whether he wrote any thing besides the Commentaries (part of which Mr. *Greaves* here publishes) is not known; but that gentleman tells us, that these alone are sufficient to correct a great many errors in astronomy; and to confute divers assertions

tions in chronology, receiv'd upon the authority of *Joseph Scaliger*; and to explain a variety of things in the *Arabian* writers, especially the mathematicians.

To this book he subjoin'd *Binæ Tabulæ Geographicæ, una* Neffir Eddini *Perfæ, altera* Ulug Beigi Tatari. *Opera & studio* Johannis Gravii *nunc primum publicatæ:* Lond. 1652. in 4to. dedicated to his friend Mr. *Edward Pocock*, and his brother Mr. *Thomas Greaves*. In the *Preface* he tells us, that having, at the follicitation of several learned men, undertaken an edition of the *Geographical Canon* of *Abulfeda*, he thought proper to publish first these two tables, by which he hop'd at present to satisfy the impatience of those, who were so importunate for the edition of *Abulfeda*, by whose assistance they imagin'd geography might be illustrated and plac'd in a right view. Mr. *Greaves* remarks, that these learned men had form'd a just notion of *Abulfeda*; but appear not to have known, that several other *Arabian* writers have treated extremely well of the subject of geography. For, to omit others, *Ebn Haukal* wrote a large work, in which he discourses very accurately of every thing remarkable in each country. *Al Edrisi*, in his book *concerning Kingdoms and Empires*, describes exactly the situation of cities and

places,

places, the boundaries of each nation, and their longitude and latitude. The same design is executed by *Ebn Chordadabah*, an eminent *Arabian* geographer. *Yacut al Hamawi* has compiled a geographical *Thesaurus*, of great use to those, who study the oriental languages. But these writers are all excell'd by *Abu al Rihan al Birun*, an admirable mathematician, who, in imitation of *Ptolemy*, wrote a geographical canon about six hundred and sixty years before Mr. *Greaves* wrote. And to pass over other writers, (about thirty of whom are cited in the geography of *Abulfeda*), *Gabriel Sionita* and *John Hesronita* publish'd the *Geographia Nubiensis*, with a *Latin* version; tho' the *Arabic* edition at *Rome*, which those learned men follow'd, is rather to be consider'd as an imperfect abridgment of *al Edrisi*, who flourish'd in the year 548 of the *Hejira*, and of the Christian *Æra* 1153, than a compleat work; as appears from two manuscripts, one bought by Dr. *Pocock* in *Syria*, and the other purchas'd by Mr. *Greaves* in *Egypt*, written in *African* letters, tho' very ancient, and with elegant maps.

The first table, publish'd by Mr. *Greaves* in this volume, was made by *Nassir Eddin*, who flourish'd about the year 660 of the *Hejira*, and was an eminent *Persian* mathematician

matician and astronomer, and is highly commended by *Gregory Abu'l Faragius*. The historians relate, that presenting a book written by himself to *Mostaasem*, the last Kalif of *Babylon*, and being treated with contempt by the Kalif, he was so exasperated, that he went to *Holach Chân*, Prince of the *Tartars*, and persuaded him to make war upon *Mostaasem*, whose army was defeated, and himself with his four sons slain by *Holac Chân*, after the taking of *Babylon*. By this event the empire and name of the *Abbassidæ*, which had flourish'd about five hundred years in *Asia*, were entirely extinguish'd. It is probable, that *Nassir Eddin* was advanc'd to great honours by *Holac*, and had a considerable share in his friendship; and under his patronage form'd the astronomical tables, which he stil'd the *Ilechan Tables* from *Ilechan* King of the *Tartars*, by the assistance of the most famous mathematicians in the city of *Maraga*. *Mahmud Shah Cholgi* prefers these tables to all others; and Mr. *Greaves* remarks, that if they had been known to the *Europeans* in the preceding ages, those monstrous hypotheses of an eighth heaven, long before introduc'd by *Thebet Ebn Corrah*, would have been exploded. Mr. *Greaves* therefore extracted this table out of his collection, which he

thinks

thinks will be of great advantage in illustrating the geography of the remotest parts of *Asia*, most of which *Naffir Eddin* had seen and travell'd over, and given an accurate account of the rest from the writings of the *Indians* and *Arabians*. The other table was made by *Ulug Beig*, King of *Parthia* and *India*, and grandson of *Timurlan* the Great, who residing in ease and affluence at *Samarkand*, his metropolis, exercis'd himself in the study of mathematicks and astronomy, and having sent from all parts for astronomers, (the principal of whom were *Giyath Eddin Jamshid*, and *Ali Kushgi*, author of a famous book concerning the Elements of Arithmetic and Astronomy) and furnish'd them with instruments, observ'd the *Phænomena* of the heavens with the utmost accuracy, and form'd from thence his tables, which are celebrated over the whole East, in the year 841 of the *Hejira*, and 1437 of the Christian *Æra*. Among these, according to the custom of astronomers, is rank'd the geographical table here publish'd by Mr. *Greaves*; who observes, that he was inform'd at *Constantinople* by some *Turkish* astronomers of no mean parts and skill, upon remarking the agreement between the observations of *Tycho Brahe* and those of *Ulug Beig*, that the latter, besides his

other

other most exact instrument, had procur'd a quadrant, the Radius of which equall'd in length the height of the dome of St. *Sophia*. This account the *Turks* had from *Persians* of credit. Mr. *Greaves* leaves the reader to believe as much of this relation as he pleases; but remarks, that very large instruments were absolutely necessary to take the height of the pole at *Samarkand*, (where *Ulug Beig* reign'd, according to *Emir Cond*, above forty years;) for he makes it to be 39 degrees, 37 minutes, and 23 seconds; from whence we may conclude his prodigious accuracy in the rest of his observations.

Mr. *Greaves* did not live long after the publication of this book, for he died *Oct.* 8, 1652 (*n*), being now fifty years of age; and was interr'd in the church of St. *Bennet Sherehog* in *London* (*o*). Dr. *Gerard Langbaine* in a Letter to Mr. *Selden*, dated at *Queen's College, Oxford, Oct.* 22, 1652, writes thus upon occasion of our author's decease: "For
" Mr. *John Greaves*, I was seized of the
" sad news of his death. I have in him lost
" a friend, and learning a great support.
" What he had of his own, as author, I hope
" his

(*n*.) *Desiderata Curiosa*. By *Francis Peck*, M. A. Vol. II. Lib XIV. p. 25. Edit. Lond. 1735. in Fol.

(*o*) Smith, p. 33. & Wood, Athen: Oxon. Vol. II. col. 158.

" his brothers, or some knowing friends,
" will be careful to preserve. You know
" he was owner of some *Arabic* books,
" which (I believe) are not to be found in
" *Europe* again. Unless you think fit to buy
" them yourself, I would willingly put in
" for this University. We shall be able
" to compass some of them, and (I hope) in
" time, by means of Mr. *Pocock* and such
" of his scholars here as are ingenious and
" studious, to make use of them. And
" methinks it is a disgrace to our nation,
" that such commodities should pass from
" hence to *France,* or *Sweden*, or the *Low*
" *Countries.*"

Besides those works, which he had publish'd, some other pieces of his were printed since his death, *viz.* I. *Lemmata* Archimedis *apud Græcos & Latinos jampridem desiderata, è vetusto codice manuscripto Arabico à* Johanne Gravio *traducta, & nunc primum cum Arabum scholiis publicata. Revisa & pluribus mendis repurgata à* Samuele Foster, Publish'd at *London* 1659. Fol. in a book intitled, *Miscellanea, sive Lucubrationes Mathematicæ* Samuelis Foster, *olim Londini in Collegio Greshamensi Astronomiæ Professoris publici. Omnia in lucem edita, & pleraq; Latinè reddita, operâ & studio* Johannis Twysden, *C. L. M. D. qui etiam ex* *suis nonnulla adjunxit.* Our author in his Letter to archbishop *Usher,* dated *Sept.* 19, 1644, speaks thus of his translation of the *Lemmata:* " I have finish'd those *Lemmata* " of *Archimedes,* ..... and, if I be not de- " ceiv'd, such as wish well to the Mathema- " ticks, will think my pains well be- " stow'd; as indeed it was no small labour " to correct the Diagrams and the Letters " (which were too often perverted in the " manuscript) and sometimes to supply what " was defective in the Demonstration itself." II. *Of the Manner of hatching of Eggs at Cairo.* Publish'd by Sir *George Ent,* in the *Philosophical Transactions* for *January* and *February* 1677, N° 137. p. 923. It is not improbable, that the Emperor *Hadrian* might allude to this custom in his Letter to *Servianus* the Consul, in which he speaks thus of the *Egyptians* [*] : *Nihil illis opto, nisi ut suis pullis alantur; quos quemadmodum fœcundant, pudet dicere.* III. *An Account of the Longitude and Latitude of* Constantinople *and* Rhodes; *directed to the most Reverend* James Usher, *Archbishop of* Armagh. Publish'd by Dr. *Thomas Smith* in the *Philosophical Transactions* N° 178. for *December* 1685. Reprinted in *A Collection of curious Travels and Voyages,* publish'd by Mr. *John Ray,*

[*] Vopiscus in Saturnino.

Ray, Tom. II. p. 84. & seqq. 2d. Edit. Lond. 1705, in 8vo. IV. *Reflexions on a Report made by the Lord Treasurer* Burleigh *to the Lords of the Council of the Consultation had and the Examination of the plain Discourse and humble Address for our gracious Queen* Elizabeth, *her most excellent Majesty to peruse and consider, as concerning the needful Reformation of the vulgar Kalendar, for the civil years and days accompting & verifying according to the time truly spent, by* John Dee, *Martii* 25. 1582. Mr. *Greaves*'s *Reflexions* were publish'd by Dr. *Thomas Smith* in the *Philosophical Transactions*, Vol. XXI. Nº. 257. for *October* 1699. V. *An Account of some Experiments for trying the Force of great Guns,* by Mr. *John Greaves.* Publish'd by Mr. *Richard Stubbs*, Rector of *East Hamsted* in *Berkshire*, in the *Philosophical Transactions*, Nº 173. p. 1090. for *July* 1685. VI. *Descriptio Peninsulæ Arabicæ ex* Abulfeda. *Arabicè & Latinè.* He design'd to have publish'd this in 1645; but was prevented by the civil wars. The translation was inserted together with the original, by Mr. *Gagnier*, in the third Volume of Dr. *John Hudson*'s *Geographiæ Veteris Scriptores Græci Minores*; from which edition chiefly M. *la Roque* made his *French* translation of the same Description of *Arabia*, subjoin'd

liv   *The LIFE of*

d'Arvieux's Journey to Palestine*. Mr. *Greaves* had likewise prepared for the press the following works. I. *Tabulæ integræ Longitudinis & Latitudinis Stellarum fixarum juxta* Ulug Beigi *Observationes.* He collated these Observations with five manuscripts, in order to render his edition as correct as possible. He left this book in the hands of Archbishop *Usher.* Dr. *Thomas Hyde*, not knowing any thing of this work of our author, publish'd the same Observations with a *Latin* translation and notes at *Oxford* in 1665, under this title: *Versio Latina e Linguâ Persicâ, & Commentarii in Observationes* Ulug Beigi *de Tabulis Longitudinis & Latitudinis Stellarum fixarum*; dedicated to Dr. *Seth Ward*, then Bishop of *Exeter*; and afterwards of *Sarum*. II. He had prepar'd a translation of *George Chrysoccoca* out of *Persian* manuscripts into *Greek*, as he found that piece among the *Baroccian* manuscripts in the *Bodleian* Library; and a Table containing the Longitude and Latitude of twenty five of the most considerable fix'd Stars; and another Table, or Κανόνιον τȣ̂ μήκȣς καὶ πλατȣ̂ς τῶν ἐπισήμων πόλεων. These tables were publish'd by *Ismael Bulliadus*, in the Appendix to his *Astronomia Philolaica* at *Paris* 1645. Dr. *Smith* tells us (*o*), that he had seen the various

---
* Printed at Paris 1717, in 8vo.   (*o*) Pag. 30.

various readings, noted down by Mr. *Greaves* in the margin, collated with the printed copy. III. *A Geographical Account of the Mountains of the Earth according to the Arabians from* Abulfeda, in *English.* IV. *Of the* Tatars *or* Moguls *from* Texeira *the* Spaniard, who borrow'd many things for *Emir Cond* the *Persian*; with a short Description of the chief cities in *Persia* by the same writer, in *English.* V. *Commentaries upon the* Epochæ, which he had publish'd an account of in the year 1650. These Commentaries were unfortunately omitted in that edition, tho' in the Title-page Mr. *Greaves* mentions them, and in the book itself refers the reader to them. Dr. *Smith* could not discover what was become of them, nor meeting with them among our author's or Archbishop *Usher*'s papers. VI. *Versio integra Tabularum Geographicarum* Abulfedæ. This could not be found by Dr. *Smith*. It appears from Mr. *Greaves*'s Preface to his edition of *Chorasmiæ & Mawaralnahræ Descriptio*, that this translation was finish'd by him. VII. *Elementa omnium Scientiarum, præsertim Mathematicarum.* This treatise comprehends a short view of all the sciences, and contains a great many things relating to Astronomy, Geography, and Chronology, collected from the *Arabic* and *Persian* writers,

ters, with several excellent astronomical observations made by himself and others. This book, written by his own hand, was given to Dr. *Dudley Loftus* by Dr. *Nicholas Greaves*, and afterwards came into the hands of Dr. *Thomas Smith*, who design'd to have publish'd it (*p*); but was prevented by death. VIII. He made several Maps from the Tables of *Naſſir Eddin*, *Abulfeda*, and *Ulug Beig* compar'd together; another of *Leſſer Aſia*, at the desire of Archbishop *Uſher*, who was then writing a learned dissertation, which was afterwards printed under the title of *Geographica & Historica Disquisitio de Minori Aſiâ proprie dicta*, &c. IX. He design'd also to publish a *Perſian Lexicon*; as appears from his Letter to Archbishop *Uſher* above quoted, where he writes thus: "According to your Grace's advice, I have "made a *Perſian Lexicon* out of such words "as I met with in the Evangelists and in "the Psalms, and in two or three *Arabian* "and *Perſian* Nomenclators; so that I have "now a stock of above six thousand words "in that language; I think, as many as *Ra-* "*phelengius* hath in his *Arabic* Dictionary. "Wherefore I have a greater mind than "ever to go to *Leyden*, and peruse their "oriental manuscripts, which were printed "by

(*p*) Smith, p. 31.

" by the expence of the States, a thing
" which long since your Grace would have
" had me to have done. But yet consider-
" ing my Lecture in *Oxford* (tho' as yet it
" cannot be read) it will not be fit for me
" to go without special leave from our ho-
" nourable Chancellor, and two or three
" more of the Lords of his Majesty's Privy
" Council, I shall therefore desire your
" Grace to procure this favour for me in
" writing, with this caution, that my ab-
" sence for a while may be no prejudice to
" me at home, especially since my journey
" is for the improvement of learning, and
" for the publishing of some of those books,
" which I long since have finished. There
" I shall have an opportunity of printing
" your Grace's Map, and of perfecting and
" publishing that discourse of Dr. *Bain-*
" *brigg* concerning the *Periodus Sotbiaca*."
X. He prepared an edition of *Ptolemy*'s Description of *Arabia*, published by Dr. *Hudson*
in the third volume of *Geographiæ Ve-*
teris Scriptores Græci minores. XI. He
propos'd likewise to have publish'd many
other tracts, particularly concerning the *Ara-*
bian Geographers, the *Weights and Measures*
of the Arabians, the *Mummies of the Egyp-*
tians and their *Hieroglyphics*, and concerning
many other antiquities of that country.

He

He left his brother Dr. *Nicholas Graves* executor of his last will and testament, which had been made the year before his death; and the latter left by will our author's astronomical instruments to the *Savilian* library in the university of *Oxford*, where they are reposited (*q*). A great many papers of our author, and letters to and from him, were sold by his brother Dr. *Nicholas*'s widow to a bookseller for an inconsiderable price, and lost, or dispersed into a variety of hands. (*r*).

He held a correspondence with several learned foreigners, particularly *William Schickard, James Golius, Claudius Hardy, Francis Junius, Peter Scarvenius,* and *Christian Ravius*; and had an intimate friendship with Archbishop *Usher*, Mr. *Selden*, Dr. *Gerard Langbaine*, Dr. *William Harvey*, Sir *John Marsham*, to whom he left by will all the coins, which he had collected in *Italy*, and the East; Dr. *Edward Pocock*, Dr. *George Ent*, Dr. *Charles Scarborough*, and other great men.

Dr. *Pocock*

(*q*) Vide Catalog. Librorum Manuscriptor. Angliæ & Hiberniæ in unum collect. Part. I. p. 302. Edit. Oxon. 1697. in Fol.

(*r*) Smith, p. 34.

Dr. *Pocock* in his *Specimen Historiæ Arabum* (*s*), *James Golius* (*t*), *George Hierom Velschius* (*u*), *Stephen le Moyne* (*x*), and Monsieur *Galland* in the Preface to the *Bibliotheque Orientale* of *D'Herbelot*, speak of him with the highest commendations. Dr. *Richard Cumberland*, afterwards Bishop of *Peterborough*, in his *Essay towards the Recovery of the* Jewish *Measures and Weights, comprehending their Monies*, having observed (*o*), " that our au-
" thor, in his book of the *Roman* foot, hath
" given us the *Egyptian Derah* or cubit ac-
" curately adjusted to the 1000 part of our
" *English* standard-foot;" proceeds thus:
" What use this very learned man intended
" to make of this *Egyptian* cubit, I find not,
" but heartily wish, that he had lived to
" finish the work he intended, about the
" measures and weights of the ancients. The
" *Jewish* cubit he hath no where stated, that
" I know of; only in his *Epistle Dedica-*
" *tory* to Mr. *Selden* he intimates it to be
" investigable by the help of the *Roman*
foot:

(*s*) Pag. 128 and 158. Edit. Oxon. 1650.
(*t*) In Additamento de Cathaia ad Atlantem Sinicum M. Martinii, p. 2, 3.
(*u*) In Commentar. in Tabulas Æquinoctiales novi Persarum & Turcarum Anni, p. 18. Edit. August. Vindelicor. 1676.
(*x*) In Observation. ad S. Barnabæ Epistol. p. 798, 799.
(*o*) Pag. 7. Edit. Lond. 1686.

"foot: how he thence could have deduced it, I know not." Dr. *George Hooper*, Bishop of *Bath* and *Wells*, in his *Inquiry into the State of the ancient Measures*, the Attick, the Roman, *and especially the* Jewish, stiles him an *accurate author* (*p*), and speaks of the known skill and accuracy of that observer (*q*); and having observed (*r*), that Mr. *Greaves* intended to prosecute the subject of the *Dirhems* and *Deinars* of the *Arabians* besides what he hath done in his *Discourse of the* Roman *Foot* (*s*), tells us, " that it is great pity for many reasons, that the accurate judgment and exquisite learning, with which he was furnished, met with those unhappy times, in which an honest man was not only discouraged, but disabled from the prosecution of such studies." Dr. *John Arbuthnot* in his *Tables of ancient Coins, Weights and Measures,* explained and exemplified in several Dissertations, tells us (*t*), that Mr. *Greaves may be justly reckoned a classical author* on the subject of the *Roman* weights and coins. Mr. *John Ward*, F.R.S. and Professor of Rhetorick in *Gresham*

(*p*) Part I. Ch. IV. Sect. 2. p. 24. Edit. Lond. 1721. in 8vo. See likewise Part II. Ch. I. Sect. 4. p. 45.
(*q*) Part III. Ch. II. Sect. 4. p. 92.
(*r*) Part IV. Ch. III. Sect. 2. p. 215, 216.
(*s*) Pag. 115.
(*t*) Chap. III. p. 15. Edit. Lond. 1727, in 4to.

Mr. JOHN GREAVES.

ham-College, in his *De Asse & Partibus ejus Commentarius*, published in Mr. *Robert Ainsworth*'s *Monumenta Vetustatis Kempiana ex vetustis Scriptoribus illustrata, eosque vicissim illustrantia,* printed at *London* 1720, in 8vo, speaks of Mr. *Greaves's Discourse of the* Roman *Foot and* Denarius, with great approbation.

He had three brothers, NICHOLAS, THOMAS, and EDWARD, all men of eminent learning.

Dr. NICHOLAS GREAVES was a commoner of St. *Mary-*hall in the university of *Oxford*, from whence in 1627 he was elected fellow of *All-Souls-*college (y). In 1640 he was proctor of that university (z). *Nov.* 1. 1642, he took the degree of batchelor of divinity (a); and *July* 6, the year following that, of doctor of divinity (b). He was dean of *Dromore* in *Ireland* (c).

Dr. THOMAS GREAVES was admitted a scholar of *Corpus Christi-*college in *Oxford*, *March* 15. 1627, and chosen fellow thereof in

(y) Wood, Athen. Oxon. Vol. II. col. 669.
(z) Id Fasti Oxon. Vol. I. col. 285.
(a) Id. ibid. Vol. II. col. 21.
(b) Id. ibid. Vol. II. col. 33.
(c) Smith, p. 34.

in 1636, and deputy reader of the *Arabick* during the abſence of Mr. *Edward Pocock* in 1637 (*d*). He took the degree of batchelor of divinity *October* 22. 1641 (*e*), and was rector of *Dunsby* in *Lincolnſhire* during the times preceding the reſtoration, and of another living near *London* (*f*). *Octob.* 19. 1661, he had the degree of doctor of divinity conferr'd upon him (*g*), and a prebend in the church of *Peterborough* in 1666 (*h*), being then rector of *Benefield* in *Northamptonſhire*, "which benefice he reſigned ſome years before his death through trouble from "his pariſhioners, who becauſe of his ſlow- "neſs of ſpeech and bad utterance held him "inſufficient for it, notwithſtanding he was "a man of great learning (*i*)." In the latter part of his life he retired to *Weldon* in *Northamptonſhire*, where he had purchaſed an eſtate, and died there *May* 22. 1676, in the 65th year of his age, and was interred in the chancel of the church there (*k*). His writings are, *De Linguæ Arabicæ Utilitate*

&

(*d*) Wood, Athen. Oxon. Vol. II. col. 556.
(*e*) Id. Faſti Oxon. Vol. II. col. 2.
(*f*) Id. Athen. Oxon. Vol. II. col. 556.
(*g*) Id. Faſti Oxon. Vol. II. col. 147.
(*h*) Id. Athen. Oxon. Vol. II. col. 556.
(*i*) Wood, Athen. ibid.
(*k*) Id. ibid.

Mr. JOHN GREAVES. lxiii

& *Præstantiâ, Oratiq Oxonii habita* 19 *Julii* 1637: Oxford 1637 in 4to. *Observationes quædam in Persicam Pentateuchi Versionem*; printed in the sixth tome of the Polyglot Bible (*l*). *Annotationes quædam in Persicam Interpretationem Evangeliorum*; printed in the same tome (*m*). These annotations were translated into *Latin* by Mr. *Samuel Clarke.* The following original Letter of his will inform us of a work, which he designed.

To Mr. RICHARD BAXTER.

Aug. 5. 1656.

'I Thanke you for your kind Letter and
' censure of my little treatise. I have
' composed another, but much larger, and
' in a different language concerning a reli-
' gion opposite to Christianity; yet (which
' is one of the great depths of *Satan*) pre-
' tending to be a confirmation of it; I meane
' the *Mahometan* religion, which hath pre-
' vailed in so great a part of the world; the
' first publisher whereof doth professe, that
' he was sent with the same message, and to
' preach the same doctrine, which *Christ*
'   before

(*l*) Pag. 48.
(*m*) Pag. 56.

' before had delivered. From whence I
' thinke it undeniably followes, that by the
' judgment of their own prophet they ought
' to embrace the Christian religion; and in
' disputation with them I conceive this ought
' to be chiefly urged and insisted on. I
' know their ordinary exception and evasion
' is, that the Scriptures are corrupted (which
' *Mahomet* often objects to the *Jews* and
' Christians) and changed, not in matters of
' small moment, but in fundamentals, as
' touching *Christ*'s prediction and expresse
' mention of *Mahomet*, as an apostle or
' messenger to be sent from God; besides
' divers other passages relating to the person
' and office of *Christ*, wherein they affirm
' our scriptures and records to be falsified,
' an error very easy to be refuted, though
' they will not easily be convinced. A trea-
' tise of their *Credenda* and *Agenda*, in part
' of both which they are diametrically op-
' posite to Christianity, I have composed out
' of their own writings; the translations now
' extant, and relations of the *Greeks* and
' *Latins* concerning *Mahomet*'s original, and
' a great part of his doctrine, being very er-
' roneous, which hath occasioned divers mi-
' stakes in *Vives*, *Grotius*, &c. Having
' therefore shewn some part of the work
' with other observations to the Reverend
                                    ' Bishop

'Bishop *Usher*, he often advised me to pub-
'lish them; but I have not yet an opportu-
'nity. This inclosed note I have sent you
'for a little taste, and especially because
'among those arguments of God's provi-
'dence, and reasons to persuade the belief
'of the Christian religion, which you and
'others produce, I think this very consider-
'able, the confession and testimony of the
'chief adversaries. What plainer or clearer
'evidence could be desired from the mouth
'of so great an enemy as this, which I have
'transcribed? To me it is a great satisfaction
'and confirmation to see God's truth and wis-
'dom justified not only by her own children,
'but even by strangers and the greatest oppo-
'sers of it; which causeth me to think of that
'expression often used in the scripture *,
'*Inimici tui* יְכַחֲשׁוּ לְךָ *mentientur tibi*, as
'many render it, *mendaciter se dedunt tibi*,
'as *Junius*; our translators sometimes,
'*Thine enemies shall be found liars unto
'thee.* The truth, which they acknow-
'ledge, shall discover them to be liars; as
''tis certain, that *Mahomet*, the more truth
'he utters in this, the more he is found a
'liar in the rest. Who knoweth whether
'they, who acknowledge our Saviour's mi-
'raculous

'raculous nativity, wonderful works, and
'miffion from heaven to preach the gospel,
'fo frequently attefted in the alcoran, may
'not at length be induced to receive the
'whole truth, of which fuch a part is al-
'ready believed by them, if Chriftians
'would ferioufly endeavour it, and labour
'to improve fuch an advantage? I fhould
'be glad to heare of your health, and to re-
'ceive an anfwer from you, if it may not
'hinder your better employments. God pre-
'ferve you for the farther benefit of his
'Church. I remaine

Your loving Brother

and Servant,

T. GREAVES.

He had a correfpondence by Letters with feverah of the moft learned men of that time, particularly Mr. *Selden* and Mr. *Abraham Wheelock*, profeffor of *Arabick* in the univerfity of *Cambridge*, as appears from the following letters to him from thofe eminent fcholars.

To my Worthy Freind Mr. THOMAS
GREAVES, at *Corpus Christi College* in
Oxford, these.

Worthy Sir,

'I Received a part of your excellent notes
'upon that *Arabique* dialogue, and
'have had some speech with the Printer con-
'cerning them. His answer is yet some-
'what uncertain. What is fit to be done, or
'may be, to second your wishes, shall
'hereafter, when you come up, be perform-
'ed as far forth as it lies in the power of

Your affectionat Freind,

March 20, 1635.
The Temple.   J. SELDEN.

Worthy Sir,

'YOU know, I doubt not, by this
'time, that God hath taken from us
'our deer freind Mr. *James* *. On *Munday*
'last he was buried at *Westminster.* He
'had divers collections and notes of history,
'and other things, which, I presume, are
'in some trunks of his in his chamber at the
'college. Into whose hands of his kindred
'   'they

* *Richard James,* B. D. Fellow of *Corpus Christi* college, *Oxford.*

' they shall come, I know not, nor could
' I tell, under that name, to whom to make
' any addresse. But because I presume they
' are yet under somme command of yours, I
' have ventured upon putting you to this
' trouble, that you would favour me so much
' as to take the best course, that might be,
' that, upon such ample satisfaction as may
' be fit, I might have them in bulk as they
' are. You shall be umpire in the businefs,
' and they shall be satisfied immediatly; if
' I may have them. If any thing ly in my
' power, wherein I may serve you, I beseech
' you command, and you shall find a very
' ready heart in

Your most affectionat Freind
and Servant,

Decemb. 13, 1638.   J. SELDEN.
The Temple.

To his much honored Friend Mr. THOMAS
GREAVES, Reader of the <i>Arabick</i> Lecture in <i>Oxford,</i> these.
   At <i>Corpus Christi College.</i>

Worthie Mr. GREAVES,

' I Am very much indebted (I confefs) to
' you, and blame myselfe for so longe
' silence. My necessities have cast me uppon
                      ' many

'many businesses of late, soe that I have al-
' most forgott myself, and before old age be-
' gin to enter into the declininge age; for
' my eye-sight, which is as deare to me as
' my life, (I feare) decays. You much re-
' vived me both by the gift of that excel-
' lent and truly eloquent speech of yours, as
' alsoe by the report of my ever honored
' friend Mr. *John Greaves*, whose presence
' (when by God's help it shal come to passe)
' together with yours, may bringe me to *Ox-*
' *ford*. I am ashamed to tell you few do
' *Arabicari* in this university; yet some doe
' yet ἅλις εἰς ἅλις ὁδεῖν. Soe that in the
' church there will be some that promote
' these studies. I shal be heartily joyful to
' see you here this vacation, and will set a-
' part a room or two for you; one in my
' howse, another in the publick schools,
' where you shal be *in gremio venerandæ*
' *materteræ vestræ matrisque nostræ*. I
' hope alsoe to be myselfe at home, and to
' enjoy your company. I thanke you again
' and aghin for that wise, learned, and rhe-
' torical panegyrick of the *Arabick* language.
' I am not able to send you mine in print,
' because not worthie. Commend me hearti-
' ly to all our freindes, to your brother with
' you; to Mr. *Jacob*, Mr. *Gregory*, Mr.
' *Chidloe*,

'Chidloe, your chaplaine, my very loving
'freind. I have heard by Sir Christopher
'Hatton of Northamptonshyre, that worthy
'Mr. Rowse was pleased to speake good
'wordes of me to him. I much thanke him
'for it; and, if you please, remember my
'service to him next after yourselfe. Now
'God præserve you ever his.

Your very lovinge Freind
and Fellow-Labourer,

Cambridge,   ABRAHAM WHEELOCK.
Julie 24. 1639.

Dr. EDWARD GREAVES, the youngest brother of Mr. *John Greaves*, was born at or near *Croydon* in *Surry*, and admitted probationer-fellow of *All-Souls*-college in *Oxford* in 1634 (*n*); and, entering in the Physick line, took the degree of doctor of that faculty, *July* 8, 1641 (*o*), in which year, and afterwards he practised with good success about *Oxford*. In 1643, he was elected superior lecturer of Physick in *Merton*-college, to read the lecture of that faculty founded by Dr. *Thomas Linacre*. He was likewise, together

---

(*n*) Wood, Athen. Oxon. Vol. II. col. 669.
(*o*) Id. Fasti Oxon. Vol. II. col. 2.

gether with Dr. *Walter Charleton*, travelling Phyſician to *Charles* I (*p*). Upon the declining of the King's cauſe, he retired to *London*, and practiſed there, and ſometimes at *Bath* (*q*). March 16, 1652, he was examined for the firſt time before the college of Phyſicians at *London*, and *October* 1, 1657, was elected fellow thereof (*r*). After the reſtoration he was appointed Phyſician in ordinary to King *Charles* II, and became a Baronet. Mr. *Wood* (*s*) ſtiles him a *pretended Baronet*; but we find, that he takes this title in his oration before the College of Phyſicians; and in the ſixth edition of *A Diſplay of Heraldry*, by John Guillim, Purſuivant of *Arms* (*t*), are the following words:
'He beareth gules, an eagle diſplay'd,
' crowned argent, by the name of *Greaves*,
' and with the arms of *Ulſter* is the coat of
' armour of Sir *Edward Greaves* of St. *Leo-*
' *nard*'s foreſt in *Suſſex*, and of *Harietſham*
' in *Kent*, Baronet. This coat, without
' the arms of *Ulſter*, and with it's due diſtance

(*p*) See a Letter of Dr. *Thomas Smith* to Mr. *Thomas Hearne*, printed in Mr. *Hearne*'s Preface to *Peter Langtoſte*'s *Chronicle*, p. 86.
(*q*) Id. Athen. Oxon. Vol. II. col. 669.
(*r*) From the Regiſter of the College, communicated by the very learned Dr. *Thomas Pellet*, Preſident of the College.
(*s*) Athen. Oxon. ubi ſupra.
(*t*) Pag. 210. Edit. Lond. 1724.

'stance is borne by his brother *Thomas
'Greaves*, D. D.' He died at his house in
Covent-Garden, London, Nov. 11, 1680,
and was interred in the Parish Church there
(*u*). He wrote and published *Morbus Epi-
demicus, ann.* 1643: *Or, the New Disease,
with Signs, Causes, Remedies*, &c. *Oxford*
1643, in 4to. written upon occasion of a
disease called *Morbus Campestris,* which
raged in *Oxford,* while the King and Court
were there. *Oratio habita in Ædibus Colle-
gii Medicorum Londinensium* 25 *Julii* 1661,
die Harvæi memoriæ dicato: Lond. 1667,
in 4to. This oration shews him to have
been a great master of the *Latin* Tongue.

(*u*) Wood, Athen. Oxon. Vol. II. col. 669.

Pyramido-

Pyramidographia:

OR, A
DESCRIPTION
OF THE
PYRAMIDS
IN
ÆGYPT.

By *JOHN GREAVES*,
Professor of Astronomy in the University of *Oxford*.

Illustrated with Cuts, engraved by a curious hand.

Romanorum Fabricæ, & antiqua opera (cum veniâ id dictum sit) nihil accedunt ad Pyramidum splendorem & superbiam.
BELLON. lib. 2. Observ. cap. 42.

LONDON:
Printed for J. BRINDLEY, Bookbinder to her Majesty, and Bookseller to his Royal Highness the Prince of *Wales*, at the *King's Arms* in *New Bondstreet*. 1736.

THE PREFACE.

HOW high an estimation the Ancients had of the Ægyptian Pyramids, appears by the several testimonies of *Herodotus, Diodorus, Strabo,* and *Pliny.* For [a] *Herodotus* acknowledges, that *tho' there were a Temple at Ephesus very renowned, as also at Samos; yet the Pyramids were worthier of relation; each of which single might be compared with many of the most sumptuous struc-*

---

[a] Καίτοι ἀξιόλογός γε κ̀ ὁ ἐν Ἐφέσῳ ἐὼν νηὸς κ̀ ὁ ἐν Σάμῳ· ἴσας μὲν νυν αἱ πυραμίδες λόγου μέζον⊙, κ̀ πολλῶν ἑκάςη αὐτέων Ἑλληνικῶν ἔργων κ̀ μεγάλων ἀνταξίη. Herod. lib. 2.

tures of the Græcians. Diodorus Siculus confirms as much: who as he prefers the works of the Ægyptians, for magnificence, before those of other nations, so he prefers the Pyramids before the rest of the Ægyptians. *It is confessed,* [b] *saith he, that these works far excell the rest in Ægypt, not only in the massiness of the structures, and in the expenses, but also in the skilfulness of the architects.* He farther adds, *The greatness of the work, and art of the workmen, strike an admiration into the spectators.* [c] *Strabo* also testifies, *that three of them are very memorable, two of these are accounted amongst the seven Miracles of the*

[b] Ὁμολογεῖται ὅ ταῦτα τὰ ἔργα πολὺ περιέχειν τῶν κατ' Αἴγυπτον, ἳ μόνον τῷ βάρει τῶν κατασκευασμάτων ἢ τ῀ δαπάναις, ἀλλὰ ὶ τῇ πολυτεχνίᾳ τῶν ἐργασαμένων. Diod. Sic. Biblioth. lib. 1. Τῷ ὅ μεγέθει τῶν ἔργων ἢ τῇ κατ' τὴν τέχνην χειρουργίᾳ θαυμαστὴν τινὰ κατάπληξιν παρέχεσθαι τοῖς θεωμένοις. Ibid.

[c] Τρεῖς δ' ἀξιόλογοι, τὰς δὲ δύο τούτων ὶ ἐν τοῖς ἑπτὰ θαύμασι καταριθμοῦνται. Strabo. lib. 17.

world.

world. Lastly, [d] *Pliny,* though he judges them *to be an idle and vain ostentation of the wealth of Kings;* yet he grants, that *three of them have filled the world with their fame.* Which three by his description, and by such indications as may be collected out of *Diodorus* and *Strabo,* must necessarily be these three, which now are extant, and of which I intend especially to discourse. For [e] *Diodorus* writes, that *they are seated on Libya side, an* cxx. *stadia* (or furlongs) *from Memphis, and from Nilus* XLV. We read in [f] *Strabo,* XL. *stadia from the city* (Memphis) *there is a certain brow of an hill, in which are many Pyramids:* who pre-

---

[d] Regum pecuniæ otiosa ac stulta ostentatio—— Tres, quæ orbem terrarum implevêre famâ. Plin. l. 36. c. 12.

[e] Αὗται δὲ κάμεναι κατὰ τὴν Λιβύην, ἢ Μέμφιος ἀπέχουσι σαδίους ἑκατὸν κ̓ εἴκοσι, τοῦ δὲ Νείλου πεντὲ πρὸς τοῖς τετταράκοντα. Diod. Sicul. lib. 1.

[f] Τετταράκοντα δ᾽ ἀπὸ τῆς πόλεως σαδίους προελθόντι ὀρεινή τις ὀφρύς ἐστιν, ἐφ᾽ ᾗ πολλαὶ μὲν Πυραμίδες εἰσί. Strab. lib. 12. Αὗται μὲν οὖν ἐγγὺς ἀλλήλων εἰσὶ τῷ αὐτῷ ἐπιπέδῳ. Idem ibid.

sently

iv The PREFACE.

sently after describing more particularly the three greatest, gives us this character: *These three stand near to one another upon the same plain.* And if this be not sufficient to point them out, [g] *Pliny* delivers many evident marks, whereby to discover them. *These three* (as he informs us) *are very conspicuous to those that sail upon the Nilus; they are seated on Africa side, upon a rocky and barren hill, between the city Memphis and that place, which we said is called the Delta, from the Nilus less than four miles, from Memphis six, there being a village opposite to them, which they name Busiris, from whence they use to ascend up to them.* All which characters were, and are, applicable to none, but only to these three.

[g] Reliquæ tres —sanè conspicuæ undique inascendentibus, sitæ sunt in parte Africæ, monte saxeo sterilique, inter Memphim oppidum, & quod appellari diximus Delta; à Nilo minus quatuor millia passuum, à Memphi sex, vico apposito, quem vocant Busirin, in quo sunt assueti scandere illas. Plin. l. 36. c. 12.

Having

The PREFACE.

Having thus discovered their true place or situation, we shall next discourse of the Authors who have written of them. Amongst the Ancients there were many, who thought it worth their labour to describe them. For *Pausanias*, as it were complaining that the Græcians had been very curious in describing these, whilst they had omitted many remarkable structures of their own, writes thus : [h] *That the Græcians admired things of strangers more than of their own ; seeing that some Historians of note had most accurately described the Pyramids of Ægypt ; whereas the Treasury of Minyas, and Walls of Tiryns (places in Bœotia) no less to be admired than these, had*

---

[h] Ἕλληνες δ' ἄρα εἰσὶ δεινοὶ τὰ ὑπέρορα ἐν θαύματι τίθεσθαι μείζονι ἢ τὰ οἰκεῖα. ὁπότε ἀνδράσιν ἐπιφανέσιν ἐς συγγραφὴν, πυραμίδας μὲν τὰς παρὰ Αἰγυπτίοις ἐπῆλθεν ἐξηγήσασθαι πρὸς τὸ ἀκριβέστατον, θησαυρὸν δὲ τὸν Μινύου ᾗ τὰ τείχη τὰ ἐν Τίρυνθι οὐδ' ἐπὶ βραχὺ ἀγαγεῖν μνήμης, οὐδ' ὄντα ἐλάττονος θαύματος. Pausaniæ Bœotica.

been omitted by them. Pliny gives us a large catalogue of Authors, that had purposely treated of this argument. [i] *Those which have writ of them, are, Herodotus, Euhemerus, Duris Samius, Aristagoras, Dionysius, Artemidorus, Alexander Polyhistor, Butorides, Antisthenes, Demetrius, Demoteles, Apion.* Where we are beholden to him for preserving the names of so many Writers, though their works (unless those of *Herodotus*) by the injury and calamity of times, have long since perished. Besides these, *Diodorus Siculus, Strabo, Pomponius Mela, Pliny, Solinus,* and *Ammianus Marcellinus* (the names of modern Authors I purposely omit) have given us some relations of them. But it may be, if the writings of *Aristides*

---

[i] Qui de iis scripserint, sunt Herodotus, Euhemerus, Duris Samius, Aristagoras, Dionysius, Artemidorus, Alexander Polyhistor, Butorides, Antisthenes, Demetrius, Demoteles, Apion. Plin. nat. hist. l. 36. c. 12.

had

The PREFACE. vii

had not perished, who in his Αἰγύπ- Αἰγύπτιος speaks thus of himself, [k] *After that I had entred into Æthiopia, and four times travelled all over Ægypt, and had left nothing unhandled, neither the Pyramids, nor labyrinth, nor temples, nor channels, and partly had procured out of their writings such measures as might be had, and partly with the Priests had measured such things as were not obvious, yet could I not preserve them entire for thee; seeing the Books, which thy servants by my appointment transcribed, have perished.* Or if we had *the sacred Commentaries of the Ægyptians,* so often cited

[k] Ἐπειδὴ καὶ γὰ μέχρι τ᾿ Αἰθιοπικῆς χώρας προσελ- θὼν ᾐ αὐτὴν διεπλωσάμην Αἰγύπτιον τετράκις τὸ σύμπαν, ᾐ παρεὶς ἰδὲν ἀνεξέτασον, ἐ πυραμίδας, ἐ λαβύρινθον, ἐχ᾿ ἱερὸν, ἐ διώρυχας, ἀλλ᾿ ὅν μὲν ἐν τ῾ βίβλοις τὰ μέρη ὑπῆρχον, ἐκεῖθεν ποιησάμενΘ· ὅν ᾐ μὴ ᾑ ἐτοίμω λαβεῖν ἦν, ἐκμετρήσας αὐτὸς μετὰ τῆς παρ᾿ ἑκάτοις ἱερέων ᾑ προφητῇ· εἶτ᾿ ἐκ ἐδυνήθω αὐτά σοι διασώσαι, τ῾ ὑπομνημάτων διαφθαρέντων, ἃ τοῖς σοῖς παισὶ προσέταξα ποιῶσαι. Aristid. λόγ. Αἰγυπτ.

by

by [1] *Diodorus*, we might receive better satisfaction, and be also more content with the loss of those other writings of the Grecians. But seeing the vicissitudes and revolutions of times have deprived us of these, whilst the Pyramids have been too great to be consumed, it will be no superfluous labour to imitate the examples of the Ancients, and to supply the loss of them, by giving a distinct narration of the several respective dimensions and proportions of these Pyramids. In which I shall tread in as even a path as I can, between truth and the traditions of such of the Ancients, as are still extant: first, putting down those relations, which by them have been transmitted to us; and next, shewing in what manner,

---

[1] Ὡς ἐν ταῖς ἱεραῖς ἀναγραφαῖς ὁρῶν ἦν καταχεχωρισμένον. Diod. Sic. lib I. Οἱ ἱερεῖς τῶν Αἰγυπτίων ἱστοροῦσιν ἐκ τῶν ἀναγραφῶν τῶν ἐν ταῖς ἱεραῖς βίβλοις. Idem ibidem.

upon examination, I found the Pyramids in the years one thousand six hundred thirty eight, and one thousand six hundred thirty nine, or in the thousand forty and eighth year of the *Hegira*. For I twice went to *Grand Cairo* from *Alexandria*, and from thence into the deserts, for the greater certainty, to view them; carrying with me a radius of ten feet most accurately divided into 10,000 parts, besides some other instruments, for the fuller discovery of the truth. But before I descend to a particular description, I shall make enquiry, by whom, at what time, and to what end these Monuments were erected.

OF THE
AUTHORS or FOUNDERS
OF THE
PYRAMIDS.

IT is the opinion of some (*a*) modern writers, that the *Ægyptian Pyramids* were erected by the *Israelites*, during their heavy pressure under the tyranny of the *Pharaohs*. And this seems to be confirmed by (*b*) *Josephus*; who relates, that when as time had extinguished the memory of the benefits of Joseph, the kingdom of Ægypt being transplanted into another family, they used the Israelites with much severity, wasting them with several labours; for they were

(*a*) Henric. Spondanus de Cœmeteriis sacris, lib. 1. par. 1. cap. 6. Brodæus Epigram. Græc. εἰς ναῦς.
(*b*) Joseph. lib. 1. Antiq. cap. 5. Ὣν τ᾽ ἦσαν ἐὖ ὑπὸ Ἰωσήφου τετυχηκότες διὰ χρόνε μῆκος λήθlω λαβόντες, ᾗ τ βασιλείας εἰς ἄλλον οἶκον μετεληλυθυίας, δεινῶς ἐνύβριζον τὰς Ἰσραηλίτας, &c.

commanded

2 Of the Authors or Founders

commanded to cut divers channels for the river (Nilus,) to raise walls, and cast up banks, whereby to hinder the inundation of the stream: they oppressed also our nation with those fabricks of the Pyramids, compelling them to learn many (mechanical) *arts, and inured them to the supporting of labours.* But the sacred Scriptures clearly expressing, the slavery of the Jews to have consisted in making and burning of brick (for the original is לבנים *Lebénim,* which the (c) *Septuagint* renders by Πλίνθος and Πλινθεία) whereas all these Pyramids consist of stone, I cannot be induced to subscribe to their assertion.

Much less can I assent to that opinion of (d) *Stephanus,* (e) *Nicetas,* (f) *Nonnus,* and the author of the Greek (g) Ἐτυμολογικὸν μέγα, with some others, who derive the name of the Pyramids ἀπὸ τοῦ πυρᾶ, that

---

(c) Exod. cap. 5. sæpè.

(d) Ὠνομάσθησαν ἢ Πυραμίδες ἀπὸ τῶν πυρῶν, ἃς ἐπὶ συναγαγὼν ὁ βασιλεὺς, ἰνδεῖαν ἐποίησε σίτου κατὰ τὴν Αἴγυπτον. Steph. *de urbibus.*

(e) Πυραμίδες, id est, ædificia quædam à Josepho, ut nonnulli opinantur, ad condenda frumenta scitè admodum elaborata, ἀπὸ τοῦ πυρᾶ, id est, à frumento, nomen consecuta. Nicetas in xx. orat. Nazianzeni.

(f) Non à vero, ut inquit Nonnus, abhorret, quin has Pyramides post Josephi tempora excessumque Judæorum ex Ægypto in Regum sepulchra converterint. Billius ex Nonno monacho ibidem.

(g) Πυραμίδες ἢ πάλιν λέγονται ὁρεία βασιλικὰ σιτοδόχα ἃ κατεσκεύασε Ἰωσήφ. Ἐτυμολ. μέγα.

is,

of the PYRAMIDS.

is, *from corn*, and not ἀπὸ τοῦ πυρὸς, *from the figure of a flame of fire*, which they resemble, because, say most of them, these were built by the Patriarch *Joseph*, as σιτοθῆκαι, *receptacles and granaries of the seven plentiful years*. For, besides that this figure is most improper for such a purpose, a Pyramid being the least capacious of any regular mathematical body, the straitness and fewness of the rooms within (the rest of the building being one solid and intire fabrick of stone) do utterly overthrow this conjecture. Wherefore the relations of *Herodotus, Diodorus Siculus*, and of some others, but especially of these two, both of them having travell'd into *Ægypt*, and conversed with the Priests, (besides that the latter made use of their Commentaries) will give us the best and clearest light, in matters of so great antiquity.

For *Herodotus* writes thus concerning the first of these Pyramids, that (b) *until King Rhampsinitus's time the Ægyptians report, the laws to have flourished in Ægypt: after whom Cheops succeeding in the kingdom, fell into all manner of vice; for, shutting up the Temples, he forbad the Ægyptians to sacrifice: besides, he commanded, that they should be employed*

(b) Herod. lib. 2. Μέχει μὲν νῦν Ῥαμψινίτε βασιλέος ἐν Αἰγύπτῳ πᾶσαν εὐνομίαν ἔλεγον, &c.

4   Of the Authors or Founders

in his works; (he means this Pyramid, of which he discourseth) *that some of them should receive the stones dug out of the quarries of the Arabian mountain, and that from thence they should carry them to the* Nilus; *these being wafted over the river, others were to receive them, and to draw them to the mountain, which is called* Libycus. *There were employed in the work ten myriads of men, every three months a myriad: the people spent ten years in the way, in which they drew the stones; which seems to me no less a work, than the building of the Pyramid itself.* (*i*) *Diodorus Siculus* discoursing of the same argument, gives the erector of this another name, different from that of *Herodotus*, styling him *Chemmis*; but in the time and person they both agree; each of them affirming him to have succeeded *Rhampsinitus*, and to have been the father of *Mycerinus*, and to have reigned over the Ægyptians fifty years. This difference of names between *Herodotus*, and *Diodorus*, concerning the same King, may probably be thus reconciled; that *Diodorus* expresses the genuine denomination in the Ægyptian language, and that *Herodotus* renders the signification in the Greek: a practice not unusual with him, and with other approved

---
(*i*) Diod. Sic. lib. 1.

of the PYRAMIDS.

Authors. Thus the Patriarch *Isaac* in the Scriptures, being denominated from פחצ that is, *laughter*, is by *Alexander Polyhistor*, as *(k)Eusebius* testifies, named ρίλως. Wherefore חם *Cham* in Hebrew (or, in the Greek flexion, *Chemmis*) signifying *adustion*, which anciently might be the same in Ægyptian, and χίαμ, or χαλαμ, signifying *swarthy visage*, or *adust*, *Herodotus* might call him *Cheops* in Greek, whom in the Ægyptian language *Diodorus* styles *Chemmis*. But I go on with *Diodorus*. *This* Chemmis, *(l)* saith he, *erected the greatest of these three Pyramids, which are reputed amongst the seven wonderful fabricks of the world:* where he also enlarges the number of the workmen employed by him, to three hundred and sixty thousand, which *Herodotus* mentions only to have been an hundred thousand; though both of them concur, and *(m) Pliny* with them both, that twenty years were spent in the building this Pyramid.

Concerning the second Pyramid, *Herodotus* and *Diodorus* assign the author of it to have been *Cephren*, brother to the former

---

(k) Euseb. lib. 9. Evangel. præpar. cap. 19.
(l) Diod. Sic. lib. 1. Χέμμις καλασκδίασι ἢ τὴν μεγίςην τ τειῶν Πυραμίδων ἣν ἐν τοῖς ἐπλά τόπον ὀπιφανεςάτοις ἔργοις ἀειθμυμένων.
(m) Pyramis amplissima ex Arabicis lapidicinis constat, Trecenta LX. hominum millia annis XX. eam construxisse produntur. Plin. lib. 36. cap. 12.

King.

King. *Diodorus* adds, that by some he is also called *Chabryis*, and was the son of *Chemmis*; a difference, which I imagine to have been occasioned out of the diversity of pronunciation, of *Chabryis* for *Cephren*; there being an easy transmutation in letters of the same organ, as Grammarians use to speak. *Cheops,* as (*n*) *Herodotus* informs us, *being deceased, his brother* Cephren *reigned after him; who imitated him, as in other things, so in the making of a Pyramid, the magnitude of which is less than that of his brother's.* And (*o*) *Diodorus* relates, *that* Chemmis *being dead, his brother* Cephren *succeeded him in the kingdom, and reigned fifty-six years. Some say, that not his brother, but his son, which was named* Chabryis, *reigned after him. This is affirmed by the consent of all, that the successor of the former king, in imitation of him, built the second Pyramid, like to the first in respect of the art and workmanship, but far inferior to it in respect of magnitude.*

The third Pyramid was erected by *(p) Mycerinus,* some call him *Mycherinus,* as it is

---

(*n*) Herodot. lib. 2. Τελδτήσαι]Θ- ἡ τότε, ἐαδέξα- ϑαι τ βασιληίην τ ἀδελφεὸν αὐτῦ Χεφρῆνα, &c.

(*o*) Diodor. lib. 1. Τελδτήσαι]Θ- ἡ τῦ βασιλέως τότε διαδέξαιο τὴν ἀρχὴν ὁ ἀδελφὸς Κεφρὴν, κὶ ἦρξεν ἔτη ἓξ πρὸς τοῖς πεντήκοντα, &c.

(*p*) Πυραμίδα δὲ κὶ ἕτι ἀπέλιπε]ο πολλὸν ἐλάσσω τῦ πατρὸς. Herodot. lib. 2.

observed by *Diodorus*, who makes him the son of *Chemmis*, as *Herodotus* doth of *Cheops*; the difference between them being, as we noted before, rather nominal than real. The same (*q*) *Herodotus* also writes, *that some of the Græcians make the third Pyramid the work of* Rhodopis *a Courtizan*; *an error in opinion of those, who seem not to know who this* Rhodopis *might be, of which they speak: for neither could she have undertaken such a Pyramid, on which so many thousand talents were to be spent; neither lived she in this man's time, but in the time of king* Amasis. Now this *Amasis*, as he elsewhere shews, lived long after these Pyramids were in being. The same story is recited by (*r*) *Strabo* and *Pliny*, both of them omitting the names of the Founders of the former two. *Strabo* gives her a double name; *The third Pyramid is the sepulchre of a Courtizan, made by her lovers, whom* Sappho *the Poetress calls* Doricha, *mistress to her brother* Charaxus; *others name her* Rhodope. But whether we name her *Doricha*, or *Rhodope*, the relation is altogether improbable, if we consider ei-

(*q*) Herodot. lib. 2. Τὴν δὴ μετεξέτεροί φασὶ Ἑλλήνων Ῥοδώπιος ἑταίρης γυναικὸς ᾖ, οὐκ ὀρθῶς λέγοντες, &c.

(*r*) Λέγεται δὲ ἡ ἑταίρης τάφος γεγονὼς ὑπὸ τῶν ἐραστῶν, ἣν Σαπφὼ μ᾽ ἡ τῶν μελῶν ποιήτρια καλεῖ Δωρίχαν ἐρωμένην τῷ ἀδελφῷ αὐτῆς Χαράξῳ γεγονυῖαν——ἄλλοι δ᾽ ὀνομάζουσι Ῥοδῶπιν. Strab. lib. 17.

ther her condition, or the infinite vastness of the expense. For *(s) Diodorus*, though he rightly acknowledges this Pyramid to be much less than either of the former two, yet in respect of the exquisite workmanship, and richness of the materials, he judges it not inferior to either of them. A structure certainly too great and sumptuous, to have been the design and undertaking of a courtizan, which could hardly have been performed by a rich and potent monarch. And yet *Diodorus* hath almost the same relation, only a little altered in the circumstances: *(t) Some say, that this is the sepulchre of the strumpet* Rhodope, *of whom some of the Nomarchæ* (or Prefects of the Provinces) *being inamoured, by a common expense to win her favour, they built this monument.* But to pass by this fable (for it is no better) and to return to our inquiry; the same author immediately before ingenuously confesses, that concerning them all three there is little agreement either amongst the natives, or amongst writers. *(u) For they say* Armæus

---

(*s*) Diod Sic. l. 1.
(*t*) Diod. Sic. l. 1. Ταύτην δ᾽ ἔνιοί λέγυσι Ροδώπιδ۞ τάφον ἢ) τ̂ ἑταίρας. ἧς φασὶ, τ̂ Νομαρχῶν τινὰς ἐgἆςας ἠυοιμύυς, διὰ φιλοςοργίαν οἰκοδομῆσαν]ας ἐπιτελέσαι κοινῇ τὸ κα]ασκδ́ασμα.

(*u*) Idem ibid. Τὴν μεγίςην ποιῆσαι λέγυςιν Αρμαῖον, τὴν ϑ δευτέραν Αμασι/ [γρ. ῎Αμμωσιν] τὴν ϑ τρίτην Ινάρωτα [γρ. Μάρωτα.]

made

made the greatest of these; the second, Amasis; *the third,* Inaron: and *(x) Pliny* informing us, that *these three were made in seventy eight years and four months,* leaves the founders of them very uncertain. For reciting the names of many authors, that had described them, he concludes: *(y) Inter omnes eos non constat, à quibus factæ sint, justissimo casu obliteratis tantæ vanitatis authoribus.*

The Arabians, whose excellencies I judge to have been in the speculative sciences, and not in the histories and occurrences of ancient times, assign other founders of these three, different from those mentioned by the Greeks. The author of the book intitled *Morat Alzeman,* writes, *they differ concerning him that built the Pyramids. Some say* Joseph, *some say* Nimrod, *some* Dalukah *the queen, and some that the Ægyptians built them before the flood. For they foresaw that it would be, and they carried thither their treasures; but it profited them nothing.* In another place he tells us, that *the Coptites* (or Ægyptians) *report, that these two greater Pyramids, and the lesser, which is coloured, are sepulchres. In the East Pyramid is king* Saurid, *in the West Pyramid his brother*

(x) Tres verò factæ annis LXXVIII. & mensibus IV. Plin. lib. 36. cap. 12.
(y) Plin. ibid.

Hougib, *and in the coloured Pyramid* Fazfarinoun, *the son of* Hougib. *The Sabæans relate, that one of them is the sepulchre of* Shiit, (that is, Seth) *and the second the sepulchre of* Hermes, *and the coloured one the sepulchre of* Sab, *the son of* Hermes, *from whom they are called* Sabæans. *They go in pilgrimage thither, and sacrifice at them a cock, and a black calf, and offer up incense.* Ibn Abd Alhokm, another Arabian, discoursing of this argument, confesses, that he could not find amongst the learned men in Ægypt any certain relation concerning them: *wherefore what is more reasonable,* saith he, *than that the Pyramids were built before the flood? For if they had been built after, there would have been some memory of them amongst men.* At last he concludes, *The greatest part of Chronologers affirm, that he which built the Pyramids was* Saurid ibn Salhouk, *the king of Ægypt, who was before the flood* 300 *years.* And this opinion he confirms out of the books of the Ægyptians. To which he adds, *The Coptites mention in their books, that upon them there is an inscription engraven;* the exposition of it in Arabick is this: *I* Saurid *the king built the Pyramids in such and such a time, and finished them in six years; he that comes after me, and says, he is equal to me, let him destroy them in six hundred*

dred years; and yet it is known, that it is easier to pluck down than to build; and when I had finished them, I covered them with sattin, and let him cover them with mats. The same relation I find in several others of them, that this *Saurid* was the founder of these three Pyramids, which the admiration of after-times inrolled amongst the miracles of the world. And these are those three which are still fair and intire, and standing near to one another; formerly not far distant from the great and ancient city *Memphis*, built by (z) *Uchoreus* (of which there is now not so much as the ruins left) and less distant from the river *Nilus*; as *Diodorus*, *Strabo*, and *Pliny* rightly describe.

Besides these three, we find mentioned in *Herodotus* and *Diodorus*, the names and authors of some others, not much inferior to these in magnitude, long since ruined, and defaced by time. On the contrary, there are many now standing in the Libyan desert, whose names and authors neither *Herodotus*, nor *Diodorus*, nor yet any of the ancients have expressed.

After *Mycerinus*, according to (a) *Herodotus* (for *Diodorus* is here silent) Asychis

---

(z) Οὐχορεὺς ἔκτισε πόλιν Μέμφιν, ἐπιφανεστάτην τ̃ κατ' Αἴγυπτον. Diodor. lib. 1.
(a) Herod. lib. 2.

12 Of the Authors or Founders

succeeded in the kingdom, (b) who being desirous to excell his predecessors, left for a monument a Pyramid made of Bricks, with these words engraven in stone: *Compare not me with the Pyramids built of stone, which I as far excell, as Jupiter doth the other gods. For striking of the bottom of the lake with long poles, and gathering the dirt which stuck to them, they made thence bricks, and formed me in this manner.*

The same author relates, that many ages after this *Asychis*, *Sanacharib*, King of the Arabians and Assyrians, who certainly is the same, which is mentioned in the Scriptures, having expelled *Sethon*, the King of the Ægyptians, and the Priest of Vulcan, (c) *the Ægyptians recovering their liberty, made choice of twelve Kings* (which is also confirmed by *Diodorus*) *dividing Ægypt into so many parts*; for they could at no time live without a King: these by a common consent built a labyrinth, above the lake of

---

(b) Ὑπερβαλέσθαι ὁ βουλόμενος τοῦτον τὸν βασιλέα τὲς πρότερον ἑαυτε βασιλέας γινομένες Αἰγύπτε, μνημόσυνον Πυραμίδα λιπέσθαι ἐκ πλίνθων ποιήσαντα, ἐν τῇ γράμματα ἐν λίθῳ ἐγκεκολαμμένα τάδε λέγοντα ἐςι. Μή με καταόνοθῆς πρὸς τὰς λιθίνας Πυραμίδας, προέχω ὁ αὐτέων τοῦτον, ὅσον ὁ Ζεὺς τῶν ἄλλων θεῶν, κοντῷ ὁ ὑποτύπτοντες ἐς λίμνω, ὅτι περχοῖτο τῶ πηλῶ τῷ κοντῷ, τοῦτο συλλέγοντες πλίνθες εἴρυσαν, καὶ με τρόπῳ τοιούτῳ ἐξεποίησαν.

(c) Herod. lib. 2.

Mœris.

Mœris. *At the angle, where the labyrinth ends, there is a Pyramid of* XL *Orgyiæ,* (that is, of CCXL feet) *in which are engraven huge resemblances of beasts; the passage to it is under ground.* And this is that Pyramid, as may evidently be collected out of (*d*) *Strabo*, in which *Imandes* lies buried, whom we may probably suppose to have been the builder of it: his words are these: *At the end of this building* (that is, of this labyrinth) *which contains a furlong in length, there is a certain* (*e*) *Sepulchre, being a quadrilateral Pyramid, each side of which is* CCCC *feet, and the altitude is the same; the name of him, that lies buried there, is* Imandes, whom the Author of the Epitome

(*d*) Strab. lib. 17.
(*e*) Diodorus *relates,* that over the sepulchre there was a circle of gold of 365 cubits compass, and a cubit in thickness, in which the days of the year were inscribed, and divided into a cubit a-piece, with a description, according to their nature, of the setting and rising of the stars, and also their operations, after the Ægyptian Astrologers. They say, this Circle was carried away by *Cambyses*, and the *Persians*, at what time they conquer'd *Ægypt*. (Diodor. Sicul. lib. 1.) [*He which shall seriously consider this, and several other passages in* Herodotus *and* Diodorus, *of the stupendous works of the Ægyptians, must needs acknowledge, that for magnificence, if not for art, they far exceeded the Græcians and Romans, even when their empires were at the highest, and most flourishing. And therefore, those* Admiranda Romæ, *collected by* Lipsius, *are scarce to be admired, if compared with some of these. At this day there is hardly any vast column or obelisk remaining in* Rome, *worthy of note, which hath not anciently been brought thither out of* Ægypt.

calls

14 Of the Authors or Founders

calls *Maindes,* and *Strabo* himself not long after, *Ifmandes*; *Diodorus* names him *Ofymanduas.* Which of these two, whether *Herodotus* or *Strabo,* hath given the truest measure of it, unless the Pyramid were now extant, cannot be decided by us. Though *Pliny* adheres to the dimensions of *Herodotus:* but whereas *Herodotus* and *Strabo* mention there but one Pyramid, he makes mention of many: and whereas *Strabo* makes this to be quadrilateral, he describes these (if I mistake not his words) to be sexangular. (*f*) *Superque Nemeses* XV. *ædiculis incluserit Pyramides complures* (that is, above this labyrinth, which he places in *Heracleopolite nomo*) *quadragenarum ulnarum, senos radice muros obtinentes.*

Long before these four Pyramids of *Cheops, Cephren, Mycerinus,* and *Asychis,* who immediately succeeded one another in the kingdom, but after this of *Ifmandes*; *Myris,* as he is called by *Diodorus,* but *Herodotus, Strabo,* and *Pliny,* name him *Mæris,* another Ægyptian King, built two admirable Pyramids; the description of which, though in *Herodotus* it immediately follows that of the twelve Kings; yet as it may evidently be collected out of him and *Diodorus,* these two of *Mæris* must

---
(*f*) Plin. lib. 36. cap. 13.

many ages have preceded. (g) For *Herodotus* tells us, that from *Menes* (the first King of the Ægyptians, whom *Diodorus* names *Menas*) the *Priests* recited out of their books, CCCXXX *Kings*, the last of which was *Mæris*; long after whom reigned *Sesostris*, who is call'd by *Manethos*, *Sethosis*; and by *Diodorus*, *Sesostris*, and *Sesoosis*; who more particularly, than *Herodotus*, expresses *Sesostris* to have been *(h)* seven ages after *Mæris*, and to have reigned long before these twelve Kings. The which *Sesostris*, or *Sethosis*, immediately succeeding *Amenophis* [according to *Manethos* in *Josephus*, as we shall shew in the ensuing discourse] must have been before *Cheops*, *Cephren*, *Mycerinus*, and *Asychis*; and therefore consequently, that *Mæris* must long have preceded these twelve Kings. This *Mæris* undertook and finished that most admirable lake, denominated after his name, as it is testified by *Herodotus*, *Diodorus*, *Strabo*, and *Pliny*. A work the most useful and wonderful, if it be rightly considered, that I think was ever by any man attempted: in the midst of which, he erected two Pyramids, the one in memory

---

(g) Herod. lib. 2. Μετὰ ῆ τῦτον [Μῆνα] κατέλεγον οἱ ἱρέες ἐκ βίβλυ ἄλλων βασιλέων τεσσερακονταῖς ἢ τετρακοσία ἐνόματα· ἐν αἱ ῶ· αὐτῷ Μοῖρις.

(h) Diod. Sic. lib. 1.

16 *Of the Authors or Founders*
of himself, the other of his wife; each of them being 100 feet in height; the description of both which, and of his lake, we have in *Herodotus*, the latter we find in *Strabo*, but in none so fully, as in (*i*) *Diodorus*, and therefore I shall relate his words. *Ten Schœnes* [that is 100 furlongs; though *Strabo*, and *Artemidorus* before him, observe a difference of *Schœnes* in *Ægypt*] *above the City* [Memphis] *Myris digged a lake of admirable use, the greatness of which work is incredible. For they relate, that the circumference of it contains* CIƆ. CIƆ. CIƆ. 100. *furlongs; the depth of it in many places is fifty fathom* [that is, two hundred cubits, or three hundred feet] *Who therefore may not deservedly ask, that shall consider the greatness of the work, how many myriads of men, and in how many years they made it? The common benefit of it to those that inhabit* Ægypt, *and the wisdom of the King, no man can sufficiently commend. For since the rising of* Nilus *is not always alike, and the country is the more fruitful by the moderateness of this; he digged a lake to receive the superfluity of the water, that neither by the greatness of the inundation unseasonably drowning the country,*

(*i*) Diod. Sic. lib. 1. Ἐπάνω ʒ̃ τ̃ πόλεως ὑπὸ δέκα χοίνων λίμνην ὤρυξε τῇ μ̃ εὐχρησίᾳ θαυμαστὴν, τῷ ʒ̃ μεγέθει τῶ ἔργων ἄπιςον, &c.

it

it should occasion marshes, or lakes; or flowing less than it should do, for want of water it should corrupt the fruits, be therefore cut a ditch, from the river to the lake, eighty furlongs long, and three hundred feet in breadth. By which sometimes receiving in, and sometimes diverting the river, he exhibited a seasonable quantity of water to the husbandmen, the mouth of it sometimes being opened, and sometimes shut, not without much art and great expences. For he that would open the bars [or sluices] or shut them, it was necessary that he spent at the least fifty talents. The lake in this manner benefiting the Ægyptians, hath continued to our times, and from the author of it at this day is called the Lake of Myris. The King, that digged it, left a place in the midst, in which he built a sepulchre, and two Pyramids, each a furlong in height; the one for himself, the other for his wife, placing upon them two marble statues, sitting on a throne, imagining by these works, he should propagate to posterity an immortal memory of his worth. The revenue of the fish of this lake he gave to his wife, for her unguents and other ornaments; the fishing being worth to her a talent a day. For they report, there are two and twenty sorts of fishes in it, and that such a multitude is taken, that those who are perpetually employ'd in salting them,

of

18 *Of the Authors or Founders*
of which there is a very great number, can hardly difpatch the work. Thus far *Diodorus*. Which defcription, as it is much more full than that of *Herodotus*, fo *Herodotus* hath this memorable obfervation, omitted by *Diodorus*: (k) *That this lake was made by hand and hollowed, it is apparent, becaufe almoft in the midft of it there ftand two Pyramids, fifty fathoms above the water, and as may fathoms of the building under water: upon the top of each of which there is a Coloffus of ftone, fitting upon a throne; fo that the Pyramids are an hundred fathoms high.* Strabo, I know not by what over-fight, omits thefe two Pyramids; whereas he acknowledges the lake of *Mæris*, in which they ftood, (*l*) to be admirable, being like a fea for greatnefs and for colour.

Befides thefe which we have handled, and whofe founders are upon record in the writings of the ancients, there are many others in the Libyan defert, where it bounds *Ægypt*, of which there is no particular mention extant, either in the Greeks, Latins, or Arabians; unlefs we fhall apply thefe

---
(*k*) Herod. lib. 2.
(*l*) Θαυμαϛὴν ὃ κỳ τ̃ λίμνlω ἔχει τ̃ Μοίριδ۞ καλυμθην, πελαγίαν τῳ μεγέθει, κỳ τῆ χρόᾳ θαλατloιδῆ. Strab. lib. 17. Vid. Schick. Taaricn. 22. & Benj. Itin. 119.

words of (*m*) *Diodorus* to some of them: *There are three other Pyramids, each side of which contain two hundred feet; the structure of them, excepting the magnitude, is like to the former:* (that is, as he there specifies, to those three Pyramids of *Chemmis, Cephren,* and *Mycerinus*) *these three kings before mentioned are reported to have erected them for their wives.* The bigness of some of these now extant, doth well answer the measure assigned by *Diodorus*. But if these three kings built them for their queens, it may be wondred why they should have placed them so remote from their own sepulchres; or why they should stand at such large and unequal differences of several miles from one another. I find as little satisfaction in (*n*) *Pliny*, where he writes, *Multa circa hoc vanitas illorum hominum fuit, vestigiaq; complurium inchoatarum extant; una est in Arsinoite nomo, duæ in Memphi, non procul labyrintho, de quo & ipsi dicemus.* For not telling us the founders of these, he leaves us still in the same darkness; only we may in

(*m*) Diod. Sic. l. 1. Εἰσὶ ἢ κ̀ ἄλλαι τρεῖς Πυραμίδες, ὧν ἑκάςη μὲν πλευρὰ δίπλεθρος ὑπάρχει, τὸ δ' ὅλον ἔργον παραπλήσιον τῇ κατασκευῇ ♃ ἄλλαις, πλὼ τῦ μεγέθυς· ταύτας ἢ φασὶ τοὺς προειρημένους τρεῖς βασιλεῖς ♃ ἰδίαις κατασκευάσαι γυναιξίν.

(*n*) Plin. lib. 36. cap. 12.

20 Of the Authors or Founders

general collect out of him, and likewise out of that ode in *Horace*,

> * *Exegi monumentum ære perrennius,*
> *Regalique situ Pyramidum altius;*

that they were the works of Ægyptian kings; but of which of them, and at what time, we are altogether uncertain. *Regum pecuniæ,* (o) saith *Pliny, otiosa ac stulta ostentatio.* Of the same opinion is *Leo Africanus,* in his accurate description of *Africa,* after many years travel in those parts. (p) *Hâc per desertum arenaceum itur ad Pyramides, nempe ad priscorum Ægypti regum sepulchra, quo in loco Memphin olim extitisse asserunt.* It may be it was the royal prerogative, and that it was prohibited to private men, how wealthy and potent soever, to be thus intombed; but without some farther light from the ancients, it would be too great a presumption to determine any thing.

(q) *Lucan,* I know not upon what ground, makes as if the *Ptolemies* had imitated the Ægyptian kings in this particular:

> *Cùm Ptolemæorum manes seriemq; pudendam*
> *Pyramides claudant.*

---

* Horat. Ode 30. lib. 3.
(o) Plin. lib. 36. cap. 12.
(p) Leo Afric. lib. 8.
(q) Lucan. lib. 8.

Surely

of the PYRAMIDS.   21

Surely if they did, thefe are none of thofe. For they would have been built at *Alexandria*, which was then the regal feat, and not at *Memphis*, the which, as (*q*) *Diodorus* affures us, began to decay after the building of *Alexandria*; like as the ancient *Thebes* (as the (*r*) Græcians ftyled it, or *the city of the Sun*, as the Ægyptians, according to (*s*) *Diodorus*, called it, or *Diofpolis*, as *Diodorus* and *Strabo* (*t*) alfo name it) did after the building of *Memphis*. Thofe who imagine the monument or fepulchre, mention'd by (*u*) *Plutarch* at *Alexandria*, into which *Cleopatra* fled for fear of *Auguftus*, to have been a Pyramid, are much deceived. For in the life of *Mark Antony*, where he informs us, that there were fepulchres near the temple of *Ifis*, of *exquifite workmanfhip, and very high*, into which fhe conveyed the richeft of her treafures, he defcribes one of them, wherein fhe hid herfelf, to have had a window above the entrance, by which fhe drew up with cords the body of *Antony*, and by which afterwards *Proculeius* entered, and furprized her. This window is not in any of thofe Pyramids which I have feen; neither can I apprehend, if thefe were of as folid and maffy ftones, and of the fame fhape as thofe

(*q*) Diodor. lib. 1   (*r*) Plato, & alii.   (*s*) Diodor. l. 1.
(*t*) Strab. lib. 17.   (*u*) Plutarch. in Antonio.

at *Memphis*, and the chambers within, as remote from the outward superficies, of what use it could be, either in respect of light or ornament; and therefore I conjecture, these monuments of the *Ptolemies* to have been of a different structure from those of the Pyramids.

In all other classical authors, I find no mention of the founders of the rest in the Libyan desert: and after such a distance of time we must be content to be silent with them.

Of the TIME in which the PYRAMIDS were built.

TO define the precise Time, in which these Pyramids were erected, as it is an inquiry of much difficulty, so of much importance, in regulating the various and uncertain traditions of the ancients concerning the *Ægyptian* chronology. For if we shall peruse those fragments of *Manethos*, an *Ægyptian* Priest, preserved by (*a*) *Josephus*, or those relations of (*b*) *Herodotus*, of 330 kings to *Mæris*, from *Menes*, the first that reigned in *Ægypt*, (who probably is (*c*) *Mizraim*, the second son of *Cham*, and (*d*) father of the *Ægyptians*;) or that computation of (*e*) *Diodorus*, borrowed from their sacred Commentaries, that to the 180th Olympiad, or to the time in which he travelled thither, there had been a succession in the royal throne for 15000 years; or that

(*a*) Joseph. lib 1. contra Apionem.
(*b*) Herodot. lib. 2.
(*c*) Gen. 10. 6.
(*d*) Joseph. lib. 1. Antiq. cap. 7.
(*e*) Diodor. lib. 1.

calcu-

calculation of (*f*) *Pomponius Mela*, of 330 *kings to the time of* Amasis, *continuing above thirteen thousand years*; or lastly those Dynasties mentioned by *Africanus* and *Eusebius*, but pretermitted by *Herodotus* and *Diodorus*, the first of which (*g*) *Joseph Scaliger* places in the seven thousand and ninth year of that *Julian* period, which by him is called *Periodus Juliana postulatitia*, and the time *Tempus prolepticum*, preceding the creation by 1336 years, we shall find our selves intangled in a labyrinth, and maze of times, out of which we cannot, without much perplexity, unwind ourselves. And if we farther consider, that amongst those many names delivered by *Manethos*, and preserved by *Josephus, Africanus, Eusebius*, and *Syncellus*, how few there are that concur with those of *Herodotus* and *Diodorus*, or with those in *Plato, Strabo, Pliny, Plutarch, Censorinus*, and some others: and that which is of greater consequence, how difficult it is to reconcile these names and times to the *Ægyptian* kings recorded in the Scriptures, we shall find ourselves beset, and as it were environed on every side, with great and inextricable doubts. What therefore, in inqui-

---

(*f*) Trecentos & triginta reges ante Amasim, & supra tredecim millium annorum ætates, certis annalibus referunt. Pompon. Mela, lib. 1. cap. 9.
(*g*) Scalig. in Eusebii Chronic.

ries of this nature, is approved as the most solid and rational foundation, that is, to find out some common and received *Epocha*, in which either all or most agree, that shall be our guide in matters of so great antiquity. Now of all the ancient *Epocha's*, which may conduce to our purpose, there is none that we may safelier rely upon, than that of the migration of the *Israelites* out of *Ægypt*; which had the same hand faithfully to pen it, that was the most active and miraculous instrument of their departure. And though profane historians differ much in the manner of this action, either as they were tainted with malice against the Hebrews, or misled with the calumnies and false reports of their enemies, the *Ægyptians*; of whom (b) *Josephus* may seem to have given a true censure, *That all the Ægyptians in general are ill-affected to the Jews*; yet all agree in this, that *Moses* was the chief author and conductor of this expedition. If therefore we shall discover the time in which *Moses* flourished, and in which this great enterprize was performed by him, it will follow by way of consequence, that knowing *what Pharaoh* or king in *Ægypt* was coetaneous and concur-

(b) Φαίνονται γὸ κỳ δὴ μάλιϛα πρὸς ὑμᾶς δυσμενῶς διατιθέντες κοινῇ μὲν ἅπαντες Αἰγύπτιοι. Joseph. l. 1. contra Apionem.

rent with him, we may by synchronism, comparing sacred and profane authors, and following the line of their successions, as it is delivered by good authority, at length fall upon the age in which *Cheops* and those other Kings reigned in *Ægypt*, whom we assigned, out of *Herodotus* and *Diodorus*, to have been the founders of these Pyramids.

And here, for our inquiry what *Ægyptian* King was concurrent with *Moses*, we must have recourse to the relations not only of the Scriptures, but also of other approved authors amongst the *Jews* and *Gentiles*; in which last, though we often find more than an *Ægyptian* darkness, yet sometimes thro' this we may discover some glimmerings of light. By the Scriptures alone it is impossible to infer, what king of *Ægypt* was coëtaneous with *Moses*; seeing the name which is there given him, of *Pharaoh*, is a common denomination, appliable to all of them; much like *Cæsar* or *Augustus* with the *Roman* Emperors, or sometime *Cosroes* with the *Persians*, and no distinctive appellation. Yet in *Herodotus* we find one king, the successor of *Sesostris*, to have been called (i) *Pheron*, which, I suppose, is *Pharaoh*, and his proper and peculiar name. But who this *Pharaoh* should be, whose

---

(i) Σεσώσει ὁ τελδυτήσαντ(Ο, ἐκδέξαδι ἔλεγον τω βασιληίω τὸν παῖδα αυτε Φερῶνα. Herodot. l. 2.

heart God hardened, and upon whom *Moses* wrought so many wonders, is worth our disquisition. *Josephus*, in his first book *contra Apionem*, out of *Manethos*, contends, that *Tethmosis* (who is termed also *Amosis* by *Africanus* and *Eusebius*) reigned then in Ægypt. The whole force of his argument lies in this, that *Manethos* mentions the expulsion of the nation of shepherds to have been by *Tethmosis*: but the *Hebrews* were a nation of shepherds; therefore the *Hebrews* were expelled out of Ægypt, or, in the Scripture phrase, departed out of Ægypt, under *Tethmosis*; and consequently, that *Moses*, who was their conductor, was coetaneous with him. That the *Hebrews* were a nation of shepherds, and so accounted of themselves, and were esteemed by others, is very perspicuous. (k) *And* Joseph *said unto his brethren, and unto his father's house, I will go up and shew* Pharaoh, *and say unto him, My brethren, and my father's house, which were in the land of* Canaan, *are come unto me. And the men are shepherds; for their trade hath been to feed cattel, and they have brought their flocks, and their herds, and all that they have. And it shall come to pass, when* Pharaoh *shall call you, and shall say, What is your occupation? that ye shall*

(k) Gen. 46. 31, 32.

say, Thy servants trade hath been about cat-tel, from our youth even until now, both we, and also our fathers: that ye may dwell in the land of Goshen. *For every shepherd is an abomination to the Ægyptians.* But before we shall disprove this assertion of *Josephus*, which carries much speciousness with it, and therefore is approved and followed by (*l*) *Tatianus*, by (*m*) *Justin Martyr*, and by (*n*) *Clemens Alexandrinus*, we shall put down the words of *Manethos* himself, as they are reported by (*o*) *Josephus* in his first book *contra Apionem*. Timaus *by name being our king, under him, I know not how, God was displeased; and beyond expectation, out of the Eastern countries, men of obscure birth incamped themselves in the country, and easily and without battel took it by force, binding the princes, and besides cruelly burning the cities, and overthrowing the temples of the Gods. Last of all they made one of themselves a king, who was named* Salatis; *he reigning nineteen years, died. After him another, named* Bæon, *reigned forty four years; next to him* Apachnas; *another, thirty six years seven months; then* Apophis *sixty one,* Janias *fifty, and one month; after all* Assis, *forty*

(*l*) In oratióne contra Græcos.
(*m*) In parænetico ad eosdem.
(*n*) Lib. 1. Stromatum.
(*o*) Joseph. lib. 1. contra Apionem. Ἐγίνετο βασιλεὺς ἡμῖν Τίμαος ὄνομα, &c.

nine years and two months. And these were the first six kings of them always conquering, and desiring to extirpate Ægypt. Their nation was called Hycsos, *that is, kingly shepherds. For* Hyc *in the sacred tongue signifies a king, and* sos *a shepherd, or shepherds in the common dialect; and thence* Hycsos *is compounded. But some say, that these were Arabians.* [**In other copies I have found, that by the denomination* Hyc, *kings are not signified, but on the contrary, captive shepherds. For* Hyc *in the Ægyptian language, when it is pronounced with a broad sound, plainly signifies captives; and this seems more probable to me, and better agreeing to the ancient history.*] *Those kings therefore which we before mentioned, and those which were called* Pastores, *and those which descended of them, ruled Ægypt five hundred and eleven years. After this he mentions, that by the kings of* Thebes, *and of the rest of Ægypt, there was an invasion made against these shepherds, and a very great and lasting war. The which, he says, were conquered by a king, whose name was* Alisfragmuthosis, *whereby they lost all Ægypt, being shut up into a place containing in circuit ten thousand acres. This space,* Manethos *says, the shepherds incompassed with a great and strong wall, that they might se-*

---

* What is here included within crotchets, are the words of *Josephus*, and not of *Manethos*.

cure

cure all their substance, and their spoils in a defensible place. But Themosis, the son of Alisfragmuthosis, endeavouring to take them, with four hundred thousand armed men beleaguered the walls, who despairing to take them by siege, made conditions with them, that they should leave Ægypt, and go without any damage whither they would. They upon this agreement, no less than two hundred and forty thousand, with all their substance, went out of Ægypt by the desert into Syria; and fearing the power of the Assyrians (who then ruled Asia) in that country which is now called Judæa, they built a city capable to receive so many myriads of men, naming it Hierusalem.

By way of answer to *Josephus*, we say, that though the *Israelites* might properly be called shepherds, yet it cannot hence be inferred out of *Manethos*, that these shepherds were *Israelites*. Nay, if we compare this relation of *Manethos* with that in *Exodus* (p), which *Josephus*, being a *Jew*, cannot but approve of, we shall find the contrary. For there they live under a heavy slavery and persecution; whereas here they are the persecutors and afflictors: there they groan under their task-masters the *Ægyptians*; here they make all *Ægypt* to groan under them: lastly, whereas there they are

(p) Exod. 1.

imployed

the PYRAMIDS *were built.* 31

imployed in the lowest offices, (*q*) *in mortar, and in brick, and in all manner of service in the field;* here, after the destruction of many cities and men, and infinite outrages committed upon the *Ægyptians*, they make one of themselves a king, and for six descents keep themselves in possession of the royal throne, of which, after a long and bloody war, they are deprived. Their building likewise of a city in *Judæa*, and naming it *Jerusalem*, according to *Manethos*, is a strong argument against *Josephus*, that those shepherds could not have been the *Israelites*. For before the enterance of the *Israelites* into *Canaan*, we find, that *Jerusalem* was a fort of the *Jebusites* upon mount *Sion*, unconquered by *Joshua*. (*r*) *As for the* Jebusites, *the inhabitants of* Jerusalem, *the children of* Israel *could not drive them out.* But they were long after subdued by David. And (*s*) *David and all Israel went to Jerusalem, which is Jebus, where the* Jebusites *were the inhabitants of the land. And the inhabitants of* Jebus *said to David, Thou shalt not come hither. Nevertheless* David *took the castle of Zion, which is the city of* David. Besides all this, the history and chronology of those ancient times, if we compare sacred and profane authors,

(*q*) Exod. 1. 14. (*r*) Josh. 15. 63. (*s*) 1 Chron. 11. 4, 5.

will

will in no sort admit, that these shepherds must have been the *Israelites*. For if these that departed out of *Ægypt* in the reign of *Tethmosis* king of *Thebais*, or of the upper part of *Ægypt*, were the children of *Israel*, then must *Moses* their conductor have been as ancient as *Tethmosis*, or *Amosis*, that is, as ancient as *Inachus* the first king of the *Argives*. For *Apion*, in his fourth book of the histories of *Ægypt*, shews out of *Ptolemæus Mendesius* an *Ægyptian* Priest, that this *Amosis* lived in the time of *Inachus*, as it is recorded by (*t*) *Tatianus*, (*u*) *Justin Martyr*, (*x*) *Clemens Alexandrinus*, and others. *Eusebius*, though he doth not approve of it, for he places *Moses* in the time of (*y*) *Cecrops*; yet he assures us, that it was a received opinion among many learned men: (*z*) *Moysen Inachi fuisse temporibus eruditissimi viri tradiderunt, ex nostris Clemens & Africanus; ex Judeis, Josephus & Justus, veteris historia monimenta replicantes.* Now *Inachus*, according to (*a*) *Castor* an ancient chronographer, with whom *Eusebius* also concurs, began to reign a thou-

(*t*) In oratione contra Græcos.
(*u*) In Parænetico ad Græcos.
(*x*) Lib. 1, Stromatum.
(*y*) And so doth St. *Austin*: Eduxit Moses ex Ægypto populum Dei novissimo tempore Cecropis, Atheniensium regis. Lib. 18. c. 11. de Civ. Dei.
(*z*) Euseb. Chron.
(*a*) Euseb. Chron.

sand

the PYRAMIDS *were built.* 33

sand and eighty years before the first *Olympiad*, that is, CIƆCCLXVIII. before the destruction of the Temple under *Zedekiah*; and before *Christ*'s nativity, after the *Dionysian* or common account, CIƆIƆCCCLVI. That of the *Olympiads* is so assured an epocha, and so strongly and clearly proved by eclipses of the sun and moon, which are the best demonstrations in chronology, these being expressed by some of the ancients to have happened in such a year of such an Olympiad, as by (*b*) *Ptolemy* others in such a year of the epocha of *Nabonassar*, that we cannot err in our calculations an hour, much less an intire day. By this therefore we shall fix the time of *Zedekiah*, and the destruction of the Temple: and consequently, if, by our continuation of the years mentioned in the sacred story, it shall appear, that from the time of *Moses*, either to the first *Olympiad*, or to *Zedekiah*, and the destruction of the Temple, there cannot be so great a distance as these suppose, we may safely then conclude, that *Moses* lived not in the time of this *Tethmosis*, and is not so ancient as *Josephus* makes him, and that these shepherds were not the *Israelites*, but very probably *Arabians*, as *Manethos* here also reports; *some say, that these*

(*b*) Ptolemæus ἐν μεγάλῃ συντάξει.

were

were *Arabians:* who to this day for the greatest part, like the *Nomades*, wander up and down, feeding their cattel, and often make incursions upon the *Ægyptians* and *Syrians*. Which occasioned *Sesostris* the Great, as we find it in (c) *Diodorus, to make a wall on the east side of* Ægypt, *a thousand and fifty furlongs in length, from* Pelusium *by the Desert to* Heliopolis, *against the inroads of the* Syrians *and* Arabians : As at this day the *Chinese* have done against the irruptions of the *Tartars* on the north and west parts of *China*, for many hundred miles; the which appears by a large map of mine of that country, made and printed in *China*. On the contrary, if the succession of times from *Moses* recorded in the holy writ, better agrees with the age of *Amenophis*, the father of *Ramesses*, whose story (d) *Josephus* hath preserved out of *Manethos*, and whose time and rank in the dynasties *Africanus* and *Eusebius* deliver out of the same *Manethos*, we may with more probability affirm, that the migration of the *Israelites*, and time of *Moses* was, when *Amenophis* was *Pharaoh*, or king of *Ægypt*, than that it was when *Tethmosis* reigned, as *Josephus* and others contend, out of a desire to make *Moses* ancienter than in truth he is.

(c) Diod. Sic. lib. 1.
(d) Joseph. lib. 1. contra Apionem.

And though this argument from the series and successions of time is so demonstrative and conclusive, that nothing can be opposed against it, and therefore might be sufficient to evince our purpose: yet if we considerately examine another relation of *Manethos*, which is slighted and depressed by *Josephus*, because it made not for his purpose, it must necessarily be, that by those shepherds he meant not the *Israelites*, but rather by the *Israelites* the leprous people, which in his computation are three hundred thirty years and six months, after the dynasty of the Shepherds. And therefore we may oppose the authority of (p) *Manethos* against himself, or rather against *Josephus*; the sum of whose discourse is this: That *Amenophis*, who was a great worshiper of the Gods, as *Orus* one of the former kings had been, being desirous to see the Gods, *one of the Priests of the same name told him he might, if he cleansed the country of leprous and polluted people*. This leprous people chose for their Captain one of the Priests of *Heliopolis*, named *Osarsiphus*, who changing his name was called *Moses*: he causing *Amenophis* for fear to fly into *Æthiopia*, was afterward by him, and by his son *Sethon*, who was also called *Ramesses* by

(d) Manethos apud Joseph. lib. 1. contra Apionem.

the name of his father, overthrown in battel, and the leprous people were pursued by them unto the confines of *Syria.* Thus far out of *Manethos.* Here, which is very remarkable, we have expresly the name of *Moses*; whereas in the former relation of *Manethos*, there is no mention of him; but of six other kings, with their peculiar names. Whereas it is not probable he would have omitted the name of *Moses*, if he had lived in that age, being a name so famous, and so well known to them; and by (*e*) *Josephus* acknowledged, *that the Ægyptians accounted him to be an admirable and divine man.* The pursuing of them unto the confines of *Syria*, doth very well intimate the following of the *Israelites* by *Pharaoh* and his host. For his terming them a leprous and polluted people, we must consider him to have been an *Ægyptian*, and therefore not unlikely to throw as many aspersions as he could upon the *Israelites*, whom they deadly hated, it may be out of memory of their former plagues. How ever it were, *Chæremon* hath almost the same history, as (*f*) *Josephus* confesses. *Chæremon professing*

(*e*) Τῦτον ὃ τὸν ἄνδρα θαυμαστὸν ὑμεῖς Αἰγύπτιοι ᾧ θεῖον νομίζουσι. Joseph. lib. 1. contra Apionem
(*f*) Lib. contra Apionem. Χαιρήμων] ᾧ ͵δ ἴτος Αἰγυπτιακὴν φάσκων ἱστορίας συγγεδφειν ᾧ ἀκολυθεῖς ταυτὸ ὄνομα τῶ βασιλέως, ὅπερ ὁ Μανεθῶς, Ἀμένωφιν ᾧ τ΄ ἥον αὐτῦ Ῥαμεσσὴν, &c.

to

the PYRAMIDS *were built.* 37

to write the history of Ægypt, says, that under Amenophis *and his son* Ramesses, *two hundred and fifty thousand leprous and polluted men were cast out of Ægypt. Their leaders were* Moses *the Scribe, and* Josephus, *who was also a sacred Scribe. The Ægyptian name of* Moses *was* Tisithen, *that of* Joseph Peteseph. *These coming to* Pelusium, *and finding there three hundred and eighty thousand men left by* Amenophis, *which he would not admit into Ægypt, making a league with them, they undertook an expedition against Ægypt.* Upon this *Amenophis* flies into Æthiopia, and his son *Messenes drives out the* Jews *into* Syria, *in number about two hundred thousand, and receives his father* Amenophis *out of* Æthiopia. I know (g) *Lysimachus* assigns another king, and another time, in which *Moses* lead the *Israelites* out of Ægypt, and that was, *when* Bocchoris *reigned in* Ægypt, *the nation of the* Jews *being infected with leprosies, and scabs, and other diseases, betook themselves to the temples to beg their living;* many being tainted with the disease, there happened a dearth in Ægypt: Whereupon *Bocchoris,* consulting with the

---
(g) Lysimachus apud Joseph. lib. 1. contra Apionem. Ἐπὶ Βοκχόρεως τῶ Αἰγυπτίων βασιλέως ☩ λαὸν ☩ Ἰουδαίων λεπρὸς ὄντας κ̀, ψευρὸς, κ̀, ἄλλα νοσήματα τινα ἔχοντας, εἰς τὰ ἱερὰ καταφεύγοντας μεταιτεν τξοφην, &c.

e   oracle

oracle of *Ammon*, received answer, *That the leprous people were to be drowned in the sea in sheets of lead; the scabbed were to be carried into the wilderness*; who choosing *Moses* for their leader, conquered that country which is now called *Judæa*. Out of which relation of *Lysimachus*, and some others of like credit, (*b*) *Tacitus* may have borrowed his in the fifth book of his histories: *Most authors agree, that there arising a contagion in Ægypt, which defiled their bodies, king* Bocchoris *consulting the oracle of* Hammon *for remedy, was bid to purge his kingdom, and to carry that sort of men, as hated of the Gods, into other countries. Thence the vulgar sort being inquired after, and collected together, after they had been left in the deserts, the rest being heavy with tears,* Moses, *one of the banish'd men, admonished them not to expect the help either of gods or men, being deserted by both; but that they should trust to him as their captain sent from heaven, to whose as-*

(*b*) Tacit. l. 5. Hist. Plurimi auctores consentiunt, ortâ per Ægyptum tabe, quæ corpora fædaret, regem Bocchorim, adito Hammonis oraculo, remedium petentem purgare regnum, & id genus hominum, ut invisum deis, alias in terras avehere jussum. Sic conquisitum collectumque vulgus, postquam vastis locis relictum sit, cæteris per lachrymas torpentibus, Mosen unum exulum monuisse, ne quam deorum hominumve opem expectarent, ab utrisque deserti, sed sibimet, ut duci cælesti, crederent, primò cujus auxilio credentes præsentes miserias pepulissent. Assensêre, atque omnium ignari fortuitum iter incipiunt.

sistance

the PYRAMIDS *were built.* 39

ſiſtance by their giving credit at the firſt, they had overcome their preſent calamities. They aſſented unto him, and being ignorant of all, they begin their journey as fortune ſhould lead them. Thus much, and more, hath *Tacitus* of *Moſes* and the *Jews.* But to paſs by his and *Lyſimachus*'s calumnies, we can no more aſſent to theſe teſtimonies of theirs, that *Moſes* lived in the time of *Bocchoris,* than we did to *Joſephus,* that he was coetaneous with *Tethmoſis.* For we find *Bocchoris* to be placed by *Africanus* and (*i*) *Euſebius,* both following *Manethos,* in the 24th dynaſty; and by (*k*) *Diodorus,* long after *Seſoſtris* the great, or *Rameſſes*; which *Rameſſes,* or *Sethoſis,* or *Sethon* (that is, *Seſoſtris* and *Seſooſis* in *Diodorus*) both in *Manethos* and *Chæremon,* is the ſon of *Amenophis,* who is the laſt king of the 18th dynaſty, according to *Africanus* and *Euſebius.* I purpoſely omit the opinion of (*l*) *Apion,* that *Moſes* (whom he makes to be of *Heliopolis*) departed with theſe lepers, and blind, and lame, in the firſt year of the ſeventh *Olympiad,* in which year, ſaith he, *the* Phœnicians *built* Carthage; and that other of (*m*) *Porphyrius*

(*i*) Ex edit. Joſ. Scaliger.   (*k*) Diod. lib. 1.
(*l*) Apud Joſeph. lib. 2. contra Apionem.
(*m*) Ex Ethnicis verò impius ille Porphyrius, in quarto operis ſui libro, quod adverſum nos caſſo labore contexuit, poſt Moyſen Semiramim fuiſſe affirmat. Euſeb. Chron.

in his fourth book against the Christians, that *Moses* was before *Semiramis:* where he places him as much too high, as *Apion* doth too low.

Laying therefore aside these vain and uncertain traditions, we have no more assured way exactly to fix the time of *Moses*, and by *Moses* the time in which the Pyramids were built, than to have recourse to the sacred Scriptures, and sometimes to compare such authors of the Gentiles with these, against whom we have no just exceptions. For by those and these conjointly, we may continue his time to the first Olympiad, and thence to the destruction of the Temple by *Nebuchadnezzar* king of *Babylon*; that of the Olympiads being a most certain and known epocha with the *Greeks*, as that of the destruction of the Temple with the *Jews*. From *Moses* then, or the migration of the *Israelites* out of Ægypt, to the building of *Solomon*'s Temple, are four hundred eighty years current, or four hundred seventy nine complete; and so also (*n*) *Eusebius* computes them. The words of the text plainly conclude this sum. (*o*) *And it came to pass in the four hundred and fourth score year after the children of* Israel *were come out of the land of* Ægypt,

---

(*n*) Eusebii Chron.   (*o*) 1 Kings 6. 1.

the PYRAMIDS *were built.* 41

in the fourth year of Solomon's *reign over* Ifrael, *in the month* Zif, *which is the second month, that he began to build the houfe of the Lord.* From the building of the Temple to the deftruction of it in the reign of *Zedekias*, by the calculation and confeffion of the beft chronologers, are betwixt four hundred and twenty, and four hundred and thirty years, which is thus deduced: After the firft foundation of the Temple, *Solomon* reigned *(p)* thirty feven years, *(q) Rehoboam* with *(r) Abiah* twenty; in whofe time we are to place *Shifhak*, or *Sefochofis*, the king of Ægypt. *(s) And it came to pafs in the firft year of king* Rehoboam, *that* Shifhak *king of* Ægypt *came up againft* Jerufalem; *and he took away the treafures of the houfe of the Lord, and the treafures of the king's houfe, he even took away all: and he took away all the fhields of gold which* Solomon *had made.* This *Shifhak* is named, by the Septuagint, Σουσακὶμ, by St. *Hierome, Sefac*, and is the fame whom *(t) Jofephus* calls Σίσακ⊙, which

---

(p) For, 1 Kings 6. 1. *In the fourth year of his reign, and the fecond month, he began to build the houfe of the Lord.* And in 1 Kings 11. 42. *The time that* Solomon *reigned in Jerufalem over all* Ifrael *was forty years.* Out of which if we fubduct three complete years that preceded the foundation of the temple, there remain thirty feven years.
(q) 1 King 14. 21. *He reigned feventeen years in* Jerufalem.
(r) 1 King 15. 2. *Three years reigned he in* Jerufalem.
(s) 1 King. 14. 25, 26.
(t) Jofeph. Antiq. lib. 8. cap. 4.

Of the Time in which

he imagines to have been *Sesostris* the great, whose victories and conquests are described at large by (*u*) *Herodotus*. But this *Sesostris*, or (*x*) *Sesoosis*, as *Diodorus* also terms him, must long have preceded *Rehoboam*'s time, as in the sequel of this discourse it will appear. Therefore the more probable opinion is that of *Scaliger*, that by *Shishak* is meant *Sesochosis*, whom *Manethos* calls Σέσογχις, and the scholiast of *Apollonius* Σεσόγχωσις: the time of the twenty second dynasty, in which we find him placed by *Africanus* and *Eusebius*, doth well agree with it; and the radical letters in *Shishak*, *Sesac*, and Σέσογχις, being the same, do very much strengthen our assertion. After *Rehoboam* and *Abiah*'s reign, (*y*) *Asah* and (*z*) *Jehosaphat* reigned sixty six years; (*a*) *Joram* and (*b*) *Ahaziah* nine; (*c*) *Athaliah* and (*d*) *Joas* forty six; (*e*) *Amasias* twenty nine, (*f*) *Uzziah* fifty

---

(*u*) Herod. lib. 2.
(*x*) *Diodorus*, in the printed copies, always names him *Sesoosis*; but in one of the MSS, as *Henr. Stephanus* observes, he is sometimes called *Sesostris*, and sometimes *Sesoosis*. Vid. edit. Diod. ab Henr. Stephan.
(*y*) 1 Kings 15. 10. *Forty one years reigned he in* Jerusalem.
(*z*) 1 Kings 22. 42. *He reigned* 25 *years in* Jerusalem.
(*a*) 2 Kings 8. 17. *He reigned eight years in* Jerusalem.
(*b*) 2 Kings 8. 26. *He reigned one year in* Jerusalem.
(*c*) 2 Kings 11. 3. *And he was with her hid in the house of the Lord six years;* and Athaliah *did reign over the land.*
(*d*) 2 Kings 12. 1. *Forty years reigned he in* Jerusalem.
(*e*) 2 Kings 14. 2. *He reigned twenty nine years in* Jerusalem.
(*f*) 2 Kings 15. 2. *He reigned fifty two years in* Jerusalem.

the PYRAMIDS *were built.* 43

two, (g) *Jotham* sixteen, (h) *Ahaz* sixteen, being contemporary with *Hoshea*, the last king of *Israel*; in whose time we find *So* to reign in *Ægypt*, 2 Kings 17. 4. After *Ahaz*, succeeded *Hezekiah*, reigning (i) twenty nine years.

Now (k) *in the fourteenth year of king* Hezekiah *did* Sennacharib *king of* Assyria *came up against all the fenced cities of* Judah, *and took them.* But afterwards when he came to besiege *Jerusalem*———(l) *it came to pass that night, that the angel of the Lord went out, and smote in the camp of the* Assyrians, *an hundred fourscore and five thousand; and when they arose early in the morning, behold they were all dead corpses. So* Sennacharib *king of* Assyria *departed, and went, and returned and dwelt at* Nineveh. In the time of this *Sennacharib*, *Sethon*, succeeding *Anysis*, reigned in *Ægypt*, according to (m) *Herodotus*, who in his *Euterpe* hath plainly the name *Sanacharib*, styling him king of the *Arabians* and *Assyrians*, and making him to have received a miraculous defeat; which, it may be, was that of *He-*

(g) 2 Kings 15. 33. *He reigned sixteen years in* Jerusalem.
(h) 2 Kings 16. 2. *He reigned sixteen years in* Jerusalem.
(i) 2 Kings 18. 2. *He reigned twenty nine years in* Jerusalem.
(k) 2 Kings 18. 13, 16.
(l) 2 Kings 19. 35, 36.
(m) Herod. lib. 2.

zekiah, tho' he applies it to *Sethon* king of the Ægyptians. His ſtory is well worth our obſervation, which runs thus: (*n*) *After this (*Anyſis*) the Prieſt of* Vulcan, *by name* Sethon, *reigned, who abuſing the men of war of the* Ægyptians, *and contemning them as not uſeful to him, beſides other ignominies, he deprived them of their lands, which had been given to every company of twelve by the former kings. Whence it happened, that when afterwards* Sanacharib *the king of the* Arabians *and* Aſſyrians *invaded* Ægypt, *the Ægyptian ſoldiers refuſed to aſſiſt him. Then the Prieſt deſtitute of counſel, ſhut himſelf up, lamenting before the image, how much he was in danger to ſuffer; in the midſt of his mourning falling aſleep, a God appeared to him, encouraging him, that he ſhould ſuffer no diſtreſs, if he would march againſt the armies of the* Arabians; *for he would ſend him ſuccour. He therefore giving credit to this dream, taking with him ſuch volunteers of the* Ægyptians *as followed him, pitched his army at* Peluſium: *For there* Ægypt *is eaſieſt invaded; neither did any of the ſoldiers follow him, but tradeſmen, and artificers, and merchants. Coming thither by night, an infinite number of mice entring upon his ene-*

(*n*) Herod. lib. 2 Μετὰ ᵹ τοῦτον βασιλεῦσαι τὸν ἱρέα τῶ Ἡφαίςυ, τῶ ὄνομα εἶναι Σεθῶν, &c.

mies,

the PYRAMIDS *were built.* 45

mies, gnawed their quivers and bows, and the feathers of their shields; so that the next day the enemies, destitute of arms, fled, many of them being slain. And therefore now this king stands in the temple of Vulcan, *in a statue of marble, holding in his hand a mouse, with this inscription:* HE THAT LOOKS UPON ME, LET HIM BE RELIGIOUS. After *Hezekiah,* (*o*) *Manasses* reigned fifty five years; (*p*) *Amon* two, (*q*) *Josiah* thirty one. (*r*) *In his days* Pharaoh Nechoh *king of Ægypt went up against the king of* Assyria *to the river* Euphrates, *and king* Josiah *went against him, and slew him at* Megiddo, *when he had seen him.* The same relation we read in *Herodotus,* if we pardon him the mistake of *Magdolo* for *Megiddo,* who writes, that (*s*) *Necus* (the king of *Ægypt*) *fighting a battle on land with the* Syrians *in* Magdolo, *obtained the victory, and after the fight he took* Cadytus, *a great city in* Syria.

Next to *Josiah* succeeded (*t*) *Joachaz*,

(*o*) 2 Kings 21. 1. *He reigned fifty five years in* Jerusalem.
(*p*) 2 Kings 22. 19 *He reigned two years in* Jerusalem.
(*q*) 2 Kings 22. 1. *He reigned thirty one years in* Jerusalem.
(*r*) 2 Kings 23. 22. and 2 Chron. 35. 20. Necho *king of Ægypt came up to fight against* Carchemish *by Euphrates, and* Josiah *went out against him.*
(*s*) Καὶ Σύριοις περὶ ὁ Νεκὼς συμϐαλὼν ἐν Μαγδώλῳ ἐνίκησε, μετὰ δ. τὴν μάχην, Κάδυτιν πόλιν τ. Συρίης ἐοῦσαν μεγάλην ἇλε. Herodot. lib. 2.
(*t*) 2 Kings 23. 31. *He reigned three months in* Jerusalem.

(*u*) *Je-*

Of the Time in which

(*u*) *Jehoiakim*, and (*x*) *Jeconiah*, or *Jehoiakin*, reigning eleven years and six months. And in the eleventh year of (*y*) *Zedekiah*, the next king after *Jechoniah*, was the Temple burnt by *Nebuzaradan, in the* (*z*) *nineteenth year of* Nebuchadnezzar *king of* Babylon, or the second of *Vaphres* king of *Ægypt*, in the computation of *Clemens Alexandrinus. This* Zedekiah, saith (*a*) *Josephus, having been a confederate of the* Babylonians *for eight years, broke his faith with them, and joining league with the* Ægyptians, *hoped to overthrow the* Babylonians. This league we find intimated in (*b*) *Ezekiel*; and we read

(*u*) 2 Kings 23. 36. *He reigned eleven years in* Jerusalem.

(*x*) 2 Kings 24. 8. *He reigned in* Jerusalem *three months*.

(*y*) *And the city was besieged unto the eleventh year of king* Zedekiah. *And on the ninth day of the fourth month the famine prevailed in the city, and there was no bread for the people of the land: And the city was broken up, and all the men of war fled by night.*

(*z*) *And in the fifth month, on the seventh day of the month (which is the nineteenth year of* Nebuchadnezzar *king of* Babylon) *came* Nebuzaradan *captain of the guard, a servant of the king of* Babylon, *unto* Jerusalem. *And he burnt the house of the Lord, and the king's house, and all the houses of* Jerusalem, *and every great man's house burnt he with fire.* 2 Kings 25. 2, 3, 4, 8, 9. The same relation we find in *Jeremiah*, chap. 53. ver. 5, 6, 7, 12, 13. almost word for word, which is remarkable.

(*a*) Joseph. Antiq. lib. 10. cap. 10. Τὴν συμμαχίαν, ἢ τὴν πρὸς τοὺς Βαβυλωνίους ἐπὶ ἔτη ὀκτὼ καλάγων, διέλυσε τὰς πρὸς αὐτοὺς σπονδὰς, ᾗ τοῖς Αἰγυπτίοις προσέθετο, καταλύσων τοὺς Βαβυλωνίους ἐλπίσας.

(*b*) Ezek. 17. 15.

the PYRAMIDS *were built.* 47

in (c) *Jeremiah* and (d) *Josephus*, of succours and assistance sent by the king of *Ægypt*, when *Zedekiah* and *Jerusalem* were first distressed by the *Chaldeans*, or forces of the king of *Babylon*: (e) *Then* Pharaoh's *army was come forth out of* Ægypt; *and when the* Chaldeans *that besieged* Jerusalem, *heard tidings of them, they departed from* Jerusalem. The same is reiterated by him: *Behold* Pharaoh's *army, which is come forth to help you, shall return to* Ægypt *to their own land. And the* Chaldeans *shall come again, and fight against this city, and take it, and burn it with fire.* All which, we see, was performed by *Nebuchadnezzar* in the eleventh year of *Zedekiah*, and a judgment also denounced against the king of *Ægypt*. (f) *Thus saith the Lord, Behold, I will give* Pharaoh Hophra *king of* Ægypt *into the hands of his enemies, and into the hand of them that seek his life: as I gave* Zedekiah *king of* Judah *into the hand of* Nebuchadrezzar *king of* Babylon *his enemy, and that sought his life.* The same is often threaten'd by the Prophet (g) Eze-

(c) Jeremiah 37. 5.
(d) Joseph. Antiq. lib. 10. c. 10. Ὁ ở Αἰγύπτιος ἀκούσας ἐν οἷς ἐστιν ὁ σύμμαχος αὐτῦ Σεδεκίας, ἀναλαβὼν πολλὴν δύναμιν, ἧκεν εἰς τὴν Ἰυδαίαν ὡς λύσων τὴν πολιορκίαν.
(e) Jer. 37. 5, 7, 8.
(f) Jer. 44. 30.
(g) Ezek. 30. 22, 23.

kiel,

kiel, who lived in the time of *Hezekiah*, as *Jeremiah* did. *I am against* Pharaoh *king of* Ægypt, *and I will scatter the Ægyptians among the nations, and will disperse them throughout the countries. And I will strengthen the arms of the king of* Babylon, *and put my sword in his hand: But I will break* Pharaoh's *arms.* Which prophecies we may discover most manifestly to have been fulfilled in the reign of *Apries*, as (*b*) *Herodotus* names him, or *Apryes*, as (*i*) *Diodorus* calls him, or *Vaphres*, as the *Septuagint* and *Eusebius* render the name of that king, which here in *Jeremiah* is called *Pharaoh Hophra*. *Who,* (*k*) saith *Herodotus, next to* Psammitichus *his grandfather was the most fortunate of all the former kings, for twenty-five years of his reign*; which might occasion *Zedekiah* to fly to him for succour: but the *Ægyptians* rebelling against him, he was overthrown in battle, taken prisoner, and afterward strangled by his own servant *Amasis,* whom they had made their king. The whole story, and manner is at large in (*l*) *Herodotus.* Neither did divine vengeance long forbear to pursue the traitor;

(*b*) Herod lib. 2.
(*i*) Diodor. lib. 1.
(*k*) Ὅς μετὰ Ψαμμίτιχον τὸν ἑαυτῦ προπάτορα ἐγένετο εὐδαιμονέςατος τῶν πρότερον βασιλέων ἐπ' ἔτεα πέντε χὶ εἴκοσι ἄρξας. Herod. l. 2.
(*l*) Herodot. lib. 2.

For

the PYRAMIDS *were built.* 49

For *Cambyses*, the king of the *Persians* and of *Babylon*, coming with an army against him, possest himself of *Ægypt*, as the Prophets had foretold. Nor could the *Ægyptians* ever to this day recover the monarchy. For after the *Persians* succeeded the *Macedonians*, after them the *Romans*, then the *Arabians*, next the *Mamalukes* or *Circassians*, and last of all the *Turks* or *Scythians*. So that we may conclude from the occurrences then happening (the relations of *Herodotus* exactly agreeing with the threatnings of the Prophets) as also from the computation of times, and from the affinity and analogy of names, that *Hophra*, and *Apries*, or *Vaphres*, must have been the very same *Ægyptian* king, coetaneous and concurrent with *Zedekiah*.

To reassume then what hath been demonstrated by us. From the migration of the *Israelites* out of *Ægypt* under the conduct of *Moses*, to the building of *Solomon*'s Temple, are four hundred seventy nine years complete; and from the building of the Temple to the destruction of it, are four hundred and thirty years, and six months. But because it is not probable, that, amongst so many kings, all of them should have reigned completely so many years as are expressed in the text, it being the usual style of kings to reckon the

years

years current of their reign as complete, I shall limit this uncertainty between four hundred twenty and four hundred thirty years, which is a sufficient latitude. If any one shall desire a more exact calculation, he may compute them by comparing other places of the Scriptures with these, to be but four hundred twenty five years current, according to the opinion of the most reverend and judicious Primate of *Ireland*, to which I willingly subscribe; though either computation be sufficient for my purpose.

This destruction of the Temple, by our best chronographers is placed in the first year of the forty eighth Olympiad, and in the hundred and sixtieth of the epocha of *Nabonaſſar*, and in the nineteenth (as the Scripture often makes mention) of *Nabuchodonoſor*, the son of *Nabolaſſar* (as (*m*) *Beroſus* in *Joſephus* names him;) which *Nabolaſſar* must necessarily be the same with him that is called *Nabopolaſſar* in *Ptolemy*, the fourteenth king of the *Babylonians* after *Nabonaſſar*; whom *Nabocolaſſar* (or (*n*) *Nabuchodonozor*, or (*o*) *Nebuchadrezzar*, or (*p*) *Nebuchadnezzar*, as the Scripture also terms

(*m*) Ναβυχοδονόσορ⸳] ὁ πατὴρ αὐτῦ Ναβολάσαρ⸳. Berof. apud Joseph. lib. 1. contra Apionem
(*n*) So *Joſephus* and the *Vetus Vulgata* always name him.
(*o*) Jer. 52. 12, 28.
(*p*) 2 Kings 25. 8. Ezra 1. 7. Esta 1. 1.

him)

the PYRAMIDS *were built.* 51

him) in his *Canon Regnorum* succeeds. The nearness of the names, and agreement of their times from *Cyrus*, in whom the sacred Scriptures and profane authors equally concur, do strongly prove them to be the same. Wherefore we may conclude, that from the time of *Moses*, or the migration of the *Israelites* out of *Ægypt*, or from the end of *Amenophis* (coetaneous with *Moses*) the last king of the eighteenth dynasty (as *Eusebius* out of *Manethos* ranks him) to the reign of *Apries*, or *Vaphres*, or *Hophra*, the eighth king of the twenty sixth dynasty (according to the same *Eusebius* following *Manethos*) being coetaneous with *Zedekiah* king of *Judah*, and *Nebuchadnezzar* king of *Babylon*, are nine hundred and four years; and from *Moses* to the first Olympiad seven hundred and fifteen, and not one thousand and eighty, as they who make *Moses* as ancient as *Inachus* affirm. In which space we may with much certainty, if we give credit to *Herodotus* and *Diodorus*, place the kings, the founders of the three greatest and fairest Pyramids; which is the principal intention of this discourse. For (*q*) both of them describe these to have reigned many ages before *Apries*, and long after *Sesostris* the great; which *Sesostris*, or *Sesoosis*, as *Dio-*

(*q*) Herodot. lib. 2. Diod. Sic. l. 1.

dorus

dorus also styles him, must have been the same king whom *Manethos* in *Josephus* calls *Sethosis*, and *Ramesses*, and (r) *Ægyptus*, son to *Amenophis* before mentioned, and brother to *Armais* or *Danaus*; and *Eusebius* of *Scaliger*'s edition in *Greek* names *Sethos*, the *Latin* translations of Saint *Hierome*, both MSS. and printed copies, *Sethus*, and by all of them is the first king of the nineteenth dynasty. The great acts and conquests assigned by *Herodotus* to *Sesostris*, and as great attributed by *Manethos* to *Sethosis*, or *Ramesses*, which cannot well be applied to any other precedent or subsequent kings; together with the relation of them both, that while he was in pursuit of his victories abroad, his brother, whom *Manethos* names *Armais*, and (s) *Danaus* (in *Herodotus* his name is omitted) rebelled against him

---

(r) Λέγει γδ, ὅτι ὁ μὲν Σέθωσις ἐκαλεῖτο ΑἴγυπῖΘ, Ἀρμαῖς ὃ ὁ ἀδελφὸς αὐτῆ Δαναός. Manethos apud Joseph. lib. 1. contra Apionem. Where in the same place *Manethos* calls this Σέθωσις also Ῥαμεσσῆς, and son of *Amenophis*. And therefore *Scaliger* rightly observes, that *Ramesses* with *Manethos* is *trinominis*. Scal. in Euseb. Chron.

(s) This *Danaus* (for his rebellion being expelled by his brother out of *Ægypt*) sailed into *Greece*, and possessed himself of *Argos*; as it is testified by *Josephus* (lib. 1. contra Apionem) by *Africanus* and *Eusebius* (vid. Euseb. Chron.) by *Pausanias*, and several others. From whom descended the *Danaidæ*, one of the races of the kings at *Argos*; of all which there is frequent mention in the *Greek* historians and chronographers: wherefore we cannot be ignorant either of *Danaus*, or of his brother's

the PYRAMIDS *were built.* 53

him at home, and the nearness of the time, which may be collected out of both, do very much confirm the probability of this assertion. *Sesostris* then, and *Sethosis* being one and the same, is by *Manethos* in *Josephus* ranked immediately after *Amenophis* (coetaneous with *Moses*, as we have proved) and in the same *Manethos*, in the tradition of *Eusebius*, after *Menophis*, that is, *Amenophis*, both in the *Greek* and *Latin* copies. Wherefore the founders of these Pyramids having lived after *Sesostris*, must likewise have been after *Amenophis*. If we will come to a greater precifeness yet of time, (for this latitude of nine hundred and four years, which we assigned from *Moses* to the destruction of the first Temple, in the time of *Zedekiah* king of *Judah*, and *Apries* king of *Ægypt*, is so great, that we may lose our selves in it) we have no other possible means left, after the revolution of so many ages,

---

brother's time. I shall only add, for further illustration, what I find in *Africanus*. Ἀρμαῖς ὁ καὶ Δαναὸς φεύγων τὸν ἀδελφὸν Ῥαμεσσῆν τὸν καὶ Αἴγυπτον ἐκπίπτει τῆς κατ' Αἴγυπτον βασιλείας αὐτῶ, εἰς Ἑλλάδα τε ἀφικνεῖται. Ῥαμεσσῆς δὲ ὁ ἀδελφὸς αὐτοῦ ὁ Αἴγυπτος καλούμενος ἐβασίλευσεν Αἰγυπτίων ἔτη ξη. Μετωνόμασεν τὴν χώραν Αἰγύπτον τῷ ἰδίῳ ὀνόματι, ἥτις πρότερον Μεσραία, παρ' Ἕλλησι δ' Ἀερία ἐλέγετο. Δαναὸς δ' ὁ καὶ Ἀρμαῖς, κρατήσας τοῦ Ἄργους, καὶ ἐκβαλὼν Σθένελον τὸν Κρότωντα Ἀργείων ἐβασίλευσεν, καὶ οἱ ὑπόγονοι αὐτῷ μετ' αὐτὸν Δαναΐδαι καλούμενοι, ἐπ' Εὐρυσθέα τὸν Σθενέλου τοῦ Περσέως, μεθ' οὓς οἱ Πελοπίδαι. African. apud Euseb. Chron.

f *and*

and the loss of so many of the commentaries and monuments of the *Ægyptians*, but by having recourse to those dynasties of *Manethos*, as they are preserved by *Africanus* and *Eusebius*. And yet in neither of these shall we find the names of *Cheops* or *Chemmis*, of *Cephren* or *Chabryis*, or of *Mycerinus*, the author of the three greater Pyramids, mentioned by *Herodotus* and *Diodorus*; or of *Asychis*, the builder of a fourth, according to *Herodotus*. Wherefore what their writings have not supplied us with, that reason must. For since these *Ægyptian* kings, as we have proved, lived between *Amenophis* and *Apries*, and by (*t*) *Eusebius* out of *Africanus*, *Amenophis* is the last of the eighteenth dynasty, and *Apries* or *Vaphres* the eighth of the twenty sixth dynasty, we must necessarily place them in one of the intermediate dynasties. But seeing all the intermediate dynasties have their peculiar kings, unless it be the twentieth, we have no reason to exclude them, and to bring these in their places as usurpers: but rather, with great probability (for I must say here with (*u*) *Livy*, *Quis rem tam veterem pro certo affirmet?*) we may assign to them the twentieth dynasty: In which we find not the name of any one king, but yet the space

(*t*) Euseb. Chron.   (*x*) Liv. lib. 1.

left

the PYRAMIDS *were built.* 55
left vacant of one hundred seventy eight years, according to *Eusebius*.

Here therefore we shall place

First, *Cheops* or *Chemmis*, the founder of the first Pyramid, who began his reign in the CIƆ IƆ CIƆ ƆCCC XLVIII year of the *Julian* period, that is, CCCCLXXXX years before the first Olympiad, and IƆCLXXVIII before the first destruction of the Temple, and CIƆ CCLXVI before the beginning of the years of our Lord. He reigned fifty years, saith *Herodotus*, and built this Pyramid, as *Diodorus* observes, a thousand years before his time, or the CLXXIX Olympiad; whereas he might have said a thousand two hundred and seven.

Secondly, *Cephren* or *Chabryis*, the builder of the second, who reigned fifty (x) six years.

Thirdly, *Mycerinus*, the erector of the third, seven years.

Fourthly, *Afychis*, the author of the fourth. } How long these two reigned is no
Fifthly, *Anyfis* the blind. } where expressed.

Sixthly, *Sabachus* the *Æthiopian*. He conquered Ægypt, and reigned (y) fifty years.

The sum is CLXIII years; this being subducted out of CLXXVIII years (the whole time allowed by *Eusebius* to this dynasty) the remainder is XV years; which space we

(x) Herod. l. 2. Diodor. l. 1. (y) Herod. & Diod. ib.

f 2 may

may without any inconvenience divide between *Asychis* and *Anysis*.

If any shall question, why the names of these kings are omitted by *Manethos*, an Ægyptian priest, in the xx dynasty, I can give no other reason, than what we read in *Herodotus*. (z) These kings (speaking of *Cheops* and *Cephren*) the Ægyptians out of hatred will not so much as name; but they call them the Pyramids of Philition a Shepherd, who in those times at that place fed his cattle. The which hatred, occasioned by their oppressions, as (a) *Diodorus* also mentions, might cause him to omit the rest, especially *Sabachus*, an Æthiopian, and an usurper.

Following this computation of *Eusebius*, of CLXXVIII years for the xx dynasty, and not that of *Africanus*, who assigns only cxxv: of whom (b) *Joseph Scaliger* hath this censure, *in istis dynastiis aliquid turbasse videtur Africanus, ut consuleret rationibus suis*; it will follow by way of consequence, as the most reverend and learned Primate of *Ireland* in his *Chronologia Sacra* hath singularly well observed,

First, that the 18th dynasty ends with the migration of the *Israelites* out of Ægypt,

(z) Τούτους ὑπὸ μίσεος οὐ κάρτα θέλουσι Αἰγύπτιοι ὀνομάζειν, ἀλλὰ καὶ τὰς πυραμίδας καλέουσι ποιμένος Φιλιτίωνος, ὃς τοῦτον τὸν χρόνον ἐνέμεσκε ὦεα κατὰ ταῦτα τὰ χωρία. Herodot. lib. 2
(a) Diodor. lib. 1. (b) Scalig. in Euseb. Chron.

and

and with the death of *Amenophis*; which is clearly signified by *Manethos*; and the times of *Belus* and *Danaus*, noted by the *Greek* chronographers, do evidently confirm it. I mean the *Ægyptian Belus* or *Amenophis*, the father of *Ægyptus* or *Sethosis*, and *Danaus*; not the *Babylonian Belus*, the father of *Ninus*, whom mythologists confound with this, feigning him to have transported colonies out of *Ægypt* to *Babylon*. The time alloted by (c) *Thallus* an ancient chronographer, to *Belus*, of cccxx years before the *Trojan* war, doth exactly agree with this *Ægyptian Belus* or *Amenophis*.

Secondly, That the twentieth dynasty will receive those six kings, which out of *Herodotus* we have placed there: the number of whose years exceed the time limited by *Africanus*.

Thirdly, That the twenty-second dynasty will fall upon the latter time of king *Solomon*, whereby *Sesonchis*, the first king of it, may be the same with *Sesac* or *Shishac*, who in the (d) fifth year of *Reboboam*, the son of *Solomon*, invaded *Judæa*. Which was the only reason that moved (e) *Scaliger* to suspect, that something had been altered by *Africanus* in these dynasties.

(c) Thallus apud Euseb.   (d) 1 King. 14, 25, 26.
(e) Scalig. in Euseb. Chron.

By the same series and deduction of times, we may conclude, that the *Labyrinth* adjoining to the Pyramid of *Ofymanduas*, raised by a common expense of the twelve kings who (f) succeeded *Sethon*, to have been CIƆ CIƆ CCC XXIV years since, or IƆCLXXX before Christ. For *Sethon* living in the time of *Sennacharib*, and these immediately following *Sethon* in the government of the kingdom, they must have reigned, either in the same age the scripture assigns to *Sennacharib*, or not long after.

Those other Pyramids, the one of *Ofymanduas* in (g) *Diodorus*, or *Ismandes* in (h) *Strabo*; and those two of *Mæris* or *Myris*, in (i) *Herodotus* and (k) *Diodorus*, it is evident they preceded *Sesostris* the great, and must therefore have been above three thousand years since; but by how many kings, or how many ages, is hard to be defined.

(f) Herodot. lib. 2.
(g) Diodor. lib. 1.
(h) Strabo lib. 17.
(i) Herodot. lib. 2.
(k) Diodor. lib. 1.

Of

Of the END or INTENTION of the Pyramids, that they were for Sepulchres: Where, by the way, is expressed the manner of Imbalming used by the Ægyptians.

THAT these Pyramids were intended for Sepulchres and Monuments of the Dead, is the constant opinion of most authors which have writ of this argument. (*a*) *Diodorus* expresly tells us, that *Chemmis* and *Cephren*, although they designed (these two greater) *for their sepulchres, yet it happened, that neither of them were buried in them.* (*b*) *Strabo* judges all those near *Memphis* to have been the sepulchres of Kings. *Forty stadia from the city* (Memphis) *there*

(*a*) Τῶν δὲ βασιλέων τῶν κατασκευασάντων αὐτὰς ἑαυτοῖς τάφους εὑρέθη μηδέτερον αὐτῶν ἐν πυραμίσιν ἐνταφῆναι. Diod. Sic. lib. 1.

(*b*) Τετλαράκοντα δ' ἀπὸ τ͂ πόλεως σαδίους ἐπελθόντι ὀρεινή τις ὀφρύς ἐςτιν, ἐφ' ᾗ πολλαὶ μὲν πυραμίδες εἰσὶ τάφοι τῶν βασιλέων. Strab. l. 17.

is a certain brow of an hill, in which are many Pyramids, the sepulchres of Kings. And in particular he calls another near the lake of *Mœris*, the (c) *sepulchre of Imandes*. To which also the writings of the *Arabians* are consonant, who make the three greater the monuments of *Saurid, Hougib,* and *Fazfarinoun.* And the *Sabæans,* the first of them the sepulchre of *Seth,* the second of *Hermes,* the third of *Sah,* from whom they suppose themselves denominated *Sabæans,* as we formerly mentioned. And if none of these authorities were extant, yet the tomb found in the greatest Pyramid to this day of *Cheops,* as *Herodotus* names him, or *Chemmis,* according to *Diodorus,* puts it out of controversy. Which may farther be confirmed by the testimony of (d) *Ibn Abd Alhokm* an *Arabian,* where he discourses of the wonders of *Ægypt,*

(c) Ἰμάνδης δ' ὄνομα ὁ τάφοις. Ibid.

(d) ابن عبد الحكم وجدوا في رس الهرم بيتا فيه حوض من الصخر و فيه صنم كالادمي مي الدهنج و في وسطه انسان عليه درج من ذهب مرصع بالجواهر و على صدره سيف لا قيمة له و عند راسه حجر ياقوت كا لبيضة صورة كضوء النهار و هيبه كبابة يقلم الطير لم يعلم احد في الد نيا ما غوره. *Ibn Abd Alhokm.*

who relates, that after *Almamon* the Calif of *Babylon* had caused this Pyramid to be opened [about eight hundred years since,] (*e*) *they found in it towards the top a chamber, with an hollow stone, in which there was a statue like a man, and within it a man, upon whom was a breast-plate of gold set with jewels; upon this breast-plate was a sword of inestimable price, and at his head a carbuncle of the bigness of an egg, shining like the light of the day, and upon him were characters writ with a pen, which no man understood.*

But why the *Ægyptian* kings should have been at so vast an expense in the building of these Pyramids, is an inquiry of a higher nature. (*f*) *Aristotle* judges them to have been the works of tyranny; and *Pliny* conjectures that they built them partly out of ostentation, and partly out of state policy, by keeping the people in imployment, to divert them from mutinies and rebellions. (*g*) *Regum pecuniæ otiosa ac stulta ostentatio. Quippe cùm faciendi eas causa à plerisque tradatur, ne pecuniam successoribus aut æmulis insidiantibus præberent, aut ne plebs esset otiosa.*

(*e*) G Almec. Hist. Arab. ex. edit. Erp.
(*f*) Arist. l. 3. Polit.
(*g*) Plin. lib. 36. c. 12.

But

But the true reason depends upon higher and more weighty considerations; though I acknowledge these alledged by *Pliny* might be secondary motives. And this sprang from the theology of the *Ægyptians*, who, as *Servius* shews in his comment upon these words of (*b*) *Virgil*, describing the funeral of *Polydorus*,

—— *animamque Sepulchro*
Condimus ——

believed, that *as long as the body endured, so long the soul continued with it*; which also was the opinion of the (*i*) Stoicks. (*k*) *Hence the Ægyptians, skilful in wisdom, do keep their dead imbalmed so much the longer, to the end that the soul may for a long while continue, and be obnoxious to the body, lest it should quickly pass to another. The Romans did the contrary, burning their dead, that the soul might suddenly return into the generality, that is, into its own nature.* Wherefore

---

(*h*) Æneid. lib. 3.
(*i*) Stoici medium sequentes, tam diu animam durare dicunt, quam diu durat & corpus. Serv. Comment. in lib. 3. Æneid.
(*k*) Unde Ægyptii periti sapientiæ condita diutius reservant cadavera, scilicet ut anima multo tempore perduret, & corpori sit obnoxia, ne cito ad aliud transeat. Romani contra faciebant, comburentes cadavera, ut statim anima in generalitatem, id est, in suam naturam rediret. Serv. Com. in l. 3. Æneid.

the PYRAMIDS *were erected.* 63

that the body might not either by putrefaction be reduced to duſt, out of which it was firſt formed; or by fire be converted into aſhes, as the manner of the *Grecians* and *Romans* was, they invented curious compoſitions, beſides the intombing them in ſtately reconditories, hereby endeavouring to preſerve them from rottenneſs, and to make them eternal: (*l*) *Nec cremare aut fodere fas putant, verùm arte medicatos intra penetralia collocant,* ſaith *Pomponius Mela.* And *Herodotus* gives the reaſon, why they did neither burn nor bury. For diſcourſing in his third book of the cruelty of *Cambyſes,* and of his commanding that the body of *Amaſis,* an *Ægyptian* king, ſhould be taken out of his ſepulchre, whipt, and uſed with all contumely, he reports, that after all he bid it to be burnt, (*m*) *commanding that which was not holy. For the Perſians imagine the Fire to be a God, and neither of them are accuſtomed to burn the dead body.* The Perſians, *for the reaſon before alledged, becauſe they conceive it unfitting for a God to devour the carcaſs of a man;* and the Ægyptians, *becauſe they are perſuaded the Fire is a living creature, devouring all things that it receives, and after it is ſatiſ-*

(*l*) Pompon. Mela, lib. 1. cap. 9.
(*m*) Herodot. lib. 3. Ἐντελλάμενος ἐν ὁσια. Πέρσαι γὰ θεὸν νομίζουσι εἶναι τὸ πῦρ, &c.

fied

fied with food, dies with that which it hath devoured. Nor is it their custom of giving the dead body *(n)* to beasts, but of imbalming [or salting] *it, not only for this reason, but that it may not be consumed with worms.* The term used by *Herodotus*, ταριχεύειν, of *salting* or *imbalming* the dead, is also used by *(o) Baruch*, and by *(p) Plato*, and by *(q) Lucian* in his discourse *de Luctu*, treating of the several sorts of burial practised by several nations. *(r) The* Grecian *doth burn* [the dead;] *the* Persian *doth bury, the* Indian *doth anoint with the fat of swine, the* Scythian *eats, and the* Ægyptian ταριχεύει, *imbalms*, or *powders.* Which manner is also alluded to by *Antoninus* under the word ταριχος· *(s) That which the other day was*

(*n*) This barbarous custom is still practised in the *East-Indies*, as *Teixeira* (who from his own travels, and the writings of *Emir Cond* a *Persian*, hath given us the best light of those countries) truly informs us. Wherefore we may give credit to that of *Tully*: *Magorum mos est non humare corpora suorum, nisi à feris sint antea laniata. In Hyrcania plebs publicos alit canes, optimates domesticos (nobile autem genus canum illud scimus esse) sed pro sua quisque facultate parat, à quibus laniatur, eamque optimam illi esse censent sepulturam.* Tusc. Quæst. l. 1.

(*o*) Baruch 6. 71.
(*p*) Plat. Phædon.
(*q*) Lucian. de Luctu. Ὁ μὲν Ἕλλην ἔκαυσεν· ὁ ὲ Πέρσης ἔθαψεν· ὁ ὲ Ἰνδὸς ὑάλῳ περιχρίει· ὁ ὲ Σκύθης κατεσθίει. ταριχεύει ὲ ὁ Αἰγύπτιος.
(*r*) De more perungendi cadavera cerâ, melle, &c. ut conservarentur, vid. Dempst. p. 634.
(*s*) M. Aurel Anto. lib. 4. Εχθὲς μὲν μυξάριον, αὔριον ὲ ταριχος ἢ τέφρα.

excre-

the PYRAMIDS *were erected.* 65
excrementitious matter, within few days shall either be ταριχ῀, *an imbalmed body, or meer ashes*; in the one expressing the custom of the *Ægyptians,* in the other of the *Romans:* where Doctor (*t*) *Casaubon,* the learned son of a learned father, hath rightly corrected the errors of those who render ταριχ῀ to be a certain sort of *fish.* By this means then of salting the body, or imbalming it (the manner of both we shall describe out of *Herodotus* and *Diodorus*) the soul was obliged (according to the belief of the *Ægyptians*) to abide with the body, and the body came to be as durable as marble. Insomuch as *Plato,* who lived in *Ægypt* with *Eudoxus* no less than thirteen years, as (*u*) *Strabo* witnesseth, brings it for an argument in his *Phædon,* to prove the immortality of the soul by the long duration of these bodies. Which surely would have been more conclusive with him, could he have imagined that to these times, that is, till two thousand years after him, they should have continued so solid and intire, as to this day we find many of them. Wherefore (*x*) Saint *Augustine* truly affirms, that the

(*t*) Casaub. ann. in l. 4. M. Aurel. Anton.
(*u*) Strabo lib. 17.
(*x*) Ægyptii vero soli credunt resurrectionem, quia diligenter curant cadavera mortuo'um; morem enim habent siccare corpora, & quasi ænea reddere, *Gabbaras* ea vocant. Aug. Serm. 120. de Diversis.

Ægyptians

Ægyptians alone believe the resurrection, because they carefully preserve their dead corpses. For they have a custom of drying up the bodies, and rendring them as durable as brass; these (in their language) they call Gabbares. Whence the gloss of *Isidore*, *Gabares mortuorum*, in *Vulcanius*'s edition; or, as (y) *Spondanus* reads, *Gabares mortuorum condita corpora*.

The manner how the *Ægyptians* prepared and imbalmed these bodies, is very copiously, and, by what I have observed, very faithfully described by *Herodotus* and *Diodorus*; and therefore I shall put down their own words: *Their mourning*, saith (z) *Herodotus*, *and the manner of their burial are in this kind. When any man of quality of the family is dead, all the women besmear their heads and faces with dirt; then leaving the body with their kindred, they go lamenting up and down the city with their kinsfolks, their apparel being girt about them, and their breasts naked. On the other side, the men, having likewise their clothes girt about them, beat themselves. These things being done, they carry it to be* (a) *imbalmed*. For this there

are

(y) Spondanus de Cœmet. sacris, lib. 1. par. 1. c. 5.
(z) Herodot. lib. 2. Θρῆνοι δὲ καὶ ταφαὶ σφέων εἰσί αἵδε, &c.
(a) Among these imbalmed bodies are found *Ægyptian* idols. *Omnigenumque Deum monstra, & latrator Anubis* to
use

the PYRAMIDS *were erected.* 67

are some appointed that profess the art; these, when the body is brought to them, shew to the bringers of it certain patterns of dead bodies in wood, like it in painting. One of these, they say, is accurately made (which I think it not lawful to name:) they shew a second inferiour to it, and of an easier price, and a third cheaper than the former: Which being seen, they ask of them, according to what pattern they will have the dead body prepared. When they have agreed upon the price, they depart thence. Those, that remain, carefully imbalm the body in this manner. First of all they draw out the brain with a crooked iron by the nostrils, which being taken out, they

use *Virgil*'s expression, *Æn.* 8. Some of these are in great, some in little portraictures, formed either of potters earth baked, or else of stone, or metal, or wood, or the like; in all which kinds I have bought some. One of them for the rarity of the matter, and for the illustration of the Scriptures, deserves to be here mentioned, being cut out of a *magnes* in the form and bigness of the κάνθαρος, or *scarabæus*, which, as † *Plutarch* testifies, was worshipped by the *Ægyptians*, and was by military men engraven as an emblem on their seals. To which sort of idols, it may be, *Moses* alluded, when, speaking of the gods of *Ægypt*, he terms them *Gillulim*, *Stercoreos Deos*; as the ‡ original is rendered by *Junius* and *Tremellius*: for such places are the unsavoury dwellings of the *Scarabæus*. That which is remarkable of it in nature is this, that the stone, though probably two thousand years since taken out of its natural bed, retains its attractive and magnetical virtue.

† *De Is. & Osir.* τοῖς δὲ μαχίμοις κάνθαρος ἦν γλυφή σφραγίδος.

גלולים

‡ *Deuter.* 29. 17. *Vidistis abominationes & stercoreos Deos illorum.*

the rock, yet still

infuse

68 *For what End or Intention*
infuse (b) medicaments. Then with a sharp Æthiopick stone they cut it about the bowels, and take out all the guts: these purged and washed with wine made of palms, they again wash with sweet odours beaten; next filling up the (c) belly, with pure myrrh beaten, and cassia, and other odours, except frankincense, they sow it up again: having done this, they salt it with nitre, hiding it seventy days; for longer it is not lawful to salt it. Seventy days being ended, after they have washed the body, binding it with fillets, or (d) ribbands, and
wrapping

(*b*) Having caused the head of one of the richer sort of these imbalmed bodies to be opened, in the hollow of the skull I found the quantity of two pounds of these medicaments; which had the consistence, blackness, and smell of a kind of *bitumen*, or pitch, and by the heat of the sun waxed soft. This infusion could not well have been made any other way, than as *Herodotus* here intimates, by the nostrils. The tongue of this imbalmed body being weighed by me, was less than seven grains *English*; so light was that member, which St. *James* calls *a world of mischief*, James 3. 6.

(*c*) *Plutarch* writes, that they first exposed the belly, being opened, to the sun, casting the bowels into the river (*Nilus*,) *tanquam inquinamentum corporis*; this being done, they filled up the belly, and the hollow of the breast, with unguents and odours, as it is manifest by those which I have seen.

(*d*) These ribbands, by what I observed, were of linnen: which was also the habit of the *Ægyptian* Priests. For *Herodotus* (*lib*. 2.) writes, that it was profane for the *Ægyptians*, either to be buried in woollen garments, or to use them in their temples. And *Plutarch* (*de Iside & Osiride*) expressly tells us, that *the Priests of* Isis *used linnen vestments, and were shaved*. Suetonius *in* Othone (c. 12.) *Sacra etiam Isidis sæpe linteâ religiosâque veste propalam celebrasse*. And therefore the goddess *Isis* is called in *Ovid* (7. *Amor. Eleg.*) *linigera*:
Nec

wrapping it in a shrowd of silk linen, they smear it with gum, which the Ægyptians often use instead of glue. The kindred receiving it thence, make (e) *a coffin of wood in the similitude of a man, in which they put the dead body; and being thus inclosed, they place it in a reconditory in the house, setting it upright against the wall. In this manner with great expenses they prepare the funerals of*

Nec tu linigeram fieri quid possit ad Isim
Quæsieris.———

Of these ribbands I have seen some so strong and perfect, as if they had been newly made. With these they bound and swathed the dead body, beginning with the head, and ending with the feet: over these again they wound others, so often one upon another, that there could not be much less than a thousand ells upon one body.

(e) These coffins are fashioned in the similitude of a man, or rather resembling one of those imbalmed bodies, which, as we described before, are bound with ribbands, and wrapped in a shrowd of linen. For as in those there is the shape of a head, with a kind of painted vizard or face fastened to it, but no appearance without of the arms and legs: so it is with these coffins, the top of them hath the shape of the head of a man, with a face painted on it resembling a woman, the residue being one continued trunk: at the end of this trunk there is a pedestal somewhat broad, upon which it stood upright in the reconditory, as *Herodotus* here mentions. Some of these coffins are handsomly painted without, with several hieroglyphicks. Opening two of them, I found within, over the body, divers scrolls fastened to the linen shrowd. These were painted with sacred characters, for the colours, very lively and fresh; amongst which were, in a larger size, the pictures of men or women, some headed like hawks, some like dogs, and sometimes dogs in chards standing alone. These scrolls either ran down the belly and sides, or else were placed upon the knees and legs. On the feet was a linen cover (and so were all the scrolls before mentioned of *linen*) painted

For what End or Intention of their dead. But those, who, avoiding too great expenses, desire a mediocrity, prepare them in this manner. They take a clyster with the juice of cedar, with which they fill the belly by the fundament, neither cutting it, nor taking it out, and salt it so many days as we mentioned before: In the last of which they take out that clyster of cedar out of the belly, which painted with hieroglyphicks, and fashioned like to a high slipper. The breast had a kind of breast-plate covering it, made with folds of linen cut scollop-wise, richly painted and gilt. In the midst of the bend, at the top of it, was the face of a woman with her arms expanded: on each side of them, at the two utmost ends, was the head of an hawk fairly gilt, by which they represented the divine nature, according to *Plutarch* (in his book *de Iside & Osiride*) as by a serpent with the tail in his mouth the revolution of the year was resembled: in which kind also I have seen fair sculptures in gemms, found at *Alexandria*: and as by the sign of the cross they did denote *vitam æternam*, in *Ruffinus*'s expression. Of these crosses I have seen several amongst their hieroglyphicks, some painted and some ingraven in this manner ☥; and some others amongst their mummies, formed of stone, or baked earth, in this figure, ☥ At *Rome* on the statue of *Osiris*, it is ingraven thus, Γ; which may serve for confirmation of what *Socrates* and *Sozomen* (*Socrat. Hist. Eccl. l.* 5. *c.* 17. & *Sozom. Hist. Eccl. l.* 7. *c* 15.) relate, That at *Alexandria* the Temple of *Serapis* or *Osiris* (for * *Plutarch* judges *Serapis* and *Osiris* to be one and the same) being by the command of *Theodosius* demolished, they found characters resembling crosses, cut in stone: these in the interpretation of the wise men of *Ægypt*, signify ζωὴν ἐπερχο-μένην, *vitam venturam*: which discovery, as the same authors report, occasion'd the conversion to Christianity of some of the Gentiles.

* Ἄμφω ἢ ἑνὸς Θεοῦ καὶ μιᾶς δυνάμεως ἠξί-ωντο. *Plut. de Is. & Osir.*

before

the PYRAMIDS *were erected.* 71
before they injected. This hath such efficacy, that it carries out with it the whole paunch and entrails corrupted. The nitre consumes the flesh, and there is only left the skin and bones of the dead body. When they have done this, they restore the body to the kindred, doing nothing more. The third manner of preparing the dead, is of them which are of meaner fortune: With lotions they wash the belly, and dry it with salt seventy days; then they deliver it to be carried away.

(*f*) Diodorus Siculus, as his manner is, more distinctly and clearly with some remarkable circumstances expresseth the same thing. *If any one die amongst the Ægyptians, all his kindred and friends casting dirt upon their heads, go lamenting about the city, till such time as the body is buried. In the mean time they abstain from baths and wine, and all delicate meat, neither do they wear costly apparel. The manner of their burial is threefold: the one is very costly, the second less, the third very mean. In the first, they say, there is spent a talent of silver; in the second, twenty* minæ; *in the last there is very little expense. Those who take care to dress the body are artizans, receiving this skill from their ancestors. These shewing a bill to the kindred of the dead of the expenses upon each*

(*f*) Diod. Sic. lib. 1.
g 2   kind

kind of burial, ask them, in what manner they will have the body to be prepared. When they have agreed upon it, they deliver the body to such as are usually appointed to this office. First he which is called the Scribe, laying it upon the ground, describes about the bowels on the left side, how much is to be cut away. Then he which is called the Cutter, taking an Æthiopick stone, and cutting away as much of the flesh as the law commands, presently flies away as fast as he can; they which are present running after him, and casting stones at him, and cursing him, [hereby] turning all the execration upon him. For whosoever doth offer violence, or wound, or do any kind of injury to a body of the same nature with himself, they think him worthy of hatred. But those which are called the Imbalmers, they esteem them worthy of honour and respect. For they are familiar with their Priests, and they go into the temples, as holy men, without any prohibition. As soon as they meet about the dressing of the dissected body, one thrusting his hand by the wound of the dead body into his intrails, takes out all the bowels within, besides the heart and kidneys; another cleanses all the entrails, washing them with wine made of palms, and with odours. Lastly, the whole body being carefully anointed with the juice of cedar, and other things,

for

the PYRAMIDS *were erected.* 73

for above thirty days, and afterward with myrrh and cinamon, and such other things, which have power not only to keep it for a long time, but also to give a sweet smell, they deliver it to the kindred. This being thus finished, every member of the body is kept so entire, that upon the brows and (g) *eye-lids the hairs remain, and the whole shape of the body* [continues] *unchanged, and the image of the countenance may be known. Hence many of the* Ægyptians *keeping the bodies of their ancestors in magnificent houses, do see so expresly the faces of them dead many ages before they were born, that beholding the bigness of each of them, and the dimensions of their bodies, and the lineaments of their faces, it affords them wonderful content of mind, no otherwise than if they were now living with them.* Thus far *Diodorus*. By which description of his and that of *Herodotus*, we see the truth of what (h) *Tully* writes: *The* Ægyptians *imbalm their dead, and keep them at home: Amongst themselves above ground,*

(g) I find in the travels of Monsieur *de Breves*, ambassador at *Constantinople*, that at his being in *Ægypt* about forty years since, they saw some of these imbalmed bodies, with hairs remaining on their heads, and with beards: which I easily believe. *Nous en vismes aucuns la teste & les pieds descouverts (à cause que les dites bandes estoient pourries) qui avoient encore le cheveux, la barbe, & les ongles.* Les Voyages de M. de Breves.

(h) Condiunt Ægyptii mortuos, & eos domi servant. *Tusc. Quæst. lib.* 1.

faith

saith *Sextus Empiricus*: and (i) *intra penetralia*, in *Pomponius Mela's* expression: and *in lectulis*, according to *Athanasius* in the life of *Antony*. *Lucian* adds farther, in his tract *de Luctu*: (k) *They bring the dried body (I speak what I have seen) as a guest to their feasts and invitations; and oftentimes one necessitous of mony is supplied by giving his brother or his father in pledge.* The former custom is intimated by (l) *Silius Italicus*, speaking of the several manners of burial practised in diverse nations:

>   ———————————*Ægyptia tellus*
> *Claudit odorato post funus stantia saxo*
> *Corpora, & à mensis exanguem haud separat umbram.*

The latter is confirmed by (m) *Diodorus Siculus*: *They have a custom of depositing for a pledge the bodies of their dead parents. It is the greatest ignominy that may be, not to redeem them; and if they do it not, they themselves are deprived of burial.* And therefore, says he immediately before, *Such as*

(i) Lib. 1. cap 9.
(k) Οὗτος μέντοι ὃ (λέγω ἢ ἰδών) ξυνεδρας ἢ τεκνῶν συνδείπνον κ᾽ συμπότην ἐποιήσατο, πολλάκις δ᾽ κ᾽ δεόμενος χρημάτων ἀνδρὶ Αἰγυπτίῳ ἔλυσε τὴν χρείαν ἐνέχυρον ἢ ὁ ἀδελφὸς ἢ ὁ πατὴρ χρόμενος ἐν καιρῷ. Lucian. περὶ πενθῶν.
(l) Lib. 3. Punicorum. Vid. Benj. Itiner. p. 107.
(m) Diodor. Sic. lib. 1.

the PYRAMIDS *were erected.*

*for any crime or debt are hindred from being buried, are kept at home without a coffin; whom afterwards their posterity growing rich, discharging their debts, and paying money in compensation of their crimes, honourably bury. For the Æ*gyptians *glory, that their parents and ancestors were buried with honour.*

This manner of the *Ægyptians* imbalming we find also practised by *Joseph* upon his father *Jacob* in *Ægypt*: and if we will believe *Tacitus*, (*n*) *The* Hebrews (*in general*) *learned from the Æ*gyptians *rather to bury their dead, than to burn them.* Where (*o*) *Spondanus*, instead of *condere cadavera*, reads *condire*, as if it had been their custom of *powdring* or *imbalming* the dead. Wash them and anoint them we know they did, by what was done to our Saviour, and to the widow *Dorcas*: and long before it was in use amongst the Gentiles, as well as *Jews*, as appears by the funeral of *Patroclus* in (*p*) *Homer*, and of *Misenus* the *Trojan* in (*q*) *Virgil*;

Corpusque lavant frigentis, & ungunt:

(*n*) Judæos ab Ægyptiis didicisse condere cadavera potius quam cremare. Tacit. Hist. lib. 5.
(*o*) Spondan. lib. 1. part. 2. cap. 5. de Coemeteriis sacris.
(*p*) Καὶ τότε δὴ λυσάντο, ᾗ ἤλειψαν λίπ' ἐλαίῳ. Iliad. lib. 19.
(*q*) Æneid. lib. 6.

And

For what End or Intention

And of *Tarquinius* the *Roman* in *Ennius*;

> *Tarquinii corpus bona fœmina lavit, &*
> *unxit.*

But certainly the *Ægyptian* manner of imbalming, which we have described out of *Herodotus* and *Diodorus*, was not received by them; or if it were, *Martha* the sister of (*r*) *Lazarus* needed not to have feared, that after four days the body should have stunk. (*s*) They which infer out of the funeral of *Asa*, king of *Judah*, that it was the custom of the *Jews* as well as *Ægyptians*, have very little probability for their assertion. (*t*) We read, that *they buried him in his own sepulchre, which he had made for himself in the city of* David, *and laid him in the bed, which was filled with sweet odours and divers kinds of spices, prepared by the apothecary's art; and they made a very great burning for him.* This very great burning is so contrary to the practice of the *Ægyptians*, to whom it was an abomination, as appears by the authorities before cited of *Herodotus* and *Mela*, besides the little affinity of filling the bed

---

(*r*) John 11. 39.

(*s*) Transtulerunt Ifraelitæ hunc ritum ex Ægypto secum in Cananæam, quo deinceps in sepulturis Principum & Regum usi dicuntur in historia Asæ. 2 Paral. 6. & alibi. D. Paræi Comment. in Gen. 50. *.

(*t*) Chron. 16. 14.

with

the PYRAMIDS *were erected.* 77

with sweet odours, and the Ægyptians filling the body and the place of the intrails with sweet odours, according both to *Herodotus* and *Diodorus*, that we shall not need to inlarge our selves in any other confutation. But as for that of *Jacob* and *Joseph*, the father and the son, both living and dying in *Ægypt*, the text is clear, that they were imbalmed after the fashion of the Ægyptians. (*u*) *And* Joseph *commanded his servants, the physicians, to imbalm his father; and the physicians imbalmed* Israel, *and forty days were fulfilled for him; (for so are fulfilled the days of those which are imbalmed.) And the* Æ*gyptians mourned for him threescore and ten days.* In the same chapter we read, (*x*) *So* Joseph *died, being an hundred and ten years old; and they imbalmed him, and he was put in a coffin in* Ægypt. Both which places are very consonant to the traditions of *Herodotus* and *Diodorus*, and may serve to shew, what necessity there is of having oft times recourse to the learning of the heathen for the illustration of the Scriptures. *Forty days were fulfilled for the imbalming of* Jacob. This, (*y*) *Diodorus* tells us,

(*u*) Gen. 50. 2, 3.   (*x*) Gen. 50. 26.
(*y*) Diod. Sic. lib. 1. Καθόλυ ὂ πᾶν τὸ σῶμα τὸ μὲν πρῶτον κεδείᾳ ᾗ τισιν ἄλλοις ἐπιμελείας ἀξιῶσιν ἐφ᾽ ἡμέρας πλείους ἢν τελακοῦσα, ὁπόια σμύρνῃ ᾗ κιναμώμῳ, &c.

was

was their cuſtom, *They anointed the dead bo(dy) with the juice of cedar, and other things, f(or) above thirty days, and afterward with myrr(h) and cinamon, and the like*; which migh(t) make up the reſidue of the forty day(s). *And the* Ægyptians *mourned for him three ſcore and ten days.* This time, out of *Herodotus*, may be collected to have been from the death of the perſon, till the body wa(s) returned by the phyſicians after ſeventy days perfectly imbalmed. The text ſays, *And* Joſeph *was put in a coffin*, which is very lively repreſented by (*z*) *Herodotus: The kindred receiving the dead body from the imbalmers, make a coffin of wood in the ſimilitude of a man, in which they put it.* This coffin then of *Joſeph*, as it is probable, was of wood, and not *marmorea theca*, as *Cajetan* imagines, the former being the cuſtom of the Ægyptians. Beſides that this was much eaſier, and fitter to be carried by the *Iſraelites* into *Canaan*, marching on foot, and, for ought we read, deſtitute of waggons and other carriages.

(*a*) The tradition of the ancient *Hebrews*,

(*z*) Herod. lib. 2.
(*a*) Veteres Hebræi commentati ſunt, duas fuiſſe arcas unâ incedentes in deſerto, alteram Divinitatis, alteram Joſephi; illam ſcilicet arcam fœderis, hanc verò loculos, quibus Joſephi oſſa ex Ægyptó aſportabantur in regionem Chanaan. Perer. Comm. in 50. cap. Geneſ.

(c) Gen. 50. 25.   (d) Exod. 13. 19.

the outside of the first Pyramid

Petr. Celect. in 50. cap. Gener.

the PYRAMIDS *were erected.*

in their commentaries, is very probable, and confonant to it. *They carried in the defert two arks, the one of God, the other of* Jofeph; *that the ark of the covenant, this the ark* [or coffin] *in which they carried* Jofeph's *bones out of* Ægypt. This coffin (if it be lawful for me to conjecture after the revolution of three thoufand years) I conceive to have been of fycomore (a great tree very plentifully growing in *Ægypt*) of which fort there are many found in the mummies, very fair, intire, and free from corruption to this day. Though I know the *Arabians* and *Perfians* have a different tradition, that his coffin was of glafs. (*b*) *They put his bleffed body, after they had wafhed it, into a coffin of glafs, and buried it in the channel of the river* Nilus, faith *Emir Cond* a Perfian.

That phrafe of *Jofeph*, where he takes an oath of the children of *Ifrael*, (*c*) *Ye fhall carry up my bones from hence*, furely is a *fynechdoche* or figurative fpeech: and fo is that in *Exodus*; (*d*) *And* Mofes *took the bones of* Jofeph *with him: for he had ftraightly fworn the children of* Ifrael, *faying*, God will

(*b*) جسم مهر مکسن بعد از غسل م تابوت
ابکینه نهاده در رود نیل نهی کم دند

(*c*) Gen. 50. 25.   (*d*) Exod. 13. 19.

furely

surely visit you, and ye shall carry up my bones away from hence with you. For his body being bowel'd, and then imbalmed after the manner of the *Ægyptians*, not only the bones, but the skin, the flesh, and all besides the intrails (which according to *(e) Plutarch* were thrown into the river) would have continued perfect and intire a much longer space, than from his death to their migration out of *Ægypt*.

Having thus by art found out ways to make the body durable, whereby the soul might continue with it, as we shewed before, which else would have been at liberty to have passed into some other body, *(f)* this also being the opinion of the *Ægyptians*, from whom *Pythagoras* borrowed his Μετεμ-ψύχωσις, or *Transanimation*, (the which made him to forbid his disciples the eating of flesh, *Ne fortè bubulam quis de aliquo proavo suo obsonaret*, as *Tertullian* wittily speaks;) the next care of the *Ægyptians* was to provide conditories, which might be as lasting as the body, and in which it might continue safe from the injury of time and men. That occasioned the ancient kings of

---

(e) Plutarch. in sept. Sapient. convivio.

(f) Πρῶτοι ᾗ ᾗ ᾗ δὲ τὸν λόγον Αἰγύπτιοί εἰσι εἰπόντες, ὡς ἀνθρώπου ψυχὴ ἀθάνατός ἐστι, τῷ σώματι ᾗ καταφθίνοντος, ἐς ἄλλο ζῶον αἰεὶ γινόμενον ἐσδύεται. Herod. lib. 2.

Thebes

Thebes in Ægypt to build thofe which (g) *Diodorus* thus defcribes: *There are, they fay, the wonderful fepulchres of the ancient kings, which in magnificence exceed the imitation of pofterity.* Of thefe in the Sacred Commentaries *forty-feven are mentioned*; but in the time of Ptolemæus Lagi *there remained but feventeen. Many of them, at our being in* Ægypt *in the hundred and eightieth* Olympiad, *were decayed*; *neither are thefe things alone reported by the* Ægyptians *out of the facred books, but by many alfo of the* Grecians, *who in the time of* Ptolemæus Lagi *went to* Thebes, *and having compiled hiftories (amongft whom is* Hecatæus) *agree with our relations.* And this might occafion alfo thofe others recorded by *Strabo*, which he calls Ἑρμαῖα, or *Mercuriales tumulos*, feen by him near *Syene*, in the upper parts of Ægypt, very ftrange and memorable. (h) *Paffing in a chariot from* Syene *to* Philæ, *over a very even plain, about an hundred ftadia, all the way almoft, of both fides, we faw in many places Mercurial tombs: a great ftone, fmooth, and almoft fpherical, of that*

(g) Diod. Sic. lib. 1. Εἶναι ἢ φασὶ ἢ τάφους ἐνταῦθα τῶν ἀρχαίων βασιλέων θαυμαςὲς, &c.

(h) Strabo. lib. 17. Ἤλθομεν δ' εἰς Φιλὰς ἐκ Συήνης ἀπήνῃ δι' ὁμαλῦ σφόδρα πεδίε ςαδίες ὁμῦ τὶ ἑκατόν. Παρ' ὅλην ἢ τ̃ ὁδὸν ἦν ἰδεῖν ἑκατέρωθεν πολλαχῦ ὥσπερ ἑρμαῖα, &c.

black

black and hard marble, out of which mortars are made, placed upon a greater stone; and on the top of this another, some of them lying by themselves: the greatest of them was no less than twelve feet diameter, all of them greater than the half of this. Many ages after, when the regal throne was removed from *Thebes* to *Memphis*, the same religion and opinion continuing amongst the *Ægyptians, that so long as the body endured, so long the soul continued with it*; not as quickning and animating it, but as an attendant or guardian, and as it were unwilling to leave her former habitation: it is not to be doubted, this incited the kings there, together with their private ambition and thirst after glory, to be at so vast expenses in the building of these Pyramids; and the *Ægyptians* of lower quality, to spare for no cost in cutting those *hypogæa*, those caves or dormitories in the *Libyan* deserts, which by the Christians now-a-days are called the *Mummies*. *Diodorus Siculus* excellently expresses their opinion and belief in this particular, together with their extreme cost of building sepulchres, in these words: (*i*) *The*

(*i*) Diod. Sic. lib. 1. Οἱ γὰ ἐγχώριοι τ̀ μὲν ἐν τῷ ζῆν χρόνον ἐυτελῆ παντελῶς ἡ̈ νομίζουσι, τὸν ἢ μετὰ τὴν τελευτὴν δι' ἀρετὴν μνημονευθησόμενον, περὶ πλείσε ποιοῦντ. Καὶ τὰς μὲν τῶν ζώντων οἰκήσεις καταλύσεις ὀνομάζουσιν, &c.

Ægyptians

Ægyptians make small account of the time of this life, being limited; but that which after death is joined with a glorious memory of virtue, they highly value. They call the houses of the living inns, because for a short space we inhabit these; but the sepulchres of the dead they name eternal mansions, because they continue with the Gods for an infinite space. Wherefore in the structures of their houses they are little sollicitous; but in exquisitely adorning their their sepulchres, they think no cost sufficient.

Now why the *Ægyptians* did build their sepulchres often in the form of Pyramids (for they were not always of this figure, as appears by those Ἑρμαῖα, or *Mercuriales tumuli*, before cited out of *Strabo*, which were spherical, and by those *hypogæa*, or caves still extant in the rocks of the desert) *Pierius* in his hieroglyphicks, or rather the anonymous author at the end of him, gives several philosophical reasons. (*k*) By a Py-

---

(*k*) Ex eruditi cujusd. lib. 2. sub finem Hieorogl. Pierii. Per *pyramidem* veteres [Ægyptii] rerum naturam, & substantiam illam informem formas recipientem significare voluerunt: quòd, ut pyramis à puncto & summo fastigio incipiens, paulatim in omnes partes dilatatur; sic rerum omnium natura ab unico principio & fonte, qui dividi non potest, nempè à Deo summo opifice, profecta, varias deinde formas suscipit, & in varia genera atque species diffunditur, omniaque apici illi & puncto conjungit, à quo omnia manant & fluunt. Verùm & alia hujus rei ratio, nempè Astronomia, reddi potest, &c.

ramid,

ramid, saith he, *the ancient Ægyptians expressed the nature of things, and that informed substance receiving all forms. Because as a Pyramid having its beginning from a point at the top, is by degrees dilated on all parts; so the nature of all things, proceeding from one fountain and beginning, which is indivisible, namely from God the chief work-master, afterwards receives several forms, and is diffused into various kinds and species; all which it conjoins to that beginning and point, from whence every thing issues and flows. There may also be given another reason for this, taken from Astronomy. For the Ægyptians were excellent Astronomers, yea, the first inventors of it;* these (dividing the Zodiac and all things under it into twelve signs) *will have each sign to be a kind of Pyramid, the basis of which shall be in the heaven (for the heaven is the foundation of Astronomy) and the point of it shall be in the center of the earth. Seeing therefore in these Pyramids all things are made, and that the coming of the sun, which is as it were a point in respect of those signs, is the cause of the production of natural things, and its departure the cause of their corruption, it seems very fitly, that by a Pyramid, Nature, the parent of all things, may be expressed. Also the same Ægyptians under the form of a Pyramid shadowed out*

the

the soul of man, making under huge Pyramids the magnificent sepulchres of their kings and heroes, to testify that the soul was still existent, notwithstanding the body was dissolved and corrupted; the which should generate and produce another body for itself, when it should seem good to the first agent; (that is, the circle of thirty six thousand years being transacted.) Like as a Pyramid (as it is known to Geometricians) the top of it standing fixt, and the base being moved about, describes a circle, and the whole body of it a cone; so that the circle expresses that space of years, and the cone that body which in that space is produced. For it was the opinion of the Ægyptians, that, in the revolution of thirty six thousand years, all things should be restored to their former state. Plato witnesseth, that he received it from them; who seems also to me in his Timæus to attest this thing, that is, that our soul hath the form of a Pyramid; which (soul), according to the same Plato, is of a fiery nature, and adhereth to the body, as a Pyramid doth to the basis, or as fire doth to the fewel. Thus far the anonymous author in *Pierius*; most of which reasons of his are but pretty fancies, without any solid proof from good authors. For he might as well say, that the Ægyptians were excellent

lent Geometricians, as well as Astronomers (as they were very skilful in both) and that they made these Pyramids to express the first and most simple of mathematical bodies; or else being excellent Arithmeticians, to represent the mysteries of pyramidal numbers; or else being well seen in the Opticks, to shadow out the manner of vision, and the emission of rays from luminous bodies, as also the *effluvium* of the *species intentionales* from the object; all which are supposed to be pyramidal. But this were to play with truth, and to indulge too much to fancy. Wherefore I conceive the reason, why they made these sepulchres in the figure of a Pyramid, was, either as apprehending this to be the most permanent form of structure, as in truth it is; (for, by reason of the contracting and lessening of it at the top, it is neither over-pressed with its own weight, nor is it so subject to the sinking in of rain, as other buildings;) or else hereby they intended to represent some of their Gods. For anciently the *Gentiles* expressed them either by columns fashioned like cones, or else by quadrilateral obelisks, the *Ægyptian* manner; in which latter kind I have seen many standing very intire, some of them plain, and some with hieroglyphicks

the PYRAMIDS *were erected.* 87

phicks inscribed. Now such obelisks are but lesser models of the Pyramids, as the Pyramids are but greater kinds of obelisks. The first institution of them, as (*a*) *Pliny* informs us, was by *Mitres*, an *Egyptian* King; whom (*b*) *Isidore* terms *Mesphres*; both of them affirming him to have consecrated them *Solis Numini*, to the Deity of the Sun. Which Deity (*c*) *Diodorus* relates the *Ægyptians* to have worshipped under the name of *Osiris*, as they did the Moon by the Goddess *Isis*, whom the *Libyans* bordering on the *Ægyptians* termed *Urania*, and the *Phœnicians Astroarches*, according to (*d*) *Herodian*. And therefore as *Isis Cornigera* (in which portraiture I have observed her statue at *Alex-*

(*a*) Trabes ex eo secere reges quodam certamine, obeliscos vocantes Solis Numini sacratos. Radiorum ejus argumentum in effigie est; & ita significatur nomine Ægyptio. Primus omnium id instituit Mitres, qui in Solis urbe regnabat, somnio jussus. Plin. lib. 36. cap. 8.

(*b*) Obeliscum Mesphres rex Ægypti primus fecisse fertur qui post cæcitatem visu recepto duos obeliscos Soli consecravit. Isid. lib. 18. cap. 31.

(*c*) Ὑπολαβεῖν τινας δύο θεοὺς ἀϊδίους τε καὶ πρώτους, τόν τε ἥλιον καὶ τὴν σελήνην, ὧν τὸν μὲν Ὄσιριν, τὴν δὲ Ἶσιν ὀνομάσαι. Diod. Sic. lib. 1.

(*d*) Λίβυες μὲν ἐν αὐτὴν Οὐρανίαν καλοῦσι, Φοίνικες δὲ Ἀστροάρχην ὀνομάζουσι, σελήνην εἶναι θέλοντες. Herod. lib. 5.

h 2 *andria*

andria to be formed) did reprefent the horns of the Moon, or *Luna falcata*; fo thefe quadrilateral Pyramids, or Obelifks, might not unfitly refemble the rays of the Sun, or their God *Ofiris*; a God denominated, as (*e*) *Plutarch* teftifies, from *Os*, fignifying in the *Ægyptian* language, *many*, and *iri*, *eyes*. For which reafon both (*f*) *Diodorus* and *Plutarch* term *Ofiris* in *Greek* πολυόφθαλμον, *many eyes* or *many rays*; the which emitted, as the Opticks demonftrate, in pyramidal or conical forms, might not unaptly by the *Gentiles* be reprefented in either figure. Hence the *Phœnicians*, next neighbours to the *Ægyptians*, and probably firft imitators of this their idolatry, worfhipped the Sun, whom they named *Elæagabalus*, or, as the ancient coins render him, *Alegabalus*, and fome infcriptions *Heliogabalus*, an idol in the fimi-

---

(*e*) Τὸν γὰρ βασιλέα καὶ κύριον Ὄσιριν ὀφθαλμῷ καὶ σκήπτρῳ γράφουσιν Ἔνιοι δὲ καὶ τοὔνομα διερμηνεύουσι πολυόφθαλμον, ὡς τὸ μὲν Ὂς τὸ πολὺ, τὸ δὲ Ἴρι τὸν ὀφθαλμὸν Αἰγυπτίᾳ γλώττῃ φράζοντες. Plut. de Ifid. & Ofir.

(*f*) Εἶναι τὸν μὲν Ὄσιριν πολυόφθαλμον, εἰκότως, πάντη γὰρ ἐπιβάλλοντα τὰς ἀκτῖνας, ὥσπερ ὀφθαλμοῖς πολλοῖς βλέπειν ἅπασαν γῆν καὶ θάλασσαν. Diod. lib. 1.

litude

the PYRAMIDS *were erected.* 89

litude of a cone. (g) *Herodian* Lib. V, *The Phœnicians worship the Sun, calling him in their language* Elæagabalus; *to whom there is erected a very spacious temple, adorn'd with gold, plenty of silver, and precious stones. It is not only worshipped by the natives, but likewise the great men and kings of the Barbarians every year, with a kind of emulation, send honourable presents to the God. There is no statue, as among the* Greeks *and* Romans, *which polish'd by hand may express the image of the God. But there is a certain great stone circular below, and ending with a sharpness above, in the figure of a cone of black colour. They report it to have fallen from heaven, and to be the image of the Sun.* This idolatry, by commerce with the *Ægyptians* and *Phœnicians*, came afterwards to be communicated to the *Grecians* and other nations; and from these, what at the first institution was proper to the Sun, came by super-

(g) Τοῦτον [τὸν Ἥλιον] οἱ ἐπιχώριοι σέβουσι τῇ Φοινίκων φωνῇ Ἐλαιαγάβαλον καλοῦντες. νεὼς δὲ αὐτῷ μέγιστος, &c. Λίθος δέ τις ἐστὶ μέγιστος, κάτωθεν περιφερὴς, λήγων εἰς ὀξύτητα κωνοειδὲς αὐτῷ σχῆμα, μέλαινά τε ἡ χρόα. Herod. lib. 5.

stition

sition to be apply'd to their other Gods. Thus (b) *Tacitus* (Lib. II. Hist.): At *Cyprus* in the temple of *Venus* at *Paphos, the image of the Goddess is not of human shape, but a figure rising continually round, from a larger bottom to a small top in conical fashion*; the reason thereof is not known. Tho' what *Tacitus* rendereth *metæ modo exurgens*, or conical, *Maximus Tyrius* termeth pyramidal. (*i*) *In* Paphos, Venus *hath the chiefest honour; howbeit her image you can liken to nothing so well as to a white Pyramid*. In like manner we find in (*k*) *Clemens Alexandrinus*, that *Callithoe* the Priestess of *Juno* decked *the column of the Goddess* with crowns and garlands; that is, saith (*l*) *Joseph Scaliger, the image of the Goddess with crowns and garlands; for at that time the statues of the*

(*b*) Simulacrum Deæ non effigie humanâ, continuus orbis latiore initio tenuem in ambitum metæ modo exurgens, & ratio in obscuro. Tacit. lib. 2. Hist.

(*i*) Πάφιαι ἡ μὲν Ἀφροδίτη τὰς τιμὰς ἔχει, τὸ δὲ ἄγαλμα οὐκ ἂν εἰκάσαις ἄλλῳ τῳ ἢ πυραμίδι λευκῇ. Max. Tyr. Διαλέξει λή.

(*k*) Clem. Alex. lib. 1. Stromatum ex Phoronidis auctore.

(*l*) Scaliger in Eusebii Chronicon.

the PYRAMIDS *were erected.* 91

Gods were κίονες πυραμοειδεῖς, *pyramidal columns,* or obelisks. And Ἀπόλλων ἀγυιεὺς was nothing else with the *Grecians* but κίων εἰς ὀξὺ λήγων, *a column ending in a point*, as (m) *Suidas* witnesseth: *which kind of column some make proper to* Apollo, *others to* Bacchus, *others to them both.* In *Pausanias* also we read, that, in the city *Corinth, Jupiter Melichius* and *Diana, surnamed Patroa, were made with little or no art*; Melichius *being represented by a Pyramid, and* Diana *by a column.* Whence not improbably the same (n) *Pausanias* in his *Corinthiaca* conjectures, this manner of representation of the Gods to have been the first and most ancient among the *Grecians*. But *Clemens Alexandrinus,* deriving the beginning of it much higher, imagines it to have been the first kind of idolatry in the world, and therefore well agreeing with the antiquity

---

(m) Ἀπόλλων] Ἀγυιεὺς δέ ἐστι κίων εἰς ὀξὺ λήγων. Οἱ ἱδρύσει πρὸ τῶν θυρῶν, ἰδίας δὲ φασιν αὐτοῖς εἶναι Ἀπόλλωνος, οἱ δὲ Διονύσου, οἱ δὲ ἀμφοῖν. Suidas.

(n) Ἔστι δὲ Ζεὺς Μειλίχιος καὶ Ἄρτεμις ὀνομαζομένη Πατρῴα, σὺν τέχνῃ πεποιημένα οὐδεμία. Πυραμίδι δὲ ὁ Μειλίχιος, ἡ δὲ κίονί ἐστιν εἰκασμένη. Pausaniæ Corinthiaca.

of

of the *Ægyptians*: (o) *Before the exact art of making statues was found out, the ancients erecting columns* [pyramidal or conical columns] *worshipped these as the images of God.*

This practice of the *Ægyptians*, I mean of erecting Pyramids for sepulchres, was but rarely imitated by other nations; though *Servius* seems to make it frequent, in his comment upon these verses of *Virgil*:

————*Fuit ingens monte sub alto*
Regis Dercenni terreno ex aggere bustum
Antiqui Laurentis, opacaq; ilice tectum.

(p) *With the ancients* (saith *Servius*) *noblemen were buried, either under mountains, or in mountains; whence the custom came, that over the dead either Pyramids were made, or huge columns erected.* In imitation of the later custom, it may be, (q) *Absalom* erected his

---

(o) Πρὶν γὰρ ἐν ἀκριβωθῆναι τῶν ἀγαλμάτων χύσις, κίονας ἱστῶσιν οἱ παλαιοὶ, ἐστὸν τίτυς, ὡς ἀρίδρυματα τῦ Θεῦ. Clem. Alex. lib. 1. Stromatum.

(p) Apud majores, Nobiles aut sub montibus, aut in montibus sepeliebantur; unde natum est, ut supra cadavera, aut Pyramides fierent; aut ingentes collocarentur columnæ. Serv. in Virgil. Vide Claudian. & Statium atque Dempst. p. 631.

(q) 2 Sam. c. 18. v. 18.

pillar.

the PYRAMIDS *were erected.* 89
pillar. And *Pausanias* describing the manner of burial amongst the ancient nation of the *Sicyonians*, tells us, (*u*) *that they covered the body with earth, and raised pillars over it.* But for the former of Pyramids, I find none out of *Ægypt* accounted miraculous, unless it be the sepulcher of *Porsena* king of *Hetruria* (with which I shall conclude) described by *Pliny* out of *Varro*; being more to be admired for the number and contrivance of the Pyramids, than for any excessive magnitude. (*x*) *We shall use* M. Varro's *own words, in the description of it. He was buried, saith he, without the city* Clusium, *in which place he left a monument of square stone. Each side of it is three hundred feet broad, and fifty feet high. Within the square basis there is an inextricable labyrinth, whither who so adventures without a clue can find no passage out. Upon this square there stand five Pyramids, four in the angles, and one in the middle; in*
the

(*u*) Pausaniæ Corinth. five lib. 2. Αὐτοὶ ᵹ Σικυῶνιοι τὰ πολλὰ ἐοίκοτι τεϳτω δάϳϵσι τὸ ϳὸ σῶμα γῇ κρύπ]ϵσιν, λίθῳ ϳ ἐποικοδομήσαϳϵς κρηπίδα, κίοκας ἐφιςᾶσι.

(*x*) Plin. l. 36. c. 13. Utemur ipsius M. Varronis in expositione ejus verbis. Sepultus est (inquit) sub urbe Clusio, in quo loco monumentum reliquit lapide quadrato, singula latera pedum lata tricenûm, alta quinquagenûm : inque basi quadratâ intùs labyrinthum inextricabilem ; quo si quis improperet sine glomere lini, exitum invenire nequeat. Supra id quadratum pyramides stant quinque, quatuor in angulis, & in medio una,

in

the bottom they are broad seventy five feet, and high an hundred and fifty. They are pointed in such a manner, that at the top there is one brass circle and covering for them all, from which there hang bells fastened to chains; these being moved by the wind, give a sound afar off, as at Dodona *it hath formerly been. Upon this circle there are four other Pyramids, each of them an hundred feet high; above which, upon one plain, there are five Pyramids, the altitude of which* Varro *was ashamed to add. The Hetruscan fables report, that it was as much as that of the whole work. With so vain a madness he sought glory by an expense useful to no man; wasting besides the wealth of his kingdom, that in the end the commendation of the artificer should be the greatest.*

In imo latæ pedum septuagenûm quinûm, altæ centum quinquagenûm: ita fastigiatæ, ut in summo orbis æneus & petasus unus omnibus sit impositus, ex quo pendeant excepta catenis tintinabula, quæ vento agitata longè sonitus referant, ut Dodonæ olim factum. Supra quem orbem quatuor pyramides insuper singulæ extant altæ pedum centenûm; supra quas uno solo quinque pyramides, quarum altitudinem Varronem puduit adjicere. Fabulæ Hetruscæ tradunt, eandem fuisse quam totius operis. Adeò vesana dementia quæsisse gloriam impendio nulli profuturo. Præterea fatigasse regni vires, ut tamen laus major artificis esset.

Porsena's

p. 89.

Porsena's Tomb at Ausium in Italy consisting of many Pyramids

Hen. Roberts Sculp.

A Description of the Pyramids *in Ægypt, as I found them in the 1048th year of the Hegira, or in the years 1638 and 1639 of our Lord, after the Dionysian account.*

HAVING discovered the Founders of these Pyramids, and the Time in which they were erected, and lastly the End for which these Monuments were built; next in the method we proposed, the Sciography of them is to be set down; where we shall begin with the dimensions of their figure without, and then we shall examine their several spaces and partitions within.

A description of the first and fairest Pyramid.

THE first and fairest of the three greater Pyramids is situated on the top of a rocky hill, in the sandy desert of *Libya*, about a quarter of a mile distant to the west from the plains of *Ægypt*, above which

which the rock riseth an hundred feet, or better, with a gentle and easy ascent. Upon this advantageous rise, and upon this solid foundation the Pyramid is erected; the heighth of the situation adding to the beauty of the work, and the solidity of the rock giving the superstructure a permanent and stable support. Each side of the Pyramid, computing it according to (a) *Herodotus*, contains in length eight hundred *Græcian* feet; and, in (b) *Diodorus Siculus*'s account, seven hundred. (c) *Strabo* reckons it less than a furlong; that is, less than six hundred *Grecian* feet, or six hundred twenty five *Roman*; and (d) *Pliny* equals it to eight hundred eighty three. That of *Diodorus Siculus*, in my judgment, comes nearest to the truth, and may serve in some kind to confirm those proportions which in another discourse I have assigned to the *Græcian* measures. For measuring the north side of it, at the basis, by an exquisite radius of ten feet in length, taking two several stations, as Mathematicians use to do when any ob-

---

(a) Herod. lib. 2.
(b) Diod. lib 1. Ἡ μὲν γὰρ μεγίστη τετράπλευρος ἴσα τῷ σχήματι, τὴν ἐπὶ τῆς βάσεως πλευρὰν ἑκάστην ἔχει πλέθρων ἑπτά.
(c) Strabo l. 17.
(d) Plin. lib. 36. c. 12. Amplissima octo jugera obtinet soli, quatuor angulorum paribus intervallis, per octingentos octoginta tres pedes singulorum laterum.

the first PYRAMID.

stacle hinders their approach, I found it to be six hundred ninety three feet, according to the *English* standard; which quantity is somewhat less than that of *Diodorus*. The rest of the sides were examined by a line, for want of an even level, and a convenient distance to place my instruments; both which the *area* on the former side afforded.

The altitude of this Pyramid was long since measured by *Thales Milesius*, who, according to (*e*) *Tatianus Assyrius*, lived about the fiftieth *Olympiad*: but his observation is no where by the ancients expressed. Only (*f*) *Pliny* tells us of a course proposed by him, how it might be found, and that is, by observing such an hour, when the shadow of the body is equal to its height. A way at the best, by reason of the faintness and scattering of the extremity of the shadow in so great an altitude, uncertain and subject unto error. And yet (*g*) *Diogenes Laertius*, in the life of *Thales*, hath the same story, from the authority of *Hieronymus*. (*h*) Hieronymus *reports, that he mea-*

(*e*) Tatiani Orat. contra Græcos.
(*f*) Plin. lib. 36. cap. 12. Mensuram altitudinis earum omniumque similium deprehendere invenit Thales Milesius, umbram metiendo, quâ horâ par esse corpori solet.
(*g*) Diog. Laert. in vitâ Thaletis, L. 1.
(*h*) Ἱερώνυμ۞ ἐκμεδῆσαι φησὶν αὐτὸν τὰς πυραμίδας ἐκ τῆς σκιᾶς παρατηρήσαντα, ὅτε ἡμῖν ἰσομεγέθεις εἰσίν.

sured

sured the Pyramids by their shadow, marking when they are of an equal quantity. Wherefore I shall pass by his, and give my own observations. The altitude is something defective of the latitude; though in (*b*) *Strabo*'s computation it exceeds; but (*i*) *Diodorus* rightly acknowledges it to be less: which, if we measure by its perpendicular, is four hundred ninety nine feet; but if we take it as the Pyramid ascends inclining, as all such figures do, then is it equal, in respect of the lines subtending the several angles, to the latitude of the basis, that is, to six hundred ninety three feet. With reference to this great altitude, (*k*) *Statius* calls them

——————— *audacia saxa Pyramidum.* ———————

And *Tacitus* (*Ann. lib. 2.*) *instar montium eductæ Pyramides.* (*l*) *Julius Solinus* goes farther yet: *The Pyramids are sharp-pointed towers in Ægypt, exceeding all height which may be made by hand.* (*m*) *Ammianus Mar-*

(*b*) Strabo lib. 17. Εἰσὶ δὲ σταδίων τὸ ὕψος: whereas the breadth he reckons less than a *stadium*.
(*i*) Diod. Τὸ ᾖ ὕψος ἕχει πλέον τῶν ἓξ πλέθρων. But to the breadth he assigns 7 *plethra*.
(*k*) Stat. d. 5. Sylv. 3.
(*l*) Pyramides sunt turres in Ægypto, fastigiatæ ultra excelsitatem omnem, quæ manu fieri potest. Jul. Solin. Polyhist. c. 35.
(*m*) Ammian. Marcell. l. 22.

cellinus

the first PYRAMID.   95

tellinus in his expreſſion aſcends as high. *The Pyramids are towers erected altogether exceeding the height which may be made by man; in the bottom they are broadeſt, ending in ſharp points at top; which figure is therefore called* Pyramidal, *becauſe in the ſimilitude of fire it is ſharpened into a cone, as we ſpeak*. (*n*) *Propertius*, with the liberty of a Poet, in an *hyperbole* flies higher yet:

Pyramidum ſumptus ad ſidera ducti.

And the (*o*) *Greek* Epigrammatiſt, in a tranſcendent expreſſion, is no way ſhort of him:

Πυραμίδες δ' ἔτι νῦν Ναυλόδεκ ἄκρα μέτωπα·
Κυρίες κρυσέοις ἄςρεσι πλησίδ'ων.

What exceſſive heights theſe fancied to themſelves, or borrowed from the relations of others, I ſhall not now examine: this I am certain of, that the ſhaft or ſpire of St. *Paul*'s in *London*, before it was caſually burnt, being as much or ſomewhat more than the altitude of the tower now ſtanding, did exceed the height of this Pyramid. For (*p*) *Camden*, in his *Elizabeth*, deſcribes

---

(*n*) Propert. l. 3. Eleg. 2.
(*o*) Græc. Epigr. l. 4. Francof. 1600, cum annot. Brodæi.
(*p*) Pyramis pulcherrima Cathedralis Eccleſiæ S. Pauli, quæ ſingulari urbis ornamento in ſuſpiciendam edita altitudinem, DXX ſcilicet pedes à ſolo, & CCLX à turre quadrata, cui impoſita erat è materia lignea plumbo veſtita, è cœlo propè faſtigium tacta deflagravit. Camdeni Elizabetha.

it

it to be, in a perpendicular, five hundred and twenty feet from the ground; and in his *(q) Britannia* to have been somewhat more than five hundred thirty four feet, whereof the tower two hundred and sixty, and the pyramid on the top two hundred seventy four.

If we imagine upon the sides of the basis, which is perfectly square, four equilateral triangles mutually propending and inclining, till they all meet on high as it were in a point (for so the top seems to them which stand below) then shall we have a true notion of the just dimension and figure of this Pyramid: the perimeter of each triangle comprehending two thousand seventy nine feet (besides the latitude of a little plain or flat on the top) and the perimeter of the basis, two thousand seven hundred seventy two feet: whereby the whole area of the basis (to proportion it to our measures) contains four hundred eighty thousand, two hundred forty nine square feet, or eleven *English* acres of ground, and 1089 of 43560 parts of an acre A proportion so monstrous, that if the ancients did not attest as much, and some of them describe it to be more, this age would hardly be induced to give credit to it. But *Herodotus* describing each side to

(q) Camdeni Britan. in Middlesex. Vide Godwinum de Præful. p. 229.

contain

the first PYRAMID.

contain eight hundred feet, the area must of necessity be greater than that by me assigned, the sum amounting to six hundred and forty thousand; or computing it as *Diodorus Siculus* doth, the area will comprehend four hundred and ninety thousand feet; and in the calculation of *Pliny*, if we shall square eight hundred eighty three (which is the number allotted by him to the measure of each side) the product, seven hundred seventy nine thousand six hundred eighty nine, will much exceed both that of *Herodotus*, and this of *Diodorus*. Though certainly *Pliny* is much mistaken, in assigning the measure of the side to be eight hundred eighty three feet, and the basis of the Pyramid to be but eight *jugera*, or *Roman* acres. For if we take the *Roman jugerum* to contain in length two hundred and forty feet, and in breadth one hundred and twenty, as may be evidently proved out of (*r*) *Varro*, and is expresly affirmed by (*s*) *Quintilian*, then will the superficies or whole extension of the *jugerum* be equal to twenty eight thousand eight hundred *Roman* feet; with which if we divide seven hun-

---

(*r*) Jugerum quadratos duos actus habet. Actus quadratus, qui & latus est pedes CXX, & longus totidem. Is modius ac mina appellatur. Varro de Re Rust. l. 1. c. 10.

(*s*) Jugeri mensuram CCXL longitudinis pedes esse, dimidiiq; in latitudinem patere, non fere quisquam est qui ignoret. Quintil. l. 1. c. 10.

dred

dred seventy nine thousand six hundred eighty nine, the result will be twenty seven *Roman jugera*, and 2089 of 28800 parts of an acre. Wherefore if we take those numbers eight hundred eighty three of *Pliny* to be true, then I suppose he writ twenty eight *jugera*, instead of eight, or else in his proportion of the side to the area of the basis he hath erred.

The ascent to the top of the Pyramid is contrived in this manner. From all the sides without we ascend by degrees; the lowermost degree is near four foot in height, and three in breadth. This runs about the Pyramid in a level; and at the first, when the stones were entire, which are now somewhat decayed, made on every side of it a long but narrow walk. The second degree is like the first, each stone amounting to almost four feet in height, and three in breadth; it retires inward from the first near three feet, and this runs about the Pyramid in a level, as the former. In the same manner is the third row placed upon the second, and so in order the rest, like so many stairs, rise one above another to the top, which ends not in a point, as mathematical Pyramids do, but in a little flat or square. Of this *Herodotus* hath no where left us the dimensions; but (t) *Henricus Ste-*

(t) Hen. Steph. in 2. lib. Herodot. *phanus,*

the first PYRAMID.   99

phanus, an able and deserving man, in his comment hath supplied it for him; for he makes it to be eight *orgyiæ*. Where if we take the *orgyia*, as both (*u*) *Hesychius* and (*x*) *Suidas* do, for the distance between the hands extended at length, that is, for the fathom or six feet, then should it be forty eight feet in breadth at the top. But the truth is, *Stephanus* in this particular, whilst he corrects the errors of *Valla*'s interpretation, is to be corrected himself. For that latitude which *Herodotus* assigns to the admirable bridge below (of which there is nothing now remaining) he hath carried up, by a mistake, to the top of the Pyramid. (*y*) *Diodorus Siculus* comes nearer to the truth, who describes it to be but nine feet. (*z*) *Pliny* makes the breadth at the top to be twenty five feet. *Altitudo* (I would rather read it *latitudo*) *à cacumine pedes* xxv. By my measure it is thirteen feet, and 280 of 1000 parts of the *English* foot. Upon this flat, if we assent to the opinion of (*a*) *Proclus*, it may be supposed that the *Ægyptian* Priests made their observations in Astronomy; and that from hence, or near

(*u*) Ὀργυιὰ ἡ ἐπ᾽ ἀμφοτέρων χερῶν τάσις. Hesych.
(*x*) Ὀργυιαὶ τὰ μετὰ τῶν ἰδίων χειρῶν. Said.
(*y*) Diodor. lib. 1.
(*z*) Plin. l. 36. c. 12.
(*a*) Procl. comm. l. 1. in Timæum Platonis.

this

this place they first discovered, by the rising of *Sirius*, their *annus κυνικὸς*, or *canicularis*, as also their *periodus Sothiaca*, or *annus magnus κυνικὸς*, or *annus heliacus*, or *annus Dei*, as it is termed by (b) *Censorinus*, consisting of 1460 sidereal years; in which space their *Thoth vagum & fixum* came to have the same beginning. That the Priests might near these Pyramids make their observations, I no way question, this rising of the hill being, in my judgment, as fit a place as any in *Ægypt* for such a design; and so much the fitter by the vicinity of *Memphis*. But that these Pyramids were designed for observatories (whereas by the testimonies of the ancients I have proved before, that they were intended for sepulchres) is no way to be credited upon the single authority of *Proclus*. Neither can I apprehend, to what purpose the Priests with so much difficulty should ascend so high; when below with more ease, and as much certainty, they might from their own lodgings hewn in the rocks, upon which the Pyramids are erected, make the same observations. For seeing all *Ægypt* is but as it were one continued plain, they might from these cliffs have, over the plains of *Ægypt*, as free and

---

(b) Censorin. de die natali. Quem Græce κυνικὸν, Latine *canicularem* vocamus. Hic *annus* etiam *heliacus* à quibusdam dicitur, & ab aliis ὁ θεοῦ ἐνιαυτός.

open

open a prospect of the heavens, as from the tops of the Pyramids themselves. And therefore *Tully* writes more truly: (c) *Ægyptii aut Babylonii, in camporum patentium æquoribus habitantes, cùm ex terra nihil emineret, quod contemplationi cœli officere posset, omnem curam in siderum cognitione posuerunt.* The top of this Pyramid is covered, not with (d) one or (e) three massy stones, as some have imagined, but with nine, besides two which are wanting at the angles. The degrees by which we ascend up (as I observed in measuring many of them) are not all of an equal depth; for some are near four feet, others want of three; and these the higher we ascend, do so much the more diminish: neither is the breadth of them alike; the difference in this kind being, as far as I could conjecture, proportionable to their depth. And therefore a right line extended from any part of the basis without to the top, will equally touch the outward angle of every degree. Of these it was impossible for me to take an exact measure, since in such a revolution of time, if the inner parts of the Pyramid have not lost any thing of their first perfection, as being not exposed to

---

(c) Cicer. de Div'n. lib. 1.
(d) Les voyages de Seign. Villamont.
(e) Sandys's Travels, l. 2.

breadth and depth of every step is one single and entire stone. The relation of *(g) Herodotus* and *(h) Pomponius Mela* is more admirable, who make *the least stone in this Pyramid to be thirty feet.* And this I can grant in some, yet surely it cannot be admitted in all, unless we interpret their words, that the least stone is thirty square (or, to speak more properly, thirty cubical) feet: which dimension, or a much greater in the exteriour ones, I can without any difficulty admit. The number of these steps is not mentioned by the ancients, and that caused me, and two that were with me, to be the more diligent in computing them; because by modern writers, and some of those too of repute, they are described with much diversity and contrariety. The degrees, saith *(i) Bellonius,* are about two hundred and fifty, each of them single contains in height forty five digits, at the top it is two paces broad. For this I take to be the meaning of what *Clusius* renders thus: *A basi autem ad cacumen ipsius supputationem facientes, comperimus circiter* CCL *gradus, singuli altitudinem habent quinque solearum*

(g) Οὐδεὶς ἦν λίθων τεληκότα ποδῶν ἐλάσσων. Herod. lib. 2.

(h) Pyramides tricenûm pedum lapidibus exstructæ. Pomp. Mel. lib. 1. cap. 9.

(i) Bellonius lib. 2. observ. c. 42.

calcei

the first PYRAMID. 105

calcei IX *pollicum longitudinis, in fastigio duos passus habet.* Where, I conceive, his *passus* is in the same sense to be understood here above, as not long before he explains himself in describing the *basis* below, which in his account is CCCXXIV *passus paululum extensis cruribus.* (*l*) *Albertus Lewenstainius* reckons the steps to be two hundred and sixty, each of them a foot and a half in depth; *Johannes Helfricus* counts them to be two hundred and thirty. (*m*) *Sebastianus Serlius,* upon a relation of *Grimano* the Patriarch of *Aquileia,* and afterwards Cardinal (who in his travels in *Ægypt* measured these degrees) computes them to be two hundred and ten, and the height of every step to be equally three palms and an half. It would be but lost labour to mention the different and repugnant relations of several others. That which by experience and by a diligent calculation I and two others found, is this; that the number of degrees from the bottom to the top is two hundred and seven; though

---

(*l*) Albertus Lewenstainius gradus ad cacumen numerat CCLX, singulos sesquipedali altitudine; Johannes Helfricus CCXXX. Raderus in Martial. epigr.

Barbara Pyramidum sileat miracula Memphis, &c.

(*m*) Il numero de pezzi dalla basa fino alla sommità sono da CXX, e sono tutti d'una altezza talmente che l'altezza di tutta la massa è quanto la sua basa. Sebast. Serl. li. 3. delle Antichità.

one of them, in defcending, reckoned two hundred and eight.

Such as pleafe may give credit to thofe fabulous traditions of *(n)* fome, that a *Turkifh* archer ftanding at the top cannot fhoot beyond the bottom, but that the arrow will neceffarily fall upon thefe fteps. If the *Turkifh* bow (which by thofe figures that I have feen in ancient monuments, is the fame with that of the *Parthians*, fo dreadful to the *Romans*) be but as fwift and ftrong as the *Englifh*; as furely it is much more, if we confider with what incredible force fome of them will pierce a plank of fix inches in thicknefs (I fpeak what I have feen) it will not feem ftrange, that they fhould carry twelvefcore in length; which diftance is beyond the bafis of this Pyramid.

The fame credit is to be given to thofe reports of the ancients, that this Pyramid and the reft caft no fhadows. *(o) Solinus* writes exprefly, *menfuram umbrarum egreffæ, nullas habent umbras.* And *(p) Aufonius,*

(n) Bellon. obferv. lib. 2. cap. 42. & alii. Peritiffimus atque validiffimus fagittarius in ejus faftigio exiftens, atque fagittam in aerem emittens, tam validè eam ejaculari non poterit, ut extra molis bafim decidat, fed in ipfos gradus cadet: adeo vaftæ magnitudinis, uti diximus, eft hæc moles.

(o) Jul. Solin. Polyh. c. 35.

(p) Aufon. eidyllio 3.

----*Quadro*

―――*Quadro cui in fastigia cono*
Surgit, & ipsa suas consumit Pyramis umbras.

(*q*) *Ammianus Marcellinus* hath almost the same relation: *Umbras quoque mechanicâ ratione consumit.* Lastly, (*r*) *Cassiodorus* confirms the same: *Pyramides in Ægypto, quarum in suo statu se umbra consumens, ultra constructionis spacia nulla parte respicitur.* All which in the winter-season I can in no sort admit to be true. For at that time I have seen them cast a shadow at noon: and if I had not seen it, yet reason and the art of measuring altitudes by shadows, and, on the contrary, of knowing the length of shadows by altitudes, doth necessarily infer as much. Besides, how could *Thales Milesius*, above two thousand years since, have taken their height by shadows, according to *Pliny* and *Laertius*, as we mentioned before, if so be these Pyramids have no shadows at all? To reconcile the difference: We may imagine *Solinus, Ausonius, Marcellinus,* and *Cassiodorus* mean in the summer-time; or, which is nearer the truth, that almost for three quarters of the year they have no shadows: and this I grant to be true at mid-day.

(*q*) Ammian. Marcell. lib. 22.
(*r*) Cassiodor. Var. 7. formula 15.

A Description of the Inside of the first PYRAMID.

HAVING finished the description of the greater Pyramid, with the figure and dimensions of it, as they present themselves to the view *without:* I shall now look *inwards,* and lead the reader into the several spaces and partitions *within:* of which if the ancients have been silent, we must chiefly impute it to a reverend and awful regard, mixed with superstition, in not presuming to enter those chambers of death, which religion and devotion had consecrated to the rest and quiet of the dead. Wherefore *Herodotus* mentions no more, but only in general, that (*a*) *some secret vaults are hewn in the rock under the Pyramid.* Diodorus Siculus is silent; tho' both enlarge themselves in other particulars less necessary. *Strabo* also is very concise, whose whole description both of this and of the second Pyramid is included in this short expression: (*b*) *Forty stadia from the city* [Memphis] *there is a certain brow of an hill, in which are many Pyramids, the sepulchres of kings: three of them are memorable; two of these are accounted amongst the*

(*a*) Herod. l. 2.   (*b*) Strabo l. 17.

seven

the first PYRAMID.

seven miracles of the world: each of these are a furlong in height; the figure is quadrilateral; the altitude somewhat exceeds each side, and the one is somewhat bigger than the other. On high as it were in the midst between the sides, there is a stone that may be removed, which being taken out, there is an oblique [or shelving] *entrance* (for so I render that which by him is termed σύειγξ σκολιά) *leading to the tomb.* Pliny expresses nothing within, but only (c) *a well* (which is still extant) *of eighty six cubits in depth*; to which he probably imagines, by some secret aquæduct the water of the river *Nilus* to be brought. *Aristides*, in his oration intitled Αιγύπ]ιος, upon a misinformation of the *Ægyptian* Priests, makes the foundation of the structure to have descended as far below, as the altitude ascends above; of which I see no necessity, seeing all of them are founded upon rocks. His words are these: (d) *Now as with admiration we behold the tops of the Pyramids, but that which is as much more under ground opposite to it, we are ignorant of: (I speak what I have received from the Priests.)* And this is that

---

(c) Plin. l. 36. c. 12.
(d) Νῦν δ' ὥσπερ τῶν πυραμίδων τὰς μὲν κορυφὰς ὁρῶντες ἐκπληττόμεθα, τὸ δ' ἀντίπαχον ᾗ ὑπὸ γῆς ἕτερον τοσοῦτον ὂν ἠγνόηται (λέγω δ' ἃ τῶν ἱερέων ἤκουον) &c. Aristid λόγ Αἰγύπ]ι .

which

A Description of

which hath been delivered to us by the ancients; which I was unwilling to pretermit, more out of reverence of antiquity, than out of any special satisfaction. The *Arabian* writers, especially such as have purposely treated of the wonders of *Ægypt*, have given us a more full description of what is within these Pyramids; but that hath been mixed with so many fictions of their own, that the truth hath been darkened, and almost quite extinguished by them. I shall put down that which is confessed by them to be the most probable relation, as it is reported by *Ibn Abd Alhokm*, whose words out of the *Arabick* are these: (e) *The greatest part of Chronologers agree, that he which built the Pyramids was* Saurid Ibn Salhouk, *king of Ægypt, who lived three hundred years before the flood. The occasion of this was, because he saw in his sleep, that the whole earth was turned over, with the inhabitants of it, the men lying upon their faces, and the stars falling down, and striking one another with a terrible noise; and being troubled, he concealed it. After this he saw the fixt stars falling to the earth in the similitude of white fowl, and they snatched up men, carrying them between two great mountains, and these mountains closed upon them, and the shining*

(e) ابن عبد الحكم

stars

the first PYRAMID. 111

stars were made dark. Awaking with great fear, he assembled the chief Priests of all the provinces of Ægypt, *an hundred and thirty Priests, the chief of whom was called* Aclimun, *relating the whole matter to them; and they took the altitude of the stars, and making their prognostication, foretold of a deluge. The king said, Will it come to our country? They answered, Yea, and will destroy it. And there remained a certain number of years for to come; and he commanded in the mean space to build the Pyramids, and a vault to be made, into which the river* Nilus *entring, it should run into the countries of the West, and into the land of* Al-Said; *and he filled them with (f)*Telesmes, *and with strange things, and with riches, and treasures, and the like. He ingraved in them all things that were told him by wise men, as also all profound sciences,*

(f) *Telesmes.*] The word used by the *Arabians* is derived from the *Greek* ἀποτέλεσμα, by an *aphæresis* of ἀπό. By the like *aphæresis*, together with an *epenthesis*, the *Arabians* call him *Bochtonassar*, whom *Ptolemy* names *Nabonassar*; as by an *aphæresis* and *syncope* the *Turks* call *Constantinople*, *Stanpol*, or *Istanbol*, from whence some of our writers term it *Stambol*; though the *Arabians* more fully express it by *Costantiniya* and *Buxantiya*, that is, *Constantinopolis*, and *Byzantium*. The various significations of τελέσματα, or ἀποτελέσματα, see in Mr. *Selden*'s learned discourse *de Diis Syris*, and in *Scaliger*'s annotations *in Apotelesmaticum Manilii*. That which the *Arabians* commonly mean by *Telesmes*, are certain *Sigills*, or *Amulets*, made under such and such an aspect, or configuration of the stars and planets, with several characters accordingly inscribed.

the

the names of (g) Alakakirs, *the uses and hurts of them ; the science of Astrology, and of Arithmetick, and of Geometry, and of Physick. All this may be interpreted by him that knows their characters and language. After he had given order for this building, they cut out vast columns and wonderful stones. They fetch massy stones from the Æthiopians, and made with these the foundations of the three Pyramids, fastening them together with lead and iron. They built the gates of them forty cubits under ground, and they made the height of the Pyramids one hundred royal cubits, which are five hundred of ours in these times ; he also made each side of them an hundred royal cubits. The beginning of this building was in a fortunate horoscope. After that he had finished it, he covered it with coloured satten from the top to the bottom ; and he appointed a solemn festival, at which were present all the inhabitants of his kingdom. Then he built in the western Pyramid thirty treasuries, filled with store of riches and utensils, and with signatures made of precious stones, and with instruments of iron, and vessels of earth, and with arms which rust not, and with glass which might be bended, and yet not broken,*

(g) *Alakakir*, amongst other significations, is the name of a precious stone ; and therefore in *Abulfeda* it is joined with *yacut*, a ruby. I imagine it here to signify some magical spell, which, it may be, was ingraven in this stone.

and

the firſt PYRAMID. 113

and with ſtrange ſpells, and with ſeveral kinds of akakirs, ſingle and double, and with deadly poiſons, and with other things beſides. He made alſo in the eaſt Pyramid divers cæleſtial ſpheres and ſtars, and what they ſeverally operate in their aſpects; and the perfumes which are to be uſed to them, and the books which treat of theſe matters. He put alſo in the coloured Pyramid the commentaries of the Prieſts in cheſts of black marble, and with every Prieſt a book, in which were the wonders of his profeſſion, and of his actions, and of his nature, and what was done in his time, and what is and what ſhall be from the beginning of time to the end of it. He placed in every Pyramid a treaſurer; the treaſurer of the weſterly Pyramid was a ſtatue of marble ſtone, ſtanding upright with a lance, and upon his head a ſerpent wreathed. He that came near it, and ſtood ſtill, the ſerpent bit him of one ſide, and wreathing round about his throat, and killing him, returned to his place. He made the treaſurer of the eaſt Pyramid an idol of black agate, his eyes open and ſhining, ſitting upon a throne with a lance: when any lookt upon him, he heard of one ſide of him a voice which took away his ſenſe, ſo that he fell proſtrate upon his face, and ceaſed not, till he died. He made the treaſurer of the coloured Pyramid a ſtatue of ſtone, called albut, ſitting. He which looked

towards

towards it was drawn by the statue, till he stuck to it, and could not be separated from it, till such time as he died. The Coptites write in their books, that there is an inscription engraven upon them, the exposition of which in Arabick *is this*: I king *Saurid* built the Pyramids in such and such a time, and finished them in six years: He that comes after me, and says that he is equal to me, let him destroy them in six hundred years; and yet, it is known, that it is easier to pluck down than to build up. I also covered them, when I had finished them, with satten; and let him cover them with mats. *After that* Almamon *the Calif entred Ægypt, and saw the Pyramids, he desired to know what was within, and therefore would have them opened. They told him, it could not possibly be done. He replied, I will have it certainly done. And that hole was opened for him, which stands open to this day, with fire and vinegar. Two smiths prepared and sharpened the iron and engines, which they forced in, and there was a great expense in the opening of it. The thickness of the wall was found to be twenty cubits; and when they came to the end of the wall behind the place where they had digged, there was an ewer* [or pot] *of green emrald; in it were a thousand dinars very weighty, every dinar was an ounce of our ounces: they wondred at it, but knew the first* PYRAMID.

knew not the meaning of it. Then Almamon *said, Cast up the account, how much hath been spent in making the entrance: they cast it up, and lo, it was the same sum which they found; it neither exceeded, nor was defective. Within they found a square well, in the square of it there were doors, every door opened into an house* [or vault] *in which there were dead bodies wrapped up in linnen. They found towards the top of the Pyramid a chamber, in which there was an hollow stone: in it was a statue of a stone like a man, and within it a man, upon whom was a breast-plate of gold set with jewels; upon his breast was a sword of invaluable price, and at his head a carbuncle of the bigness of an egg, shining like the light of the day; and upon him were characters written with a pen, no man knows what they signify. After* Almamon *had opened it, men entred into it for many years, and descended by the slippery passage which is in it; and some of them came out safe, and others died.* Thus far the *Arabians*: which traditions of theirs are little better than a Romance; and therefore leaving these, I shall give a more true and particular description out of mine own experience and observations.

On the north side ascending thirty eight feet, upon an artificial bank of earth, there is a square and narrow passage leading into the

the Pyramid, through the mouth of which (being equidistant from the two sides of the Pyramid) we enter as it were down the steep of an hill, declining with an angle of twenty six degrees. The breadth of this entrance is exactly three feet, and 463 parts of 1000 of the *English* foot: the length of it, beginning from the first declivity, which is some ten palms without, to the utmost extremity of the neck or streight within, where it contracts it self almost nine feet continued, with scarce half the depth it had at the first entrance (though it keep still the same breadth) is ninety two feet and an half. The structure of it hath been the labour of an exquisite hand, as appears by the smoothness and evenness of the work, and by the close knitting of the joints; a property long since observed and commended by *Diodorus (b)* to have run through the fabrick of the whole body of this Pyramid. Having passed with tapers in our hands this narrow streight, though with some difficulty (for at the farther end of it we must serpent-like creep upon our bellies) we land in a place somewhat larger, and of a pretty height, but lying incomposed; having been dug away either by the curiosity or avarice of some, in hope to discover an hidden treasure;

(b) Diodor. Sic. lib. 1.

the first PYRAMID.

treasure; or rather by the command of *Almamon*, the deservedly renowned Calif of *Babylon*. By whomsoever it were, it is not worth the inquiry; nor doth the place merit describing, but that I was unwilling to pretermit any thing, being only an habitation for bats, and those so ugly, and of so large a size, exceeding a foot in length, that I have not elsewhere seen the like. The length of this obscure and broken place containeth eighty nine feet; the breadth and height is various, and not worth consideration. On the left hand of this, adjoining to that narrow entrance through which we passed, we climb up a steep and massy stone, eight or nine feet in height, where we immediately enter upon the lower end of the first gallery. The pavement of this rises with a gentle acclivity, consisting of smooth and polish'd marble, and, where not smeared with filth, appearing of a white and alabaster colour: the sides and roof, as *Titus Livius Burretinus* a *Venetian*, an ingenious young man, who accompany'd me thither, observed, was of impolished stone, not so hard and compact as that of the pavement, but more soft and tender; the breadth almost five feet, and about the same quantity the height, if he have not mistaken. He likewise discover'd some irregularity in the breadth, it opening a little wider in some places than in others: but this inequality could not be discerned by the eye, but only by measuring it with a careful hand. By my observation with a line, this gallery contained in length an hundred and ten feet. At the end of this begins the second gallery, a very stately piece of work, and not inferiour either in respect of the curiosity of art, or richness of materials, to the most sumptuous and magnificent buildings. It is divided from the former by a wall, through which stooping we passed in a square hole, much about the same bigness as that by which we entred into the Pyramid, but of no considerable length. This narrow passage lieth level, not rising with an acclivity, as doth the pavement below, and roof above, of both these galleries. At the end of it, on the right hand, is the well mentioned by *Pliny*; the which is circular, and not square, as the *Arabian* writers describe: the diameter of it exceeds three feet; the sides are lined with white marble, and the descent into it is by fastening the hands and feet in little open spaces cut in the sides within, opposite and answerable to one another, in a perpendicular. (*This Well is described in Plate* 2. *Fig.* 1.) In the same manner are almost all the wells and passages into the cisterns at *Alexandria* contrived, without stairs or windings, but only

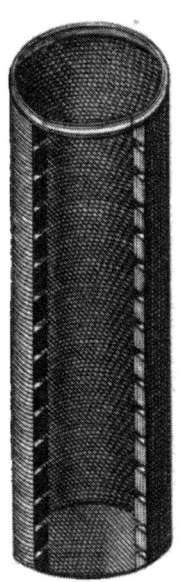

fig. 1. p. 118.

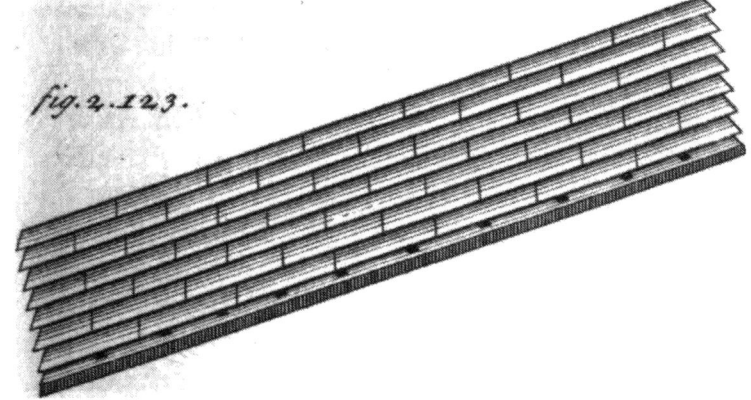

fig. 2. 123.

the first PYRAMID.

only with inlets and square holes on each side within; by which, using the feet and hands, one may with ease descend. Many of these cisterns are with open and double arches, the lowermost arch being supported by a row of speckled and *Thebaick* marble pillars, upon the top of which stands a second row, bearing the upper and higher arch: the walls within are cover'd with a sort of plaster, for the colour white, but of so durable a substance, that neither by time, nor by the water, is it yet corrupted and impaired. But I return from the cisterns and wells there, to this in the Pyramid; which, in (*i*) *Pliny*'s calculation, is *eighty six cubits in depth*; and, it may be, was the passage to those secret vaults mentioned but not described by *Herodotus*, that were hewn out of the rock, over which this Pyramid is erected. By my measure founding it with a line, it contains twenty feet in depth. The reason of the difference between *Pliny*'s observation and mine, I suppose to be this; that since his time it hath almost been dammed up, and choaked with rubbish; which I plainly discovered at the bottom, by throwing down some combustible matter set on fire. Leaving the well, and going on strait upon a level the distance

(*i*) In pyramide maxima est intus puteus LXXXVI. cubitorum, flumen illo admissum arbitrantur. Plin. l. 36. c. 12.

of fifteen feet, we entred another square passage, opening against the former, and of the same bigness. The stones are very massy, and exquisitely joined, I know not whether of that glistering and speckled marble I mentioned in the columns of the cisterns at *Alexandria*. This leadeth (running in length upon a level an hundred and ten feet) into an arched vault, or little chamber; which, by reason it was of a grave-like smell, and half full of rubbish, occasioned my lesser stay. This chamber stands east and west; the length of it is less than twenty feet, the breadth about seventeen, and the height less than fifteen. The walls are entire, and plaster'd over with lime; the roof is covered with large smooth stones, not lying flat, but shelving, and meeting above in a kind of arch, or rather an angle. On the east side of this room, in the middle of it, there seems to have been a passage leading to some other place. Whether this way the Priests went into the hollow of that *sphinx*, as *Strabo* and (k) *Pliny* term it, or *androsphinx*, as *Herodotus* calls such kinds (being by *Pliny*'s calculation CII feet in compass about the head, in height LXII, in length CXLIII, and, by my observation, made of one entire stone) which stands not far

(k) Plin. lib. 36. cap. 12.

distant

the first PYRAMID.

distant without the Pyramid, south-east of it, or into any other private retirement, I cannot determine; and it may be too, this served for no such purpose, but rather as a *theca* or *nicchio*, as the *Italians* speak, wherein some idol might be placed, or else for a piece of ornament (for it is made of polished stone) in the architecture of those times, which ours may no more understand, than they do the reason of the rest of those strange proportions that appear in the passages and inner rooms of this Pyramid. Returning back the same way we came, as soon as we are out of this narrow and square passage, we climb over it, and going strait on, in the trace of the second gallery, upon a shelving pavement (like that of the first) rising with an angle of twenty six degrees, we at length come to another partition. The length of the gallery, from the well below to this partition above, is an hundred fifty and four feet: but if we measure the pavement of the floor, it is somewhat less, by reason of a little vacuity (some fifteen feet in length) as we described before, between the well and the square hole we climbed over. And here, to reassume some part of that which hath been spoken, if we consider the narrow entrance at the mouth of the Pyramid, by which we descend; and the length of the first and second galleries, by which we ascend,

ascend, all of them lying as it were in the same continued line, and leading to the middle of the Pyramid, we may easily apprehend a reason of that strange echo within of four or five voices, mentioned by (*l*) *Plutarch* in his fourth book *De placitis Philosophorum*; or rather of a long-continued sound, as I found by experience, discharging a musket at the entrance. For the sound being shut in, and carried in those close and smooth passages, like as in so many pipes or trunks, finding no issue out, reflects upon itself, and causes a confused noise, and circulation of the air, which by degrees vanishes, as the motion of it ceases. This gallery or corridor, or whatsoever else I may call it, is built of white and polished marble, the which is very evenly cut in spacious squares or tables. Of such materials as is the pavement, such is the roof, and such are the side-walls that flank it: the coagmentation or knitting of the joints is so close, that they are scarce discernable to a curious eye; and that which adds grace to the whole structure, though it makes the passage the more slippery and difficult, is the acclivity and rising of the ascent. The height of this gallery is twenty six feet, the

---

(*l*) Ἐν γύπταις κατ' Αἴγυπτον συρμάτων ἔνδον φωνὴ ῥηγνυμένη τέτρακις ἢ ᾗ πέντε ἤχυς ἀπεργάζεται. Plut. lib. 4. de Philos. plac. cap. 20.

breadth

the first PYRAMID. 123

breadth is six feet, and 870 parts of the foot divided into 1000; of which, three feet, and 435 of 1000 parts of a foot, are to be allowed for the way in the midst, which is set and bounded on both sides with two banks (like benches) of sleek and polished stone; each of these hath one foot, 717 of 1000 parts of a foot in breadth, and as much in depth. Upon the top of these benches, near the angle, where they close and join with the wall, are little spaces cut in right-angled parallel figures, set on each side opposite to one another; intended, no question, for some other end than ornament. In the casting and ranging of the marbles in both the side-walls, there is one piece of architecture, in my judgment, very graceful, and that is, that all the courses or ranges, which are but seven (so great are those stones) do set and flag over one another about three inches; the bottom of the uppermost course over-setting the higher part of the second, and the lower part of this overflagging the top of the third; and so in order the rest, as they descend. Which will better be conceived by the representation of it to the eye, as in *Plate* 2. *Fig* 2. than by any other description.

Having passed this gallery, we enter another square hole, of the same dimensions with the former, which brings us into two

anti-

anticamerette, as the *Italians* would call them, or anticlosets (give me leave, in so unusual a structure, to frame some (*m*) unusual terms) lined with a rich and speckled kind of *Thebaick* marble. The first of these hath the dimensions almost equal to the second. The second is thus proportioned; the area is level, the figure of it is oblong, the one side containing seven feet, the other three and an half, the height is ten feet. On the east and west sides, within two feet and an half of the top, which is somewhat larger than the bottom, are three cavities or little seats, in the manner described in *Plate* 2. *Fig.* 3.

This inner anticloset is separated from the former, by a stone of red speckled marble, which hangs in two mortises (like the leaf of a sluice) between two walls, more than three feet above the pavement, and wanting two of the roof. Out of this closet we enter another square hole, over which are five lines cut parallel and perpendicular, in the manner described in *Plate* 2. *Fig.* 4.

Besides these I have not observed any other sculptures or ingravings in the whole Pyramid And therefore it may justly be wondred, whence the *Arabians* borrowed

---

(*m*) Sunt enim rebus novis nova ponenda nomina. Cic. lib. 1. de naturâ Deorum.

those

p. 124.

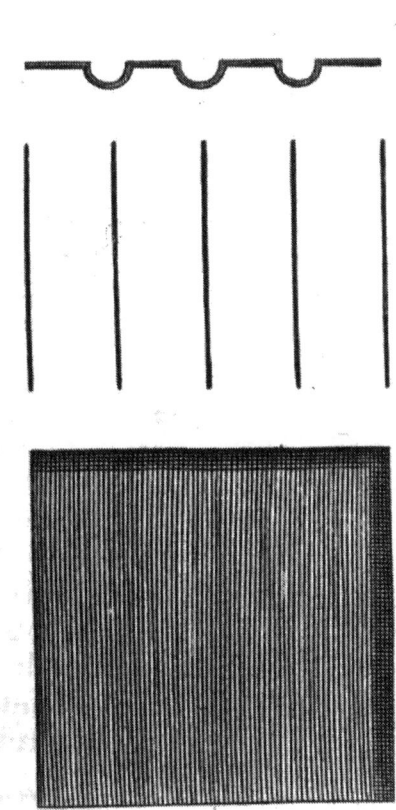

the first PYRAMID. 125

those traditions I before related, that *all sciences are inscribed within in hieroglyphicks.* And as justly it may be questioned, upon what authority *Dio*, or his epitomizer *Xiphilinus* reports, that *Cornelius Gallus* (whom (n) *Strabo* more truly names *Ælius Gallus*, with whom he travelled into *Ægypt* as a friend and companion) *(o) engraved in the Pyramids his victories,* unless we understand some other Pyramids not now existent. This square passage is of the same wideness and dimensions as the rest, and is in length near nine feet (being all of *Thebaick* marble, most exquisitely cut) which lands us at the north end of a very sumptuous and well-proportioned room. The distance from the end of the second gallery to this entry, running upon the same level, is twenty four feet. This rich and spacious chamber, in which art may seem to have contended with nature, the curious work being not inferior to the rich materials, stands as it were in the heart and center of the Pyramid, equidistant from all the sides, and almost in the midst between the basis and the top. The floor, the sides, the roof of it, are all made of vast and exquisite tables of *Thebaick* marble, which, if they were not vailed and obscured

---

(n) Strabo lib. 17.
(o) Xiphil. in Cæs. Aug. Τὰ ἔργα ὅσα ἐπεποιήκει, ἐς τὰς πυραμίδας ἐσέγραψε.

by

by the steam of tapers, would appear glistering and shining. From the top of it descending to the bottom there are but six ranges of stone, all which being respectively sized to an equal height, very gracefully in one and the same altitude run round the room. The stones, which cover this place, are of a strange and stupendous length, like so many huge beams lying flat, and traversing the room, and withall supporting that infinite mass and weight of the Pyramid above. Of these there are nine, which cover the roof; two of them are less by half in breadth than the rest; the one at the east end, the other at the west. The length of this *(p)* chamber on the south-side, most accurately taken at the joint or line where the

---

(p) These proportions of the chamber, and those which follow, of the length and breadth of the hollow part of the tomb, were taken by me with as much exactness as it was possible to do; which I did so much the more diligently, as judging this to be the fittest place for the fixing of measures for posterity: a thing which hath been much desired by learned men; but the manner how it might be exactly done, hath been thought of by none. I am of opinion, that as this Pyramid hath stood three thousand years almost, and is no whit decayed within, so it may continue many thousand years longer: and therefore, that after-times measuring these places by me assigned, may hereby not only find out the just dimensions of the *English* foot, but also the feet of several nations in these times, which in my travels abroad I have taken from the originals, and have compared them at home with the *English* standard. Had some of the ancient Mathematicians thought of this way, these times would not have been so much perplexed in discovering the measures of the *Hebrews, Babylonians,*

the first and second row of stones meet, is thirty four *English* feet, and 380 parts of the foot divided into a thousand (that is, 34 feet, and 380 of 1000 parts of a foot.) The breadth of the west side, at the joint or line where the first and second row of stones meet, is seventeen feet, and an hundred and ninety parts of the foot divided into a thousand (that is, 17 feet, and 190 of 1000 parts of a foot.) The height is nineteen feet and an half.

Within this glorious room (for so I may justly call it) as within some consecrated oratory, stands the monument of *Cheops* or *Chemmis*, of one piece of marble, hollow within, and uncovered at the top, and sounding like a bell: which I mention not as any rarity either in nature or in art (for I have observed the like found in other tombs of (q) marble cut hollow like this) but because I find modern authors to take notice of it as a wonder. Some write, that the body hath

---

ans, *Ægyptians*, *Greeks*, and other nations. Such parts as the *English* foot contains a thousand, the *Roman* foot on *Cossutius*'s monument, commonly called by writers *pes Cossutianus*, contains 967; the *Paris* foot, 1068; the *Spanish* foot, 920; the *Venetian* foot, 1062; the *Rhinland* foot, or that of *Snellius*, 1033; the *braccio* at *Florence*, 1913; the *braccio* at *Naples*, 2100; the *derah* at *Cairo*, 1824; the greater *Turkish* pike at *Constantinople*, 2200.

(q) As appears by a fair and ancient monument, brought from *Smyrna* to my very worthy friend *Edward Roll* Esq; which stands in his park at *Woolwich*.

been

been removed hence; whereas *Diodorus* hath left above sixteen hundred years since a memorable passage concerning *Chemmis*, the builder of this Pyramid, and *Cephren* the founder of the next adjoining: *(r) Although* (saith he) *these kings intended these for their sepulchers, yet it happened that neither of them were buried there. For the people being exasperated against them by reason of the toilsomness of these works, and for their cruelty and oppression, threatned to tear in pieces their dead bodies, and with ignominy to throw them out of their sepulchres. Wherefore both of them dying, commanded their friends privately to bury them in an obscure place.* This monument, in respect to the nature and quality of the stone, is the same with which the whole room is lined, as by breaking a little fragment of it I plainly discover'd, being a speckled kind of marble, with black and white and red spots as it were equally mixed, which some writers call *Thebaick* marble; though I conceive it to be that sort of Porphyry, which *Pliny* calls *Leucostictos*, and describes thus: (s) *Rubet porphyrites in eâdem Ægypto; ex eo candidis intervenientibus punctis leucostictos appellatur. Quantislibet molibus cædendis sufficiunt lapi-*

(r) Diod. Sic. lib. 1. Τῶν δὲ βασιλέων τῶν κατασκευασάντων αὐτὰς ἑαυτοῖς τάφους, συνέβη μηδέτερον αὐτῶν ἢ συρμίσιν ἐνταφῆναι, &c.

(s) Plin. lib. 36. cap. 7.

the first PYRAMID. 129

dicinæ. Of this kind of marble there was, and still are, an infinite quantity of columns in *Ægypt*. But *Venetian*, a man very curious, who accompanied me thither, imagined, that this sort of marble came from mount (*t*) *Sina*, where he had lived amongst the rocks, which he affirmed to be speckled with party colours of black and white and red, like this: and to confirm his assertion, he alledged, that he had seen a great column, left imperfect amongst the cliffs, almost as big as that huge and admirable (*u*) *Corinthian* pillar standing to the south of *Alexandria*, which by my measure is near four times as big as any of those vast *Corinthian* pillars in the *Porticus* before the *Pantheon* at *Rome*, all which are of the same coloured marble with this monument; and so are all the obelisks with hieroglyphicks, both in *Rome* and *Alexandria*. Which opi-

(*t*) Which may also be confirmed by *Bellonius*'s observations, who describing the rock, out of which, upon *Moses*'s striking it, there gushed out waters, makes it to be such a speckled kind of *Thebaick* marble: *Est une grosse pierre massive, droicte de mesme grain & de sa couleur, qu'est la pierre Thebaique.*

(*u*) The compass of the *scapus* of this column at *Alexandria*, near the *torus*, is twenty four *English* feet: the compass of the *scapus* of those at *Rome* is fifteen *English* feet and three inches. By these proportions, and by those rules which are expressed in *Vitruvius* and in other books of architecture, the ingenious reader may compute the true dimensions of those before the *Pantheon*, and of this at *Alexandria*, being in my calculation the most magnificent column that ever was made of one entire stone.

nion

nion of his doth well correspond with the tradition of *Aristides*, who reports, that in *Arabia there is a quarry of excellent porphyry*. The figure of this tomb without is like an altar, or, more nearly to express it, like two cubes finely set together, and hollowed within: it is cut smooth and plain, without any sculpture and ingraving, or any relevy and imbossment. The exteriour superficies of it contains in length seven feet three inches and a half. (*x*) *Bellonius* makes it twelve feet, and (*y*) Monsieur *de Bréves* nine; but both of them have exceeded. In depth it is three feet, three inches, and three quarters, and is the same in breadth. The hollow part within is in length, on the west side, six feet, and four hundred eighty eight parts of the *English* foot divided into a thousand parts (that is, (*z*) 6 feet, and 488 of 1000 parts of a foot) in breadth: at the north end two feet, and two hundred and eighteen parts of the foot divided into a thousand parts (that is, (*a*) 2 feet, and 218

of

(*x*) Pervenitur in elegans cubiculum quadrangulum sex passus longum, & quatuor latum, quatuor veró vel sex orgyiis altum, in quo marmor nigrum solidum in cistæ formam excisum invenimus, duodecim pedes longum, quinque altum, & totidem latum, sine operculo. Bellon. observ. lib. 2. cap. 42.

(*y*) Les voyages de Monsieur de Breves.

(*z*) 6 feet $\frac{488}{1000}$.   (*a*) 2 feet $\frac{218}{1000}$. In the reiteration of these numbers, if any shall be offended, either with the novelty or tediousness of expressing them so often, I must justify my self by the example of *Vlug Beg*, nephew to

Timur-

the first PYRAMID.   131

of 1000 parts of a foot) The depth is 2 feet, and 860 of 1000 parts of the *English* foot. A narrow space, yet large enough to contain a most potent and dreadful monarch being dead, to whom living all *Ægypt* was too streight and narrow a circuit. By these dimensions, and by such other observations as have been taken by me from several imbalmed bodies in *Ægypt*, we may conclude, that there is no decay in nature (though the question is as old as *(b) Homer*) but that the men of this age are of the same stature they were near three thousand years ago; not-

Timurlanc the great (for so is his name, and not *Tamerlane*) and emperor of the *Moguls* or *Tatars* (whom we term amiss the *Tartars*.) For I find in his astronomical tables (the most accurate of any in the east) made about two hundred years since, the same course observed by him, when he writes of the *Grecian, Arabian, Persian,* and *Gelalean* epocha's, as also of those of *Cataia* and *Turkistan*. He expresseth the numbers at large, as I have done, then in figures, such as we call *Arabian*, because we first learned these from them; but the *Arabians* themselves fetch them higher, acknowledging, that they received this useful invention from the *Indians*; and therefore from their authors they name them *Indian* figures: lastly, he renders them again in particular tables. Which manner I judge worthy the imitation, in all such numbers as are radical, and of more than ordinary use. For if they be only twice expressed, if any difference shall happen by the neglect of scribes or printers, it may often so fall out, that we shall not know which to make choice of: whereas if they be thrice expressed, it will be a rare chance but that two of them will agree; which two we may generally presume to be the truth.

(*b*) Jam vero ante annos prope mille, vates ille Homerus non cessavit minora corpora mortalium quam prisca conqueri. Plin.   *Nam genus hoc vivo jam decrescebat Homero.*
Terra malos homines nunc educat atque pusillos.
                                          Juvenal. sat. 15.

withstanding

withstanding (c) St. *Augustine* and others are of a different opinion. *Quis jam ævo isto non minor suis parentibus nascitur?* is the complaint of *Solinus* above 1500 years since. And yet in those *cryptæ sepulchrales* at *Rome* of the primitive Christians, resembling cities under ground, admired anciently by St. *Hierome*; and very faithfully of late described by *Bosius* in his *Roma subterranea* (I took so much pains for my own satisfaction to enter these wonderful grotto's, and to compare his descriptions) I find the bodies entombed, some of them being as ancient as *Solinus* himself, no way to exceed the proportions of our times.

It may justly be questioned how this monument of *Cheops* could be brought hither, seeing it is an impossibility, that by those narrow passages, before described, it should have entred. Wherefore we must imagine, that by some *machina* it was raised and conveyed up without, before this oratory or chamber was finished, and the roof closed. The position of it is thus; it stands exactly in the meridian, north and south, and is as it were equidistant from all sides of the chamber, except the east, from whence it is doubly remoter than from the west. Under it I found a little hollow space to have

(c) August. de Civ. Dei, l. 15. c. 9.

the first PYRAMID. 133

been dug away, and a large stone in the pavement removed, at the angle next adjoining to it; which *(d) Sandys* erroneously imagines to be a passage into some other compartment; dug away, no doubt, by the avarice of some, who might not improbably conjecture an hidden treasure to be reposited there. An expenseful prodigality, out of superstition used by the ancients, and with the same blind devotion taken up and continued to this day in the *East Indies*. And yet it seems by *Josephus*'s relation, that by the wisest king, in a time as clear and unclouded as any, it was put in practice, who thus describes the funeral of king *David*: *(e) His son* Solomon *buried him magnificently in* Hierusalem, *who, besides the usual solemnities at the funerals of kings, brought into his monument very great riches, the multitude of which we may easily collect by that which shall be spoken. For thirteen hundred years after,* Hyrcanus *the High Priest being besieged by* Antiochus, *surnamed* Pius, *the son of* Demetrius, *and being willing to give mony to raise the siege, and to lead away his army, not knowing where to procure it, he opened one of the vaults of the sepulchre*

(d) Sandys's Travels.
(e) Jos. lib. 7. Antiq. Jud. cap. 12. "Ἔθαψε δ' αὐτὸν ὁ παῖς Σολομὼν ἐν Ἱεροσολύμοις διαπρεπῶς, τοῖς τ' ἄλλοις οἷς δεῖ κηδεῖαν νομίζεσθαι βασιλικὴν ἅπασι, καὶ δὴ καὶ πλοῦτον αὐτῷ πολὺν καὶ ἄφθονον συνεκήδευσεν, &c.

of

of David, *and took thence three thousand talents, part whereof being given to* Antiochus, *he freed himself from the danger of the siege, as we have elsewhere declared. And again, after many years king* Herod *opening another vault, took out a great quantity of money; yet neither of them came to the coffins of the Kings; for they were with much art hid under ground, that they might not be found by such as entred into the sepulcher.*

The ingenious reader will excuse my curiosity, if before I conclude my description of this Pyramid, I pretermit not any thing within, of how light a consequence soever. This made me take notice of two inlets or spaces in the south and north sides of this chamber, just opposite to one another; that on the north was in breadth 700 of 1000 parts of the *English* foot, in depth 400 of 1000 parts, evenly cut, and running in a strait line six feet, and farther, into the thickness of the wall; that on the south is larger, and somewhat round, not so long as the former, and, by the blackness within it, seems to have been a receptacle for the burning of lamps. *T. Livius Burretinus* would gladly have believed, that it had been an hearth for one of those eternal lamps, such as have been found in *Tulliola's* tomb

in

in *Italy*, and, if *(f) Camden* be not misinformed, in *England*, in the *Cryptoporticus* of *Flavius Valerius Constantius*, father to *Constantine* the great, dedicated to the urns and ashes of the dead: but I imagine the invention not to be so ancient as this Pyramid. However, certainly a noble invention; and therefore pity it is, it should have been smother'd by the negligence of writers, as with a damp. How much better might *Pliny*, if he knew the composition of it, have described it, than he hath done the *linum asbestinum*, a sort of linen spun out of the veins, as some suppose, of the *Carystian* or *Cyprian* stone (which in my travels I have often seen:) though *(g) Salmasius*, with more probability, contends the true *asbestinum* to be the *linum vivum*, or *linum Indicum*; in the folds and wreaths of which they inclosed the dead body of the prince, (for saith *(h) Pliny, Regum inde funebres tunicæ*; and no wonder, seeing not long after he adds, *æquat pretia excellentium margaritarum)* committing it to the fire and flames, till it were consumed to ashes; while in the same flames this shrowd of linen, as if it had only been bathed and washed (to allude to his expression) by the fire, became more

---

(f) Camd. Brit. ubi agit de Brigantibus.
(g) Salmasii exercit. Plinian.
(h) Plin. lib. 19. cap. 1.

white and refined. Surely a rare and commendable piece of skill, which (*i*) *Pancirollus* juftly reckons amongft the *deperdita*; but infinitely inferiour, either in refpect of art or ufe, unto the former.

And thus have I finifhed my defcription of all the inner parts of this Pyramid; in which I could neither borrow light to conduct me from the ancients, nor receive any manuduction from the uncertain informations of modern travellers in thofe dark and hidden paths. We are now come abroad into the light and fun, where I found my Janizary, and an *Englifh* Captain, a little impatient to have waited above (*k*) three hours without, in expectation of my return, who imagined what they underftood not, to be an impertinent and vain curiofity.

(*i*) Pancirol tit. 4. Rerum deperditarum.
(*k*) That I and my company fhould have continued fo many hours in the Pyramid, and live (whereas we found no inconvenience) was much wonder'd at by Doctor *Harvey*, his Majefty's learned Phyfician. For, faid he, feeing we never breathe the fame air twice, but ftill new air is required to a new refpiration (the *fuccus alibilis* of it being fpent in every expiration) it could not be, but by long breathing we fhould have fpent the aliment of that fmall ftock of air within, and have been ftifled; unlefs there were fome fecret tunnels conveying it to the top of the Pyramid, whereby it might pafs out, and make way for frefh air to come in at the entrance below. To which I return'd him this anfwer: That it might be doubted, whether the fame numerical air could not be breathed more than once; and whether the *fuccus* and aliment of it could be fpent in one fingle refpiration; feeing thofe *urinatores*, or divers under water for fpunges in the *Mediterranean*

The inside.

a b the *entrance into* the **Pyramid**
the midst b *cent into the first* **Gallery**
to the South-first **Gallery**. d r *the* **Well**
with the Sev passage to the arched **Chamber**
arched **Chamber**. f k *the second* **Gallery**
l *the first* **Anticloset**
o *the second* **Anticloset**
p *the* **Chamber** *in which the Tomb stands*

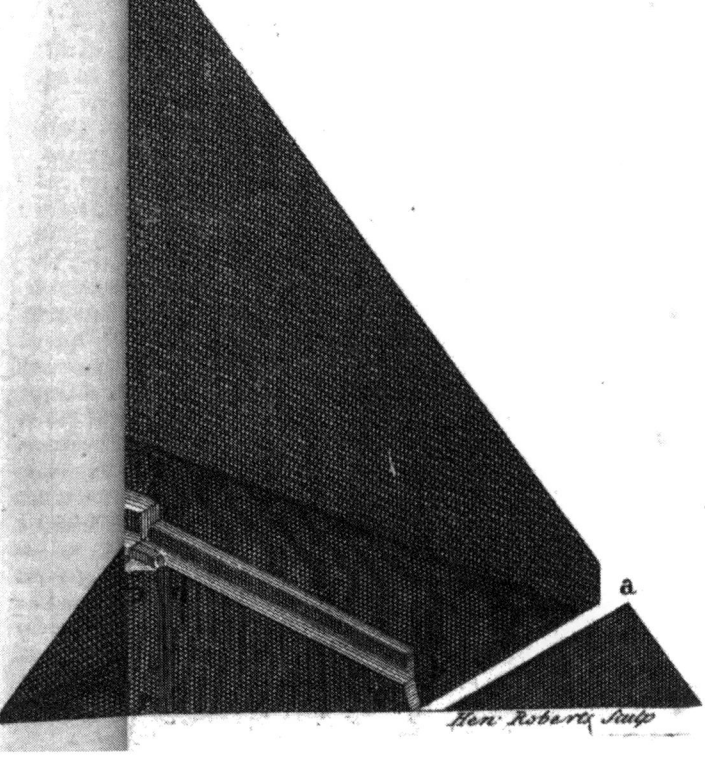

Hen. Roberts Sculp.

the first PYRAMID.

diterranean sea, and those for pearls in the *Sinus Arabicus* and *Persicus*, continuing above half an hour under water, must needs often breathe in and out the same air. He gave me an ingenious answer, that they did it by the help of spunges filled with oil, which still corrected and fed this air; the which oil being once evaporated, they were able to continue no longer, but must ascend up, or die: an experiment most certain and true. Wherefore I gave him this second answer, that the fuliginous air we breathed out in the Pyramid, might pass thorough those galleries we came up, and so thorough the streight neck or entrance leading into the Pyramid; and by the same, fresh air might enter in, and come up to us: which I illustrated with this similitude; as at the streights of *Gibraltar*, the sea is reported by some to enter on *Europe* side, and to pass out on *Africa* side; so in this strait passage, being not much above three feet broad, on the one side air might pass out, and at the other side fresh air might enter in. And this might no more mix with the former air, than the *Rhodanus*, as *Pomponius Mela* and some others report, passing through the *Lacus Lemanus*, or lake of *Geneva*, doth mix and incorporate with the water of the lake. For as for any *tubuli* to let out the fuliginous air at the top of the Pyramid, none could be discovered within or without. He replied, they might be so small, as that they could not easily be discerned, and yet might be sufficient to make way for the air, being a thin and subtil body. To which I answer'd, that the less they were, the sooner they would be obstructed with those tempests of sands, to which these deserts are frequently exposed: and therefore the narrow entrance into the Pyramid is often so choaked up with drifts of sand (which I may term the rain of the deserts) that there is no entrance into it. Wherefore we hire *Moors* to remove them, and open the passage, before we can enter into the Pyramid: with which he rested satisfied. But I could not so easily be satisfied with that received opinion, that at the streights of *Gibraltar* the sea enters in at the one side, and at the same time passes out at the other. For besides that in twice passing those streights I could observe no such thing, but only an in-let, without any out-let of the sea; I inquired of a captain of a ship, being captain of one of the six that I was then in company with, and an understanding man, who had often passed that way with the Pirates of *Algier*, whether ever he observed any outlet of the sea on *Africa* side; he answered, no. Being asked why then the Pirates went out into the *Atlantick* sea on *Africa* side, if it were not, as the opinion is, to make use of the current; he answer'd, it was rather to secure themselves from the Christians, who had near the mouth of the streights the port of *Gibraltar*, on the other side, to harbour in. Wherefore, when I consider with my self the great draught of waters that enter at this streight, and the swift current of waters which pass out of the *Pontus Euxinus* by the *Bosphorus Thracius* into the *Mediterranean* sea (both which I have seen) besides the many rivers that fall into it, and have no visible passage out; I cannot conceive but that the *Mediterranean* sea, or *Urinal* (as the *Arabians* call it from its figure) must long since have been filled up, and swelling higher, have drowned the plains of *Ægypt*, which it hath never done. Wherefore I imagine it to be no absurdity in Philosophy, to say that the earth is tubulous, and that there is a large passage under ground from one sea to another. Which being granted, we may easily thence apprehend the reason why the *Mediterranean* sea rises no higher, notwithstanding the fall into it of so many waters; and also know the reason why the *Caspian* sea, though it hath not in appearance any commerce with other seas, continues salt (for so it is, whatsoever *Polycletus* in *Strabo* says to the contrary) and swells not over its banks, notwithstanding the fall of the great river *Volga* and of others into it. That which gave me occasion of entring into the speculation was this; that in the longitude of eleven degrees, and latitude of forty one degrees, having borrowed the tackling of six ships, and in a calm day sounded with a plummet of almost twenty pounds weight, carefully steering the boat, and keeping the plummet in a just perpendicular, at a thousand forty five *English* fathoms, that is, at above an *English* mile and a quarter in depth, I could find no land or bottom.

A Description of the Second Pyramid.

FROM the first Pyramid we went to the second, being scarce distant the flight of an arrow. By the way I observed, on the west side of the first, the ruins of a pile of building all of square and polished stone, such as *(a) Pliny* calls *basaltes*, and describes to be *ferrei coloris & duritiæ*, of an iron colour and hardness. Formerly it may be some habitation of the Priests, or some monument of the dead. To the right hand of this, tending to the south, stands this second Pyramid, of which besides the miracle the ancient and modern writers have delivered little. *(b) Herodotus* relates, that *Cephren*, in imitation of his brother *Cheops*, built this; but that he fell short in respect of the magnitude; *for* (saith he) *we have measured them*. It were to be wished for fuller satisfaction of the reader, he had expressed the quantity, and also the manner how he took his measure. He adds; *It hath no subterraneous structures, neither is the* Nilus *by a channel derived into it, as in the*

(a) Plin. l. 36. cap. 7.
(b) Herodot. lib. 2.

former. *(c) Diodorus* somewhat more particularly describes it thus; that *for the architecture it is like unto the former, but much inferiour to it in respect of magnitude: Each side of the basis contains a stadium in length:* The same measure by *(d) Strabo* is assigned to the altitude; *Each of these* (discoursing of the first and second Pyramids) *is a furlong in height.* That is, to comment on their words, of *Grecian* feet six hundred, of *Roman* six hundred twenty five. So that by this computation, each side should want an hundred *Grecian* feet of the former Pyramid. *(e) Pliny* makes the difference to be greater, for assigning eight hundred eighty three feet to the former, he allows to the side of the basis of this but seven hundred thirty seven. By my observation the stones are of colour white, nothing so great and vast as those of the first and fairest Pyramid; the sides rise not with degrees like that, but are all of them plain

---

(c) Diodor. Sic. lib. 1. Τῇ μὲν κατὰ τὴν τέχνην χαςργίᾳ παραπλησίαν τῇ προειρημένῃ, τῷ δὲ μεγέθει πολὺ λειπομένην, ὡς ἂν τ̔ ἐν τῇ βάσει πλευρᾶς ἑκάστης ἴσης ςαδιαίας.

(d) Εἰσὶ γὰ ςαδιαῖαι τὸ ὕψ<tt>Ο</tt>. Lib. 17.

(e) Plin. l. 36. cap. 12. Alterius intervalla singula per quatuor angulos pares DCCXXXVII [pedes] comprehendunt.

p. 242.

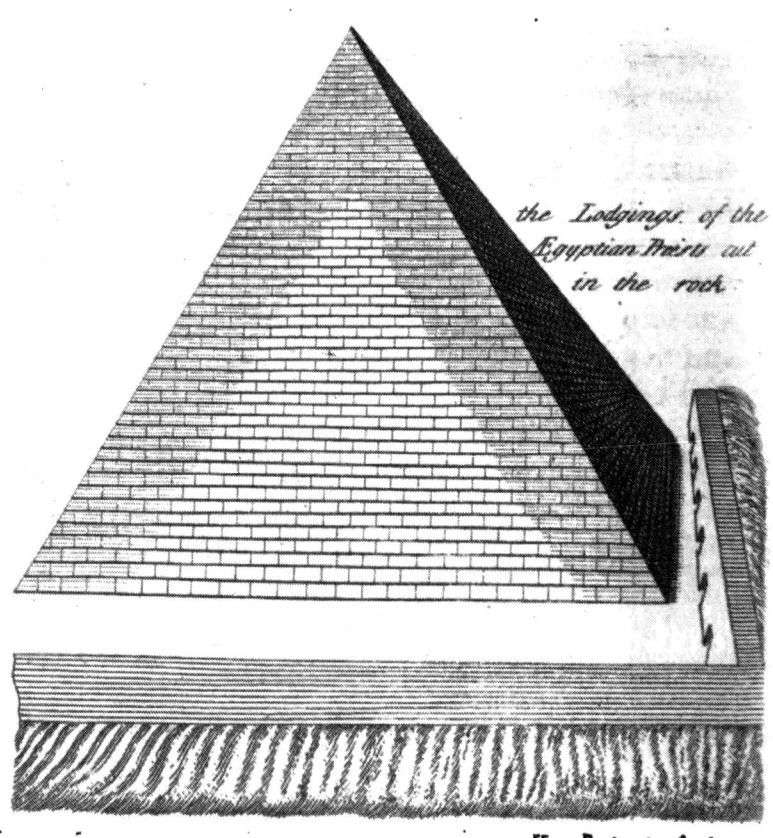

The second Pyramid

the Lodgings of the
Egyptian Priests cut
in the rock.

Hen: Roberts Sculp.

the second PYRAMID. 141

and smooth, the whole fabrick (except where it is opposed to the south) seeming very entire, free from any deformed ruptures or breaches. The height of it, taken by as deliberate a conjecture as I could make (which it was easy to do, by reason of the nearness of this and the former, being both upon the same plain) is not inferiour to it; and therefore *Strabo* hath rightly judged them to be equal. The sides also of the basis of both are alike, as, besides the authority of *(e) Strabo*, the *Venetian* Doctor assured me, who measured it with a line. There is no entry leading into it, and therefore what may be within, whether such spaces and compartiments as I observed in the former, or whether different, or none, I must leave to the conjecture of travellers, and to the discovery of after-times.

This Pyramid is bounded on the north and west sides with two very stately and elaborate pieces; which I do not so much admire, as that by all writers they have been pretermitted. About thirty feet in depth, and more than a thousand and four hundred in length, out of the hard rock these buildings have been cut in a perpendicular, and squared by the chizel, as I suppose, for lodgings of the Priests. They run along at

(e) Strabo lib. 17.

a convenient distance, parallel to the two sides we mentioned of this Pyramid, meeting in a right angle, and making a very fair and graceful prospect. The entrance into them is by square openings, hewn out of the rock, much of the same bigness with those I described in the first Pyramid. Whether these were symbolical (as the Theology of the *Ægyptians* consisted much in mysterious figures) and the depressure and lowness of these were to teach the Priests humility, and the squareness and evenness of them an uniform and regular deportment in their actions, I leave to such as have written of their Hieroglyphicks to determine. The hollow space within, of them all, is somewhat like to a square and well-proportion'd chamber, covered and arched above with the natural rock; in most of which (as I remember) there was a passage opening into some other compartiment, which the rubbish and darkness hinder'd me from viewing. On the north side without, I observed a line, and only one, engraven with sacred and *Ægyptian* characters, such as are mentioned by *(f) Herodotus* and *(g) Diodorus* to have been used by the Priests, and were

(f) Herodot. lib. 2.

(g) Παιδεύουσι ἢ τοὺς υἱὸς οἱ μὲν ἱερᾶς γεάμματα διτ]ὰ τάτε ἱερὰ καλέμενα, ἢ κοινότερα ἔχοντα τὴν μάθησιν. Diod. lib. 1.

different

the second PYRAMID. 143

different from the vulgar characters in civil affairs, in which former kind *(b) Justin Martyr* makes *Moses* to have been skilful; as the Scripture makes him to have been, *(i) learned in all the wisdom of the Ægyptians.* These ran not downwards, as the *Chinese* in our times write, but were continued in a strait line, as we use to write; and are to be read (if any understand those mysterious sculptures) by proceeding from the right hand to the left, and as it were imitating the motion and course of the Planets. For so *(k) Herodotus* expresly informs us, that *the* Grecians *write and cast account, going from the left hand to the right, the* Ægyptians *from the right hand to the left.* And this is that which in an obscure expression is also intimated by *(l) Pomponius Mela,* [*Ægyptii*] *suis literis perversè utuntur.* A manner practised by the *Hebrews, Chaldeans,* and *Syrians* to this day; and not unlikely to have been borrowed by them from the *Ægyptians*; to whom the *Chaldæans* also owed

---

(*b*) Ὃν ὁ προφήτης εἰ καὶ τὴν ἄθνησιν ἔχεν, ἀλλ᾽ ἐκ ἔτι καὶ τὴν χρῆσιν, &c. Just. Martyr. Quæst. & Responf. ad Orthodoxos.

(*i*) Act. 7. 22.

(*k*) Γράμματα γράφουσι καὶ λογίζονται ψήφοισι, Ἕλληνες μὲν ἀπὸ τῶν ἀριστερῶν ἐπὶ τὰ δεξιὰ φέροντες τὴν χεῖρα. Αἰγύπτιοι δὲ, ἀπὸ τῶν δεξιῶν ἐπὶ τὰ ἀριστερά. Herodot. lib. 2.

(*l*) Pompon. Mel. lib. 1. c. 9.

their

their firſt skill in Aſtrology, as the *Grecians* did their knowledge in Geometry; the former being atteſted by (*m*) *Diodorus*, and the latter confeſſed by (*n*) *Proclus* and other *Grecians*. And ſurely in imitation of theſe, or of the *Jews*, the *Arabians*, neighbouring upon both, have taken up this manner of writing, and continued it to our times, communicating it alſo by their conqueſts to the *Perſians* and *Turks*.

(*m*) Diodor. Sic. l. 1.
(*n*) Secund. lib. Comment. Procli in prim. lib. Eucl.

A Description of the Third Pyramid.

THE third Pyramid stands distant from the second about a furlong, upon an advantageous height, and rising of the rock, whereby afar off it seems equal to the former; though the whole pile is much less and lower. The time was so much spent with my other observations, that I could not take so exact a view as I desired, and the work deserved; yet I took so much of both, as to be able to confute the errors of others. But before I perform this, I shall relate what the ancients, and one or two of our best writers, which have travelled thither, have delivered concerning this. (a) Herodotus discoursing of it, tells us, that [Mycerinus] *left a Pyramid much less than that of his father, wanting of all sides (for it is quadrangular) twenty feet: it is three hundred feet on every side, being to the middle of it built with*

(a) Herodot. lib. 2. Πυραμίδα ἢ κ̀ ἔτ۞ ἀπελίπετο πολλὸν ἐλάσσω τῆ πατρὸς, εἴκοσι ποδῶν καταδέουσαν, κῶλον ἕκαστον τειῶν πλέθρων, ἐούσης τετραγώνε· λίθε ἢ ἐς τὸ ἥμισυ Αἰθιοπικῦ.

Æthio-

Æthiopick *marble*. *(b) Diodorus Siculus* is somewhat larger and clearer. *Every side of the basis* [Mycerinus] *caused to be made three hundred feet in length; he raised the walls fifteen stories with black stone, like* Thebaick *marble; the rest of it he finished with such materials as the other Pyramids are built. This work, although it is exceeded by the rest in magnitude, yet for the structure, art, and magnificence of the marble, it very far excells them. In the side towards the north,* Mycerinus, *the name of the founder, is engraven.* To *Diodorus* I shall adjoin the testimony of (*e*) *Strabo: Farther, upon a higher rise of the hill, is the third* [Pyramid,] *much less than the two former, but built with a greater expense. For almost from the foundation of it to the middle it consists of black stone, with which they make mortars, brought from the remotest mountains of* Æthiopia; *which being hard, and not easy to be wrought, hath made the work the more costly.* Pliny also, not as a spectator and eye-witness, as the former, but as an historian writes thus: *(d) The third* [Pyramid] *is less than the former we mentioned, but much more beautiful: it is*

(*b*) Diod. Sic. lib. 1.
(*c*) Strabo l. 17. Geogr.
(*d*) Plin. l. 36. c. 12. Tertia minor prædictis, sed multo spectatior, Æthiopicis lapidicibus assurgit cccLxIII pedibus inter angulos.

erected

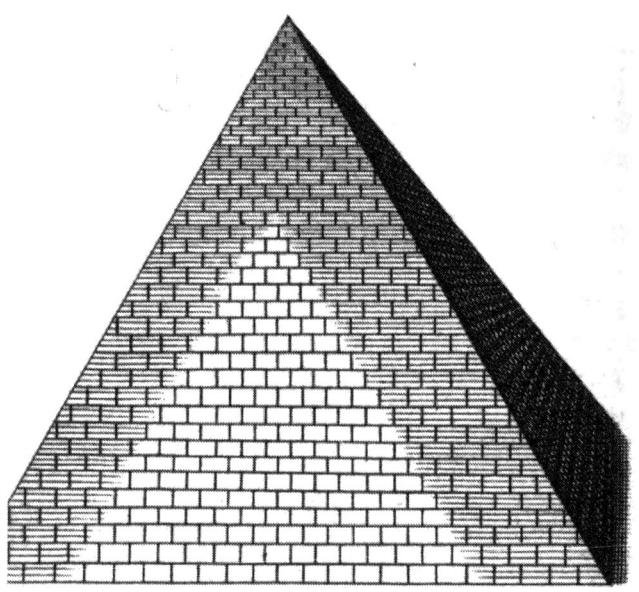

erected with Æthiopick *marble, and is three hundred sixty three feet between the angles.* And this is all that hath been preserved of the ancients concerning this Pyramid. Amongst modern writers none deserves to be placed before *Bellonius,* or rather before *P. Gillius.* For (*e*) *Thuanus* makes the other to have been a *plagiarius,* and to have published in his own name the observations of *P. Gillius,* a man very curious and inquisitive after truth, as appears by his Topography of *Constantinople,* and his *Bosphorus Thracius,* to whom *Bellonius* served as an amanuensis. (*f*) *The third Pyramid is much less than the former two, but is a third part greater than that which is at* Rome, *near the* mons Testaceus, *as you pass to St.* Paul's *in the* Ostian *way. It is still perfect, and no more corrupted, than if it had been newly built. For it is made of a kind of marble, called* basaltes, *or* Æthiopick *marble, harder than iron itself.*

It will be in vain to repeat the traditions and descriptions of several others, all which

---

(*e*) Thuan. hist. l. 16.
(*f*) Bellon. observ. l. 2. c. 24. Tertia Pyramis duabus superioribus longè minor. Tertia est autem parte major eâ, quæ apud Testaceum montem est Romæ, quâ ad D. Pauli eundum est itinere Ostiensi. Adhuc integra est, neo magis rimis corrupta, quàm si jam recens exstructa esset. Marmoris enim genere constat, quod *basaltes* nuncupatur; vel lapis Æthiopicus, ipso ferro duriore.

by

by a kind of confederacy agree in the same tale for the substance, only differing in some circumstances; so that I shrewdly suspect, that *Diodorus* hath borrowed most of his relation from *Herodotus*, and *Strabo* and *Pliny* from *Diodorus*, or from them both, and the more learned moderns from them all. For else how can it be imagined, they should so constantly agree in that, which if my eyes and (g) memory extreamly fail me not, is most evidently false? And therefore I have a strong jealousy, that they never came near this Pyramid; but that they did, as I have observed all travellers in my time in *Ægypt* to do, fill themselves so full, and as it were so surfeit with the sight of the greater and fairer Pyramid, that they had no appetite to be spectators of the rest, where they should only see the same miracle (for the Pyramids are all of the same figure) the farther they went, decreasing, and presented as it were in a less form; or, if they did view this, it was *quasi per transennam*, very perfunctorily and slightly, and that through a false and coloured glass; for they have mistaken both in the quality of the stone and colour of the Pyramid. I

(g) I have since conferred with an *English* captain, who having been four times at *Alexandria*, and as often at the Pyramids, assures me that I am not mistaken.

the third PYRAMID.

begin with (*h*) *Herodotus*, who by a notable piece of forgetfulness, if it be not a σφάλμα in the copies, makes the dimensions of each of the sides in the basis of this, to be three hundred feet, and yet to want but twenty of the first Pyramid, to which he assigned before eight hundred feet: an impossibility in arithmetick. And therefore it will be no presumption to correct the place, and instead of ἴκοσι ποδῶν καταδέουσαν, to write πεντηκοσίων ποδῶν καταδέουσαν. I know not how to palliate or excuse his other errour, where he makes this Pyramid to be built, as far as to the middle of it, with *Æthiopick* marble. If this sort of marble be *ferrei coloris*, as it is described by (*i*) *Pliny*, and granted by (*k*) *Diodorus* and (*l*) *Strabo*, both of them expressing the colour to be black, and the latter bringing it from the remotest mountains of *Æthiopia*, where the marble hath the same tincture and colour with the inhabitants, then can this relation of *Herodotus* no way be admitted. For the whole Pyramid seems to be of clear and white stone, somewhat choicer and brighter than that in either of the two other Pyramids.

(*h*) Herod. lib. 1.
(*i*) Plin. lib. 36. cap. 7.
(*k*) Diodor. lib. 1.
(*l*) Strab. lib. 17. Geog.

And therefore I wonder that *Diodorus*, *Strabo*, and *Pliny*, and, amongst later authors, *Bellonius*, *Gillius*, and several others, should have all followed *Herodotus*; when with a little pains and circumspection they might have reformed his and their own errour. It may perhaps be alledged in their defence, that they mean the buildings within are erected with black and *Æthiopick* marble: and yet if this be granted, since there is no entrance leading into this, no more than is into the second Pyramid, what may be within depends upon the uncertainty of tradition or conjecture, both which are very fallible. Though it cannot be denied, but that close by, on the east side of it, there are the ruins of a pile of building, with a sad and dusky colour, much like that we described in passing to the second Pyramid, which might be the ground and occasion of this errour. I cannot excuse the ancients; but *Bellonius* or *Gillius* (for it is no matter which of them owns the relation, when both of them have erred) are far more inexcusable; because it might have been expected from them, what (*m*) *Livy* supposes, *Novi semper scriptores, aut in rebus certius aliquid allaturos se, aut scribendi arte rudem vetustatem superaturos credunt.* Whereas

(*m*) Tit. Liv. lib. 1.

these

these, on the contrary, have depraved what hath been, in this particular, with truth delivered by the ancients. For whereas *Herodotus* and *Diodorus* equal the side of the basis to 300 feet, and *Pliny* extends it to 363, they make it only a third part greater than the Pyramid at *Rome* of *C. Cæstius*, near the *mons testaceus*. So that either they have much enlarged that at *Rome*, or shrunk and contracted this. For the Pyramid at *Rome*, exactly measured on that side which stands within the city, is completely seventy eight feet *English* in breadth; to which if we add a third part of it, the result will be an hundred and four: which should be equal to this *Ægyptian* Pyramid, in the notion and acception of *Bellonius*. An unpardonable oversight, no less than two hundred feet, in a very little more than three hundred. For so much, besides the authority of *Herodotus* and *Diodorus* before cited, I take the side of this Pyramid to be, and the altitude to have much the same proportion.

I would gladly have seen in this the name of *Mycerinus*, the founder of it, engraven, as (n) *Diodorus* mentions; or that other inscription in the first, whereof *Herodotus* procured the interpretation; but both have been defaced by time. His words

(n) Diodor. lib. i.

are these: (*o*) *In the Pyramid there are Ægyptian characters inscribed, which shew how much was expended upon the workmen, in radishes, onions, and garlick, which an interpreter (as I well remember) said, was the sum of a thousand and six hundred talents of silver; which if it be so, how much is it credible was spent in iron, and in meat, and in clothes for the labourers?* Hereby I might have known what to determine of the ancient *Ægyptian* letters: I mean not the sacred ones (for those were all symbolical, expressing the abstractest notions of the mind, by visible similitudes of (*p*) birds and beasts, or by representations of some other familiar objects) but those used in civil affairs. By such sculptures, which I have seen in gems found at *Alexandria*, and amongst the *Mummies*, I can no way subscribe to the assertion of *Kircherus*, though an able man, who in his *Prodromus Coptus* contends, that the

---

(*o*) Herodot. lib. 2. Ἐσήμαν]αι ᾗ διὰ γραμμάτων Αἰγυπτίων ἐν τῇ πυραμίδι ὅσα ἔς τε συρμαίω ᾗ κρόμμυα, ᾗ σκόροδα ἀναισίμωθη τοῖσι ἐργαζομένοισι. Καὶ ὡς ἐμὲ εὖ μεμνῆσθαι τὰ ὁ ἑρμηνεύς μοι ἐπιλεγόμενος τὰ γράμματα ἔφη, ἑξακόσια ᾗ χίλια τάλαντα ἀργυρίου τετελέσθαι, &c.

(*p*) Phœnices primi, famæ si creditur, ausi,
Mansuram rudibus vocem signare figuris.
Nondum flumineas Memphis contexere biblos
Noverat, & saxis tantùm volucresque feræque,
Sculptaque servabant magicas animalia linguas.
                                        Lucan. l. 3.

present

present *Ægyptian* or *Coptite* character (which certainly is nothing but a corruption and distortion of the *Greek*) is the same with that of the ancient *Ægyptians*. But surely the *Ægyptian* character is of a much higher descent; and, if we believe (*q*) *Tacitus*, whose opinion is very probable, they were the first inventors of Letters; though some ascribe the honour of this invention to the *Phœnicians*.

(*q*) Primi per figuras animalium Ægypti sensus mentis effingebant, & antiquissima monimenta memoriæ humanæ impressa saxis cernuntur, & literarum semet inventores perhibent. Inde Phœnicas, quia mari præpollebant, intulisse Græciæ, gloriamque adeptos, tanquam repererint, quæ acceperant. Tac lib. 11. Annalium.

Of the rest of the Pyramids in the Libyan Desert.

I HAVE done with these three Pyramids, each of them being very remarkable, and the two first reckoned amongst the miracles of the world. The rest in the *Libyan* desert, lying scatter'd here and there, are (excepting one of them) but lesser copies, and as it were models of these; and therefore I shall neither much trouble my self nor the reader with the description of them. Though to speak the truth, did not the three first standing so near together obscure the lustre of the rest, which lie far scattered, some of them were very considerable. And therefore I cannot but tax the omission of the ancients, and the inadvertency of all modern writers and travellers, who with too much supineness have neglected the description of one of them, which, in my judgment is as worthy of memory, and as near a miracle as any of those three which I have mentioned. And this stands from these south and by west at twenty miles distance, more within the sandy desert, up-

on

on a rocky level like these, and not far from the village whence we enter the *Mummies*. This, as the *Venetian* Doctor assured me, and as I could judge by conjecture at a distance, hath the same dimensions as the first and fairest of these; hath graduations or ascents without, and of the same colour like that, but more decayed, especially at the top, and an entrance into it on the north side, which is barred up within; and therefore whatsoever is spoken of the first in respect of the exteriour figure, is appliable to this. (*a*) *Bellonius* extremely exceeds in his computation of the number of them, who thus writes: *Above an hundred others are seen dispersed up and down in that plain.* I could not discover twenty. And long since, *Ibn Almataug*, in his book of the miracles of *Ægypt*, reckons them to be but eighteen: *There are in the west side no more famous buildings than the Pyramids; the number of them is eighteen; of these, there are three in that part which is opposite to* Fostat, *or* (*b*) Cairo.

(*a*) Plusquàm centum per eam planitiem hinc indè sparsæ conspiciantur. Bellon. l. 2. c. 44.
(*b*) That *Fostat, Metzr,* and *Cahira* (or, as we usually term it, *Cairo*) are three distinct names as it were of one and the same city, appears by the *Geographia Nubienfis*, and *Abulfeda* in *Arabick*: though *Abulfeda* more particularly describes *Alkahira* to be on the north side of *Fostat*, and *Fostat* to be seated upon the river *Nilus*.

In what Manner the PYRAMIDS were built.

E had ended our discourse of the Pyramids, but that I find one scruple toucht upon by *Herodotus*, *Diodorus*, and *Pliny*, which is worth the discussion, as a point of some concernment in architecture: and that is, In what manner these Pyramids were built, and with what art and contrivance the stones, especially those vast ones in the first, were conveyed up. (*a*) *Herodotus*, who first raised the doubt, gives this solution: *They carried up the rest of the stones with little engines made of wood, raising them from the ground upon the first row: when the stone was lodged upon this row, it was put into another engine, standing upon the first step, from thence it was conveyed to the second row by another. For so many rows and orders of steps as there were, so many engines were there: or else they removed the engine, which was one, and easy to be carried to every particular row, as often as they moved a stone.*

(*a*) Ἥιρεν τοὺ ἐπὶ λοιπὲς λίθες μηχανῆσι ξύλων βραχέων πεποιημένοισι, &c. Herod. l. 2.

We will relate that which is spoken of either part. Therefore those in the Pyramid were first made which were the highest, then by degrees the rest, last of all those which are nearest to the ground, and are the lowest. The first part of this solution of *Herodotus* is full of difficulty. How, in erecting and placing of so many *machinæ*, charged with such massy stones, and those continually passing over the lower degrees, could it be avoided, but that they must either unsettle them, or endanger the breaking of some portions of them? which mutilations would have been like scars in the face of so magnificent a building. His second answer is the sounder; but I conceive the text to be imperfect. (b) *Diodorus* hath another fancy: *The stones* (saith he) *at a great distance off were prepared in* Arabia: *and they report, that by the help of* aggeres (*engines not being then invented*) *the work was erected. And that which begets the greatest admiration is, that so vast a structure was perfected in that place, which is all about replenished with sand,*

where

(b) Λέγεται δὲ τ̀ μὲν λίθον ἐκ τ̀ Ἀραβίας ἀπὸ πολλῦ διαςήματ۞ κομιδῆναι, τ̀ ϳ κατασκευὴν διὰ χωμάτων γιϳθαι, μήπω ὠβ μηχανῶν εὑρημἑνων κατ᾽ ἐκείνους τοῦ χρόνους. Καὶ τὸ θαυμασιώτατον, τι τὸ τηλικοῦτον ἔργον κατασκευασμὲνον ὴ τῶ ἀπέχον۞ τόπω παντός ἀμμώδους ὄν۞, ὐδὲν ἴχνυ۞ ὗτε τῦ χώματ۞, ὗτε τ̀ τῶ λίθων ξεςυργίας ὴ λαξευςεως ὑπολείπεϳαι, ὡςε δοκεῖν μὴ

where there appears not any reliques either of the aggeres, *or of the hewing and polishing of the stones. So that it seems not piece-meal by the industry of men, but altogether and at once, the whole pile, as it were by some God, was erected in the midst of the sands. Some of the* Ægyptians *relate wonders of it, and endeavour to obtrude I know not what fables; namely, that these* aggeres, *consisting of salt and nitre, were dissolved by letting in the river, which wholly consumed them without the labour of hands, leaving this structure* (intire.) *But the truth of the business is not so, but that those multitudes of men, which were imployed in raising the* aggeres, *carried them away unto their former places. For as they report, three hundred and sixty thousand men were employ'd in these offices, and the whole work was scarce finished in the space of twenty years.* Pliny *partly agrees with him,*

μὴ κατ' ὀλίγον ὑπ' ἀνθρώπων ἐργασίας, ἀλλὰ συλ-
λήβδην κὶ ὁμοῦ, ὥσπερ ὑπὸ θεοῦ τινὸς τὸ κατασκεύασμα
τεθῆναι πᾶν εἰς τὴν περίχυσαν ἄμμον· ἐπιχειροῦσι δέ
τινες τῶν Αἰγυπτίων τερατολογεῖν κὶ μυθεύεσθαι, ὑπὲρ τούτων, λέγοντες, ὡς ἐξ ἁλῶν κὶ νίτρου τῶν χωμάτων
γεγονότων, ἐπαφεθεὶς ὁ ποταμὸς ἔτηξεν κὶ διέλυσεν
αὐτὰ, κὶ παντελῶς ἠφάνισεν ἄνευ τῆς χειροποιήτου πραγ-
ματείας· οὐ μὴν κὶ τἀληθὲς οὕτως ἔχει, διὰ δὲ τῆς πολυ-
χειρείας τῶν τὰ χώματα βαλόντων πάλιν τὸ πᾶν ἔργον
εἰς τὴν προϋπάρχουσαν ἀποκατεστάθη τάξιν· τριάκοντα
μὲν γὰρ κὶ ἓξ μυριάδες ἀνδρῶν, ὥς φασι, ταῖς τῶν ἔργων
λειτουργίαις προσήδρευσαν, τὸ δὲ πᾶν κατασκεύασμα τέ-
λος ἔσχε μόγις ἐτῶν εἴκοσι. Diod. Biblioth. Hist. l. 1.

and

PYRAMIDS *were built.* 159

and partly gives another anfwer : (*c*) *The queſtion is, by what means the cement was conveyed up to ſuch a height.* (He rather might have queſtioned, how thoſe vaſt ſtones were conveyed up.) *Some ſay, that banks of nitre and ſalt were made up, as the work roſe, which being finiſhed, they were waſhed away by the river* Nilus. *Others imagine, that bridges were made with brick; which the work being ended, were diſtributed into private houſes. For they conceive that the* Nilus, *being much lower, could not come to waſh them* (away.) If I may aſſume the liberty of a traveller, I imagine that they were erected, neither as *Herodotus* deſcribes, nor as *Diodorus* reports, nor as *Pliny* relates: but that firſt they made a large and ſpacious (*d*) tower in the midſt reaching to the top; to the ſides of this tower I conceive the reſt of the building to have been applied piece

---

(*c*) Quæſtionum ſumma eſt, quanam ratione in tantam altitudinem ſubvecta ſint cæmenta. Alii enim nitro ac ſale adaggeratis cum creſcente opere, ac peracto, fluminis irrigatione dilutis : alii lateribus è luto factis extructos pontes, peracto opere in privatas domos diſtributos. Nilum enim non putant rigare potuiſſe multò humiliorem. Plin. l. 36. c. 12.

(*d*) Admitting this ſuppoſition, we may eaſily apprehend, how thoſe huge ſtones might by engines be raiſed in a perpendicular, as the work roſe, with leſs difficulty and expenſe, than either in a ſlope or traverſe line, upon banks of nitre or bridges of brick, according to the traditions of *Diodorus* and *Pliny :* both which muſt have been of a ſtupendous and almoſt incredible height.

after

after piece, like so many buttresses or supporters, still lessening in height, till at last they came to the lowermost degree. A difficult piece of building, taken in the best and easiest projection: and therefore it is no wonder if it were not often imitated by the ancients, and no where expressed or commended by the great master of Architecture, *Vitruvius*. Yet surely if we judge of things by the events, and if we reflect upon the intention of monuments, which are raised by the living to perpetuate the memory of the dead, then is this as commendable a way as any. And therefore we see at *Rome*, that though by the revolution of so many ages the (e) *Mausoleum of Augustus* be almost decayed, and the (f) *Septizonium of Severus* be utterly lost, both intended for lasting and stately sepulchres; yet the *Pyramid of C. Cestius* stands fair and almost intire: which is no more to be compared, either for the vastness of the stones, or the whole bulk and fabrick of it with these, than are the limbs and body of a dwarf to the dimensions of a giant, or some large *colossus*.

I have done with the *Work*, but the *Artizans* deserve not to be pretermitted: concerning whom the observation of *Diodorus* is as true, as it is boldly delivered by him:

(e) Sueton. in Augusto.   (f) Spartianus in Severo.

(g) It

PYRAMIDS *were built.*

(g) *It is confessed that these works (speaking of the Pyramids) far excell the rest in Ægypt, not only in the massiness of the structures, and in the expenses, but also in the industry (and skill) of the artificers. The Ægyptians think, the architects are more to be admired than the kings who were at the expense. For they by their abilities and study, these by their wealth received by inheritance, and by the labours of others, erected them.*

The CONCLUSION.

AND thus much of the *Sciography*, or of the artificial and architectonical part. I shall shut up all with one observation in nature, for the recreation of the reader, recited by *Strabo* in these words: (*h*) *We ought not to omit one of the strange*

(g) Diod. Sic. l. 1. Ὁμολογεῖται ὃ ταῦτα τὰ ἔργα πολύ ἐρέχειν τῶν κατ' Αἰγυπτον ὐ μόνον τῷ βάρει τῶν κατασκευασμάτων κ̀ τ̀ δαπάναις, ἀλλὰ κ̀ τῇ πολυτεχνίᾳ τῶν ἐργασαμένων· κ̀ φασί δεῖν θαυμάζειν μᾶλλον τοὺς ἀρχιτέκτονας τῶν ἔργων ἢ τὺς βασιλεῖς τοὺς ὁρμωμένους τὰς εἰς ταῦτα χορηγίας· τοὺς μὲν γ̀ τ̀ ἰδίαις ψυχαῖς κ̀ τ̀ φιλοτιμίαις, τοὺς δ̀ τ̀ κληρονομηθείσῃ πλούτῳ κ̀ τ̀ ἀλλοτρίαις κακίαις ἐπὶ τελ. ἀγαθὴν τ̀ ἐργαίρεσιν.

(*h*) Ἐν δέ τι τῶν ὀρθουμένων ὑφ' ἡμῶν ἐν τ̀ πυραμίσι παράδοξον ὐκ ἄξιον παραλιπεῖν. Ἐκ γ̀ τ̀ λατύπης σωροί τινες πρὸ τῶν πυραμίδων κεῖνται. ἐν τούτοις δ' ἐνίοτε αἱ ψήγματα κ̀ τύπῳ κ̀ μεγέθει φακοειδῆ. ἐνίοις δὲ, κ̀ ὡς ἂν πτίσμα οἷον ἡμιλεπίσων ὑπόρχει. φασὶ δ' ἀπολιθωθῆναι λείψανα τ̀ τῶν ἐργαζομένων τροφῆς. ἐκ ἀπίοικε δέ. Strab. lib. 17. Geog.

things

things seen by us at the Pyramids. Some heaps of stones, being fragments hewn off, lie before the Pyramids; amongst these are found little stones, some in the similitude and bigness of lentils, some as of grains of barley, which appear half unscaled: they report, these are some reliques of the provisions which were given to the workmen, and have been petrified: which seems probable enough.

These, if there were ever any such, are either consumed by time, or scattered by the winds, or buried with those tempests of sand, to which the deserts are perpetually exposed: but *Diodorus*, who not long preceded him, was not so curious, as to deliver this relation. And were not *Strabo* a writer of much gravity and judgment, I should suspect, that these petrified grains (though I know such petrefactions to be no impossibility in nature; for I have seen at *Venice* the bones and flesh of a man, and the whole head, except the teeth, intirely transmuted into stone; and at *Rome* clear conduit water, by long standing in aqueducts, hath been turned into perfect alabaster) are like those loaves of bread which are reported to be found by the *Red Sea*, converted into stone, and by the inhabitants supposed to be some of the bread the *Israelites* left behind them, when they passed
over

The Conclusion.　163

over for fear of *Pharaoh*. They are fold at *Grand Cairo* handſomly made up in the manner of the bread of theſe times, which is enough to diſcover the impoſture. For the ſcripture makes them to have been unleavened cakes: *(i) And they baked unleavened cakes of the dough, which they brought forth out of* Ægypt. Or elſe *Strabo*'s relation may be like the tradition of the riſing of dead mens bones every *(k)* year in *Ægypt*: a thing ſuperſtitiouſly believed by the Chriſtians; and by the Prieſts, either out of ignorance or policy, maintained as an argument of the reſurrection. The poſſibility and truth of it, *Metrophanes* the Patriarch of *Alexandria* thought (but very illogically) might be proved out of the Prophet *Eſay*: *(l) And they ſhall go forth, and look upon the carcaſſes of the men that have tranſgreſſed againſt me: for their worm ſhall not die, neither ſhall their fire be quenched; and they ſhall be an abhorring unto all fleſh.*

(i) Exod. 12. 39.

(k) Sandys in his travels writes, that *they are ſeen to riſe on Good-Friday.* A *Frenchman* at *Grand Cairo*, who had been preſent at the reſurrection, ſhewed me an arm which he brought from thence: the fleſh ſhrivel'd, and dried like that of the Mummies. He obſerved the miracle to have been always behind him: once caſually looking back, he diſcover'd ſome bones carried privately by an *Ægyptian* under his veſt; whereby he underſtood the myſtery.

(l) Eſay 66. 24.

But

But I have digressed too far. The confutation of these, and the description of the *Mummies*, or of the rest of the *Ægyptian* sepulchres (for from thence comes the matter of this their supposed resurrection) and that infinite mass and variety of hieroglyphicks, which I have either seen there, or bought or transcribed elsewhere, may be the (*m*) argument of another discourse.

(*m*) An argument intended by me, and for which I made a collection of several antiquities in my travels abroad; but these (and would only these!) have unfortunately perished at home amidst the sad distractions of the time.

The E N D.

A DISCOURSE
OF THE
ROMAN FOOT
AND
DENARIUS:

From whence, as from two Principles,

The MEASURES and WEIGHTS used by the Ancients may be deduced.

By *JOHN GREAVES*,
Professor of Astronomy in the University of
OXFORD.

Σπυδαςίον ὅπως δειθῶσι καλῶς αἱ ἀρχαί. μεγάλω
ῥδ ἰχύσι ῥοπὴν πρὸς ἐπίδραμα.

*Una Fides, Pondus, Mensura, Moneta sit una,
Et status illæsus totius Orbis erit.*
BUDELIUS *de Monetis.*

LONDON:
Printed for J. BRINDLEY, Bookbinder to her Majesty, and Bookseller to his Royal Highness the Prince of Wales, at the *King's Arms* in *New Bondstreet.* 1736.

TO

His truly Noble and learned Friend,

John Selden, Esq;

Burgess of the University of *Oxford* in the Hon. *House of Commons.*

SIR,

THAT I should present you, who have so honourably deserved of antiquity and of your country, and, if I may add mine own obligations, in particular of me, with so small a retribution as a *Roman Foot*, and *Denarius*, may seem

seem more proportionable to mine abilities, than to the eminency of your place and worth. But you who, to the honour of your profession, have joined the wisdom of the ancients, and justly have merited this elogy,

——Anglorum gloria gentis Seldenus,

an elogy long since given you by a man, who is deservedly esteemed πολλῶν ἀντάξιος ἄλλων, the learned *Hugo Grotius*; you are best able to judge of what importance these two are, in the discovery of the weights and measures used by the antients.

And first, for measures, the אמה or *cubit of the Sanctuary*, in the *Scriptures, Josephus,* and the *Rabbines:* the Αιγύπτιος and Βαβυλώνιος πῆχυς in *Herodotus* (the former equal to that of *Samos,* the latter misrendred

red

red by *Pliny* and *Solinus*, *Pes Babylonius*) : the παρασάγγης Περσικὸς in *Herodotus*, containing xxx. ςάδια, in *Strabo*, sometimes LX. sometimes XL. and sometimes xxx. (but in *Hesychius* ὁ παρασάγγης ἔχει μίλια τέτταρα, and in *Abulfeda* three miles; with whom, and with the *Persians* to this day it is called the (a) فرسخ *farsach :*) the σχοῖνος Αἰγύπτιος in *Herodotus*, *Artemidorus*, and *Strabo*: the πᾶς βασιλικὸς, καὶ Φιλεταίρειος in *Hero*: the *pes Ptolemaicus* and *Drusianus* in *Hyginus*: besides infinite others depending upon the proportions of some of these: I say these cannot, after the destruction of those ancient monarchies and republicks, any other way be restored, than from such monuments, as, by divine pro-

(a) دامــــا الفرسخ فهو عند القدما ىعند المحدثين ثلثة اميال

The *farsach*, with the ancients and moderns, contains three miles. Abulf. Geogr. MS.

vidence,

vidence, have escaped the hands of ruin, and continued to these latter ages. For were it not that the *pes Romanus*, or *Monetalis*, as *Hyginus* terms it, were still extant in *Rome*, on the monuments of *Cossutius*, and of *Tit. Statilius Vol. Aper* (for those two columns, the one with the inscription ΠΟΔ. Θ. mentioned by *Marlianus*, and *Philander*; the other with ΠΟΔ. ΙΒ. seen by the same *Philander*, are both lost) we might utterly despair of knowing the measures of the *Hebrews, Babylonians, Persians, Ægyptians, Grecians, Romans,* and of all others described in classical authors: who could not transmit to posterity the individual measures themselves, but only the proportions they respectively had to one another; which proportions being pure habitudes, cannot, as mathematicians observe, be reduced to the measures of these times,

[171]

times, unless either some of the ὑποκείμενα themselves were existent, or else exact copies taken from the originals were derived to us.

In like manner it is for weights, the מנה, the ככר, the שקל, or σίκλος of the *Hebrews*, or מלעא of the *Chaldeans*, which *Aruck* renders by four זוזים *zuzim*, that is, four *denarii* (from whence, the *Persian* σίγλος in *Xenophon* and *Hesychius* may have received its denomination:) the τάλαντον Βαβυλώνιον, containing seven thousand *Attick* drachms, the τάλαντον Αἰγιναῖον ten thousand, the τάλαντον Σύρον a thousand five hundred, the τάλαντον Ἀττικὸν six thousand, all mentioned by *Julius Pollux*; the *Talentum Ægyptium* in *Varro*, containing eighty *pondo*, or pounds; the *talentum Euboicum* in *Festus*, four thousand *denarii*: these, with infinite others, both *mensuræ* and *pondera*, whether considered as *Medica*,

dica, or *Georgica*, or *Veterinaria*, cannot in our times be restored, but only by such weights of the antients as are still extant; that is, either by the *denarius* of the *Romans*, or δραχμὴ of the *Grecians*, or by the *congius* of *Vespasian*, or by the *libræ* and *unciæ Romanæ*, and the like, that have been preserved by antiquaries.

Seeing therefore the *Denarius* is of as great moment for the discovery of weights, as the *Roman* Foot for the knowledge of measures, I have taken these two, as two irrefragable principles, from whence the rest used by the ancients may be deduced. And because the *Denarius* may be considered in a double respect, either as *nummus*, or as *pondus*; the first acception conducing to the valuation of coins, the second to the certainty of weights: it was therefore necessary

that

that both the weight and valuation of the *Denarius* should be exactly known. To which purpose, in *Italy* I examined with a balance (the scale of which the eightieth part of a grain would sensibly turn) many hundred fair *denarii*, both *Consulares* and *Cæsarei*, as also *quinarii*, or *victoriati* in silver; several *aurei* of the former, and later Emperors; besides the original standard of the *congius*, placed by *Vespasian* in the Capitol; and many *unciæ* and *libræ* in brass. From whence I collected the weight of the *denarius Consularis* and *Cæsareus*; that to be the seventh part of the *Roman* ounce, as *Celsus*, *Scribonius Largus*, and *Pliny* rightly describe; and this to be sometimes the eighth part, and sometimes the seventh, but most frequently in a middle proportion betwixt eight and seven, till *Seve-*

O *rus*

rus and *Gordianus*'s times: under whom, and the succeeding Emperors, it recovered the weight of the *denarius Consularis*, but lost much of its fineness by the mixture of allay.

With these *denarii*, for the greater certainty, I compared such *Grecian* coins (especially *Athenian*) as I had either seen in choice cabinets, or bought of mine own; and those were the χρυσοῖ, or ϛατῆρες absolutely taken, which, as *Julius Pollux*, and *Hesychius*, out of *Polemarchus* testifie, weighed two drachms; the τετράδραχμα, or τέτραχμα, or ϛατῆρες ἀργυρίȣ, four drachms; the δραχμαὶ, the τρίωβολα, or, as *Pollux* names them, the ἡμίδραχμα, with several others.

By which comparison I first discovered, that howsoever the *Romans* (as *Pliny* and *A. Gellius* expresly;

presly; *Valerius* and *Suetonius*, by way of consequence) equal the *denarius* to the *drachma*; and tho' the *Greeks* (as *Strabo, Cleopatra, Plutarch, Galen, Dio* and many more) equal the *drachma* to the *denarius*, speaking in a popular estimation, and as they vulgarly passed in way of commerce; yet if we shall put on the resolution of him in the comedy,

Oculatæ nostræ sunt manus, credunt quod vident:

we may evidently discern in the scale, the *drachma Attica* to be heavier than the *denarius*; and therefore all such writers of the ancients as equal them, if we speak strictly of weight, and not of estimation, have been deceived; and con-

consequently all modern writers, following their traditions in discourses *de ponderibus, & de re nummaria*, have erred.

But because it is not probable that the ancients, both *Greeks* and *Romans*, should be deceived in their own coins, and in their own times, it occasioned my observing the practise abroad of the κολλυβιςαὶ in exchanges, with whom the same specifical coins in different states pass with different estimations, to think of some means how I might reconcile the traditions of the *Greeks* and *Romans*, concerning the weight and valuation of the *drachma Attica* and *denarius*, notwithstanding the difference in the balance of such as are now found at *Athens* and at *Rome*.

And

And this drew from me that discourse which I have inserted at the end of this book, *Of some directions to be observed in comparing the valuations of coins:* which may serve, not only to reconcile the *Greek* and *Roman* writers, but especially the traditions of *Philo, Josephus, Epiphanius,* St. *Hierome,* and *Hesychius,* who make the *Hebrew* שקל *shekel* equal to the *Attick* tetradrachm; whereas in the scale, which is the best judge of this controversy, I find them manifestly unequal, the *Hebrew* or *Samaritan* shekel being much less than the *Attick* tetradrachm.

But it may be questioned, why after the labours of *Portius, Budæus, Alciatus, Agricola, Montanus, Mariana, Budælius, Alcasar, Villalpandus, Jo. Scaliger, Capellus, Snellius,* and of many other eminent

eminent men, who have writ either *dedita opera*, or ἐν παρέργῳ, *de ponderibus & menfuris*, I fhould undertake any thing of this nature. My anfwer is, that obferving in them fo great a variety, and contradiction of opinions, I was willing to ufe mine own judgment, how mean foever, in giving myfelf private fatisfaction; and tho' I intended this work as a πάρεργον to other employments; yet, having by the advantage of travelling in foreign parts, perufed in *Italy, Greece,* and *Ægypt,* more antiquities than I think any of them above named fingle, I thought it would not be unacceptable, if I did, as it is the manner of travellers, publifh at home fuch obfervations and difcoveries as I made abroad. The which I humbly dedicate to you, as out of a
desire

desire to express my gratitude for many noble favours; so out of an assurance, that if they receive your approbation, I need not to fear the censure of others.

Your most obliged friend,

and humble servant,

John Greaves.

OF THE Roman FOOT.

HAT the Foot was the most received, and usual measure amongst the *Romans*, as the Cubit amongst the *Jews*, is a thing not controverted by any. For *(a) Polybius* describing their *scutum*, makes it *in breadth over the bend two* [Roman] *feet and an half, and in length four feet: or, if it be of a greater sort, a palm more is to be added to this measure.* And not long after expressing the manner of their castrametation, or encamping, he *(b)* writes; that *as often as a place is designed for the camp,* the Prætorium (or General's lodging)

(*a*) Polyb. lib. 6.
(*b*) Polyb. ibid. Τεθείσης δὲ τ͂ σημαίας, ᾗ μέλλυσί ἐπηγνύωαι ταύτην, ὑπομετρεῖται πλευξ τ͂ σημαίας τετράγωνος τόπ©. ὅς τε πάσας τὰς πλδυξς ἑκατὸν ἀπέχειν πόδας τ͂ σημαίας, &c.

takes

takes up that part, which is fittest for prospect and direction. Setting therefore up the standard, where they intend to fix the Prætorium, *they so measure out a square about the standard, that each side may be distant from it an hundred feet, and the whole* area *contain four* jugera. In like manner (c) *Cæsar*, in the description of his bridge over the *Rhine*, makes the binders, or transversary beams, to be *bipedales*. (d) *Tully* also judges the quantity of the apparent diameter of the sun to be *pedalis*. And, not to produce more authorities, (e) *Suetonius* relates, that *Augustus presented before the people of* Rome, Lucius *a young gentleman, well descended, only for to shew that he was less than two feet in height, seventeen pounds in weight, and of an immense voice*. But concerning the precise quantity of this Foot, there is not any one thing, after which learned men have more enquired, or in which they do less agree. For *Budæus* equals it to the *Paris* foot; *Latinus Latinius, Maffæus, Ursinus*, and others, deduce it from an ancient monument in the *Vatican* of *T. Statilius Vol. Aper: Portius Vi-*

(c) Cæs. Comm. lib. 4.
(d) Cicero l. 2. Academ. quæst.
(e) Suetonius in Augusto. Adolescentulum Lucium honestè natum exhibuit, tantùm ut ostenderet, quod erat bipedali minor, librarum XVII. ac vocis immensæ.

centinus,

tentinus, Philander, Georgius Agricola, Ghetaldus, Donatus, and several others, contend, the foot on *Coffutius*'s monument in *Rome*, to be the *Roman* foot: *Marlianus* describes it out of a porphyry column, with this inscription, ΠΟΔ. Θ: *Lucas Pætus* defines it from some brass feet found amongst the *rudera* in *Rome*: *Villalpandus* derives it from the measure of the *congius*, placed by *Vespasian* in the *Capitl* (the original standard being still extant:) *Willebrordus Snellius* equals it to the *pes Rhinlandicus*: and several others have had several fancies and conjectures. In such a variety and uncertainty of opinions, we have no more solid foundation of our inquiry, than either to have recourse to the writings of the ancients; or else to such other monuments of antiquity, as having escaped the injury and calamity of time, have continued entire to this present age.

And first for the ancients. (*f*) *Vitruvius*, in his third book of Architecture, gives this description of the *Roman* foot: *E cubito cùm dempti sunt palmi duo, relinquitur pes quatuor palmorum. Palmus autem habet quatuor digitos, ita efficitur uti pes habeat* xvi. *digitos, & totidem asses æreos*

(*f*) Vitruvius l. 3.

denarius. (g) *Columella* shews, that it was the basis and foundation to all their other measures: *Modus omnis areæ pedali mensurâ comprehenditur, qui digitorum est* XVI. *Pes multiplicatus in passus, & actus, & climata, & jugera, & stadia, centuriasque, mox etiam in majora spatia procedit. Passus pedes habet quinque.* (h) *Frontinus* more clearly and distinctly expresseth the several parts and divisions of it. *Pes habet palmos* IV. *uncias* XII. *digitos* XVI. *Palmus habet digitos* IV. *uncias* III. *Sextans, quæ eadem dodrans appellatur, habet palmos* III. *uncias* IX. *digitos* XII. From which authority of *Frontinus,* and the place before cited of *Vitruvius,* we may collect some analogy to have been observed in the proportions of the *Roman* Foot, and of the *Roman* Coins. For as the *denarius* contained XVI. *asses,* so the foot contained XVI. *digitos:* And as the *assis* was divided in XII. *uncias,* so likewise the foot was divided in XII. *uncias;* and therefore the *dodrans* is used by *Frontinus,* and the *semiuncia* and *ficilicus* by *Pliny,* for proportionable parts of the *Roman* foot; as the same are used by other classical authors for proportionable parts of the *Roman assis* and *uncia.* From

(g) Columella, l. 5. de R. Rust.
(h) Frontin. de limitibus agrorum.

Of the Roman Foot.

which analogy the *pes Romanus*, I suppose, is termed by (*k*) *Hyginus pes Monetalis*. Likewise in the ancient laws of the XII. tables, (which *Tully* calls the fountains of the Civil Law) the *sestertius pes* hath the same proportion with the *sestertius* in Coins; for as the *sestertius*, according to (*l*) *Arruntius*, was *olim dupondius & semis*, anciently *two pounds of brass and a half*; so the *sestertius pes* was two feet and an half. (*m*) *Volusius Mætianus: Sestertius duos asses & semissem, quasi semis tertius; Græca figura* ἕβδομον ἡμιτάλαντον. *Nam sex talenta & semitalentum eo verbo significantur. Lex etiam* XII. *Tabularum argumento est, in qua duo pedes & semissis, sestertius pes vocatur.* But to return to *Frontinus*, who farther discoursing of the *Roman* foot, gives a distinction of three sorts of feet: and those were first, *pes porrectus*, next, *pes constratus*, or as (*n*) *Agricola* reads it, *contractus*, and lastly, *pes quadratus*. The first was the measure of longitudes, the other two of superficies. There were, writes (*o*) *Frontinus, In pede porrecto semipedes duo, in pede constrato semipedes quatuor, in pede*

(*k*) Hygin. de limit. constit.
(*l*) Arruntius ex editione Gotofredi.
(*m*) Vol. Mæt. de assis distrib.
(*n*) Agricola de mensuris quibus intervalla metimur.
(*o*) Frontinus de limitibus agrorum.

quadrato

quadrato femipedes octo. Which words of his are to be thus explicated; the *pes porrectus* was the *Roman* foot extended in length, and therefore there were in it *femipedes duo:* the *pes conftratus* was the fquare of the *femipes*, and therefore the perimeter of it contained *femipedes quatuor*, or, which is all one, two entire *Roman* feet: the *pes quadratus* was the fquare of the *Roman* foot; wherefore of necessity there muft be four feet in the perimeter, or in *Frontinus*'s expreffion, eight *femipedes*. The fame (*p*) author likewife in his book *de aquæductibus*, defcribing the digit and *uncia* of this (*eft autem digitus,* fays he, *ut convenit, fexta decima pars pedis, uncia duodecima*) ufeth a diftinction of digits, as he did of feet before, not mentioned by any other author: *Quemadmodum autem inter unciam & digitum diverfitas, ita & ipfius digiti fimplex obfervatio non eft; nam alius vocatur quadratus, alius rotundus. Quadratus tribus quartis decimis fuis rotundo major: rotundus tribus undecimis fuis quadrato minor eft.* The proportions here affigned by him to the *digitus quadratus* and *rotundus*, are the fame which (*q*) *Archimedes* long before ufed: and thofe are,

---

(*p*) Frontinus de Aquæductibus.
(*q*) Archim. de circ. dimenf. prop. 2.

that

Of the Roman Foot.

that a circle hath the same proportion to the square of the diameter, that xi hath to xiv. *Hero* also discoursing of several sorts of measures, informs us thus concerning the foot: Ὁ μὲν δάκτυλος, μέτρον ἐςι σμικρότατον. ἡ δὲ δοχμὴ ἐςι δακτύλων δ', ὅπερ μέτρον καὶ δακτυλοδόχμη, παλαιςήτε, καὶ δῶρον καλεῖται. ἡ δὲ λιχὰς ἐςι δακτύλων ἰ, τὸ δ' ὀρθόδωρον ιά, ἡ δὲ σπιθαμὴ ιβ', ὁ δὲ πῦς δοχμῶν δ', ἤτοι δακτύλων ις', ἡ δὲ πυγμὴ δακτύλων ιή, ὁ δὲ πυγὼν κ', ὁ δὲ πῆχυς κδ', ἤτοι δοχμῶν ς', ἡ δὲ ὀργυιὰ πήχεων δ', ἤτοι ποδῶν ς'. *The digit is the least measure; the palm consists of* iv *digits, and is called dactylodochme, palaiste, and doron. The lichas is* x *digits, the orthodoron* xi, *the span* xii. *The foot hath* iv *palms, or* xvi *digits, the pygme* xviii *digits; the pygon* xx; *the cubit* xxiv, *or* vi *palms; the orgyia* iv *cubits, or* vi *feet.* Most of which measures the *Romans* borrowed from the *Greeks*; as on the contrary the *Greeks* borrowed the ἰύγερον and μίλιον from the *Roman jugerum* and *milliare*. The same *Hero* describes another sort of foot used in *Italy.* Ὁ δὲ Ἰταλικὸς πῦς δακτύλως ἔχει τρεῖς καὶ δέκα καὶ τρίτον. *The Italian foot contains thirteen digits, and one third.* Whence (r) *Salmasius* concludes, that the *Romans* used one sort of foot in *Rome*, con-

---

(r) Salmasii Exercit. Plinianæ. p. 684.

sisting of XVI *digits*, and in some parts of *Italy* another, being but XIII *digits* and one third. Which might be granted, did not (s) *Hyginus*, who is much ancienter, in his tract *de Limitibus constituendis* contradict it. His words are these: *Item dicitur in Germaniâ in Tungris pes Drusianus, qui habet monetalem & sescunciam, ita ut ubicunque extra fines legésque Romanorum, id est, ut solicitiùs proferam, ubicunque extra Italiam aliquid agitatur inquirendum; & de hâc ipsâ conditione diligenter præmoneo, ne quid sit quod præteriisse videamur.* Where speaking immediately before of the *pes Romanus*, or as he also calls it, the *pes monetalis*, by which he measures and defines the *limits*, he gives us this caution, that out of *Italy* (for in *Italy* he supposes one measure to be generally received) we are to observe the quantity of the foot, or measure of the country; and for this reason, to avoid ambiguity, he assigns the proportions of the *pes Drusianus*, at *Tongeren* in *Germany*, to be a *sescuncia* more than the *pes monetalis* used at *Rome* and in *Italy*; and so in another part about *Cyrene*, which *Ptolemy* gave to the *Romans*. (t) *Pes eorum, qui Ptolemaicus appellatur, habet monetalem pedem &*

(s) Hyginus de Limit. Constit.
(t) Hyginus ib.

semun-

femunciam. But to omit the *pes Ptolemaicus* (for our enquiry is only of the *Roman* Foot) I cannot but wonder at the mistake of (*u*) *Joseph Scaliger,* concerning the *pes Drusianus* and *Romanus,* who thus writes: *Pes igitur ille Drusianus major est Romano sescunciâ; fuit enim* XXII *digitorum, quantorum* XVI *est pes Romanus.* If it were but a *sescuncia* greater than the *Roman* foot, as *Hyginus* and he also make it, how can it possibly be XXII *digitorum?* or how can he excuse his words which immediately follow? *Ex quo colligimus pedem Drusianum omnino esse eum, qui hodie in Galliâ & Belgio in usu est, qui profectò major est* VI *digitis, quantorum* XVI *est pes, qui Romæ in hortis Angeli Colotii sculptus in saxo visitur. Eum enim nos cum pede Gallicano comparantes, id verissimum esse deprehendimus.* Neither is the error of some others much less, in making the *pes monetalis* or *Romanus,* and *pes Regius Philetærius* to be equal. Because the *Roman* foot consisted of XVI *digits*, as *Frontinus* writes, and the *pes Philetærius* of as many, as (*x*) *Hero* shews: ὁ πᾶς ὁ μὲν βασιλικὸς, καὶ Φιλεταίριος λεγόμενος ἔχει παλαισὰς δ', δακτύλες ις'. Therefore both these are equal. The error is in supposing all

---

(*u*) Jos. Scaliger, de re Nummariâ.
(*x*) Hero in Isagoge.

digits

digits to be alike; and therefore the same number of *digits* being in both, that both are equal. By the same argument we may conclude the *Roman* foot, the *Arabian* foot, and the *derah* or cubit of these, to be equal to the cubit or *sesquipes* of the *Romans*; seeing (*y*) *Abulfeda*, an *Arabian* Geographer, defines the derah to consist of xxiv digits, and so many also did the *Roman sesquipes* contain. But the observation of (*z*) *Rhemnius Fannius* in this particular is much better; which he applies to weights, and we may by analogy assign to measures.

Semina sex alii siliquis latitantia curvis
Attribuunt scripulo, lentes veraciter octo,
Aut totidem speltas, numerant, tristésve lupinos
Bis duo; sed si par generatim bis pondus inesset,
Servarent eadem diversæ pondera gentes:
Nunc variant. Etenim cuncta non fœdere certo
Naturæ, sed lege valent, hominúmque repertis.

But to return to the *Roman* Foot: lastly, we may alledge (*a*) *Isidorus Hispalensis*: *Palmus autem quatuor habet digitos, Pes* xvi *digitos, Passus pedes quinque, Pertica passus duos, id est, decem pedes.* And this is that which I find delivered by such of the an-

(*y*) Abulfedæ Geogr. Arab. MS.
(*z*) Rhemnii Fannii fragmentum.
(*a*) Isid. Hispal. l. 15. c. 15.

tients as are extant. Out of which bare and naked defcriptions, it is as impoffible to recover the *Roman* foot, as it is for Mathematicians to take either the diftance or altitude of places, by the proportions of triangles alone, or by tables of fines and tangents, without having fome certain and pofitive meafure given, which muft be the foundation of their enquiry. All that can be collected by thefe defcriptions is this, that we may know into how many parts the *Romans* ufually divided their feet; and all thefe divifions I have feen in fome antient ones. But fuppofe there were no *Roman* foot extant, how by XVI *digits*, or by IV *palms*, or by XII *unciæ* (which is the moft uncertain of all, feeing whatfoever hath quantity, how great or fmall foever it is, may be divided in XII *uncias*) could it be precifely reftored? For if that of (*b*) *Protagoras* be true, as well in meafures, as in intellectual notions, that Man is πάντων χρημάτων μέτρον; whence (*c*) *Vitruvius* obferves, that the *Latins* denominated moft of their meafures, as their *digit, palm, foot* and *cubit*, from the parts and mem-

---

(*b*) Protagoras apud Ariftot. l. 13. cap. 5. Metaphyf. πάντων ἕιναι χρημάτων μέτρον τ͂ ἀνθρωπων.

(*c*) Nec minus menfurarum rationes, quæ in omnibus videntur neceffariæ effe, ex corporis membris collegerunt: uti digitum, palmum, pedem, cubitum. Vitruv. l. 3. c. 1.

bers of a man; who shall be that perfect and square man, from whom we may take a pattern of these measures? or if there be any such, how shall we know him? or how shall we be certain the ancients ever made choice of any such? Unless, as some fancy, that the cubit of the Sanctuary was taken from the cubit of *Adam*, he being created in an excellent state of perfection; so we shall imagine these *digits* and *palms* to have been taken from some particular man of compleater lineaments than others. On the other side, if this *foot* may be restored by the *digits* and *palms* of any man at pleasure, since there is such a difference in the proportions of men, that it is as difficult to find two of the same dimensions, as two that have the same likeness of faces, how will it be possible, out of such a diversity, to produce a certain and positive measure, consisting in an indivisibility, not as a point doth in respect of parts, but in an indivisibility of application, as all originals and standards should do? The *Arabians*, to avoid this difficulty, shew us a more certain way, as they suppose, how to make this commensural digit, and consequently the foot; and that is, by the breadth of six barly-corns laid one contiguous

tiguous to another. For thus (d) *Muhammed Ibn Meſoud*, in his book intituled in the *Perſian, Gehandaniſh*, relates; that *in the time of Almamon* (the learned Calif of *Babylon*) by the elevation of the pole of the æquator, they meaſured the quantity of a degree upon the globe of the earth, and found it to be fifty ſix miles, and two thirds of a mile: every mile containing four thouſand cubits, and each cubit twenty-four digits, and every digit ſix barly corns. The ſame proportions are aſſigned in the Geographia Nubienſis, printed in *Arabick* at *Rome*:

الذراع اربعة وعشرون اصبعا و الاصبع ست حبات شعير

The cubit is 24 *digits, and every digit is ſix barly-corns.* But this is as uncertain as the former, and is built upon a ſuppoſition, that all ſuch are of the ſame dimenſion. Whereas thoſe of one country differ much from thoſe of another; and thoſe of the ſame country (as I have made trial in *Ægypt*, more out of curioſity, than as hoping this way to give my ſelf ſatisfaction) are not all of the ſame bigneſs: and not only ſo, but in the ſelf-ſame ear there is a ſenſible difference, as experience doth ſhew. And yet *Snellius*, a man much to be commended for his abilities in the Mathematicks, and to be blamed for his ſupine negligence, both

(d) محمد ابن مسعود MS.

Of the Roman Foot.

in his meafure of the magnitude of the earth, and in his dimenfions of the *Roman* foot, upon thefe flight and weak principles deduces the *Arabian* foot, *(e) this containing ninety fix grains, fuch as his* Roman *foot* (for none befides himfelf will own it) *contains ninety.* Wherefore fome other *Arabians*, to mend the matter, limit the breadth of one of them *(f) by fix hairs of a camel evenly joined one by another:* by which invention their *derah* being almoft anfwerable to the *Roman fefquipes* or cubit, fhall confift of twenty four digits, and every digit of fix barly-corns, and every barly-corn of fix hairs of a camel. So that in conclufion the hair of a camel fhall be the *minimum* in refpect of meafures. But this invention, however at the firft it may feem fomewhat fubtil (for we are come now almoft as low as atoms) is leaft of all to be approved. For tho' the fuppofition were true, that all hairs are of a like bignefs in all camels,

---

(e) Snellius in Eratofth. Batav. lib. 2. cap. 2.
(f) Aly Kufhgy, who affifted *Vlug Beg* in compiling his aftronomical tables in *Perfian* (tables the moft exact of any in the eaft) limits their breadth by fix hairs of an horfe.

هر اصبع مقدار شش جو معتدل وعوض هر جو مقدار شش تار موي بال اسب.

Every digit is fix barly-corns laid evenly together, and the breadth of every barly-corn is fix hairs of an horfe's tail. Inftit. Aftron. Aly Kufhgy, MS.

whereas

whereas they are different in one and the same; yet this objection is unanswerable, that seeing hairs are not perfectly round, though the sense judges them so, but angular, and that with some inequality, as magnifying-glasses plainly demonstrate, it will be very difficult so to size them together, that they shall always take up the same breadth: and if they do not, little errors committed in such small bodies, though at the first insensible, will infinitely increase and multiply in the measuring of great distances, to which these are supposed the foundation. And therefore I cannot but approve the counsel of (g) *Villalpandus*, who adviseth such as will examine measures and weights, to begin with the greater, and not with the lesser. And that there is reason for his assertion may be made evident, especially in weights, to such as shall make an experiment. For admit there were a standard of ten thousand grains, and another of one grain, it will be easy, by a continued subdivision of the former with a good balance, to produce a weight equal to the

---

(g) Villalpandus de apparatu orbis ac templi, par. 2. l. 3. c. 25. Atque in universum illud unum monitos velim eos omnes, qui mensurarum ac ponderum cognoscendorum desiderio tenentur, ne à minimis incipiant examinare majora: nam vel minimus quisque error sæpius multiplicatus in magnum adducit errorum cumulum.

standard

standard of one grain: yea, though at the beginning some little error had been committed, which after many divisions will vanish and become imperceptible. Whereas on the contrary, the most curious man alive, with the exactest scale that the industry of the most skilful artizan can invent, shall never be able, out of the standard of one grain, to produce a weight equal to the weight of ten thousand grains, but that there shall be a sensible and apparent difference; yea, though he had that excellent scale mentioned by (*h*) *Capellus* at *Sedan*, which would sensibly be turned with the four hundredth part of a grain. The like difference as we find in weights, we may conceive by analogy to be in measures, when they shall be made out of such little parts, as hairs, barly-corns, digits, and the like; and therefore I cannot but disapprove the ordinary course of most Geographers, whether *Greeks*, *Latins*, or *Arabians*, that from such nice beginnings measure out a degree upon earth, and consequently the magnitude of this globe. On the contrary, the enterprize of (*i*) *Snellius* in his *Eratosthenes Batavus*, and of our countryman (*k*) M. *Wright*, hath been more commendable;

(*h*) Capellus de Pond. & Nummis lib. 1.
(*i*) Snell. in Eratosth Bat. lib. 2.
(*k*) Wright, of the Errors of Navigation.

Of the Roman FOOT.

mendable; who by the space of a degree on earth (or which were better, of many degrees) have endeavoured to fix measures with more exactness and certainty for posterity. But of this argument I shall have occasion to speak hereafter; and therefore to return to the business in hand.

Since the *Roman* foot cannot be recovered by hairs, grains, digits, palms, and such like physical bodies, which being of a various and indeterminate magnitude, cannot give, unless by accident, the commensuration of that which ought to be precisely limited and determined: some relinquishing the former way as erroneous, have endeavoured, with much ingeniousness, by weights, to find out the *Roman* foot. For there is the same analogy between measures and weights, as between continued and discrete quantities: and as Mathematicians by numbers demonstrate, or rather illustrate the affections of lines, superficies, and geometrical bodies; so by weights measuring some physical bodies, especially such as are liquid, in cubical vessels (which are easiest commensurable), we may render the exact quantity of the *Roman* foot, and by consequence of all their other measures. And therefore

therefore (*l*) *Lucas Pætus* and (*m*) *Villalpandus* have attempted with more probable reasons to difcover the *Roman* foot, the one by the *fextarius*, the other by the *Roman congius*. For the *fextarius* being the fixth part of the *congius*, and the *congius* containing x. *libræ*, or pounds, as it is manifeft by that exquifite ftandard in *Rome* with this infcription:

IMP. CÆSARE.

VESPAS. VI

T. CÆS. AUG. F. IIII cos.

MENSURÆ

EXACTÆ IN

CAPITOLIO

(*n*) P X

Again, the *congius* being the eighth part of the *amphora*, or *quadrantal*, filled with water or wine, as by the teftimonies of (*o*) *Diofcorides*, (*p*) *Sextus Pompeius*, and of an ancient anonymous *Greek* author, tranflated by *Alciat*, it doth appear: if therefore a veffel be made of a cubical figure,

---

(*l*) Luc. Pætus l. 3. de Menfur. & Pond. Rom.
(*m*) Villalp. de appar. Urb. ac Temp. par. 2. l. 3. c. 25.
(*n*) P X fignifies *pondo decem*. (*o*) Fragm. Diofcor.
(*p*) Sext. Pomp. Feft. de Verb. fignif.

which

which may receive VIII. *congii*, or XLVIII. *sextarii*, or LXXXIV. pounds of water or of wine, out of the sides of this cube, by (*q*) *Rhemnius Fannius*'s description, or rather by *Sextus Pompeius*, who is ancienter, will the *Roman* foot be deduced. For both these write (neither is it as yet contradicted by any man) that the longitude of one of the sides of the *amphora* (being a cube) is answerable to the *Roman* Foot. And here our inquiry would be at an end (supposing the authorities of *Festus* and *Fannius* to be unquestionable) were there not farther some objections, which cannot easily be removed; and those are, first, a supposition that we have the true *Roman libra* (for by this we are to find the *congius*, admitting there were none extant, as by the *congius*, the *amphora*, or *quadrantal*) a thing of as great difficulty as the foot itself; and besides, if this were obtained, yet we cannot have an absolute certainty, that water or wine shall in all places alike ponderate, by reason of the different gravity which is observed in natural bodies, though they be homogenous and of a like substance. Wherefore laying aside all such speculations, as being far from that accurateness which is required,

---

(*q*) Rhemn. Fann. fragm.

there is no other possible means left for this discovery, but to have recourse to such monuments of antiquity, as have escaped the injury and calamity of time, which is our next and second inquiry.

And here it will not be amiss to see what learned men, who not long preceded our age, have observed out of ancient monuments concerning the *Roman* Foot; and then to relate what course I took to give my self private satisfaction, which I hope will be also satisfactory to others. *Philander* in his Commentaries upon *Vitruvius*, being one of the first that had seen and diligently perused many ancient measures in *Rome*, (whereas *Portius*, *Agricola*, *Glareanus*, and some others, received them upon trust) gives us so much the more certain information. His words are these: (r) *Veruntamen quoniam non statim ex cujuscunque pollicibus, aut digitis, quis fuerit apud antiquos Romanus pes sciri potest, facturum me studiosis rem gratam putavi, si ad marginem libri semipedem apponerem, dimensum ex antiquo pede, in marmore, quod est in hortis Angeli Colotii Romæ sculpto, cujus etiam, nisi me fallit memoria, meminit Leonardus Porcius lib. de Sestertio. Eum*

(r) Philander in lib. 3. cap. 3. Vitruvii.

enim

enim pedem, nos cæteris, qui circumferuntur, prætulimus, quòd conveniret cum eo, quem fculptum invenimus in alio marmoreo epitaphio T. Statilii Vol. Apri menforis ædificiorum, quod operâ Jacobi Meleghini fummi Pont. Architecti ex Janiculo non ita pridem refoffum, in Vaticanum hortum tranflatum eft. Quamvis jacentem in Bafilicâ Apoftolorum columnam ex porphyrite, cum his Græcis in calce literis Π Ο Δ. Θ. *id eft pedum novem, nos cum dimenfi effemus, deprehenderimus non refpondere noftro eum, quo ufus fuerat ejus columnæ artifex, fed noftro effe majorem duobus fcrupulis & beffe, id eft unciæ parte nonâ. Ut argumentum aliquod effe poffit, pedis Græci fuiffe modulo fcapum columnæ factum; quod facilius conjicere potuiffem, fi integra effet alia ex eodem lapide columna, quam in viâ latâ eft confpicere jacentem, his in calce literis* Π Ο Δ I B *infignitam. Verùm quando ftadium Herodoto lib. 2. Heroni, Suidæ, cæteris Græcis fit fexcentorum pedum; Plinio, Columellæ, cæteris Latinis fexcentorum viginti quinque noftrorum, neceffe eft Romanum à Græco femunciâ fuperari.* Thus far *Philander.* Not long after him *Lucas Pætus,* having examined the foot on *T. Statilius*'s tomb, and that other of *Coffutius,* together with feveral ancient ones in brafs, found amongft the *rudera* at *Rome*, concludes, That the (s) true *Roman* Foot *dictis duobus marmoreis comparatus, septimâ unciæ parte, sive unciæ scripulis tribus, & duabus scripuli sextulis, & sextulæ semisse brevior est.* Much about the same time I found in *Ciaconius*, out of *Latinus Latinius*, another experiment to have been made by many eminent men together at *Rome*. *Superioribus autem annis,* (t) saith he, *Ant. Augustinus, qui postmodum fuit Archiepiscopus Tarraconensis, Jo. Baptista Sighicellus Episcopus Faventinus, P. Octavius Pacatus, Achilles Maffæus, Achilles Statius, Benedictus Ægius, Fulvius Ursinus, Latinus Latinius, cùm veram pedis Rom. quantitatem statuere vellent, plures ejusd. pedis mensuras simul contulerunt, & earum octo cum antiquissimâ dicti pedis formâ, quæ in basi quâdam in hortis Vaticanis extat, adamussim convenire videntes, ex hoc pede quadrato vas confecerunt, quod etiam nunc octoginta aquæ vel vini libras, quibus publicè signatis civitas utitur, omnino capere invenerunt, & cum octo congiis antiquis congruere, ut neque minus quidquam, neque amplius inter utraque esset. Quo experimento evidentissimè cognoverunt, & libras*

(s) Luc. Pætus l. 1. de Antiq. Rom. & Græc. intervall. mensuris.

(t) Ciaconius è Lat. Latinii Observationibus de pede Rom.

nostri

nostri temporis cum antiquis Romanis esse easdem, cùm congii antiqui vas sub Vespasiano Imp. signatum decem libras contineret, quot etiam nostri temporis libras capit; & hunc esse justum pedem Romanum, cùm ex ejus modulo perfectum quadrantal octoginta libras contineat, quæ cum congii antiqui libris ad momentum respondent. Notwithstanding these observations, *Villalpandus* knowing how necessary it was to have the true dimensions of the *Roman* foot, to find out the proportions of the *Hebrew* cubit, made new experiments; and after examination of the measures and weights at *Rome*, he thus concludes: (*u*) *Sed iis omnibus tam variis, aliisque multis sententiis prætermissis, in hâc unâ conquiescimus, ut arbitremur unum Farnesianum congium posse omnes antiquas Romanorum, atque aliarum gentium mensuras, omniáque pondera pristinæ integritati restituere.* And in another place: *Quapropter aliis omnibus conjecturis, argumentationibus, æreis pedibus, marmoreis dimensionibus, aut sculpturis, quasi maris fluctibus prætermissis, in hâc unâ pedis longitudine, quasi in portu conquiescere jam tandem decrevimus.* Yet *Snellius*, in his *Eratosthenes Batavus*, could not rest satisfied with this foot of *Villal-*

(*u*) Villalpandi Apparatus Urbis ac Templi. par. 2. l. 3. c. 25.

pandus, how exquisite soever he imagines it: for he had a mind to discover it nearer home, making the *Rhinland* foot equal to the *Roman*. The proof of his assertion is taken from an ancient *Roman armamentarium*, or fort near the sea, not far from *Leyden*, which by the natives is called *bet huys te Briten*, and is supposed by *Ortelius* to have been built by *Claudius Cæsar* in his intended voyage for *Britain*, of which (*x*) *Suetonius* and *Dio* make mention: *five in commodiorem legionum cohortiumque transvectionem, sive quo milites hibernarent,* saith *Ortelius. Arcis ipsius fundamenta* (according to (*y*) *Snellius*) *quadratâ sunt formâ, & quaquaversum ducentis quadraginta Rhinlandicis pedibus patent. Ut vel hinc Romanæ mensuræ vestigia quàm planissimè agnoscas. Nam ipsius podismus duorum Romanorum jugerum magnitudinem complectitur. Jugeri enim mensuram ducentos & quadraginta longitudinis pedes esse, non est ferè quisquam qui ignoret, inquit Quintilianus l.* 1. *cap.* 10. *Varro de Re Rustica, lib.* 1. *cap.* 10. *Jugerum quod quadratos duos actus habet. Actus quadratus, qui & latus est pedes* 120. *& longus totidem. Is modius, ac mina Latina appellatur; ut mihi planè dubium non*

(*x*) Suetonius in Claudio. Dio Hist. Rom. lib. 60.
(*y*) Snell. in Eratosth. Bat. l. 2. c. 2.

videa-

videatur, eos hic Romanæ menfuræ modum fecutos, hujus ftructuræ podifmum ita comprebendiffe fecundum jugeri menfuram, ut duo jugera, vel actus quatuor contineret. Frontinus de limitibus. Hi duo fundi juncti jugerum definiunt, deinde hæc duo jugera juncta in unum quadratum agrum efficiunt, quòd fint omnes actus bini: ut fingula ideò latera ducentos & quadraginta pedes in longum patêre neceffe fit. Atqui totidem pedibus Rhinlandicis fingula latera exporrigi geodætarum experientia confirmat. Unde efficitur Romanum antiquum pedem noftro Rhinlandico planè æquari.

After thefe experiments of fo many able and learned men, and thofe too taken from ancient monuments, it may feem ftrange, that we fhould not be able as yet to define the true quantity of the *Roman* foot. For this I can affign no other reafons than thefe. Firft, that thofe which have defcribed it, have either not exactly, and with fuch diligence as was requifite, performed it; or elfe, if they have been circumfpect in this kind, they have omitted to compare it with the ftandards for meafures of other nations. On the contrary, thofe which have compared it with the prefent ftandards, never took it from the ancient monuments and originals which are at *Rome*, but only from fome draughts or fchemes delineated in

books.

books. Now how uncertain a way this is, doth appear by (z) *Villalpandus*, who thus writes: *Ego dum hæc scriberem, hunc Colotianum pedem circino expendi, & in annotationibus Guil. Philandri solertissimi viri, & apud Georgium Agricolam, & apud Lucam Pætum, & Stanislaum Grsepsium, & nullum potui reperire alteri æqualem, imo verò neque ejusdem pedis assignatas similes partes.* The same have I observ'd in those *Roman* feet described by *Portius, Agricola, Philander, Pætus, Ciaconius,* and *Villalpandus* himself, that they differ one from another; and not only so, but those of the same author, in the same impression, are likewise different. Which last must arise, either by the diverse extension of the paper in the press when it is moist, or by the inequal contraction of it when it grows dry, or by some other accident in the beating and binding. So that though it were granted, that so many learned men had found out what we inquire after, the *Roman* foot; yet it is impossible, out of those schemes and draughts deliver'd in their books, for the reasons before specified, to attain an absolute certainty. But *Snellius* shews us a remedy of this difficulty, which, in my opinion, is as vain as his *Roman* foot (seeing by his supposition

(z) Villalpand. de Apparatu Urbis ac Templi, par. 2. l. 3. c. 25.

all

Of the Roman Foot.

all paper muſt ſhrink alike, be it thick or thin) and that is, to allow one part in ſixty for the ſhrinking of the paper: *For ſo much (a)* ſaith he, *do Typographers obſerve, that letters contract themſelves, when they are taken off wet from the types.*

Wherefore having received ſmall ſatisfaction from the writings of the ancients, and not much better from the imperfect deſignations of the *Roman* foot by modern authors, I propoſed to my ſelf in my travels abroad theſe ways, which no reaſonable man but muſt approve of. And thoſe were, firſt, to examine as many ancient meaſures and monuments in *Italy*, and other parts, as it was poſſible; and ſecondly, to compare theſe with as many ſtandards and originals, as I could procure the ſight of. And laſt of all, to tranſmit both theſe and them to poſterity, I exactly meaſured ſome of the moſt laſting monuments of the ancients. To this purpoſe, in the year 1639 I went into *Italy*, to view, as the other antiquities of the *Romans*, ſo eſpecially thoſe of weights and meaſures; and to take them with as much exactneſs as it was poſſible, I carried inſtruments with me made by the beſt artizans.

(a) Pars ſexageſima typorum & formarum longitudini excuſis decedit, quemadmodum à diligentibus & peritis typographis ſciſcitando edoctus ſum. Snell. in Eratoſth. Batav. l. 2 c. 1.

Where

Of the Roman Foot.

Where my first inquiry was after that monument of *T. Statilius Vol. Aper*, in the *Vatican* gardens, from whence (b) *Philander* took the dimensions of the *Roman* foot, as others have since borrowed it from him. In the copying out of this upon an *English* foot in brass, divided into 2000 parts, I spent at least two hours (which I mention to shew with what diligence I proceeded in this and the rest) so often comparing the several divisions and digits of it respectively one with another, that I think more circumspection could not have been used; by which I plainly discovered the rudeness and insufficiency of that foot. For besides that the length of it is somewhat too much (whatsoever (c) *Latinius* out of an observation made by *Ant. Augustinus, Sighicellus, Pacatus, Maffæus, Statius, Ægius,* and *Fulvius Ursinus*, pretends to the contrary) there is never a digit that is precisely answerable to one another. Howsoever, it contains 1944 such parts as the *English* foot contains 2000.

My next search was for the foot on the monument of *Coffutius, in hortis Colotianis,* from whence it hath since received its denomination (though it be now removed) being termed by writers *pes Colotianus*. This foot

---

(b) Philand. in l. 3. c. 3. Vitruvii.
(c) Ciaconius è Latino Latinio.

I took

Of the Roman Foot.

I took with great care, as it did well deserve, being very fair and perfect; afterwards collating it with that *Roman* foot which *Lucas Pætus* caused to be ingraven in the *Capitol* in a white marble stone, I found them exactly to agree; and therefore I did wonder, why he should condemn this with his pen (for he makes some *(d)* objections against it) which notwithstanding he hath erected with his hands, as appears by the inscription in the *Capitol*, CURANTE LU. PAETO. It may be, upon second thoughts, he afterward privately retracted his error, which he was not willing to publish to the world. Now this of *Cossutius* is 1934 such parts as the *English* foot contains 2000.

Next I sought after that porphyry column mentioned by *(e) Marlianus*, as also by *(f) Philander* and others, with this inscription, ΠΟΔ. Θ. For if the length of that column were assigned according to the proportion of the *Greek* foot, then would the *Roman* foot be thence deduced; this (as I shall elsewhere shew) containing 24 such parts, as that contained 25. Or if it were made according to the *Roman* foot, as the

---

(d) Luc. Pætus l. 1. de Antiq. Rom. & Græc. intervall. mensuris.
(e) Marlianus de Antiqit. Urbis.
(f) Philander in lib. 3. c. 3. Vitruvii.

Grecians

Grecians after their subjection to the *Roman* empire often used the same measures that the *Romans* did, then had I my desire. But the column being defaced, or lost, my labour was in vain: And it seems, (*g*) *Pætus* about seventy years before made the same inquiry with as little satisfaction.

I should be too tedious in describing the several feet which I have perused in brass, found amongst the *rudera* at *Rome*, and carefully preserved by antiquaries; of most of which *Peireskius* hath given a good character in some letters of his, which I have seen in the hands of *Buchardus*, a learned man, not yet printed, who thus writes: (*h*) *I cannot sufficiently wonder at the inequality which I have found in the divisions by digits and inches of the ancient* Roman *feet; which seem to me to have been made for fashion sake,* & dicis causâ *(as lamps that are found in tombs, incapable of oil) more to express the mystery and profession of those that were to use them, than for to regulate the measure of any thing besides them.*

Besides these, I examined the antient structures of the *Romans*, hoping, by collating one with another, to deduce the

---

(*g*) Luc. Pætus l. 1. de Antiq. Rom. & Græc. intervall. mensuris.
(*h*) Ex Epistolis Peireskii MSS.

dimension

Of the Roman Foot.

dimension of their foot. For I presumed that those excellent Architects, before they began their work, must necessarily propose some models to themselves, according to the proportions of which, they meant to raise their fabricks: which proportions could not be assigned, but in the parts of some common and received quantity; and this in all probability was the *Roman* Foot, being a measure generally used, and by publick authority prescribed. Upon which grounds I measured the stones in the foundation of the *Capitol*, *Domitian*'s, or rather *Vespasian*'s Amphitheatre, the triumphal Arcs of *Titus* and *Severus*, together with that of *Constantine* the Great, and above all, that exquisite Temple of the *Pantheon*, built by *Agrippa*, I know not whether with more cost or art; concerning which (*i*) *Sebastianus Serlius* is of opinion, *that if all rules of Architecture were lost, they might be revived out of this monument alone.* And in truth this place gave me more satisfaction than any other. For most of the white marble stones on the pavement contained exactly three of those *Roman* feet on *Cossutius*'s monument, and the lesser stones in porphyry contained one and a half.

(*i*) Sebast. Serl. delle Antichita.

But

But yet I thought this was not sufficient, unless I went to *Tarracina*, which is the antient *Anxur*, fifty three miles distant from *Rome*: having read in (k) *Andreas Schottus*, out of *Pighius*'s *Hercules Prodicius*, that near the sea by the *via Appia*, in the height of a white rock (whence that of (l) *Horace*,

Impositum saxis latè candentibus Anxur)

there are described the *Roman decempedæ*. And indeed the place is very memorable for the whiteness, altitude, and hardness of the rock, which notwithstanding is cut away perpendicularly, on the side towards the *Tyrrhene* Sea, above a hundred and twenty feet in depth, to make passage for the *Appian* Way; and at the space of every *decempeda*, these characters X, XX, XXX, &c. (being almost *cubitales*) are fairly engraven in a continued order descending to CXX. Measuring below the distance between CXX and CX, it amounted to 9 *English* feet, and $\frac{1114}{1000}$ of a foot, computing it from the (m) line engraven above CXX, to the line next under CX. The rest I examined with

---

(k) Andr. Schott. itinerar. (l) Horat. l. 1. Serm. Sat. 5.
(m) See at the end of this book the figure of these characters as they are cut in the rock at *Anxur*, with lines incompassing them.

Of the Roman FOOT.

my eyes, by often comparing the distance between CXX and CX, whether it were equal to that between CX and C, and this again (ascending upwards) to that between C and XC; which manner, tho' it be uncertain and conjectural, and far from that exactness I used in all others, yet it was the best means I could then put in practise; and I am confident that whosoever shall measure those spaces, shall find a manifest inequality. To which opinion I am the rather induced, because measuring there in several places the breadth of the *Appian* Way, cut out of the same rock, I found a difference sometimes of one or two inches, or more; it being in one place 13 *English* feet, and $\frac{1642}{1000}$ of a foot; in another, 13 feet and $\frac{1818}{1000}$; in a third, 13 and $\frac{1771}{1000}$. Whereby I concluded that the ancients, in making that way, had not respect to a mathematical point (as it was not necessary) but only that if any difference were, it should not be sensible. And such differences have I observed in the white *Corinthian* pillars, in the *Pantheon* before mentioned, of above an inch or two in the circuit of the *scapus*, near the *torus*; which inequality, seeing no eye could discover, the masters of that exquisite work did justly contemn. Whereas the porphyry stones,

stones, and those of white marble on the pavement, are sized so even, and so exactly to the proportions of the *Roman* foot, that nothing can be more accurate: and this the nature of the work required. For the temple being round (which hath occasioned the *Italians* vulgarly to call it the *Rotundo*) the circle within could not so exquisitely have been filled up, if there had not been a special care taken in observing the true dimensions in every particular stone. But to return to the rock at *Anxur*; the spaces between those characters, to an eye that shall be intentively fixt upon them, will be apparently different. So that I concur in opinion with (*n*) *Schottus*, that those figures were placed there *to give notice to posterity how much of the rock had been removed to make passage for the* Appian *way*; and not for any memorial of the *Roman* measures.

Having measured those places in the *Appian* way at *Tarracina*, I made trial of at least twenty others between *Tarracina* and *Naples*, without any great satisfaction; and therefore partly the incertainty that I found there, and partly the danger of thieves, discouraged me from measuring the *Roman milliare*, a work conceived by some to be of

(*n*) Schotti itiner.

great

Of the Roman Foot. 215

great use for the discovery of the *Roman* foot. Seeing the *milliare*, containing *mille passus*, as the very name imports, and every *passus* consisting of five feet, as (*o*) *Columella* and (*p*) *Isidorus* expresly tell us, here therefore would be 5000 feet to help us to one, could there be but found out a perfect *Roman* mile. And this I imagined might probably be discovered amongst those many *vestigia* of *Roman* ways which to this day are frequently seen in *Italy*. Wherefore conferring with *Gasparo Berti*, a man curious and judicious, (as appears by his ichnography of *Roma subterranea* in *Bosius*) as also with *Lucas Holstenius*, a learned companion of *Cluverius*, in those honourable travels of his for the restauration of the ancient Geography; they both informed me, that there are still in the *Appian* way, where it passes over the *Pomptinæ paludes*, several *columnæ* or *lapides milliarii* standing, whereby the *Romans* divided and distinguished their miles; and which occasioned those phrases, *ad primum, ad quartum, ad centesimum lapidem*, and the like. And these, it may be, at the first were ordinary stones, till *C. Gracchus* caused columns to be erected in their places: Διαμετρήσας κατὰ μίλιον

(*o*) Columella de Re Rust. l. 5.
(*p*) Isidor. l. 15. c. 15. Origin.

ὁδὸν πᾶσαν (τὸ ἢ μίλιον ὀκτὼ ϛαδίων ὀλίγον ἀποδεῖ) κίονας λιθίνες σημεῖα τῦ μέτρε κατέϛησεν. *He meaſured out* (faith *(q) Plutarch*) *by miles all the ways, the mile containing little leſs than eight* ſtadia, *and placed columns of ſtone to deſign the meaſure.* The thing was of that ornament and uſe, as that it was afterwards taken up, and continued by the *Roman* Emperors; as appears by theſe inſcriptions, which are fairly ingraven on the firſt column, found amongſt the ruins in the *Appian* way, and from thence lately removed into the *Capitol* by order of the *(r)* ſenate and people of *Rome*.

I

IMP. CAESAR
VESPASIANVS. AVG.
PONTIF. MAXIM
TRIB. POTESTAT. V̄Ī̄Ī
IMP. X̄V̄Ī̄Ī P. P. CENSOR
COS. V̄Ī̄Ī DESIGN. V̄Ī̄Ī̄Ī

(q) Plutarchus in Gracchis.

(r) S. P. Q. R.
COLVMNAM. MILIARIAM
PRIMI. AB. VRBE. LAPIDIS. INDICEM
AB. IMPP. VESPASIANO. ET. NERVA
RESTITVTAM
DE. RVINIS. SVBVRBANIS. VIAE. APPIAE
IN. CAPITOLIVM. TRANSTVLIT

Below

Of the Roman FOOT. 217

Below this, on the end of the *scapus:*

IMP. NERVA. CAESAR
AVGVSTVS. PONTIFEX
MAXIMVS. TRIBVNICIA
POTESTATE. COS. III PATER
PATRIAE. REFECIT

Below this, on the *basis* of the same pillar:

IMP. CAESARI. DIVI
TRAIANI. PARTHICI. F
DIVI. NERVAE. NEPOTI
TRAIANO. HADRIANO
AVG. PONTIF. MAXIM
TRIB. POTEST. II COS. II
VIATORES. QVI. IPSI. ET. COS. ET
PR. CETERISQVE. MAGISTRATIB
APPARENT. ET. H. V.

To these I shall also add the inscription of another *columna milliaria*, not extant in *Gruterus*, or any other, that I know, which I have seen at *Tarracina*; the column being exactly of the same magnitude with the former, but wanting, by the injury of time, a *basis* below, and a globe of nigh three feet diameter on the top, serving instead of a capital, both which the former hath:

218   *Of the Roman* Foot.

X

Imp. Caesar
dIvI. Nervae
Filius. Nerva
Traianvs. Avg
Germanicvs
Pontif. Max
Trib. Pot. x̄iiii
Imp. v̄i Cos. v̄ P. P
x̄viii Silice. Sua. Pecvnia
Stravit

LIII   If

The figure X fignifies the diſtance of *Tarracina* from the next city or town in the way to *Rome*; and that was, *Ad medias*, a place ſo called, either becauſe it was *ad medias paludes*, or elſe becauſe it was in the midway almoſt between *Tarracina* and *Appii Forum*. For it was ten miles from *Tarracina*, and nine from *Appii Forum*, as appears by the *Itinerarium Hieroſolymitanum* in *Bertius*.

  Appii Forum
  Ad medias IX.
  Tarracina X.

The figure LIII below ſignifies the diſtance of *Tarracina* from *Rome*: which diſtance may be farther proved out of *Appian*, in his third book of the Civil Wars, ſpeaking of *Auguſtus*: *Ὅτι αὐτῷ περὶ Ταρρακίνας ἀπὸ τετρακοσίων σταδίων Ῥώμης ϛαδίων* Being about Tarracina, *which is diſtant* 400 ſtadia *from* Rome. Theſe *ſtadia* reduced to miles, if we allow ſeven *Greek ſtadia* and an half to a *Roman* mile, as *Suidas* doth, will make up fifty three miles, and one third part of a mile; that is, two *ſtadia* and an half over and above; which fraction *Appian* neglects, and therefore uſes the round number four hundred *ſtadia* for fifty three miles.

The figure XVIIII ſignifies the *Decennovium*, or way paſſing over the fens between *Appii Forum* and *Tarracina*; ſo denominated, becauſe it contained nineteen miles in length:
which

Of the Roman FOOT. 219

If therefore two such columns were found entire (as I am informed there are four or five in the *Decennovium*, standing in a continued order) the distance between two such being exactly measured, would much conduce to the discovery of the *Roman* foot. Upon which supposition, I had almost resolved to have gone thither, as I did to other places, with no other intention, but only to have been a spectator of those columns, and to have trusted to mine own hands in taking their distances. But which may also be proved out of *Procopius*, where he speaks of the Δεκεννόβιον. This way was paved by *Trajan*, as the inscription shews, and, I think, first of all by him. Long after it was repaired by *Theodoricus*, according to another inscription that I have seen at *Tarracina*, of which *Gruterus* and *Cluverius* also make mention; where, omitting the titles of *Theodoricus*, in the marble we find these words engraven:

DECENNOVII. VIAE. APPIAE. ID. EST. A. TRIP
VSQVE. TERRACENAM. ITER. ET. LOCA. QVAE
CONFLVENTIBVS. AB. VTRAQVE. PARTE. PALVDVM
PER. OMNES. RETRO. PRINCIPVM. INVNDAVERANT
VSVI. PVBLICO. ET. SECVRITATI. VIANTIVM
RESTITVIT. - - - - - - - - PER
PLVRIMOS. QVI. ANTE. NON. ERANT. ALBEOS
- - - - - DEDVCTA. IN. MARE. AQVA

By this number XVIIII. signifying the *Decennovium*, and by the *Itinerarium Hierosolymitanum*, we may safely correct the *Itinerarium Antonini*, in which *Tarracina* is placed but eighteen miles distant from *Appii Forum*; and from hence likewise we may certainly know, how far the Christians went to meet St. *Paul*, and that was thirty four miles. For so much was *Appii Forum* distant from *Rome*, if we subduct nineteen out of fifty-three; whereas the Itineraries of *Bertius*'s Edition make it more.

upon a more deliberate examination of the bufiness, I perceived that this enquiry did depend upon a very nice fuppofition. For if the *Decempedatores*, or *Curatores viarum*, proceeded not with extreme caution, and aimed almoft at a mathematical point, in defigning the juft fpace of each particular mile (which in a work of that length is not probable; where the inequality of many feet could not be difcerned by the eye, and might be admitted without any blemifh; for in (*u*) *Varro*'s judgment, *Senfus nullus quod abeft mille paffus fentire poteft*) it could not be, but the fame differences, or fomewhat like muft have crept in with them, which have been obferved amongft us in our meafured and ftatute miles, out of which it would be a vain attempt exactly to demonftrate the *Englifh* foot. The neglect of which circumfpection, amongft fome other reafons that may be affigned, I take to be one, of the diverfity which Aftronomers made in that memorable obfervation, made in the planes of *Singiar*, or *Sinar*, by the command of *Almamon* the renowned Calif of *Babylon*, about eight hundred years fince, in proportioning the magnitude of a degree upon earth. For having taken the altitude of the pole at

---

(*u*) Varro de L. L. lib. 5.

two several stations, differing a degree in the heavens, they measured the distance between these stations on earth, going on in the same meridian; where *(x) some of them,* says Abulfeda, *found it to be fifty-six miles, and two thirds, others fifty-six, without any fraction.* If therefore the *Roman Decempedatores,* or *Geodætæ,* used not more circumspection than the *Babylonian* Astronomers (which is not likely) there can be no trust given to their miles, and less trust to the foot that shall be deduced from thence.

Wherefore to come to a conclusion; having made enquiry more ways than, it may be, any man hath done, and I think with as much caution and exactness as any, it will be necessary after all, to shew amongst so many feet as are taken to be *Roman,* which I conceive to be the most genuine and true. And tho' in such an incertainty and scarcity of ancient monuments, and in such a diversity of opinions amongst modern writers, it may seem too great a presumption positively to define the magnitude of the *Roman* foot; yet having had the opportunity to have perused, in this kind, more antiquities than any that have

(x) فكان مع اجذيهما ستة وخمسون ميلا وثلثا ومع الاخرى ستة وخمسون ميل بغير كسر.
Abulf. Geogr. Arab. MS.

preceded,

preceded, I may with the more confidence conclude, that the *pes Colotianus*, in my judgment, is the true *Roman* Foot; and that for these reasons:

For first, it most exactly agrees with some very antient and perfect *Roman* feet in brass, found long since amongst the *rudera* at *Rome*; especially with that excellent one (as I remember) of *F. Ursinus*, a learned Antiquary. Tho' I cannot deny but that I have seen two ancient feet in brass, different from this; the one of *Gualdus*, a very fair one, wanting two parts and an half of such as this contains 1000, a small and inconsiderable difference: the second of *Gottifridus*, a gentleman of honourable quality (to whom I stand obliged for the free donation of several antiquities) which exceeds it by eight parts; but this last hath been made by a very rude and unskilful hand.

Next, the proportions of almost all the white marble stones, as also of those lesser in porphyry, in the pavement of that admirable temple of the *Pantheon*, are either completely three of these feet, or one and an half; which, it is not probable, in a structure of so much art, should have been the work of chance. Add to this the dimensions of several stones, in the foundation

tion of the *Capitol*, in *Titus* and *Severus*'s triumphal arcs, correfponding either to the whole foot, or conjointly to the whole, and fome *unciæ* or digits of it.

Thirdly, the infcription on the fame monument where this foot is found, of the *circinus*, the *libella*, the *norma*, and the like, plainly fhew that thefe were intended to exprefs *Coffutius*'s profeffion, whom (y) *Pætus* imagines to have been a Sculptor; and this being intended, I fee no reafon why the *Roman* foot fhould have been cut in fo fair a relevy, either too fhort or too long, when the fame hand, and the fame pains might have made it exact. It is true, that the foot upon *Statilius*'s tomb, is 1944 fuch parts as this is but 1934, whereof the *Englifh* foot taken by me from the iron yard, or ftandard of three feet in *Guildhall* in *London*, contains 2000; but how rudely, in refpect of digits, that foot of *Statilius* is defcribed, I have before difcovered. And therefore I wonder that (z) *Philander*, in his Commentaries upon *Vitruvius*, fhould in a matter of fuch high concernment in Architecture, proceed with fo much inadvertency, affirming, that be-

---

(y) Luc. Pætus, l. 1. de Antiq. Rom. & Græc. interval. menfuris.

(z) Philand. in l. 3. c. 3. Vitruvii.

224 Of the Roman Foot.

tween this of *Statilius*, and that of *Coſſutius*, there is no difference. And if he, a Mathematician, hath thus erred (tho' commonly men verſed in thoſe ſciences, take not up things at too cheap a rate, without due examination) what opinion may we conceive of another obſervation, made at the ſame monument by (*a*) *Ant. Auguſtinus, Jo. Baptiſta Sighicellus, P. Octavius Pacatus, Achilles Maffæus, Achilles Statius, Benedictus Ægius, Fulvius Urſinus, Latinus Latinius*, with as many ancient feet, as there were men preſent? I ſhrewdly ſuſpect they ſlubbered over their obſervation, as not regarding in nineteen hundred parts, and better, the ſmall exceſs or defect of ten parts; or not rightly apprehending what might be the conſequences of ſuch an error, how little ſoever, in meaſuring the vaſt magnitude of the terreſtrial globe, or of the celeſtial bodies.

Laſtly, beſides the authorities of *Portius Vicentinus, Georgius Agricola, Glareanus, Ghetaldus, Donatus*, and of many other learned and judicious men, who approve of this *pes Colotianus*, (tho' bare authority is the worſt, becauſe the weakeſt kind of argument) that excellent *congius* of *Veſpaſian*, now extant in *Rome*, ſo highly and ſo

---

(*a*) Ciaconius è Latini Latinii Obſerv. de Pede Rom.

juſtly

justly magnified by *(b) Villalpandus*, may likewise serve to confirm, if not totally, my assertion, yet thus far, that I have not exceeded in assigning the true longitude: For by the clear evidences of *(c) Dioscorides*, and of an *anonymous Author* before cited, eight *congii* are the just measure of the *Roman amphora*, or *quadrantal*; and again, by as many testimonies of *(d) Sextus Pompeius*, and *(e) Rhemnius Fannius*, each of the sides of the *amphora* is equal in longitude to the *Roman* foot. Wherefore having procured by special favour the *congius* of *Vespasian*, I took the measure of it with *(f) milium*, (being next to water, very proper for such a work) carefully prepared and cleansed; which being done with much diligence, I caused a cube to be made answerable to the true dimension of the *pes Colotianus*; filling up the capacity of which, and often reiterating the same experiment, I found continually the excess of about half a *congius* to re-

(b) Villalpandus l. 2. Disp. 2. c. 11. de Apparatu Urbis ac Templi.
(c) Fragmenta Dioscoridis.
(d) Sext. Pomp. Festus de Verb. signif.
(e) Rhemn. Fann. carm. fragm.
(f) It had been better to have made my experiment with water, and then to have weighed it with an exact balance; but because no balances are found in *Rome* so exact as with us, I was fain to measure it with *milium*.

main, and that an *amphora* made by the *pes Colotianus* would contain but seven *congii* and about an half. And therefore I cannot sufficiently wonder at the observation of (g) *Ant. Augustinus, Pacatus, Maffæus, Statius, Urfinus,* and others, with a cube of that foot which is described on *Statilius's* monument; who affirm the *quadrantal* of this exactly to contain eight of these *congii* of *Vespasian*: whereas upon due examination, I confidently affirm that they have erred. And therefore (h) *Villalpandus* in this particular, with more judgment and ingenuity, hath published his observation concerning the measure and precise weight of *Vespasian's congius*, than any other whatsoever. Altho' I cannot be induced to assent to that deduction, which he infers of the *Roman* foot (from the side of a *quadrantal* containing eight of these *congii*) relying upon the authorities of *Festus* and *Fannius*, against so many evidences produced to the contrary. Wherefore as he is singular in his opinion (for there is

---

(g) Ciaconius è Latini Latinii Observationibus de Pede Rom. Cùm veram pedis Rom. quantitatem statuere vellent, ejusd. pedis mensuras simul contulerunt, & earum octo cum antiquissima dicti pedis forma, quæ in basi quadam in hortis Vaticanis exstat, adamussim convenire videntes, ex hoc pede quadrato vas confecerunt, &c. Vide supra.

(h) Villalpand. de Apparatu Urbis ac Templi. par. 2. lib. 3. cap. 25.

not one author of credit which follows his assertion) so is his foot as singular, there being not one, of at least ten ancient ones in the hands of several antiquaries (besides those inscribed on two monuments in *Rome*) which arrive to the proportions of his, by 27 parts in 2000. As for those other fancies of his (for they are no better) of describing also the *Roman* foot by the altitude of *Vespasian*'s *congius*, and assigning the *(i) latus cubicum* of the *modius*, the *semicongius*, the *sextarius*, and *hemina*, from certain parallel circles circumscribed about it (which certainly, as the scheme of the *congius* it self, drawn by me to the full proportion, shews, were delineated without any farther intention than for ornament) I do not think them worth the confutation.

And therefore it will be much better to give some solution to those authorities of *Sextus Pompeius*, and *Rhemnius Fannius*, alledged by him. For the objection which may be raised thence, is very material; How the *pes Colotianus* can be the true *Roman* foot, since it is confessed by me, that it doth not precisely answer to the sides of a *quadrantal*, or cube, containing eight of those *congii* of *Vespasian*, or forty eight *sextarii*?

(i) Vides etiam latus cubicum modii, semicongii, sextarii, heminæ, &c. Villalpand. ib.

Whereas on the contrary, *Festus* expresly writes, that the *quadrantal* was the square (he means the cube) of the *Roman* foot. (k) *Quadrantal vocabant Antiqui, quam ex Græco amphoram dicunt, quod vas pedis quadrati, octo & quadraginta capit sextarios.* And (l) *Fannius* confirms the same:

Pes longo spatio, latóque notetur in anglo,
Angulus ut par sit, quem claudit linea triplex.
Quattuor ex quadris medium cingatur inane:
Amphora fit cubus: quam ne violare liceret,
Sacravere Iovi Tarpeio in monte Quirites.

We might elevate their authorities, by saying, these are only the testimonies of two Grammarians, better versed in disputes of words, than critical in measures, which more properly are the speculation of Mathematicians; and therefore if *Vitruvius* had affirmed it, much more credit might have been given. But we shall rather say, they wrote what was vulgarly and commonly upon tradition believed, that the length of one of the sides of the *amphora* was equal to the *Roman* foot: not that it was precisely and exactly equal, but that of any known measure whatsoever then extant, this came the nearest to it, as indeed

(k) Sext. Pomp. Festus de Verb. signif.
(l) Rhemn. Fann. carmina de Pond. & Mensuris.

it doth; yea, ſo near, that if at this day the *amphora* and *Roman* foot were in uſe amongſt us, many a writer that had never been ſo curious, as diligently to compare them, would not be ſcrupulous to affirm as much. Which may appear by the practiſe of *Ant. Auguſtinus, Pacatus, Maſ‐ fæus, Statius, Urſinus,* and of ſeveral other learned men, not long before our times; who, tho' they purpoſely made it their en‐ quiry to diſcover the true *Roman* weights and meaſures, and therefore made ſpecial uſe of this *congius* of *Veſpaſian*, yet have no leſs erred, as we ſhewed before in the dimenſion of the *amphora*, than both *Feſtus* and *Fannius* have done. Neither will this anſwer ſeem improbable concerning mea‐ ſures, if we ſhall examine a place or two concerning coins, in which the ancients, and thoſe too of the better ſort of authors, have in the very ſame manner erred. For (*m*) *Livy* writing, that *Marcellus* gave to *L. Bantius* (or *Bandius*) 10. *bigati,* that is, *denarii* (ſo called becauſe the *biga* was or‐ dinarily ſtamped upon the reverſe of the *denarius*); (*n*) *Plutarch* deſcribing the ſame gift, renders it by ſo many *drachmæ*, the

---

(*m*) Liv. l. 23.
(*n*) Plutarchus in Marcello.

Grecian manner of computation; not that the *drachma*, in the exact and intrinsecal valuation, was equal then to the *denarius*, or the *denarius* to the *drachma* (as we shall shew in the ensuing discourse) but that in the vulgar and popular estimation the one passed for the other, being both not much different in their weight, as well as valuation. Likewise *(o) Dio* informs us, that *Octavius* promised the *Veteran* soldiers 10. *drachmæ* a man: whereas *(p) Cicero* expressing the same thing to *Atticus*, terms them 10. *denarii*. And *Suetonius* writes, that *Cæsar* by testament gave to each of the common people *sestertia trecenta*, that is, seventy-five *denarios*, which *(q) Plutarch*, both in the life of *Brutus*, and of *Antonius*, renders δραχμὰς ἑβδομήκοντα πέντε, *seventy-five drachmes*. In like manner we may say, that *Festus* and *Fannius* have described the *amphora* by the *Roman* foot; not as if this were the exact measure of it, but as being the most known, and nearest proportion, in which, without falling into fractions, it might evenly and roundly be expressed.

(o) Dio. l. 45. in Cæs. Octav.
(p) Cic. l. 16. 8. ep. ad Atticum.
(q) Plut. in Bruto. Idem in Antonio.

And

Of the Roman Foot.

SEMIPES. ROM.

And thus have we finished our enquiry after the *Roman* Foot: our next labour should be to compare it with the present standards and originals for measures of divers nations. For which I must refer the Reader to this ensuing table.

Of the Roman FOOT.

The Roman FOOT compared with the Measures of divers Nations.

		hundr. pts
THE foot on the monument of *Statilius* in *Rome* contains	1005	17
The foot of *Villalpandus*, deduced from the *congius* of *Vespasian*, contains	1019	65
The ancient *Greek* foot being in proportion to the ancient *Roman* foot, as 25 to 24, contains	1041	67
The *English* foot	1034	13
The *Paris* foot	1104	45
The *Venetian* foot	1201	65
The *Rhinland* foot, or that of *Snellius*	1068	25
The *derah* or cubit at *Cairo* in *Ægypt*	1886	25
The *Persian* arish	3306	10
The greater *Turkish* pike at *Constantinople*	2275	08
The lesser *Turkish* pike at *Constantinople* is in proportion to the greater, as 31 to 32.		
The braccio at *Florence*	1908	28
The braccio for woollen at *Siena*	1284	38
The braccio for linnen at *Siena*	2041	37
The braccio at *Naples*	2071	66
The canna at *Naples*	7114	79
The vara at *Almaria* and at *Gibraltar* in *Spain*	2854	19
Il palmo di Architetti at *Rome*, whereof 10 make the *canna di Architetti*	756	98
Il palmo del braccio di Mercantia, & di Tessito di Tela at *Rome*; this and the former are both ingraven in a white marble stone in the *Capitol* with this inscription, *Curante Lu. Pæto*	719	24
The *Genoa* palm	842	81
The *Antwerp* ell	2360	91
The *Amsterdam* ell	2345	40
The *Leyden* ell	2337	13

Such parts as the *Roman* Foot, or that on the monument of *Cossutius* in *Rome*, contains 1000.

Of the Roman FOOT.

The English FOOT, *taken from the Iron-Standard at* Guild-hall *in* London, *and compared with the Standards for Measures of divers Nations.*

Such parts as the English foot contains 1000,	THE *Roman* foot, or that on the monument of *Coffutius* in *Rome*, contains	967
	The foot on the monument of *Statilius* in *Rome* contains	972
	The foot of *Villalpandus*, deduced from the *congius* of *Vespasian*, contains	986
	The *Greek* foot	1007 $\frac{42}{100}$
	The *Paris* foot	1068
	The *Venetian* foot	1162
	The *Rhinland* foot, or that of *Snellius*	1033
	The derah or cubit at *Cairo* in *Ægypt*	1824
	The *Persian* arish	3197
	The greater *Turkish* pike at *Constantinople*	2200
	The lesser *Turkish* pike at *Constantinople* is in proportion to the greater, as 31 to 32.	
	The braccio at *Florence*	1913
	The braccio for woollen at *Siena*	1242
	The braccio for linnen at *Siena*	1974
	The braccio at *Naples*	2100
	The canna at *Naples*	6880
	The vara at *Almaria* and at *Gibraltar* in *Spain*	2760
	Il *palmo di Architetti* at *Rome*, whereof 10 make the *canna di Architetti*	732
	Il *palmo del braccio di Mercantia, & di Tessito di Tela* at *Rome*; this and the former are both ingraven in a white marble stone in the *Capitol*, with this inscription, *Curante Lu. Pæto*	695 $\frac{1}{2}$
	The *Genoa* palm	815
	The *Antwerp* ell	2283
	The *Amsterdam* ell	2268
	The *Leyden* ell	2260

☞ *This Table I made by the Standards, the former by Proportion.*

OF THE
DENARIUS.

AS I have made for Measures the *Roman* foot the foundation of my enquiry, and therefore have handled it in the precedent Treatise: so for finding out of Weights, I shall take the *denarius* as an undeniable principle, from whence those of the antients, by a necessary consequence, may be inferred. For as the unity is in respect of numbers, or the *sestertius* in discourses *de re nummariâ*; so is the *denarius*, for weights, a fit rise or beginning, from whence the rest may be deduced. Not but that it were better (as I gave the caution before) if we absolutely consider the exactest ways of discovering weights, to begin with the greater, and by them to find out the less, than by the less to produce the greater; but if we look upon the condition of times,

and

and consider the means that are left after so many revolutions and changes of the *Roman* Empire, it will be safer to alter our method: for to this day there are many thousand *denarii* left, and, amongst these, some so perfect and entire, as if they had been but newly brought from the mint; whereas of the *Roman libræ*, and ounces, there are but few extant, if compared with these. *Lipsius* and *Gruterus* in their inscriptions mention some, and *Pætus* some others, besides such as I have seen in the hands of Antiquaries, and many of mine own; most of which differ from one another, either as having been consumed by rust and time, or it may be also by the men that then lived, for their advantage lessened; a thing too often practised amongst us. Wherefore I think it more convenient by the *denarius* to deduce the proof, and evidence of these, than by the diversity and uncertainty of these to conclude the *denarius*: and yet if some of the best and fairest of them shall agree with this, I shall think my self so much the more assured.

Now seeing the *denarius* may be consider'd in a double respect, either as *nummus*, or as *pondus*: in the first acception, the valuation of it in civil affairs is remarkable; in the latter, the gravity and pon-

ponderousness: I shall speak no farther of the former, than as it may conduce in some sort to illustrate the latter. The *denarius* was a silver coin in use amongst the *Romans*, passing at the first institution for *dena æra*, or ten *asses*. And so *(a) Vitruvius* expresly writes: *Nostri autem primò decem fecerunt antiquuum numerum, & in denario denos æreos asses constituerunt.* The same thing is attested by *(b) Volusius Metianus: Denarius primò asses decem valebat, unde & nomen traxit.* *(c) Pliny*, besides a confirmation of the same valuation, assigns also the time in which it was first stamped: *Argentum signatum est anno Urbis (d) quingentesimo octogesimo quinto, Q. Fabio consule, quinque annis ante primum bellum Punicum, & placuit denarius pro decem libris æris;* that is, for ten *asses*. For the *asses*, both then, and under the first Consuls, were *librales*. *Dionysius Halicarnasseus:* Ἦν δὲ ἀσσάριον, χάλκεον νόμισμα, βάρος λιτραῖον· *The assis was a brass coin, weighing a pound.* Where by the way it is worth the observation, the strange, and, in my opinion, the unadvised proportion betwixt the

(a) Vitruv. l. 3. c. 1.
(b) Vol. Metianus de Assis distributione.
(c) Plin. l. 33. c. 3.
(d) Budæus (l. v. de Asse) corrects these numbers by *Livy* (l. xxx.) and reads them 478.

brass and silver monies of those times: that ten pounds of brass should be but answerable to the 84th part (for so much, or near it, was the *denarius*) of a pound of silver; or to speak more clearly, that one pound in silver, should be equal in valuation to 840 pounds in brass. Neither can there be any excuse of that error, unless this, that there then was an infinite plenty of the one, and as great a scarcity of the other. However it were, the same proportion is testified by *Varro*, who farther adds, that the *Romans* took the first use and invention of the *denarius* from the *Sicilians*: (e) *In argento nummi, id à Siculis, denarii quòd denos æris valebant*. And according to this valuation, the *denarius* had an impress upon it of the figure X, denoting the *decussis*, or number of the *asses*, as *Valerius Probus* witnesses, and sometimes this character X̶; both which I have seen, and can shew in several ancient ones. This latter, by the ignorance of scribes formerly in MSS. and of our printers of late in the edition of *Celsus*, and of *Scribonius Largus*, is represented by an asterisc *; and by a worse error in the same authors, the figure X expressing the *denarius* as a *pondus*, is confounded with the figure X expressing

(e) Varro l. 4. de Ling. Lat.

a number.

Of the DENARIUS. 239

a number. From this figure on the *denarius*, or *decuffis*; (f) *Vitruvius* calls the interfections of lines, *decuffes*, and *decuffationes*; and (g) *Columella* ufeth the phrafe *in ftellam decuffari*, when lines meet diamond-wife, or lozenge-like, as thefe in the character X or ✡. Neither did the *denarius* long pafs at the valuation of ten *affes*, nor the *affes*, which before and then were *librales*, continue at one ftay, but with the exigencies of the *Roman* State the rate of the *denarius* rofe, and the weight of the *affes* fell; that is in effect, both the filver and the brafs monies came to be augmented in their eftimation. For by a publick edict of *Fabius Maximus* the Dictator, the Common-wealth being hardly preffed upon by *Hannibal*, the *denarius* came to be priced at fixteen *affes*, and the *affes* which were then *fextantarii*, or the fixth part of the *Roman* pound (for in the firft *Punick* war, by reafon of the exceffive expenfes of the ftate, they firft fell from being *librales*, to be *fextantarii*) came now in the fecond *Punick* war to be *unciales*. The whole progrefs, and manner of this alteration, is by none fo well and fully

(f) Vitruv. l. 10.
(g) Columella l. 5.

expreft,

exprest, as by (*h*) *Pliny*, and therefore I shall a little insist upon his words: *Silver, says he, came to be coined in the 585th year of the City,* Q. Fabius *being Consul, five years before the first* Punick *war, and then the* denarius *passed for ten pounds of brass, the* quinarius *for five, the* sestertius *for two pounds and an half. The weight of the* assis *in brass, was diminished in the first* Punick *war, the Common-wealth not being able to support the expenses; and then it was decreed that the asses should be coined* sextantario pondere; *that is, with the weight of the sixth part of a pound, or two ounces, whereas before they were* librales. Tho' *Alciatus* here, upon a very gross mistake, contends that they were then coined *dextantario pondere*, and not *sextantario*, but yet that they were called *asses sextantarii*, because the *sextans*, or sixth part of an ounce was wanting. Whereas (*i*) *Festus* expresly writes: *Grave æs dictum à pondere, quia deni asses singuli pondo libræ efficiebant, denarium ab hoc ipso numero*

(*h*) Argentum signatum est Anno Urbis DLXXXV. Q. Fabio Cos. quinque annis ante primum bellum Punicum. Et placuit denarius pro X libris æris, quinarius pro quinque, sestertium pro dupondio ac semisse. Libræ autem pondus æris imminutum bello Punico primo, cum impensis Resp. non sufficeret, constitutumque ut asses sextantario pondere ferirentur. Plin. l. 33. c. 3.

(*i*) Sext. Pompeius Fest. de verb. signif.

dictum:

dictum: sed bello Punico populus Romanus pressus ære alieno, ex singulis assibus libralibus senos fecit, qui tantundem valerent. And these words of *Pliny*, which immediately follow those before recited, put it out of controversy: (*k*) *Whereby,* says he, *five parts were gained, and the debts (of the Commonwealth) discharged.* I would gladly see by what arithmetick *Alciatus* can demonstrate, that the Common-wealth shall gain five parts, making the *asses sextantarii* in his sense; whereas on the contrary, taking them in this interpretation (as both (*l*) *Agricola* and (*m*) *Villalpandus* do) it is a thing most evident. For the whole pound, or *asses*, before consisting of twelve ounces, being now reduced to two ounces, and these two passing at as high a rate in the valuation of things vendible, as the whole *libra* did, it is plain that the Commonwealth by this diminution of weight, keeping the same constant tenure of the estimation of the *asses*, gained ten parts in twelve, that is, five in six; and not one in six, as *Alciatus* would have it. But to omit this digression, and to re-

---

(*k*) Plin. l. 33. c. 3. Ita quinque partes factæ lucri, dissolutumque æs alienum.

(*l*) Agricola l. 2. de Pondere & Temperat. Monetarum.

(*m*) Villalp. de Appar. Urbis ac Templi. par. 2 lib. 2. Disp. cap. 9.

turn to *Pliny*. (n) *Afterwards being oppress'd by* Hannibal, *under* Q. Fabius Maximus *the Dictator, the* asses *were made* unciales, *and the* denarius *passed for sixteen* asses, *the* quinarius *for eight, and the* sestertius *for four. And hereby the Common-wealth gained half; yet in the pay of the Militia, the* denarius *was always accounted for ten* asses. *The impress of the silver* (that is, of the *denarius*) *were the* bigæ, *and* quadrigæ; *from whence they are called* bigati, *and* quadrati. *Not long after, by the* lex Papiria, *the* asses *came to be* semunciales. Livius Drusus, *Tribune of the people, mixed an eighth part of brass with the silver.* Thus far *Pliny*. Out of which words it is most evident (omitting many passages of his, worth our consideration) that as the *denarius* at the first institution passed for ten *asses*, so afterwards it was valued at sixteen. And *Vitruvius* gives a reason, why next to ten, they made choice of sixteen, rather than of twelve, or any other proportion: (o) *Quo-*

(*n*) Postea Hannibale urgente, Q. Fabio Maximo Dictatore, asses unciales facti: placuitque denarium x.vi. assibus permutari, quinarium octonis, sestertium quaternis: Ita Resp. dimidium lucrata est. In militari tamen stipendio semper denarius pro x. assibus datus. Notæ argenti fuere bigæ atque quadrigæ, & inde bigati quadrigatique dicti. Mox lege Papiria semunciales asses facti. Livius Drusus in Tribunatu plebis octavam partem æris argento miscuit. Plin. l. 33. c. 3.
(*o*) Vitruv. l. 3. c. 1.

Of the DENARIUS. 243

niam animadverterunt utrosque numeros esse perfectos, & sex, & decem, utrosque in unum conjecerunt, & fecerunt perfectissimum decussissexi; where *(p) Budæus* reads *decussissexis*, but *(q) Villalpandus decussi sex*, that it may the better, as he imagines, answer to the Greek δέκα ἕξ. *(r) Hujus autem rei*, saith *Vitruvius, autorem invenerunt pedem. E cubito enim cùm dempti sint palmi duo, relinquitur pes quatuor palmorum; palmus autem habet quatuor digitos, ita efficitur uti pes habeat sexdecim digitos, & totidem asses æreos denarius.* (s) *Metianus* also purposely treating of this argument, after that he had related that the *denarius*, at the first institution, was valued at ten *asses*, adds, *now it is worth sixteen*. And not to cite more authorities, the impress of XVI, as well as of X, found upon several *denarii*, and seen both by *(t) Antonius Augustinus* (a man very accurate in coins, as appears by his Dialogues) and by *Villalpandus*, besides one with the inscription of *C. Titinius* with the same character, mentioned by *Fulvius Urfinus* and *(t) Dalechampius*, puts it out

---

(p) Budæus. l. 5. de Asse.
(q) Villalp. de Apparatu Urbis ac Templi.
(r) Vitruv. l. 3. c. 1.
(s) Vol. Metianus de Assis Distrib.
(t) Anton. August. Dialogo. 1.
(u) Dalechampius in Plin. l. 33. c. 3.

of controversy; and this valuation of the *denarius*, as it is more than probable, continued from the first institution of it in the second *Punick* war, without any interruption to *Justinian*'s time, and it is likely longer, since there is no proof out of any ancient author, nor any character on any ancient *denarius*, found to the contrary. As for those authorities which are alledged and pressed by *Budæus* and *Alciatus*, of *Varro*, *Apuleius*, *Arruntius*, and *Pompeius*, affirming, that after the second *Punick* war, the *denarius* contained ten *asses*, the *quinarius* or *Victoriatus* five, the *sestertius* two and an half; we may give a true and easy solution, that these writers expressed the valuation of them, as they were in their first original and beginning, with reflection to their primitive denomination; in which respect, the *Treviri monetales*, or officers of the mint, usually imprinted on the *denarius* the character X, rather than XVI, the former being the impress of its first institution, and the latter of its after-valuation. And so in like manner may those citations be answer'd of *Plutarch*, *Dionysius*, and others, produced by some learned men to strengthen their assertion, that the *denarius*, after the second *Punick* war, returned to its first estimation. Which thing could not

not have been effected, without extreme loss and prejudice to particular men, in their private fortunes and estates; which the justice and wisdom of the *Roman* Senate, under the Consuls, was not likely to have introduced, or the people to have admitted.

To conclude: The *denarius*, as it is evident by many irrefragable authorities before alledged, in the highest valuation passed for sixteen *asses*, and, according to that proportion, the *quinarius* or *Victoriatus* for eight, the *sestertius* for four: but in the lowest valuation, or first institution, it passed for ten *asses*; and then the proportion of the *quinarius* was five, of the *sestertius* two *asses* and an half, and therefore was thus marked, IIS, or thus, HS; as the *quinarius* had this character, V, and also this, X, as it is to be seen in a *Victoriatus* of mine own (besides several others) with the face and inscription of *M. Cato*. By which coin that place may not unfitly be explained, which troubled (*x*) *Budæus*, why the *ordo decussatus* and *ordo quincuncialis* signify in the ranking of trees the same thing, although the *quinarius* or *quincunx* give the denomination to the one, and the *denarius* or *decussis* to the other. The reason is, because the *quinarius*

(*x*) Budæus l. 1. de Asse.

had the character X imprinted on it, as well as the *denarius* or *decuſſis*. Besides, in (*y*) *Temporarius* we find the *quincunx* to be thus ∶-∶ repreſented, as the *uncia* thus, -; ſo that five of theſe *unciæ* making the *quincunx*, and theſe five being ranged like the figure X (the character of the *decuſſis*) it is no wonder if the *ordo decuſſatus* and *quincuncialis* were taken for the ſame.

That the *denarius* ſhould have paſſed at any other rate between ſixteen and ten *aſſes*, as there is no coin extant to prove it, ſo there is no expreſs authority to conclude it. Though ſome infer out of (*z*) *Polybius*, that it was valued alſo at twelve *aſſes*; becauſe he defines the ἡμιασσάριον, or *ſemiſſis*, to be τέταρτον μέρος ὀβολῦ, *the fourth part of the* Attick *obolus*; and ſix *oboli* being in the δραχμὴ, to which *drachma* they ſuppoſe the *denarius* equal, therefore there muſt be twenty four *ſemiſſes*, or twelve *aſſes*, in the *denarius*. But with much better reaſon we may hence infer, that the *drachma* was ſomewhat bigger than the *denarius*, as we ſhall prove in this enſuing diſcourſe; and therefore *Polybius* allows twelve *aſſes* to it: whereas if it had been preciſely equal to the *denarius*, he would have valued it at ten, or elſe ſixteen of the leſſer ſort of *aſſes*. So

(*y*) Cod. MS. Temporarii.   (*z*) Polyb. lib. 2.

that

that Sir *H. Savile*, a man of exquisite judgment and learning, in his discourse at the end of *Tacitus*, justly blames *Hottoman* for altering the text of *Polybius*; and is himself to be censured, as also (*a*) *Lipsius*, in inferring thence, that the *denarius* contained twelve *asses*.

The several parts of the *denarius*, excepting the *quinarius* and *sestertius*, of both which I have spoken before, are all comprized in this description of (*b*) *Varro*, with which I shall conclude. *Nummi denarii decima libella, quòd libram pondo as valebat, & erat ex argento parva; sembella, quòd sit libellæ dimidium, quòd semis assis. Teruncius à tribus unciis sembellæ quod valet dimidium, & est quarta pars sicut quadrans assis.* By which proportions it appears, that the *libella* was the tenth part of the *denarius*, when it was current at ten *asses*, the *sembella* the twentieth, the *teruncius* the fortieth. And thus much of the *denarius*, as it is *nummus*.

The second, and our principal consideration of the *denarius*, is, as it is *pondus*. In which acception it will be necessary to premise a second distinction, that the *denarius*

(*a*) Lipsius Elector. 1. c. 2.
(*b*) Varro lib. 4. de Ling. Lat.

was either (*c*) *Confularis* or *Cæfareus*. The *Confularis* was that which was made under the government of the city by the Confuls, the *Cæfareus* under the *Cæfars*. The *Confularis* (I mean, the *Confularis* after the second *Punick* war, and under the later Confuls) contained precifely the feventh part of the *Roman* ounce, as the other did the eighth part, or fomewhat near it.

Firft, that the *denarius Confularis* of the later Confuls was the feventh part of the *Roman* ounce: This fhall be our principal enquiry, becaufe it is more evident of the two, and will give us the beft light to difcover the true weight of the *denarius*, in the notion and acception of the ancients, both *Greeks* and *Latins*. It is moft apparent, both by feveral fair coins which I have perufed of

---

(*c*) The *Confularis* again may be confidered, either in the time of the former or of the later Confuls. That of the former Confuls, at the firft inftitution of it by *Q. Fabius*, five years before the firft *Punick* war, *Peireskius* not improbably imagines to have been the fixth part of the *Roman* ounce: and *Agricola* by comparing it with the *talentum Atticum*, which *Varro* values at 15000 *feftertii*, and with the *tetradrachme*, which *Livy* (*lib.* 34.) eftimates *trium fere denariorum*; as alfo upon the authority of the fcholiaft of *Nicander*, who equals the *denarius* to a drachm and an half, as *Prifcian* doth to a drachm and a third part; I fay, *Agricola* affigns to it almoft the fame proportion with *Peireskius*. But becaufe I have feen no *denarii Confulares* of fo great antiquity, and thefe authorities may perchance admit of other conftructions, I fhall leave this opinion as only probable, and follow what is more certain and demonftrative, of the later Confuls.

the

Of the DENARIUS. 249

the later Confuls, as alfo by *Cornelius Celfus*, who lived in the beginning of the *Roman* Emperors, before there happened a general diminution of the *denarius*, that it was then the feventh part of the ounce, who thus writes: (*d*) *Sed & antea fciri volo in unciâ pondus denariorum effe feptem.* The fame proportion is alfo expreffed by (*e*) *Scribonius Largus,* who lived not long after *Celfus*, as fome imagine; his words are thefe: *Erit autem nota denarii unius pro Græcâ drachmâ; æquè enim in librâ denarii octoginta quatuor apud nos, quot drachmæ apud Græcos incurrunt:* (*f*) *Pliny* alfo confirms the fame: *Mifcuit denario triumvir Antonius ferrum, alii* (he means under the Emperors) *è pondere fubtrahunt, cùm fit juftum octoginta quatuor è libris fignari.* Out of which words of his, and of *Scribonius Largus*, it will by a neceffary confequence be inferred, that the true weight of the *denarius Confularis* is the feventh part of an ounce. For if we multiply twelve, the number of the ounces in the *Roman libra* (as by all it is confeft) by feven the number of the *denarii*, of which the ounce then confifted, the fum will be eighty-four *denarii*; and fo many, fay *Scribonius*

(*d*) Celfus lib. 5. c. 17.
(*e*) Scribon. Largus in Præfatione.
(*f*) Plinius l. 33. c. 9.

and

and *Pliny*, ought juftly to be in the *Roman* pound. And thefe are the only clear and pofitive authorities that are to be found in claffical authors; moft of the writings of the ancients *de ponderibus & menfuris* having long fince been loft; or elfe thofe few fragments that are left of *Cleopatra, Diofcorides,* and of others, are fo corrupted, that little truth with any certainty can be collected. From whence it will by way of corollary follow, that if either the *denarius Confularis* be given, the *Roman* ounce and *libra* in the fame proportion will neceffarily be thence deduced; or, if the *Roman* ounce and *libra* be given, the *denarius* will as neceffarily be concluded.

But before we farther treat of this argument, we fhall endeavour alfo to demonftrate the *denarius* by the *drachma Attica.* For *Scribonius* feems, and fo do other ancients, to make them equal. And therefore *Pliny* writes: (g) *Drachma Attica denarii argentei habet pondus:* whereas the *drachma Æginæa* was much larger, this containing ten fuch *oboli,* as the *Attick* contained fix; and therefore the *Athenians,* in hatred of the *Æginæans,* called it παχεῖαν δραχμὴν, as (h) *Pollux* teftifies. And here as we

(g) Plin. lib. 21. cap. 34. (h) Jul. Poll. l. 9. c. 6.

confidered

considered the *denarius* as *nummus*, and as *pondus*; so likewise must we take the *drachma Attica* as *nummus*, and as *pondus*: in the prosecution of both which relatively to the *denarius*, I shall insist so much the longer, because it is an argument that hath scarce at all, or very perfunctorily been handled. The *drachma*, as *nummus*, was a silver coin in use amongst the *Athenians* (for I intend only to speak of the *drachma Attica*, for the same reason that *Pliny* doth: (*i*) *Ferè enim Attica observatione utuntur medici*) and so it was the measure of things vendible, as all coins are: and as *pondus*, so was it the measure of their gravity and weight. Now the *drachma*, as *nummus*, passed in the estimation of the best authors, both *Greek* and *Latin*, at the same rate and valuation as the *denarius* did. And therefore as often as the *Latins* are to express the *Greek drachma*, they render it by the *denarius*, and on the contrary, the *Greeks* the *denarius* by the *drachma*. Thus what (*k*) *Tully* renders by the *denarius*, *Dio* in his 45*th* book expresseth by the *drachma*. Their words, both speaking of *Augustus*, are these: *Veteranos quique Casilini, & Calatiæ sunt* (as *Tully* relates) *perduxit ad suam*

(*i*) Plin. l. 21. c. 34.   (*k*) Cic. 16. l. 8. ep. ad Attic.

t 4   *sententiam;*

sententiam; nec mirum, quingenos denarios dat. Καὶ ἔδωκεν εὐθὺς τότε, saith *(l) Dio,* κατὰ πεντακοσίας δραχμάς. In like manner *(m) Pliny* writes: *Veniſſe murem ducentis nummis,* (that is, *denariis;* for *nummus* abſolutely put is often, though not always, taken for the *denarius,* as on the contrary, the *denarius* is taken for *nummus* in *Heſychius: (n)* Δενάριον τὸ νόμισμα, ἢ εἶδος ἀργυρίʉ.) *Caſilinum obſidente Annibale, eúmque qui vendiderat fame interiſſe, emptorem vixiſſe annales tradunt.* The ſame thing *(o) Valerius Maximus* reports in his 7*th* book, and 6*th chap.* and *(p) Strabo* in his 5*th* book; the former writing, that it was ſold for 200 *denarii,* and the latter, that it was bought for 200 *drachmæ.* To theſe authorities I ſhall adjoin *'q) Cleopatra :* Τὸ Ἰταλικὸν δηνάριον ἔχει δραχμὴν ἁ· *The* Italian *denarius containeth one drachma.* And *(r) A. Gellius: Lais* μυρίας δραχμὰς ἢ τάλαντον *popoſcit, hoc facit nummi noſtratis denariûm decem millia.*

Theſe two thus paſſing the one for the other, being alſo at the firſt inſtitution much of the ſame fineneſs in reſpect of ſilver, it muſt neceſſarily be admitted, either that

---

(l) Dio lib. 45. *(m)* Plin. lib. 8. cap. 57. *(n)* Heſychius in voce δηνάειον. *(o)* Val. Maxim. lib. 7. cap. 6. *(p)* Strabo lib. 5. Geograph. *(q)* Fragmenta Cleopatræ. *(r)* Aul. Gellius lib. 1. c. 8. Noct. Att.

they

they were exactly the same for weight, which is our next enquiry, or else that they were not much different. For in comparing of foreign coins, the κολλυβιϛαὶ, or *nummularii*, in ancient times, must have taken the same course which our most knowing bankers do practise now. First, to respect the pureness and fineness of the coins, whether they be alike for the *intrinseck*; and next, whether they have the same weight; and if they differ in either, or both of these, according to those differences to proportion their exchanges. Those other accidental causes of the rising and falling of exchanges of monies, since they are meerly contingent, depending upon the necessities either of times, or places, or persons, I purposely pretermit, as not so proper and essential to our enquiry. As for the *extrinseck* of coins, by which I mean the outward form or character, and inscription of the prince or state, though this may raise the valuation of them in those countries which are subject to the prince or state, and lessen them in those which are out of their dominions; yet this can produce no remarkable difference, more than what is usually assigned by the masters of the mint for the waste in coining, and for the labour of the work.

With

With these cautions if we shall examine the *Attick drachma*, and by such writings of the ancients, or by such coins as are extant, enquire their true weight, we shall come to such a precisenefs, as may be hoped for in a work of this nature. (s) *Suidas* tells us in general, Δραχμὴ δὲ ὁλκὴ νομίσματος ἀργυρίȣ· *The drachma is the weight of the silver money.* And (t) *Hesychius* more particularly informs us, Δραχμὴ τὸ ὄγδοον τῆς ȣ̓γγίας· *The drachma is the eighth part of the ounce.* And (u) *Fannius* yet more distinctly writes,

In scrupulis ternis drachmam, quo pondere doctis
Argenti facilis signatur pondus Athenis.

To which we may add (x) *Cleopatra*: Ἡ δραχμὴ ἔχει γράμματα γ´. ὀβολȣ̀ς ϛ´. θερμȣ̀ς θ´. κεράτια ιη´. χαλκȣ̀ς μη´· *The drachma hath three scruples, six oboli, nine lupini, eighteen siliquæ, forty-eight æreola.* The (y) *Scholiast* of *Nicander* also makes the δίδραχμον to be τὸ τέταρτον τῆς ȣ̓γγίας, *the fourth part of the* [Attick] *ounce.* In the same proportion are we to take those other silver *Athenian* coins mentioned by (z) *Julius Pollux*,

---

(s) Suidas in voce δραχμή. (t) Hesychius in voce δραχμή. (u) Rhemn. Fann. (x) Fragmenta Cleopatræ. (y) Scholiastes Nicandri. (z) Jul. Poll. l. 9. c. 6.

Of the Denarius) 255

namely, the τρίδραχμον, which consisted of three drachmes; the τετράδραχμον, or τέτραχμον, which by a syncope is the same with the τετράδραχμον, containing four drachmes, or the half ounce. Τέτραχμον, τετράδραχμον, saith (*a*) *Hesychius*; though (*b*) *Ammonius* puts a distinction between 'em. τέτραχμον μὲν γὰρ ἐςὶ τὸ νόμισμα, τετράδραχμον ἢ τῶν τεσσάρων δραχμῶν [ἄξιον.] This the *Greeks* also called ςατὴρ, as (*c*) *Cleopatra* and (*d*) *Epiphanius* witness. Ὁ ςατὴρ, in *Cleopatra*, ἄγει δ. καλοῦσι ἢ αὐτὸν τετράδραχμον. *The stater weighs four drachmes; this they call the tetradrachme.* And this also may most clearly be collected out of (*e*) St. *Matthew*, where, seeing the original expresseth it more fully than our translation, I shall recite the words as they are in the *Greek*. Ἐλθόντων ἢ αὐτῶν εἰς Καπερναὺμ, προσῆλθον οἱ τὰ δίδραχμα λαμβάνοντες τῷ Πέτρῳ, καὶ εἶπον, ὁ διδάσκαλος ὑμῶν ὒ τελεῖ τὰ δίδραχμα; which the vulgar renders thus: *Et cùm venissent Capernaum, accesserunt, qui didrachma accipiebant, ad Petrum, & dixerunt ei, Magister vester non solvit didrachma?* and our translation thus: *And when they were come to Capernaum,*

(*a*) Hesychius in voce τέτραχμα. (*b*) Ammonius περὶ ὁμοίων κ διαφόρων λέξεων. (*c*) Fragmenta Cleopatræ. (*d*) Epiphanius περὶ ςαθμῶν. (*e*) Matth. cap. 17. v. 24.

they

they that received tribute-money came to Peter, and said, Doth not your Master pay tribute? In the 27th verse of the same chapter, our Saviour answers: Ἵνα μὴ σκανδαλίζωμεν αὐτὸς, πορευθεὶς εἰς τὴν θάλασσαν βάλε ἄγκιςρον, καὶ τὸν ἀναβαίνοντα πρῶτον ἰχθὺν ἆρον, καὶ ἀνοίξας τὸ ςόμα αὐτῦ, εὑρήσεις ςατῆρα· ἐκεῖνον λαβὼν δὸς αὐτοῖς ἀντὶ ἐμῦ καὶ σῦ. *Notwithstanding, lest we should offend them, go thou to the sea, and cast an hook, and take up the fish that first cometh up: and when thou hast opened his mouth, thou shalt find a piece of money; that take, and give unto them for me and thee.* This, which our translation calls *tribute-money* in the 24th verse, is called in the original δίδραχμον, or *two drachmes*; and so much was paid by the poll, according to (*f*) *Josephus*, for each particular person. Our Saviour therefore paying for himself and St. *Peter*, in the 27th verse, bids him to give a *stater*, that is, a τετράδραχμον, or *four drachmes*, namely, the double to the δίδραχμον, which our translation renders too generally by *a piece of money*: but the (*g*) *Persian* translation interprets it distinctly by *four drachmes:*

جهل درم سره بيابى انرا بيارى عوض منه عوض تو بده ۞

Thou shalt find four drachmes in it, that take, and give for thee and me.

(*f*) Joseph. lib. 1. de bell. Jud. c. 27.   (*g*) Evangelia Persi.
MSS. eruditissimi viri D. Pocockii.

With

Of the DENARIUS. 257

With this *Attick tetradrachme*, or silver *ſtater*, the *Hebrew* and *Samaritan* שקר *ſhekel*, that is, *ſicle*, did alſo agree. For if we give credit to *Joſephus*, who in (*h*) *Scaliger*'s eſteem is, *diligentiſſimus καὶ Φιλαληθέςατος omnium ſcriptorum*, we ſhall find them to be the ſame. (*i*) Ὁ ὃ σίκλος νόμισμα Ἑβραίων ὧν Ἀττικὰς δέχεται δραχμὰς τέσσαρας *The* ſicle *is a ſort of mony amongſt the* Hebrews, *that contains four* Attick *drachmes*. The ſame proportion is evidently collected out of (*k*) *Philo*, where for fifty ſhekels mentioned in the law, he renders two hundred drachmes; and for thirty, an hundred and twenty. (*l*) *Heſychius* likewiſe teſtifies as much: Σίκλος τετράδραχμον Ἀττικὸν, *the ſicle is* [in valuation] *the* Attick *tetradrachme*. And (*m*) St. *Hierom*, the ableſt of the Fathers in the *Jewiſh* Antiquities, tells us, (*n*) *Siclus, id eſt ſtater, habet quatuor drachmas Atticas*. Theſe

---

(*h*) Scalig. σερλεγομ. in libr. de Emend. Temp.
(*i*) Joſephus lib. 3. Antiq. Judaic.
(*k*) Philo de Decalogo.
(*l*) Heſychius in voce σίκλ℗.
(*m*) Hieronym. in Ezek 3.
(*n*) Such ſicles, I conceive, were thoſe τειακοντα ἀργύεια, *the thirty pieces of ſilver*, which were given to *Judas* as the reward of his treaſon. *Euſebius* relating the ſtory, expreſly terms them *ſilver-ſtaters*, which an *Hebrew* would have termed כסף *ceſef*, this in the ſcripture phraſe being frequently put for the ſhekel; and therefore the *Syriack* tranſlation of the New Teſtament reads it כספא. Whence *Tremellius* hath this

Of the DENARIUS.

These testimonies are so positive, and from so good authors (to which also I might adjoin (*o*) *Epiphanius*, in his book περὶ ςαθμῶν, did I not conceive him to be full of errors in that discourse) that I cannot sufficiently wonder at that strange opinion of (*p*) *Grsepsius*, and some others, introduced out of affectation of novelty, of a double *shekel*, the one sacred, equal to the *tetradrachme*, the other profane,

---

this annotation: *Observant Hebræi, ubicunque in Scripturis argenteorum fit mentio, non expressâ numismatis argentei specie, intelligi siclum sanctuarii æquivalentem quatuor denariis.* Some modern writers imagine them to have been but thirty *denarii*; but *Baronius* contends that they were, *vel librarum argenti triginta, vel aureorum coronatorum trecentorum*; and *Arias Montanus*, that they were either *triginta libræ*, or *triginta talenta*. The most probable opinion is, that this sum was neither so great as *Baronius* and *Montanus* make it, nor yet so little as some moderns would have it, but between both, and that is, *thirty shekels*. M. *Casaubon*, in his Exercitations upon *Baronius*, hath a probable conjecture to strengthen this assertion: *Non enim temerè factum videtur, quòd filius Dei qui sese exinanivit, assumptâ servi formâ,* (Phil. 2. 7.) *triginta argenteis venderetur, sicut lege Dei mancipia totidem siclis æstimantur* (Exod. 21. 32.) *Et apud* Josephum, (*l.* 4. *c.* 8.) *Facit hoc quoque non parum ad Domini abjectionem declarandum, quando caput ejus tam parvi æstimatum est.* A small price, I confess, thirty shekels being less than fifteen of our ordinary crowns. But *Hierome* upon St. *Matthew* thought it to be as little, who thus writes, as M. *Casaubon* renders him: *Infelicem Judam non cogitasse quanti pretii rem venderet: sed Christum mundi Salvatorem, Dei filium, ceu vile aliquod mancipium minimo pretio addixisse.* Now the price of a servant we find in *Exodus* to have been thirty shekels.

(*o*) Epiphanius περὶ ςαθμῶν.
(*p*) Grsepsius de multiplici Siclo, & Talento.

weighing

weighing the *didrachme*; that used in the Sanctuary, this in Civil Commerce, without any solid foundation in the writ, or without any probability of reason, that in any wise state the prince and people should have one sort of coin, and the priests should have another; and that this of the Sanctuary should be in a double proportion to the other, and yet that both should concur in the same name. It is true, there is often mention in the (*q*) Scriptures of the *weights of the Sanctuary*, not as if these were different from what were used vulgarly in the city, but because the standards and originals, the rules of commutative justice, and therefore of an high and sacred use, were kept (as it is more than probable) in the Sanctuary; for God himself makes this one of the priest's offices, (*r*) *ut sint super omne pondus atq; mensuram*. And it is no wonder that God, who so much hated a (*s*) *false balance*, and a *false measure*, should commit the charge of these to the priests, as things most holy; since the heathens themselves, out of a reverent estimation of them, placed them in their temples, as appears by that inscrip-

(*q*) And all thy estimation shall be according to the shekel of the Sanctuary. *Levit.* 27. v. 25. *Vet. vulg.* Siclo Sanctuarii ponderabitur. (*r*) 1 *Paral.* 23. 29.
(*s*) *Prov.* 11. 1. Item cap. 20. v. 10. 23.

tion of the *congius* of *Vespasian* before alledged, and now extant in *Rome*; and by these verses of (*t*) *Fannius*, treating of the *Roman* measures:

Amphora fit cubus, quam, ne violare liceret,
Sacravere Iovi Tarpeio in monte Quirites.

And afterwards in the times of Christianity, they were kept in churches, as it is to be seen in the (*u*) *Authenticks of Justinian*, where he commands, that the weights and measures should be kept, *in sacratissimâ cujusvis civitatis ecclesiâ*. As for those allegations, taken out of the interpretation of the LXX. whereby *Grsepsius* and others go about to prove a double *shekel*, they are all well and solidly, in my judgment, answered by (*x*) *Villalpandus* and others, to whom I shall refer the judicious Reader: For I intend not here to speak of the *Hebrew shekel*, or *Attick drachme*, more than what may serve to illustrate the *denarius*.

Seeing therefore, as we have proved, that the *Attick drachma* was equal in the notion and acception of the ancients, to the

---

(*t*) Rhemn. Fann. Carmina de Pond. & Mensuris.
(*u*) Authen. collat. 9. de Collatoribus tit. 11. novel. 128. c. 15. (*x*) Villalpand. de Appar. Urbis ac Templi. par. 2. lib. 2. disp. 4. c. 28. Item par. 2. lib. 2. disp. 4.

denarius;

denarius; if therefore an entire, either *Attick* δραχμὴ, or δίδραχμον, or τετράδραχμον were found, we might thence conclude the *denarius*. Again, since the *Hebrew shekel* hath likewise been demonstrated to be equal to the *Attick* τετράδραχμον, and this *Attick* τετράδραχμον to four *denarii*, by the common and received *(y)* axiom of Geometricians we may conclude, that the *Hebrew shekel* was also equal to four *denarii*; that is, that four *Roman denarii*, the *Attick* τετράδραχμον, and the *Hebrew* שקל, were all respectively equal to one another. If therefore an *Hebrew shekel*, fair and entire, were found, we might as necessarily thence infer the *denarius*, as by the τετράδραχμον.

We shall endeavour by both these to enquire out the truth, and first, by the *Attick tetradrachmes* in silver; because of these I have seen and weighed many, some of them very fair and perfect, and found at many several places, as *Athens, Constantinople, Tenedos,* and other parts: where the art of counterfeiting coins is not as yet crept in, and where it is to little purpose to practise it, seeing in those places there are few so curious as to buy them,

---

(y) Quæ eidem æqualia, sunt æqualia inter se. Eucl. axiom. 1. l. 1.

or that will give a greater valuation, than what they are worth in the *intrinsick*. Wherefore having in *Italy*, and elsewhere, perused many hundred *denarii Consulares*, I find, by a frequent and exact trial, the best of them to amount to sixty-two grains *English*, such as I have carefully taken from the standards of the *Troy* or silver weights kept in the Tower of *London*, in *Goldsmiths-hall*, and in the University of *Oxford:* on the other side weighing many *Attick tetradrachmes*, with the image of *Pallas* on the fore part, and of the *noctua* on the reverse, I find the best of these to be two hundred sixty-eight grains, that is, each particular *drachme* sixty-seven grains.

And that no man may doubt whether these were true *Athenian tetradrachmes*, we are to observe, that the ancients used several impresses on their coins, by which they might be known and distinguished. And therefore *argentum signatum*, in the description of *Quintius*'s triumph over *Philip*, is by (z) *Livy* opposed to *argentum infectum*, which (a) *Pollux* terms ἄσημον; as (b) *Tully* calls the former sort *factum atque signatum*, and the (c) *Greeks* ἐντετυπωμένον. Thus the *denarius* had the impress of the

---

(z) Liv. l. 34. (a) Jul. Pol. l. 9. c. 6. (b) Cicer. 6. Verr. (c) Jul. Pol. l. 9. c. 6.

biga,

biga, or *quadriga*, as *Pliny* informs us; and therefore (d) *Livy* uses the word *bigati* for *denarii*, and (e) *Pliny* both *bigati* and *quadrigati*. The brass coins of the *Romans* were thus marked: (f) *Nota æris fuit ex alterâ parte Janus geminus, ex alterâ rostrum navis, in triente vero & quadrante rates.* The *Persians* stamped on the reverse an (g) archer, which occasioned that conceit of *Agesilaus*, mentioned by (g) *Plutarch, That the King of* Persia *had beaten him back with ten thousand archers*, when with so much money he had corrupted the *Grecians*. The *Carthaginians*, on the one side signed the face of a woman, (I suppose in memory of Queen *Dido*) on the reverse the head of an horse, or, in *Virgil*'s expression, (i) *caput acris equi*, both which I have seen. The *Peloponnesians* had the impress of a tortoise on their money, whence that witty *Greek* proverb took its original: (k) Τὰν ἀρετὰν, καὶ τὰν σοφίαν νικᾶντι χελῶναι. The money at *Tenedos* had on the one side a double hatchet, and on the other side two heads, one of a man, and another of a woman, arising from the same stem, or neck, in memory of a law

---

(d) Liv. l. 34. (e) Plin. l. 33. c. 3. (f) Plin. ib.
(g) Plutarchus in Artaxerxe. Τὸ ᵹ Περσικὸν νόμισμα τοξίτην ἐπίσημον εἶχεν. (h) Plut. Agesil.
(i) Virg. 1. Æneid. (k) Jul. Pol. l. 9. c. 6.

264 Of the DENARIUS.

made by the King of that island (whom (*l*) *Heraclides* names Τέννης, placing him ancienter than the *Trojan* war) that a man and a woman, taken in adultery, should have their heads struck off with an hatchet. In which kind I met with two very rare and ancient coins in silver, at *Constantinople*, both made with a very fair relevy, and both agreeing in the same image and inscription; the one weighed less than the *Attick tetradrachme*, the other wanted somewhat of the *drachme*. And because the coin hath not, I think, been seen by any antiquary, and the history is remarkable, I shall here express the figure of the fairest of these.

And the history I shall relate out of (*m*) *Heraclides*. Νόμον δέ τινά φασι τὸν βασιλέα Τέννην διαθέσθαι, εἴ τις λάβοι μοιχὸν ἀποκτείνειν τοῦτον πελέκει. ἁλόντος ἢ τῦ υἱοῦ αὐτῦ, καὶ τοῦ λαβόντος ἐρομένο τὸν βασιλέα τί χρὴ ποιεῖν, ἀποκρίνασθαι τῷ νόμῳ χρῆσθαι. καὶ

(*l*) Heraclides περὶ πολιτειῶν.
(*m*) Heraclides περὶ πολιτειῶν.

διὰ

διὰ τῆτο τῦ νομίσματος ἀυτῦ ἐπὶ θάτερα πέλεκυς κεχάρακται, ἐπὶ θάτερα ἢ ἐξ ἑνὸς ἀυχένος πρόσωπον ἀνδρὸς καὶ γυναικός. καὶ ἐκ τῆτυ λέγεται ἐπὶ τῶν ἀποτόμων, τὸ ἀποκεκόφθαι Τενηδίῳ πελέκει. *They say, King Tennes made a law, that if one took another in adultery, he should kill him with an hatchet. His son being found so, and he that took him asking the King what he should do, he answered, Execute the law: and for this reason, of one side of his money there was an hatchet imprinted, on the other the face of a man and of a woman, arising out of one neck. From hence it is said of severe actions, to be cut with a* Tenedian *hatchet.* For which exemplary justice, those of *Tenedos*, as it is probable, deified King *Tennes*. (n) *Tully* writes, *Tenedij Tenem Deum appellant:* and again, *Tenem apud Tenedios putant esse sanctissimum Deum, ac eorum urbem condidisse;* where his name is truer writ, than in *Heraclides.* For the coin hath only a single N, and so hath (o) *Eustathius.*

The money of *Chios*, as *Julius Pollux* witnesses, had the *effigies* or resemblance of *Homer*, no doubt in honour of his memory; though (p) *Herodotus* relates, that

(n) Cicer. lib. 3. de Natura Deorum.
(o) Eustathii παρεκβολαὶ εἰς τ̄ ἁ ῥαψωδ. Ιλιαδ.
(p) Herodot. in vita Homeri.

whilst he was living, he found at first but cold entertainment in that island. *Theseus*, the tenth King of the *Athenians*, signed his money with the impress of an ox; hence that proverb, βοῦς ἐπὶ γλώσσῃ βέβηκεν. This, as (*q*) *Julius Pollux* testifies, was the δίδραχμον: who farther adds, τὸ ἢ παλαιὸν τοῦτο ἦν Ἀθηναίοις νόμισμα, καὶ ἐκαλεῖτο βοῦς ὅτι βοῦν εἶχεν ἐντετυπωμένον. εἰδέναι ἢ αὐτὸ καὶ Ὅμηρον νομίζουσιν εἰπόντα, ἑκατόμβι' ἐν- νεαβοίων. καὶ μὲν κἂν τοῖς Δράκοντος νόμοις ἔςιν ἀποτείνειν δεκάβοιον, καὶ ἐν τῇ παρὰ Δη- λίας θεωρίᾳ τὸν κήρυκα κηρύτ7ειν φασὶν ὁπότε δωρεάν τινι ἐδίδοτο, ὅτι δοθήσονται αὐτῷ τοσοῦ- τοι βόες. καὶ δίδοσθαι καθ' ἕκαςον βοῦν δύο δραχμὰς Ἀττικάς. *This was an ancient coin amongst the* Athenians, *and was called* βοῦς, *because it had the figure of an ox instamped. They imagine that* Homer *knew this, when he said, nine hecatombs of oxen; and also in the laws of* Draco, *it is to pay the mulct of ten oxen. And they say, that at the solemn shew at* Delos, *the crier, when any gift is to be given, cries so many oxen shall be given, and for every ox, so many* Attick *didrachmes are given.* The same (*r*) author writes, that the *Attick tetradrachme* was stamped with the face of *Minerva*, and he might have added, with the *noctua* on the re-

(*q*) Jul. Pol. l. 9. c. 6.   (*r*) Jul. Pol. ibid.

verse.

Of the DENARIUS.

verſe. This (s) *Eubúlus* pleaſantly calls Παλλάδος πῶλον, *Minervæ pullum.* The Διώβολον had the face of *Jupiter* (it may be it is an error in *Pollux,* for *Pallas*) and on the other ſide the *noctua.* The τετρώβολον had on the one ſide *Jupiter,* according to *(t) Pollux* (I conceive it to be a miſtake for *Pallas* or *Minerva*) on the other ſide two *noctuæ,* becauſe it was the double to the διώβολον. From the *diobolum,* (u) *Plautus* uſes the term *diobolaris ſervorum ſordidulorum, ſcorta diabolaria;* which (x) *Feſtus* interprets thus, *meretrices diobolares appellatas, ex eo quòd duobus obolis ducerentur.* To which I may adjoin, out of ſuch ancient coins as I have ſeen, that the *triobolum* (whence that phraſe of *(y) Plautus, homo trioboli,* and of the *Greeks,* ἄξιος τριωβόλε) which by (z) *Pollux* is called the ἡμίδραχμον, had the face of *Pallas* on the one ſide, and the *noctua* on the other; and ſo likewiſe had the *obolus* and *drachma,* of ſuch as I peruſed, and all of them on the reverſe the inſcription ΑΘΕ. And I think I may ſafely add, that on ſuch coins as we find the *noctua,* with a deep relevy, we may

(s) In Anchiſe. (t) Jul. Pol. l. 9. c. 6. (u) Plautus in Pœnulo. (x) Sextus Pompeius Feſtus de Verb. ſignif. (y) Plautus in Pœnulo. (z) Jul. Pol. l. 9. c. 6.

conclude them to be *Athenian* coins. (a) *Plutarch* is of the same opinion, in the life of *Lysander*, where he discourses of *Gylippus* a commander, as famous for defeating the *Athenians* in *Sicily*, as infamous for stealing the silver consigned to him by *Lysander* for the city *Sparta*. *When he arrived*, saith Plutarch, *at Sparta, he hid the silver that he had stolen, under the tiles of his house, and delivered into the hands of the* Ephori *the bags, shewing them the seals* [intire]: *Which being opened, and the money told, they found the sums to disagree from the labels: wherewith being troubled, a servant of* Gylippus, *in obscure terms intimated to them, that under the tiles of his master's house there were hid many* noctuæ, *or owls;* ἦν γὰρ (ὡς ἔοικε) τὸ χάραγμα τȣ̃ πλείςȣ τότε νομίσματος, διὰ τȣ̀ς Ἀθηναίȣς γλαȣ̃κες. *For the greatest part (as it seems) of the money then had the stamp of the* noctua, *by reason of the* Athenians; who not long before, as *Thucydides* and the best historians of those times shew, were the richest and most flourishing state amongst the Grecians.

Having therefore had the opportunity to have bought, or else the favour to have weighed, many fair and perfect *Attick tetradrachmes*,

---

(a) Plutarchus in Lysandro.

Of the DENARIUS. 269

tradrachmes, found at remote places, with the *Pallas galeata* on the one side, and the *noctua* with the inscription ΑΘΕ on the reverse, where E being placed for H proves the antiquity of them: (for the *Atticks* at the first used not H, but only E, for both E and H) I find by the best of these (to re-assume what I said before) that the *Attick tetradrachme* is 268 grains, and the *drachme* 67 of our *Troy* or *English* standard: which may farther be confirmed by an *Attick drachme* of mine own, found in the *Black Sea*, with this inscription, ΑΘΕ ΤΙΝΑΡΝΙΚΑ ΑΡΧΕ, and by a (b) τριώβολον, or *semidrachme* bought by me at *Alexandria*, that weighing near 66 grains, and this 30 and better: the face of *Minerva*, either by use or time, being a little diminished in both; but yet so little, that they cannot have lost above 2 or 3 grains of their primitive weight. And as this single *Attick drachme* of mine is much to be valued by antiquaries for the weight, and therefore was desired by the learned *Piereskius*; so is the inscription ΤΙΝΑΡ-ΝΙΚΑ ΑΡΧΕ no less worth consideration,

---

(b) I have since perused a fair *Athenian* τετώβολον of my very worthy and learned friend, *John Marsham* Esq; weighing completely thirty-three grains *English*; as also another of Sir *Thomas Roe's*, together with an ὲβολὲς of his, weighing eleven grains.

for the explication of a place in (*c*) *Livy*: who describing the naval triumph of *L. Æmilius*, writes thus: *Pecunia translata nequaquam tanta pro specie regii triumphi. Tetracina Attica* CCXXXIII *millia, Cistophori* CCCXXII *mill.* Where (*d*) *Budæus* and *Rhodiginus*, instead of *tetracina*, read *tetradrachma. Tetracinum enim quid sit, nemo, ut arbitror, novit,* saith *Budæus*: I would rather read it, as the coin doth, *Tinarnica*, this having almost the same letters with *Tetracina*, which by the scribes, I suppose, have been inverted. Neither is there any reason, why *Livy* might not as well mention in this triumph, *Attica Tinarnica*, as *Tetradrachma*; these being the fourth part of the *tetradrachme*, and therefore better agreeing with his description: *Pecunia translata nequaquam tanta pro specie regii triumphi*; and also better agreeing with the *Cistophori* he here mentions, a sort of coin about half of these *Attica Tinarnica*, whereas the *tetradrachma* were eight times as great. For (*e*) *Festus* expressing the *talentum Euboicum*, renders it by 7500 *cistophori*, and by 4000 *denarii*, or *Attick drachmes*, that is CIƆ. *tetradrachmes: Euboicum ta-*

(*c*) Livius l. 37. (*d*) Bud. l. 2. de Asse. Rhodigin. Lect. Antiq. l. 10. c. 2. (*e*) Sextus Pompeius Festus de Verb. signif.

lentum

Of the DENARIUS. 271

lentum nummo Græco septem millium & quingentorum cistophorûm est: nostro quatuor millium denariorum.

And as these testimonies above alledged are beyond all exceptions, so the gold coins of the *Grecians*, which I have examined, do most evidently prove this proportion assigned to the *Attick drachme*. Which, that we may the better understand, we are to observe what proportion the valuation of the gold of those times had to the silver; and next, what proportion it had in respect of weight.

For the first, (f) *Julius Pollux*, in very perspicuous terms puts it down: Τὸ ἢ χρυσίον ὅτι τῶ ἀργυρίω δεκαπλάσιον ἦν σαφῶς ἄν τις ἐκ τῆς Μενάνδρω παρακαταθήκης μάθῃ. *That the gold was in a tenfold proportion to the silver, one may evidently learn out of* Menander's Paracatathece. (g) The *Scholiast* of *Aristophanes* implies as much: Εἰσὶ μὲν χρυσοῖ ςατῆρες οἱ Δαρεικοί. ἐδύνατο ἢ ἕκαςος αὐτῶν, ὅπερ ὁ παρὰ τοῖς Ἀττικοῖς ὀνομαζόμενος χρυσῦς, ἐκ ἀπὸ Δαρείω τῶ Ξέρξω πατρὸς ἀλλ' ἀφ' ἑτέρω τινὸς παλαιοτέρω βασιλέως ὠνομάσθησαν. Λέγωσι δέ τινες δύνασθαι τὸν Δαρεικὸν δραχμὰς ἀργυρίω εἴκοσιν. ὡς τὺς πέντε Δαρεικὺς δύνασθαι μνᾶν ἀργυρίω. *The* Darics *are golden staters, each of them is worth as much*

(f) Jul. Pol. l. 9. c. 3. (h) Scholiastes Aristophanis.

as

as that which is named by the Atticks the χρυσῦς. They are called so, not from Darius the father of Xerxes, but from another King more ancient than he. Some say, that the Daric is valued at twenty drachmes of silver, so that five Darics are worth a mina of silver. For the *Attick* μνᾶ, or *mina*, containing an hundred *drachmes* in weight, as it is very clear out of (*b*) *Pliny*, (*i*) *Pollux*, and others: *Mna* (saith *Pliny*) *quam nostri minam vocant, pendet drachmas* Atticas *centum*: And *Pollux*, Ἡ μνᾶ ἡ παρ' Ἀθηναίοις ἑκατὸν εἶχεν δραχμὰς Ἀττικὰς: The mina, with the Athenians, containeth an hundred Attick *drachmes*: and the χρυσῦς Δαρεικός, or ϛατὴρ χρυσῦς of *Darius*, consisting of two *drachmes* in weight, as we shall presently prove; it will necessarily follow, that the proportion of the δραχμὴ χρυσίο, was to the δραχμὴ ἀργύριο in *decuplâ ratione*; and therefore that five *Daricks*, or ten *drachmes* of gold, were equal in valuation to an hundred *drachmes* in silver, that is, to the μνᾶ. The same proportion may be collected out of (*k*) *Polybius*, when the *Romans*, upon a sum of money to be received, concluded a peace

---

(*b*) Plin. l. 21. c. 34.   (*i*) Jul. Pol. l. 9. c. 3.
(*k*) Polybii ἐκλογαὶ περὶ πρεσβειῶν, c. 28. Ex Biblioth. Fulvii Ursini, Ant. 1582.

with

Of the DENARIUS. 273

with the *Ætolians.* Ἀντὶ τρίτε μέρες τȣ͂ ἀργυρίȣ χρυσίȣ, χρυσίον ἐὰν βȣ́λωνται διδόντες τȣ͂ δέκα μνῶν ἀργυρίȣ, χρυσίȣ μνᾶν. Which words (*l*) *Livy* renders thus: *Pro argento si aurum dare mallent, dare convenit, dum pro argenteis decem aureus unus valeret.* This being granted, as certainly of neceffity it muſt, I would correct that place of (*m*) *Hesychius*, concerning the δραχμὴ χρυσίȣ, and read it thus: Δραχμὴ ᾗ χρυσίȣ ὁλκὴ νομίσματος εἰς ἀργυρίȣ λόγον δραχμῶν ι´. and not διδράχμων ι´. as it is in the printed copies. And by this of *Hesychius*, I would fupply the defect of (*n*) *Suidas*, who writes: Δραχμὴ ᾗ ὁλκὴ νομίσματος εἰς ἀργυρίȣ δραχμὰς ι´. and make it thus: Δραχμὴ ᾗ χρυσίȣ ὁλκὴ νομίσματος εἰς ἀργυρίȣ λόγον·δραχμὰς ι´. For without the addition of χρυσίȣ, and λόγον, there is no ſenſe: and I believe *Suidas* took theſe very words out of *Hesychius*.

Having thus found the proportion that the δραχμὴ χρυσίȣ had to the ſilver, our next inquiry is, how many of theſe *drachmes* in weight the χρυσȣ͂ς, or χρυσȣ͂ς ςατὴρ, or *aureus* contained. (*o*) *Julius Pollux* gives us in this particular the beſt and moſt poſitive

(*l*) Liv. l. 38. ἔρα ᾗ τοῖς Ἕλλησιν κ´ δραχμῶν τὸ χρυσȣ͂ν ἀλλάτ]εται νόμισμα. Zonaras.
(*m*) Hesychius in voce δραχμή.
(*n*) Suidas in voce δραχμή. (*o*) Jul. Pol. l. 4. c. 24.

information of any: Ὁ ἢ χρυσᾶς ςατὴρ δύο εἶχε δραχμὰς. Ἀττικάς. *The golden* stater [*or* aureus] *contains two* Attick *drachmes*. The same is confirmed by (*p*) *Hesychius*: Πολέμαρχος φησὶ δυνάσθαι τὸν χρυσᾶν παρὰ τοῖς Ἀττικοῖς δραχμὰς δύο· τὴν ᾖ τᾶ χρυσᾶ δραχμὴν νομίσματος ἀργυρίᾰ, δραχμὰς δέκα· *Polemarchus says, that the* aureus *amongst the* Athenians *contains two drachmes, and that the drachme of gold is worth ten drachmes of silver*. And to this of *Pollux* and *Hesychius* all the *aurei* of the ancient *Grecians*, which have passed through my hands, do very well correspond. Now these *aurei*, as they had several impresses upon them, so had they several names by which they are distinguished: for they were either Ἀττικοὶ, or Δαρεικοὶ, or Φιλίππειοι, or Ἀλεξάνδρειοι, or the like; all which we may prove by *Xenophon*, (*q*) *Harpocratio*, the Scholiast of *Aristophanes*, and others, to have been equal to two *Attick drachmes*, and therefore respectively equal to one another. Neither is this much to be wonder'd at, that the *Gre-*

(*p*) Hesychius in voce χρυσᾶς.

(*q*) Λέγυσι δέ τινες δύνασθαι τ̄ Δαρεικὸν ἀργυρᾶς δραχμὰς κ′ (as *Joseph Scaliger* rightly corrects the printed copies, which render it ή or ὀκτὼ) ὡς τὺς πέντε Δαρεικὺς δύνασθαι μνᾶν ἀργυρείᾰ. Harpocr. Τετρᾰκίλιοι Δαρεικοὶ Xenophonti sunt δέκα τάλαντα. Talentum autem 600 drachmæ. Ergo Δαρεικὸς sunt 20 drachmæ. *Scal. de re Num.*

cians

cians and *Persians*, though at enmity amongst themselves, yet should agree in the *aurei*; seeing that in our times the *Venetian chequeen*, the *Barbary ducat*, the *Ægyptian* and *Turkish sherif*, are almost all of the same pureness in respect of the gold, and not differing above a grain in the weight; which difference we may also allow to those of the ancients, without any prejudice to our inquiry. Concerning these *aurei*, or golden *staters*, the observation of (r) *Julius Pollux* is worth our consideration: Καὶ οἱ μὲν Δαρεικοὶ ἐκαλοῦντο ςατῆρες, οἱ ἢ Φιλίππειοι, οἱ ἢ Ἀλεξάνδρειοι, χρυσοῖ πάντες ὄντες, καὶ εἰ μὲν χρυσοῦς εἴποις προσακούεται ὁ ςατήρ, εἰ ἢ ςατὴρ εἴποις πάντως ὁ χρυσοῦς· *Of the* staters *some were denominated from* Darius, *some from* Philip, *some from* Alexander, *and were all of gold: and when you say the* aureus, *the* stater *is understood; but if you say the* stater, *the* aureus *is not always meant.* And this is most true; for the χρυσοῦς, or *aureus* (I speak not here of the *aureus Romanus*, this being somewhat less than these mentioned by *Pollux*) did always imply the ςατήρ, but the ςατὴρ did not always infer the *aureus*: the *stater* being more general, signifying as well the *argenteus* as the *aureus*, and that was double to this; the *stater argenteus* be-

(r) Jul. Pol. l. 9. c. 6.

ing

ing *four drachmes*, as we proved before, and therefore the same with the *tetradrachme*; and the *aureus* two *drachmes*, and therefore equal in weight to the *didrachme*. Wherefore every *aureus* was rightly called a *stater*, but every *stater* could not rightly be called an *aureus*.

From these *aurei* then, or χρυσοῖ ϛατῆρες, we may deduce the silver *Attick drachme*, if we either had the Δαρεικοὶ, some of which to this day are found in *Persia*; or if we had the Φιλίππειοι, or the Ἀλεξάνδρειοι. To pass by the Δαρεικοὶ, because I have not perused any of them, and to speak only of the Φιλίππειοι and Ἀλεξάνδρειοι, of which there are many extant.

Concerning the Φιλίππειοι, (s) *Snellius* writes thus: *Philippi nummum unicum, & Alexandri Macedonum, solertissimus veterum nummorum æstimator Nicolaus Rockoxius possidet, utrumque eodem pondere granorum* 179. Now one hundred seventy-nine grains of gold in *Holland*, such as *Snellius* used, are answerable to an hundred thirty-four grains *English*, and an half. Near which proportion, I have observed two others, with the inscription ΦΙΛΙΠΠΟΥ, excepting only a grain or two.

(s) Snellius de re Nummaria.

Of the DENARIUS. 277

As for the Ἀλεξανδρεινοὶ, I find the weight of one of the fairest for impression and character, I think, in the world, which I bought at *Alexandria*, with the image and inscription ΑΛΕΞΑΝΔΡΟΥ, to be exactly of *English* grains 133½, and another at *Constantinople* 133, and in the same proportion several others. With which comparing one of mine honoured and learned friend, *John Marsham* Esq; I find his a grain defective: and weighing since some others, out of that choice and rare κειμήλιον of ancient coins, collected by the noble Sir *Simonds D'Ewes*, Knt. Bart. I observed two of his to exceed 133, by half a grain.

Wherefore I may conclude (allowing only half a grain for so much wanting by time, or by the mint) from the *aureus* being double to the *Attick drachme*, that it hath been rightly assigned by me to be sixty-seven grains; and from this, with those limitations abovementioned, I may conclude the *denarius Consularis*, (which is our principal enquiry) seeing (*t*) *Galen*, l. 8. c. 3. *de Compositione Medicam.* according to the *Latin* manner of division, speaking of an antidote prescribed by *Asclepiades*, whereof the *dosis* was to be one *drachme*, or *denarius*,

(*t*) Galenus l. 8. de Compofit. Medicam.

writes thus: Ἡγῦμαι ἢ λέγειν αὐτὸν δραχμὴν ἀργυρᾶν, καὶ γὰρ ὕτω σχεδὸν ἅπασι τοῖς νεωτέροις ἰατροῖς ἔθος ὀνομάζειν. ἄλλο ἢ νοεῖν ἡμᾶς ὐδὲν ἡ τῦ πράγματος φύσις ἀναγκάζει. πρόδηλον δ' ὅτι δραχμὴν λέγομεν νῦν ἐν τοῖς τοιὑτοις ἅπαντες, ὅπερ Ῥωμαῖοι δηνάριον ὀνομάζυσιν. *I suppose that he means the silver* drachme, *for so all the later Physicians are wont to call it, neither will the nature of the thing suffer us to understand any other. And it is manifest, that in such things as we all now name the* drachme, *the* Romans *name the* denarius.

The *denarius* also, as we proved before out of *Philo*, *Josephus*, Saint *Hierome*, and *Hesychius*, may be inferred by the *Hebrew* or *Samaritan shekel*; the *shekel*, by the joint testimony of all of them, being equal in valuation to the *Attick stater argenteus*, or *tetradrachme*; and the *Attick tetradrachme*, as we have shewed, to *quatuor denarii Consulares*. If therefore an *Hebrew* or *Samaritan shekel* in silver, fair, and not impaired, were found, we might by this as well discover the *denarius*, as by the *tetradrachme*, or the *aureus*. And here I must confess I have not seen so many perfect and entire, with the *Samaritan* characters, which certainly are the best and truest (for those with the later characters,

invented,

Of the DENARIUS. 279

invented, as some suppose by *Esdras*, are most of them counterfeit) as to give my self satisfaction. For though I have perused that of *Arias Montanus*, now in the University of *Oxford*, which he describes in his tract *de Siclo*, and from whence he deduces the proportion of the *Hebrew shekel*, yet, to speak the truth, there is no trust to be given to it: Not but that the coin is very ancient, and the inscription upon it in *Samaritan* characters well made; but the sides of it have been so filed away, that it hath very much lost of the true weight: for I find it to be scarce the weight of twenty pence of our *English* standard. Whereas *Montanus*, if he made his observation exactly, equals it to almost four *Spanish rials*, or to four *Roman Julio's*, both which exceed two of our *English* shillings. So that till such time as I may procure out of the East (whither I have often sent) some perfect *shekels*, I must be content to take up the relations of others. And here I shall begin with *Moses Nehemani Gerundensis* a Jew, a learned expositor of the *Pentateuch*, who, as *Arias Montanus* tells us, flourished in *Catalonia* above 400 years since. His words, as *Montanus* hath delivered them in his tract *de Siclo*, are these: (*u*) *In comment. Exod.* 39. *multis verbis differens, significabat, se non facile ad Salomonis Iarrhæi, qui ante illum in Galliâ scripserat, sententiam de siclo accedere; cum Salomon affirmasset, Siclum esse dimidiam argenti unciam. Postea jam absoluto in omnem Legem Commentariorum opere, idem Moses Gerundensis capite ad eam rem propriè addito, sicli æstimationem à Salomone illo indicatam, re ipsâ doctus, ingenuè, & apertè, ut viros doctos, & veri inveniendi atque docendi cupidos decet, comprobavit. Narrat autem se eo anno, quo illa scriberet, in Palæstinam ex Hispaniâ sacrorum locorum visendi causâ navi delatum Acconam, quam nunc Iachan vocant, devenisse; ibidémque sibi ab incolis ostensum fuisse nummum argenteum antiquissimum, expressis tamen signis & literis conspicuum; in cujus altero latere forma esset vasculi illius, quod mannâ plenum in sacra arca ad sæculorum monumentum, Dei jussu, & Mosis procuratione fuerat repositum: & in altero ramus ille admirabilis, quem in fasciculum virgularum plurimarum Aaronis nomine illatum (cùm illius sacerdotali dignitati ab æmulis quibusdam obtrectaretur) posterâ die populus omnis florentem, amygdalàque explicantem vidit; in-*

(*u*) Arias Montanus de Siclo, in libro qui inscribitur Thubal Kain, sive de Mensuris.

scriptiones

scriptiones etiam fuisse in eodem nummo Samaritanis characteribus, quæ olim communes totius Israelis literæ fuerant, ante discessionem decem tribuum à duabus, lingua planè Hebraica, quarum exemplum ex alterâ parte erat SEKEL ISRAEL, quod Latinè sonat Siclus Israelis: ex alterâ verò JERVSALEM KEDESSAH, hoc est Jerusalem sancta: qui nummus antiquitatem cùm primis magnam probabat, utpote cujus nomine Israelis, eo tempore quo omnes XII. tribus communi concordia Israelis nomen obtinebant; quóque Hierosolyma ipsis omnibus regia urbs, sanctaque erat; eademque communis omnibus & religionis, & publicæ rei, & monetæ, atque literarum ratio, quæ, postea discessione factâ, alia atque alia utrique parti fuit. Namque Judæi, ut omnes ferè scriptores asserunt, ne cum schismaticis Israelitis ullo sacrorum usu communicarent, eam literarum formam, quæ nunc etiam in usu est, hoc est quadratam, mutatis valde alterius prioris figuris, adinvenêre. Affirmat præterea idem Gerundensis, nummum illum, qui Siclus inscribebatur, sibi in staterâ pensum dimidiæ argenti unciæ pondus reddidisse; ostensam quoque alteram monetam dimidiato pondere minorem, iisdem omnino vasis & rami figuris, quæ tamen non SEKEL, sed HHASZI SEKEL, hoc est dimidius Siclus diceretur: probari itaque

sibi

sibi vel maximè Salomonis Iarrhæi, de sicli pondere & valore, sententiam. Thus far *Gerundensis:* who if he had expressed with what half ounce he compared his *shekel*, or if *Montanus* had done it for him, they had given the judicious Reader better satisfaction. But this, I suppose, by a probable conjecture may be supplied, in saying, that he living in *Catalonia*, weighed it with the *Catalonian* or *Spanish* half ounce; which (x) *Villalpandus* and (y) *Ciaconius*, both of them *Spaniards*, make equal to the half ounce now used at *Rome*, that is, to two shillings, three-pence farthing, of our money. This conjecture of mine will exceeding well confirm those many observations of *Villalpandus*, a man in this kind very curious, which he made of several ancient *shekels* in silver, who thus writes: (z) *Igitur ante aliquot annos appendimus Siclum unum apud F. Ursinum, & postmodum eos omnes, quos præcedenti capite percensuimus, atque comperimus singulos argenti siclos ex æquo semunciæ Romanæ antiquæ respondere; ita ut ne minimum quidem hordei aut*

(x) Eædem omnino sunt unciæ, quibus olim **Romani** Hispanique utuntur, &c. Villalp. de Appar. Urb. ac Templi, par. 2. l. 3. c. 20.

(y) Ciaconius de Ponderibus, pag. 45.

(z) Villalpand. de Appar. Urbis ac Templi, par. 2. l. 2. disp. 4. c. 28.

frumenti

frumenti granulum, huic vel illi lanci addi potuerit, quin in eam examen propenderet. Nec mirum cuiquam videri debet, antiquissimos nummos suo pristino ponderi nunc respondere, neque ullam argenti partem vetustate consumptam·tot sæculis fuisse. Nam singulari Dei beneficio nobis contigit, tot integros appendere potuisse siclos. Id quod nummi ipsi integri vetustatem maximè præ se ferentes, literæ expressæ extantésque, argenti color, atque alia id genus multa, facile probant. With these observations of *Villalpandus*, I find the weight of a *Samaritan shekel* of the truly noble and learned *M. Selden* to agree; to whom I stand obliged for this favour, as he doth for the coin to the honourable antiquary Sir *Robert Cotton*. To these testimonies, though (it may be) sufficient of themselves, I shall add (*a*) one more, for farther illustration of the weight of the *Hebrew* or *Samaritan shekel*; and that is, of an ancient and fair one in silver, amongst his majesty's coins, perused by the most reverend Primate of *Ireland*, a man of exquisite learning and judgment, who hath often assured me, that it

---

(*a*) We may also insert the observation of *Anton. August. dialogo* 2. *Ne ho uno* [*siclo*] *che è d'argento, & è di peso di quattro dramme conforme à quello che dice San Girolamo sopra Ezechielle*: where, by four *drams*, he means half the *Roman* ounce.

weighs 2 ſhill. and 5 pence of the *Engliſh* ſtandard; which proportion, excepting ſome few grains, in which it doth exceed, does well correſpond with thoſe of *Villalpandus*. And this may farther be confirm'd out of the *Talmud*, (*b*) כל כסף האמורח בתורה כסף צורי ושל דברי חם כסף מדינה *Argentum omne cujus in Lege fit mentio, intelligitur argentum Tyrium (ponderis & bonitatis ut in urbe Tyri,* as (*c*) *Schlinder* interprets it;) *ſed Rabbinorum argentum intelligitur argentum commune provinciale.* Taking therefore the ſilver money of *Judea*, as the *Talmud* doth, to be equal to the *Tyrian*, and that of *Carthage* to be equal to that of *Tyre*; as it is very probable that the *Carthaginians*, being a plantation of the *Tyrians*, might obſerve their proportions in coins, as well as their cuſtoms in religion, we may by theſe diſcover the *ſhekel* to be much about the ſame weight that hath been aſſigned. For (*d*) *Ant. Auguſtinus*, deſcribing in his Dialogues the weight of two fair *Carthaginian* coins in ſilver, writes, *That they are each of them ſomewhat more than four* drachmes; that is, as he elſewhere explains himſelf, a little more than half the *Roman* ounce. If there-

(*b*) Kidduſh f. 11. (*c*) Schindlerus in Pentaglotto.
(*d*) Ant. Auguſt. dialog. 6.

fore we shall adhere to the observation of *Gerundenfis*, made four hundred years since, or to these later of *Villalpandus* and others, or to this conjecture of mine; the *Hebrew shekel*, and half the present *Roman* ounce, are either both the same, or else very near in proportion.

And this may easily be granted; but if it be, how will four *denarii Consulares*, four *Attick drachmes*, and the *Hebrew shekel*, be reciprocally equal to one another, as they should be by those several testimonies before alledged? Whereas by many hundred *denarii Consulares* tried by an exact balance, I find the best of these to contain sixty-two grains *English*, and the best *Attick drachme* sixty-seven, and the fourth part of the *shekel* to be but fifty-four grains and three quarters, if we admit of *Gerundenfis*'s and *Villalpandus*'s observations: which notwithstanding according to *Philo*, *Josephus*, St. *Hierome*, *Epiphanius*, and *Hesychius*, should be equal to the *Attick drachme*; and the *Attick drachme*, by the testimonies of the ancients, should be likewise equal to the *denarius*. For the solution of this objection, I answer, first, That the *denarius* and *Attick drachme*, being distinct coins of different states, and not much unequal in the true weight, it is no wonder, especially in *Italy* and in the *Ro-*

man dominions, that they should pass one for another; no more than that the *Spanish rials*, in our sea-towns in *England*, should pass for testers, or the quarters of the *dollar* be exchanged for our shillings: whereas the *rial* in the intrinsecal valuation is better than our *tester* by four grains, and somewhat more; and the quarter of the *dollar* is better than our *shilling* by more than eight grains, or a penny; but because they want the valuation, character, and impression of our princes, which I call the *extrinseck of coins*, therefore doth the *Spanish* mony fall from its true value with us, and so would ours do in *Spain*. By the same analogy must we conceive the *Attick drachmes*, though in the *intrinseck* they were somewhat better worth than the *denarius*, yet, for want of the *extrinseck*, to have lost in *Italy*, and thereby to have become equal in valuation to the *denarius*. And this seems to be implied by (e) *Volusius Metianus: Victoriatus enim nunc tantundem valet, quantum quinarius olim. At peregrinus nummus loco mercis, ut nunc tetradrachmum & drachma, habe-*

(e) *Vol. Metianus de Assis distributione.* These words of *Metianus* I find in a MS. of *Temporarius* thus corrected: *Victoriatus enim nunc tantundem valet, quantum quinarius. Olim ut peregrinus nummus loco mercis, ut nunc tetradrachmum & drachma, habebatur.* Whether it be by conjecture, or that he found it in some ancient MS. I know not, but the emendation I cannot but approve.

batur.

batur. Which words of his, *loco mercis,* plainly shew, they made some gain of the *tetradrachmum* and *drachma,* as our merchants and goldsmiths do of the *Spanish rials,* and quarters of a *dollar*; which they could not do, if they were precisely equal, but must rather be losers in the melting or new coining of them. And therefore all (*f*) modern writers that have treated of this argument, some of them making the *drachma* less than the *denarius,* others equal, but none greater, have been deceived by a double paralogism, in standing too nicely upon the bare words of the ancients, without carefully examining the things themselves. First, in making the *denarius* and *Attick drachme* precisely equal, because all ancient authors generally express the *Attick drachme* by the *denarius,* or the *denarius* by the *drachme*; either because in ordinary commerce and in vulgar estimation they passed one for another in the *Roman* state; or else if any were so curious to observe their difference, as surely the κολλυβιϛαὶ were, yet by

---

(*f*) Budæus drachmam putat ejusdem ponderis esse cum denario, Onuphrius verò inter utrumque statuit rationem sesquitertiam, Agricola sesquiseptimam; ut Panvinio tres denarii quatuor drachmas, Agricolæ verò septem denarii octo drachmas efficiant. *Capell. de Pond. & Nummis, libr.* I. LXXXIV. denarii, quæ est libra Romana, sunt æquales XCVI. drachmis, quæ est libra Italica, & medica. *Scal. de re Nummaria.*

reason of their nearness, and to avoid fractions, and having no other names of coins that were precisely equal, whereby to render them, therefore all *Greek* and *Latin* authors mutually used one for the other. And secondly, because some writers, as *Dioscorides* and *Cleopatra*, affirm that the *Roman* ounce contained eight *drachmes*, therefore modern authors infer, that the *denarius* being equal to the *drachme*, and eight *drachmes* being in the *Roman* ounce (as so many were in the *Attick*) that therefore there are eight *denarii* in the *Roman*, and consequently that the *Roman* and *Attick* ounces are equal. Whereas *Celsus*, *Scribonius Largus*, and *Pliny*, as we shewed before, expresly write, that the *Roman* ounce contained in their time, which was after *Diascorides*, seven *denarii*. And being natural *Romans*, and purposely mentioning the proportion of the *denarius* to the ounce, thereby the better to regulate their doses in physick, it is not probable but they must better have known it than the *Grecians*. Besides, who with any certainty can collect out of these imperfect fragments of *Dioscorides* and *Cleopatra* (for those tracts of theirs *de ponderibus* are no better) whether at the first they wrote in that manner, as they are now printed? Or if they did, why might not

Of the DENARIUS.

not they endeavour to introduce into the *Roman* ounce, in imitation of the *Attick*, that manner of divifion which is now generally received in our times, of making the ounce, of what kind foever it be, to contain eight drachms? And furely this of eight being a *compound number*, as Arithmeticians ufe to fpeak, was much fitter than feven, ufed by the *Romans*, which being a *prime number*, is therefore incapable of any other divifion. And then for to conclude, that becaufe the *Attick* ounce had eight drachms, and the *Roman* as many, that therefore their ounces are equal; is all one as to conclude, that the *Paris* and *Englifh* ounces are equal, becaufe the *French* as well as we (and fo do all Phyficians of all countries that I know) divide their ounce by eight drachms. And thus, I fuppofe, I have fufficiently anfwered the firft part of the objection concerning the *denarius* and the *Attick drachme*: that if we refpect the vulgar and popular eftimation, in which fenfe claffical authors underftood them (for they could not well otherwife render them, than as they were current) fo were they equal; but if we refpect the intrinfecal valuation, which depends upon the weight, efpecially when coins are of a like finenefs, fo were they unequal; the *Attick drachme* being of our

money

money eight pence farthing, and the *denarius Consularis* seven pence half-penny farthing, allowing for the standard (g) eight *English* grains to the silver penny.

Neither do I know any authority, that either expresly, or by a true and logical consequence, can be produced out of classical authors to infringe this assertion of mine, unless it be one in *Fannius*, which being a fragment, is the less to be valued; and another in *Livy*, who thus writes, *lib.* 34. in his description of the triumph of *Quinctius: Signati argenti octoginta quatuor millia fuere Atticorum, tetradrachmum vocant; trium ferè denariorum in singulis argenti est pondus.* Which words of his occasioned (h) *Georgius Agricola*, not knowing how to answer them, to bring in a distinc-

---

(g) These proportions, with those before and those which follow, are taken from the *English* standard at five shillings the ounce (as it was formerly coined) to avoid fractions; that is, eight grains to the silver penny: whereas in these times it is five shillings and two pence. Not that the ounce is increased, for this is always constant and fixt; but that for reasons of state our silver coins are diminished, and consequently contain fewer grains. And this diminution must necessarily be, as often as other nations, with whom we have commerce, rebate in the proportions of their coins; or else we must be content to be losers.

(h) G. *Agricolæ responsio ad Alciatum de Pond. & Mensuris.* Argentei Romanorum denarii triplices sunt: *graves*, qui pendunt drachmam Atticam cum dimidia; *mediocres*, qui drachmam & septimam ejus partem; *leves*, qui plerumque drachmam.

tion

Of the DENARIUS.

tion of three sorts of *denarii*; the *gravis*, weighing an *Attick drachme* and an half; the *mediocris*, one and a seventh part; the *levis*, most commonly one; without any clear proof in any ancient author, and directly contrary to all ancient coins of the *Atticks* and *Romans* which I have seen: of which error he would not have been guilty (for there is no man that hath writ either *de ponderibus & mensuris*, or *de re metallica*, more solidly and judiciously than he) if he had been so happy as to have perused many intire *Grecian aurei* and *tetradrachmes*, or else to have examined a greater and more select quantity of *Roman* coins. To satisfy my self concerning that place of *Livy*, I had recourse to our MSS. here (and I could wish I had done the like in *Italy)* and these I find to agree with the printed copies; though the coins, which are much ancienter than any MSS. constantly disagree. Wherefore if it be not a mistake in *Livy* himself, which I am not to believe in so grave an author, I would correct the copies by the coins, and instead of III. *ferè denariorum*, make it thus, IV. *ferè denariorum*. Where the figure V. being resolved into two lines, and left a little open at the bottom, might easily be taken for the figure II. And this I do certainly believe is the true ground of

that

that error, wherewith so many of late have been perplext *(i)*. However it were, it is as ancient as *Priscian*, or *Pseudo-Priscian* (as *Capellus* stiles him) who, in his tract *de Ponderibus*, reads those words of *Livy* in the same manner, *trium ferè denariorum*.

As for the *denarius aureus*, a name I think not known to the ancients, which *Salmasius* and others collect out of *(k) Livy, de fœdere Ætolico: Pro argento si aurum dare mallent, dare convenit, dum pro argenteis decem aureus unus valeret*. I see no solid foundation for that opinion; all that can be collected from thence is, that the gold then was *in decuplâ ratione* to the silver, which I have proved before. And whereas *(l) Plautus* hath his *denaria Philippea*,

Nummi octinginti aurei in marsupio infuerunt,
Præterea centum denaria Philippea;

this is a metaphorical, or comical expression of him, and no certain sort of coin;

(i) If this answer be not satisfactory, we may say, as some have done, that *Livy, Fannius*, and the Scholiast of *Nicander*, speak of the *denarii* of the former Consuls immediately succeeding *Q. Fabius*: For there being but six of those in the ounce, (as they suppose) the *denarius* will be greater than the *drachma*, as it will be less when seven were coined under the later Consuls, which is our assertion.

(k) Livius, l. 38. *(l)* Plautus in Rudente.

which

which he pleasantly calls *denarii*, because half the χρυσοῖ Φιλίππειοι were equal in weight to the *drachma*, and so also was the *Roman denarius* supposed to be.

Nor are we to take the κῆνσος, which is thrice mentioned by St. *Matthew*, and once by St. *Mark*, for the *denarius*, as some have done; no, nor for any other sort of coin: for it is precisely the *Latin* word *census*; that is, ὁ Φόρος, *tributum*; and so is it render'd by St. *Luke*, Ἔξεςι Καίσαρι Φόρον δῦναι, ἢ ὔ; where St. *Matthew* and St. *Mark* have it: Ἔξεςι δῦναι κῆνσον Καίσαρι, ἢ ὔ; though *Hesychius* and *Moschopulus*, both upon an error, interpret it a sort of coin. *Hesychius*, Κῆνσος εἶδος νομίσματος ἐπικεφάλαιον, or νομίσματος ἐπικεφαλαίῳ, as M. *Casaubon* corrects it: and *Moschopulus*, Κῆνσος νόμισμα δραχμῆς ἰσοςάσιον. *The* census *is a coin equal in weight to the* drachme; that is, in the notion of the *Greeks*, equal to the *denarius*. The error of these two *Greek* Grammarians is a misunderstanding the propriety of the *Latin* word *census*; and that occasioned them to take κῆνσος, and νόμισμα τῦ κήνσυ, for the same. But the Evangelist *Matthew* puts a manifest difference between κῆνσος *tributum*, and νόμισμα, the money that was paid for tribute. Ἐπιδείξατέ μοι τὸ νόμισμα τῦ κήνσυ, writes St. *Matthew*; *shew me the money of the tribute*; or, as our new tranflation renders it, *fhew me the tribute money*. And the three Evangelifts, *Matthew*, *Mark*, and *Luke*, immediately after expreſly term this money the δηνάριον. Οἱ δὲ προσήνεγκαν αὐτῷ δηνάριον, *and they brought unto him a penny*; which being a *Roman* coin, and current amongſt the *Jews*, being then in ſubjection to the *Romans*, it is more than probable, that they paid their tribute to *Cæſar* in the ſame ſpecies of money that was uſed by *Cæſar*, and not with any new or peculiar ſort of coin, according to *Baronius* (which M. *Caſaubon* hath juſtly confuted) but with the ordinary current money of *Rome*, and that was the *denarius*.

Our next ſolution ſhould be of the *ſhekel*, how it could be equal to the *tetradrachme*, and conſequently to four *denarii*, when by the conſtant weight of the beſt *Hebrew* or *Samaritan ſhekels* extant, we find them to be much leſs. And here I am a little unſatisfied, how to reconcile the coins to *Philo*, *Joſephus*, *Epiphanius*, Saint *Hierome*, and *Heſychius*; or elſe, if we admit of the coins (as I know no juſt exceptions againſt them) how to excuſe theſe authors of too ſupine negligence in comparing them, if ſo be they ever were ſo curious as to collate

late them with the *Attick tetradrachmes*. For if we shall say that the silver *stater*, or *Attick tetradrachme*, was a foreign coin in respect of the republick of the *Jews*, and therefore that in *Judea* it might somewhat fall from its true valuation, we shall say no more than what reason and experience confirm. But then, that the *tetradrachme* should sink so low, as to lose fourpence half-penny, if we take the reverend Primate's observation before-mentioned, or which is more, six-pence, *q.* if we follow that of *Gerundenfis* and *Villalpandus*, or those of mine, upon two shillings nine-pence half-penny, for so much was the *tetradrachme* of our money, it may seem too great a diminution, especially the *Attick* money being as pure and fine as that of the *shekel*; and therefore no Goldsmith amongst the *Jews*, but would have given a greater rate only to melt it, and turn it into bullion. Yet on the other side, when I consider the practise of the money-changers amongst the *Jews* at this day, which it may be was as bad in *Philo's* and *Josephus's* time, and might occasion our Saviour, not long before, to whip them out of the temple, which they by their extortions had made a den of thieves, who now make it a trade at *Alexandria*, and elsewhere,

elsewhere, in changing *Spanish dollars* into *(m) madines* (or the small silver money current in *Ægypt*) to gain one or two *madines* upon every *dollar*, notwithstanding the *Spanish* money is as frequent, and as well known in *Turky*, as their own; I can the better imagine they might make the same advantage, or a little more, upon the *Attick tetradrachmes*; which, it may be also, were not permitted, being contrary to their law, to pass so generally with them, as the *Spanish* money now doth (by reason of the image of *Pallas*, and the *noctua* instamped): or if they were permitted, yet they might not be so common and so well known; and therefore upon strangers in *Judea*, in giving them current money for that which was foreign, they would gain so much the more. So that *Philo* and *Josephus*, when they equal the *shekel* to the *tetradrachme*, may have taken it upon the relation and practise of these money changers, and not upon any experiment of their own. The same answer may serve for *Epiphanius*, Saint *Hierome*, and *Hesychius*; though it may be these borrowed their descriptions from *Philo* or *Josephus*, who long preceeded them; and being *Jews*, and living in the time when

---

(m) At my being in *Ægypt*, thirty-five *madines* passed for a *dollar*: Sandys, in his *Travels*, writes forty.

the

the state of the *Jews* was in being, whereas these did not, their authority is the more to be credited. And thus have we finished our enquiry of the *denarius Consularis*, by comparing it with the *Attick drachmes* and the *Hebrew shekels*.

The last, and best way to discover the true weight of it, is by the *congius Romanus*, whereof, by a special providence, as (*n*) *Pætus* and *Villalpandus* have well observed, the original standard of *Vespasian* is still extant in *Rome*. This, as the superscription upon it, X P demonstrates, contains the weight of ten *Roman* pounds, and is equal (by the joint confession of all authors treating this argument) to six *sextarii*. Again, the *sextarius*, as (*o*) *Galen* writes, ἔχει μίαν λίτραν καὶ ἡμίσειαν καὶ ἕκτον, ὡς ἐἶναι τὰς πάσας ἐγγίας κ'. *contains one pound and an half, and a sixth part, so that it hath in all twenty ounces:* Or, as (*p*) *Oribasius*, physician to *Julian* the Apostate, informs us, is equal to the *Roman* pound, and eight ounces: Ἰταλικὸν κεράμιον ἔχει ξέςας μή. ξήςης λίτραν μίαν, καὶ ἐγγίας ή. *The* Italian amphora *contains forty-eight* sextarii, *and the* sextarius *one pound*

(*n*) Pætus l. 3. de Antiq. liquid. aridisque Mensuris. Villalp. de Appar. Urbis ac Templi, par. 2. l. 3. c. 25.
(*o*) Galen. l. 1. de Compos. Medicam.
(*p*) Oribasius l. 2. ad Eustathium filium.

and eight ounces. The capacity therefore of this *congius*, being filled up with six *sextarii* of some certain sort of liquors (for it is *liquorum mensura*) will give us ten *Roman* pounds, and consequently their ounces and *denarii*. The only difficulty is, with what sort of liquor we must measure it; for all liquors are not of the same gravity; and this is well cleared by *(q) Rhemnius Fannius*, and others.

> *Illud præterea tecum cohibere memento*
> *Finitum pondus varios servare liquores.*
> *Nam Libræ, ut memorant, beſſem sexta-*
>   *rius addet,*
> *Seu puros pendas latices, seu dona Lyæi.*

The *sextarius* (saith *Fannius*) contains one pound and eight ounces, whether we weigh clear water or wine; where by wine, according to *(r) Agricola*, is to be understood, *vinum fulvum*, such as the *Greeks* call κιῤῥὸν· rather I imagine that wine, which *Galen* calls λευκὸν, καὶ ὀλιγόφορον. The *sextarius* then being one pound eight ounces of clear water, or pure wine, and six *sextarii* being in the *congius*, it is most evident that the *congius* contains ten pounds of water or of wine. This also appears by a *Ple-*

(q) Rhemn. Fann. Carmina de Pond. & Menſ.
(r) Agricola l. 3. de Ponder. Rerum.

biſcitum

Of the Denarius.

biscitum of the two *Silii*, *Publius* and *Marius*, which is to be seen in the best copies of (*s*) *Sextus Pompeius*.

VTI. QVADRANTAL. VINI. OCTOGINTA. PONDO. SIET

CONGIVS. VINI. DECEM. IS. SIET

DVO. DE. QVINQVAGINTA. SEXTARII. QUADRANTAL. SIET. VINI

SEXTARIVS. ÆQVVS. ÆQVO. CVM. LIBRA-RIO. SIET.

The same is confirmed by (*t*) *Dioscorides*, who, for farther certainty, mentions with what sort of water we should measure it; and that is with rain (*u*) water, which he makes to be the most infallible of all. Ὁ χῦς τυτέςι τὸ κόγγιον ἔχει λι. ῑ. τὸ ἡμικόγγιον ἔχει λι. ε̄. ὁ ξέςης ἔχει λίτραν μίαν γο ν̄, &c. ὁ αυτὸς ἢ ςαθμός ἐςι καὶ ὕδατος καὶ ὄξες. Φασὶ ἢ τῦ ὀμβρίυ ὕδατος πληρωθῆναι ἀψευδέςατον εἶναι τὸν ςαθμὸν, ἄγεινδὲ ὁλκὰς ξ̄κ τὸν κῦν. *The* chus *(that is, the* congius*) contains ten pounds, the* semicongius *five,*

(*s*) Sext. Pomp. de Verb. signif.

(*t*) Fragmenta Dioscoridis.

(*u*) The proportion that rain water hath to fountain water is as 1000000 to 1007522; and the proportion that it hath to water distilled, is as 1000000 to 997065, as it hath been observed by *Snellius in Eratosth. Batav. l.* 2. *c.* 5. *Est in æquali mole ratio aquæ pluviæ ad distillatam, quemadmodum* 1000000 *ad* 997065; *pluviæ autem ad putealem ut* 1000000 *ad* 1007522.

the sextarius *one pound, and eight ounces, &c. The weight of water and of vinegar is the same. They say, that if it be filled up with rain water, the weight will be most certain.* (*x*) *The congius weighs seven hundred and twenty drachmes.* An anonymous *Greek* author, falsly reputed to be *Galen* in the edition at *Venice*, confirms the same; (*y*) Πα-

---

(*x*) This authority of *Dioscorides*, with that other citation following out of an anonymous author, strongly proves my assertion, that the *drachma Attica* was more ponderous than the *denarius Consularis*. For there being LXXXIV of these *denarii* in the *Roman* pound, as we have elsewhere proved, and X *Roman* pounds in the *congius*, it is most evident there are IƆCCCXL *denarii* in the whole *congius*. Again, IƆCCXX *drachmes*, by the testimonies of *Dioscorides* and this anonymous writer, being equal to the *congius*, and the *congius* being equal to IƆCCCXL *denarii*, therefore IƆCCXX *drachmes* are equal to IƆCCCXL *denarii*; and therefore of necessity every particular *drachme* of these must be greater than each particular *denarius*. And though, according to my assertion, the *congius* containeth some few *drachmes* more than are by them assigned; yet that difference, seeing it might many ways happen, as I afterwards shew in the like experiments of *Villalpandus* and *Gassendus*, it cannot any way overthrow my conclusion. For the *drachmes* are still fewer than the *denarii Consulares*, and therefore greater, which was the thing intended to be proved. And this may farther be confirmed, in that both *Cleopatra* and this anonymous author make also the ξέςης, or *sextarius* (being the sixth part of the *congius*) to contain an hundred twenty *drachmes* of fountain water. Whereby it appears there is no error committed in the former numbers: ὁ ξέςης μέτρῳ μὲν ἔχει κοτυλὰς ϛ´ ςαθμῷ δὲ < ρκ´. The *sextarius* (saith Cleopatra) *contains in measure two cotyls, but in weight an hundred and twenty* drachmes. And the anonymous writer: Ἔχει δὲ ὁ ξέςης ςαθμῷ δραχμὰς ρκ´. *The* sextarius *contains in weight an hundred and twenty* drachmes.

(*y*) Anonymus Græc.

ρὰ

Of the DENARIUS.

ρα ἢ τοῖς Ἰταλοῖς εὑρίσκεται ὁ χȣς μέτρῳ μὲν ἔχων ξ ϛ. κοτύλας ιβ. ϛαθμὸν ἢ ὕδατος ὀμβρίȣ, ὅπερ ἐϛιν ἀψευδέϛατον, δραχμὰς ͵Ιχ: *Amongst the* Romans *is found the* congius, *containing in measure fix* sextarii *(that is)* XII. cotylæ: *but in weight of rain water, which is most infallible*, IƆCCXX. *drachmes.* And whereas (z) *Dioscorides* elsewhere writes: Τὸ κόγγιον ἔχει λίτρας θ'. τὸ ἡμικόγγιον λ'. δ' S. ὁ ξέϛης ἔχει λ'. ἀ S. *The* congius *hath nine pounds, the* semicongius *four and an half, the* sextarius *one and an half;* there is no repugnancy between this and his former assertion. For here he speaks of the *congius* filled with oyl, and before of the same *congius* filled with water or wine: and that this should be but nine pounds, whereas the former is ten, is no more repugnant to reason, than it is to nature, that oil should be lighter than water or wine; which (a) *Ghetaldus*, in his *Archimedes promotus*, hath demonstrated the most accurately of any man, to be in the proportion that 1 is to $1 \frac{1}{11}$ in respect of water, and as 1 is to $1 \frac{4}{75}$ in respect of wine; which is almost the same with *Dioscorides*. The not observing this difference of weight, arising from the different gravity of seve-

(z) Fragmenta Dioscoridis.
(a) Ghetaldus in Archim. promoto.

ral liquors, in vessels of one and the same capacity, is that which hath occasioned much incertainty and confusion in modern writers. And therefore we shall, for farther perspicuity, insert that distinction which is often inculcated by (b) *Galen*, that the *Romans* used two sorts of ounces and pounds; and those were either ςαθμικαὶ, or μετρικαὶ, *ponderal* or *mensural*: the one had respect solely to the gravity, the other to the *moles* and gravity conjointly: the former were always certain and fixt, consisting of solid matter; the later were *vasa* (frequently ἐκ κέρασι) being receptacles and measures of liquid substances; and therefore the *libræ* and *unciæ mensurales* in these were greater or less, according as the liquor to be measured was heavier or lighter. Whence (c) *Galen* blames Physicians for not expressing this difference: Διὸ γράφειν ἐχρῆν ἐπιμελέςερον ἐν ταῖς Φαρμακίτισι βίβλοις τὰς ἰατρὰς ὁποίας τινὰς κελεύεσι βάλλεσθαι τὰς ἐγγίας ἢ τὰς λίτρας τῶν ὑγρῶν Φαρμάκων, πότερον τὰς μετρικὰς, ἢ τὰς ςαθμικάς. And he gives the reason of it; (d) Αἱ μὲν γὰρ ςαθμικαὶ τὸ βάρος κρίνεσι τῶν σωμάτων, αἱ δ μετρικαὶ τὸν ὄγκον. *For the ponderal examine the weight of bodies, but the mensural*

(b) Galenus l. 1. & 6. de Comp. Medicam secun. genera.
(c) Lib. 6. de Compos. Medic. secun. genera.
(d) Lib. 1. de Compos. Medic. secund. genera.

Of the DENARIUS.

the moles. But to return to the *congius*, and by it to our discovery of the *denarius*. The water then must be natural, either of some fountain, or of rain. For if it be artificial, such as are made by distillations, whether by a strong reverberation, or by a gentle in an alembick, these having somewhat of the property of fire, will be lighter than the natural, as (e) *Agricola* and others observe: I shall produce two observations of the *congius* with fountain water, made by two very eminent and able men, *Villalpandus* and *Gassendus*, the one at *Rome*, with the *Roman* weights, from the (f) original *congius* itself, the other at *Aix*,

---

(e) Perinde verò ut vinum hoc factitium omni nativo est levius, sic aquæ ferè omnes, quæ ignis calore rebus quibuscunque excoctis distillarint, quas ob id distillatas appellant, cæteris aquis leviores sunt. *Agricola l. 3. de Pond. Rerum.*

(f) This *congius* I had weighed, if I could have procured a balance of such exactness as was fitting for such a work. The want of which occasioned *Villalpandus* to suspect the observation of *Pætus*, tho' *Pætus* writes thus of himself: *Plenum, cum justissimâ trutinâ, quâ hodie Romæ utimur, cùm appendissem* [congium,] *inveni aquam, quâ eam compleveram, libras nostri temporis novem, uncias sex semis efficere, quibus uncias quinque, drachmas quatuor, scripulum unum, & grana* XIV. *(quæ amplius sunt in his nostris, quam in antiquis libris, computando eum congium libras decem) & ultra scripulum unum, & grana* XIV. *(de quibus nullam rationem habendam esse judicavi) ex antiquis libris prædictis pendere inveni.* But *Villalpandus* trying it long after *Pætus*, with more care, and with a balance made of purpose, found it to be exactly ten such pounds as are now used in *Rome*. All that I could do, was to fill the capacity of it with *mi-*
lium

Aix, with the *Paris* weights, from a model, or copy of that at *Rome*, procured by *Peireskius*. And here to compare the *denarius Consularis* with their observations, it is necessary to have exactly both the *Roman* and *Paris* weights. The former, with as much accurateness as possible, were taken in *Rome*; the other were sent me by Monf. *Hardy*, a learned man of honourable quality in *Paris*, who compared them with the standard. To begin with that of *Villalpandus*, who gives us a large description, with how much caution and circumspection, and with how exquisite a balance

lium well cleansed, and to compare it with the *English* measures taken from the standards. It contained of our measures for wine, three quarts, one pint, and one eighth part of a pint. Of our corn, or dry measures, three quarts, and about one sixth part of a pint. At my being in *Italy*, there was found amongst the ruins at *Rome* a *Semicongius* in brass, of the same figure with this of *Vespasian*, the sides much consumed by rust. This I also measured, and found it to be the half of *Vespasian's congius*. From this measure of the *congius*, we may rightly apprehend how vast that draught was of *Novellus Torquatus*, who drank three of these *congii* at once, from whence he was called *Novellus Tricongius*. The story is recited by *Pliny*, l. 14. c. 22. *Apud nos cognomen etiam Novellus Torquatus Mediolanensis ad Proconsulatum usque è praeturâ honoribus gestis, tribus congiis (unde & nomen illi fuit) epotis uno impetu, spectante miraculi gratiâ Tiberio principe in senectâ jam severo, atque etiam aliàs saevo, sed ipsâ juventâ ad merum pronior fuerat.* In the same chapter, *Pliny* likewise discourses thus of *Cicero*, son to that famous orator: *Tergilla Ciceronem Marci filium binos congios simul haurire solitum ipsi objicit, Marcoque Agrippae à temulento scyphum impactum.*

he

he twice made his experiment, whereby he discovered the weight of it in water to be exactly answerable to ten such pounds as are now used in *Rome*. Whence he concludes: *(g) Constanter asserimus antiquam Romanorum libram, unciam, ac pondera, tot ætatum successione, ac Romani imperii perturbationibus minimè immutata fuisse, sed eadem per manus tradita usque ad nostra tempora perdurasse.* This *Roman* pound of his reduced to the *English* standard for silver, or *Troy* weight, with which I have faithfully collated it, is 5256 grains *English*, such as the *Troy* pound is 5760: the whole *congius* therefore consisting of ten pounds, will be 52560 *English* grains. The other observation is related by *(h) Gassendus*, in his elegant discourse *de vitâ Peireskii. Ut paucis ergo res dicatur, cautiones adhibuimus easdem, quas Lucas Pætus & Villalpandus, dum vas ipsum ad summum collum puteali aquâ opplevimus, expendimus, vasis pondus subduximus. Deprehendimus autem aquam, quæ Romano pondere esse debuit decem librarum, seu unciarum centum viginti, esse pondere Parisiensi (quale nempe Parisiis exploratum missumque est) librarum septem, minus unciæ quadrante: seu unciarum cen-*

(g) Villalpandus l. 2. disp. 2. c. 11. de Appar. Urbis ac Templi.
(h) Gassendus in vitâ Peireskii.

tum

tum undecim, & quadrantum unciæ trium. Deinde ex hac proportione collegimus unciam Romanam continere grana quingenta, & triginta sex, qualium quingenta septuaginta sex in Parisiensi continentur: unde & illis in drachmas collectis, obvenere cuilibet drachmæ grana sexaginta septem: idque proinde censuimus pondus denarii Cæsarei, quem dictum est fuisse (i) drachmalem. Now the *Paris* ounce sent to me by Monſ. *Hardy*, containing four hundred seventy-two grains *English*, and an half, and the *congius*, according to *Gassendus*, of the *Paris* ounces 111¼, the compleat weight of the *congius* in grains will be 5280 ⅞; which sum exceeds that of *Villalpandus* by 241 ⅞, that is, by more than half a *Roman* ounce. This difference (though it is not great) be-

---

(i) The inference of *Gassendus* I easily grant, that the *denarius* under some of the *Cæsars* was *drachmalis*, that is, the eighth part of the *Roman* ounce. But neither was it always so under the *Cæsars*, nor if it had been so, will it therefore follow that it was *drachmalis*, or the eighth part in respect of the *Attick* ounce. Seeing the *Athenian* ounce was greater than the *Roman*, as we have before proved; and therefore the *denarius Consularis*, which was the seventh part of the *Roman* ounce, was scarce the eighth part of the *Attick*. Wherefore he must see how he can make it good, where he brings *Peireskius* in the second book of his life thus discoursing. —— *Denarium, cùm tempore Regum pependisset trientem unciæ, sub antiquâ tamen rep. pependisse solùm sextantem, sub recentiore partem septimam, sub primis Cæsaribus octavam, seu drachmam (Atticæ nempe drachmæ æqualem.)*

tween

Of the DENARIUS. 307

tween these two observations of theirs might arise, either from the unequal swelling of the water in the *congius*; or from the different gravity of fountain water at *Rome*, and at *Aix*; or from some inequality of the model and original; or from some defect in the *jugum*, or beam of the balance, which if it were not made by a very skilful hand, by the pressure of so great a weight would suffer some alteration. Which way soever it was, either by some, or all of these, the difference cannot prejudice my conclusion a compleat grain, which no reasonable man but will allow, either for coining, or for waste. For if I divide 52560, the number of the grains in the *congius*, according to *Villalpandus*, by IƆCCCXL. the number of the *denarii* in ten pounds, the sum will be LXII. $\frac{5}{7}$. Or if we shall follow *Gassendus*, though I should rather prefer *Villalpandus*, because he took his immediately from the original, then will the weight of the *denarius Consularis* be LXII. $\frac{361}{420}$. The fraction in both without any inconvenience may be omitted. And this proportion of the weight of the *denarius Consularis*, if it were necessary, I could farther prove by some of the *aurei Consulares*, which often were double in weight to the *denarii*, as the χρυσοῖ Ἀττικοὶ

308 *Of the* DENARIUS.

καὶ were double to the δραχμαὶ ἀργυρίȣ; as also by several *quinarii* in silver (which are the half of the *denarii*) by a very ancient and perfect (*k*) *semuncia*, by a *quadrans* and *triens*, all of them in brass of mine own, and by several other weights examined abroad. One of them I cannot pretermit, being near five *Roman* pounds, and very remarkable for this inscription. EX. AUCTORITATE. Q. JUNI. RUSTICI. PR. VR. but the weight of it is a little defective; part of the *silex* (as many of the ancient *Roman* weights, that I have seen were (*l*) *ex silice*, which is as hard, or harder than marble) being broken away; else the rest is very entire, and well polished. But I conceive that, by those former ways, I have so irrefragably demonstrated the true ponderousness of the *denarius Consularis*, that it would be thought superfluous, or a vain ostentation, to endeavour any farther to prove it. Wherefore instead of that, I shall handle the *denarius Cæsareus*, which is our second enquiry.

(*k*) Of these *Roman semunciæ*, I have bought, and seen several in brass; besides one, which I owe to my very worthy and learned friend, Dr. *Ent*.

(*l*) *Pætus*, l. 1. de Antiq. Rom. & Græc. interv. mensuris, makes mention of a *libra Romana* in brass, procured by *Fulvius Ursinus*, of singular rarity: *in cujus supremâ planitie argenteis literis hæc erat nota* I, & *in circumferentiâ hæ aliæ* EX. AVC. D. CAES. but this I had not the happiness to see in *Italy*.

Of the DENARIUS.

The *denarius Cæsareus* was that which was made under the government of the *Cæsars*; and this, instead of the face and inscription ROMA, with the character X or ✶ on the fore part, and the impress of the *biga* or *quadriga* on the reverse (in which kind most of the *denarii Consulares* were stamped) had on the reverse several impresses, and on the other side the image or resemblance of the Emperor: which occasioned our Saviour to ask the question, when a δηνάριον or *Roman* penny was shewed to him, (m) *Whose is this image and superscription? They say unto him*, Cæsar's. This *denarius Cæsareus*, if we respect some definitive quantity and weight, was as various and uncertain, as the *denarius Consularis* of the later Consuls was constant and fixt; being under the first Emperors sometimes more, sometimes less, as the reasons and exigencies of the state did require, or the profuseness and prodigality of those times. Yet this uncertainty, as far as I have observed, was limited within some certain and determinate bounds; the *denarius Cæsareus* never exceeding the seventh part of the *Roman* ounce, and never being less than the eighth part, but often in a middle proportion between both, and that with much

(m) Matth. 22. 16.

inequality.

inequality. And this made (*n*) *Villalpandus*, after many experiments at *Rome*, to conclude, that out of the *denarii* nothing concerning the *Roman* weights could be determined. Though *Portius*, *Agricola*, *Ciaconius*, *Snellius*, and several others before and after him, are of a contrary opinion. And it may be, if *Villalpandus* had distinguished between the difference of times, and in them of the different coins, and considered those of the Consuls distinctly from those of the *Cæsars*, and those of the former *Cæsars* from those of the later, he would have reformed his judgment. For it plainly appears upon examination, that the diminution of their weight was an invention introduced after *Antonius* the Triumvir's time, whereas before the *denarius* was fixt. *Miscuit*, saith (*o*) *Pliny*, *denario Triumvir Antonius ferrum, alii è pondere subtrahunt* (his meaning is, under the Emperors to *Vespasian*'s, or his own time) *cùm sit justum octoginta quatuor è libris signari*. Where he says very well in speaking so generally, *alii è pondere subtrahunt*, without precisely limiting the proportion. For this, as we observed, was very various and undeterminate; so that whereas the just number of

---

(*n*) Villalpand. de Apparat. Urb. ac Templ. par. 2. l. 2. disp. 2. c. 13. (*o*) Plin. l. 33. c. 9.

Of the DENARIUS.

the *denarii*, according to the practife of the later Confuls, fhould be eighty-four in the *Roman* pound, we find by the weight of the beft of them under the former *Cæfars*, that they coined fometimes eighty-fix, eighty-eight, &c. till at laft there came to be ninety-fix *denarii* in the *Roman* pound, that is, eight in the ounce. And this, by a very neceffary confequence, may be inferred out of another place of *Pliny*, if we take for granted what fome moderns confefs, and the gold and filver coins found to this day, of the later Confuls and firft Emperors, ftrongly prove, that as the *Atticks* made their χρυσᾶς, or *aureus*, double in weight to the δραχμὴ ἀργυρὶς, fo did the *Romans* make their *aureus* double in weight to the *denarius*. Which proportion they might borrow from the *Athenians* and other *Grecians*, who, as (p) *Arias Montanus* imagines, firft received it from the practife of the *Hebrews*; or rather, as I fuppofe, from the *Phenicians*, and thefe from the *Hebrews*. From whencefoever it came, it is not much material in our inquiry: that which we may fafely conclude from thence is this, that the gold being in refpect of weight double to the filver, the *aureus Romanus*

(p) Arias Montanus in *Thubal Cain*, five de Menfuris.

falling

falling in its weight, the *denarius* likewise of necessity must fall, else could they not have continued *in duplâ ratione.* Now in what manner the *aureus* was first coined, and how afterwards it lost of its primitive weight, *Pliny* informs us: *(q) Aureus nummus post annum* LXII. *percussus est, quam argenteus, ita ut scrupulum valeret sestertiis vicenis, quod efficit in libras ratione sestertiorum, qui tunc erant, sestertios* IƆCCCC. *Post hæc placuit* XL. M. *signari ex auri libris; paulatimque principes imminuere pondus, imminuisse verò ad* XLV. M. For this testimony and the former we are to thank *Pliny*, seeing there is neither *Greek* nor *Latin* author extant, from his time to *Theodosius*, that gives us any certainty what to conclude concerning the ancient coins. And therefore since this later is of great consequence, but somewhat corrupted, I compared it with the MSS. in the *Vatican* and *Florentine* libraries, and with a fair one in *Baliol* college, which renders the later part of it thus: *Postea placuit* X. XL. *signari ex auri libris, paulatimque principes imminuere pondus, imminuisse verò ad* XLVIII. Where for XLVIII. *(r) Villalpandus* corrects, or rather corrupts the text, in writing XLV. But *Agricola* and

(q) Plin. l. 33. c. 3. *(r)* Villalp. de Apparat. Urbis ac Templ. par. 2. l. 2. disp. 2. c. 12.

(s) Snellius

Of the DENARIUS.   313

(*s*) *Snellius* read it by conjecture thus: *Post hæc placuit* XLII. *signari ex auri libris, paulatimque principes imminuere pondus, minutissimè verò ad* XLVIII. And (*t*) *Snellius* gives a reason of it in his *Eratosthenes Batavus: Nam ita argentei denarii, & aurei nummi eadem manet analogia, pondere subduplo, ut quamdiu octoginta quatuor argentei è libra, & è singulis unciis septem cudebantur, tamdiu quoque aurei duo & quadraginta libram implerent. Postquam verò argentei nummi pondus imminutum est, ut sex & nonaginta in libram constituerentur, tum quoque duo de quinquaginta aurei, pondere tanto leviore, in singulis libris cudi cœperunt.* Which conjecture seems not altogether improbable, if we respect the later Consuls and first *Cæsars*, in whose times we find the *aurei* to have been double to the *denarii Cæsarei*: but surely long before *Justinian*, the *aurei*, or as they were then also called, the *solidi*, lost that proportion to the silver, and kept it only to the *semisses aurei*, to which they were double, as they were in a treble proportion to the *tremisses*.

Wherefore instead of these conjectures (which have been the bane of many a good author) of *Agricola, Villalpandus,* and *Snellius*, I would read the later part of those

(*s*) Snell. in Eratosth. Batav. l. 2. c. 5.   (*t*) Ibid.

words of *Pliny* as the MSS. do, till I can see some concluding reason, or good authority of ancient authors to the contrary. For I do not see why the *Romans* at the first might not coin forty *aurei* out of the *libra*, as well as forty silver *teruncii* out of the *denarius*; which (*u*) *Varro* assures us they did. And who knows whether at the first making of their gold coins, which was sixty two years, according to *Pliny*, after the first coining of silver, they endeavoured to keep them *in duplâ ratione* in respect of weight; which graceful manner they might afterwards introduce by commerce with the *Grecians*.

And here, e'er I proceed any farther in my inquiry after the *denarius Cæsareus*, I cannot but complain either of the negligence of former times, or unhappiness of ours; in that not one author extant mentions the true weight of the *denarii* under the *Cæsars*. (*x*) *Xiphilinus* relates in his epitome of *Dio*, how *Antonius Caracalla* corrupted and abased the coins, but makes no mention of the weight: Τῷ ᾖν Ἀντωνίνῳ, τάτε ἄλλα καὶ τὸ νόμισμα κίβδηλον ἦν, τόδε ἀγύριον καὶ τὸ χρυσίον· ὁ παρεῖχεν ἡμῖν, τὸ μὲν ἐκ μολίβδȣ καταργυρȣμενον, τὸ δὲ καὶ ἐκ χαλκȣ καταχρυσȣμενον ἐσκευάζετο· *To An-*

(*u*) Varro l. 4. de Ling. Latin.
(*x*) Xiphilinus in Anton. Caracalla.

toninus,

Of the DENARIUS.

toninus, *as other things, so also his money was adulterated. For the silver and gold which he gave us, the one was prepared of lead silvered over, and the other of brass gilt.* (y) Suidas also, speaking of the *monetarii*, writes thus: Μονιτάριοι δι περὶ τὸ νόμισμα τεχνῖται, δι ἐπὶ Αὐρηλιανῷ διέφθειραν τὸ νόμισμα, καὶ τὸν ἴδιον ἄρχοντα Φιλικήσιμον ἀνελόντες ἐμφύλιον ἐγείρυσι πόλεμον, ὓς μόλις Αὐρηλιανὸς χειρωσάμενος ὑπερβαλλύσῃ κολάσεων ὠμότητι κατειργάσατο· The monetarii *are artizans employed in the making of money: these in* Aurelian's *time corrupted the money, and having slain their governor* Felicissimus, *raised a civil war; whom* Aurelianus *with much difficulty conquering, put to death with exquisite torments.* And many good laws were made, by several Emperors, against adulterating and corrupting of coins, and those executed with much severity, even in the time of Christianity. For we find under the Emperor *Constantine,* that such as offended in this kind were not only put to death, but to a cruel and bitter death by fire. L. OMNES SOLIDI. C. THEOD. *SIQVIS SOLIDI CIRCVLVM EXTERIOREM INCIDERIT, VEL ADVLTERATVM IN VENDENDO SVBJECERIT.* Omnes solidi, in quibus nostri

---

(y) Suidas in voce Μονιτάριοι, sive Μονητάριοι.

vultus,

vultus, ac veneratio una est, uno pretio æstimandi sunt atque vendendi, quanquam diversa formæ mensura sit: quod siquis aliter fecerit, aut capite puniri debet, aut flammis tradi, vel aliâ pœnâ mortiferâ. Quod ille etiam patietur, qui mensuram circuli exterioris adraserit, ut ponderis minuat quantitatem, vel figuratum solidum adulterâ imitatione in vendendo subjecerit. In *Constantius*'s time the same punishment was inflicted. *L. PRÆMIO. C. THEOD. DE FALSA MONETA. Præmio accusatoribus proposito, quicunque solidorum adulter potuerit reperiri, vel à quoquam fuerit publicatus, illicò omni dilatione submotâ flammarum exustionibus mancipetur.* And afterwards under *Valentinianus*, *Theodosius*, and *Arcadius*, they were accounted and suffered as *rei læsæ Majestatis. L. FALSÆ MONETÆ. COD. EODEM. Falsæ monetæ rei, quos vulgò paracharactas vocant, Majestatis crimine tenentur obnoxii.* But no where is it mentioned concerning the *denarii* and *quinarii*, which were the silver coins in common use, how much should be their weight. Wherefore in such a silence of ancient authors, we have no more solid and sure foundation of our inquiry, than either by our selves to examine the weight of the fairest coins under the Emperors, or else to relate what others long before our time have

Of the DENARIUS. 317

have obferved. *Antonius Auguftinus* in general informs us, when coins were at their higheft perfection, and how they began to decline with the *Roman* empire: as commonly when money comes to be abafed, and that the mint, like the pulfe, beats too flowly and irregularly, it is an evident fymptom of fome diftemper in the bowels of a ftate. (z) *The medals of all times* (faith he) [*are worthy to be obferved by artizans*] *beginning from* Alexander *the Great, in whofe time they principally flourifhed, till the Emperor* Gallienus, *when they chiefly fell together with the empire. From thence to the end of* Juftinian *there are found good medals of all the Emperors, but with a notable diminution of their politenefs and ancient perfection. Thofe which we have after* Juftinian *are unfufferably bad. The fault by all men is affigned to the* Huns, *and* Vandals, *and* Alanes, *and* Goths, *and* Longobards, *and to*

(z) Le medaglie di tutti i tempi [fono degne da effer offervate degli artifeci] comminciando de Aleffandro magno, nell' età del quale principalmente fiorirono, per fin al tempo dell' Imperador Gallieno, nel quale caddero affatto infieme con l' imperio. Da indi poi in finà Giuftiniano fi trovano bon medaglie di tutti gli Imperadori, ma con notabil perdita della politezza & perfettione antica. Quel poi che habbiamo doppo Giuftiniano, è tanto cattivo che non fi può fofferire. Et fe ne dà quafi da ognano la colpa à gli Unni, à i Vandali, à gli Alani, à i Goti, à i Longobardi, & ad altre barbare & fiere nationi, che fignoreggiarono gran parte d'Europa. *Ant. Auguft. dialog.* 1.

other

other barbarous and savage nations, who conquered the greatest part of Europe. *Erizzo,* who lived almost an hundred years since, a very diligent man in the *Roman* coins, but it is to be wished that he had used more judgment in the explication of them, more particularly informs us: *(a) Having compared the weight of those sorts of money which are equal in weight to the* Roman denarius, *with the medals of silver which have the heads of the* Roman *Emperors imprinted, I have found them not a little different, so that as it were all those medals weigh less than the* denarius. *And having also weighed those medals which have the effigies of the* Cæsars, *I have continually found them different amongst themselves in weight.* This uncertainty so troubled *Villalpandus,* after many experiments made at *Rome,* that he knew not what to determine. And it seems *(b) Blondus* long before conceived it impossible: *Hæc omnia qualia per singulas ætates fuerint, examussim ostendere non magis difficile quàm impossibile fuerit; non solùm quia obscuris, & nostrâ ætate*

(a) Havendo io tali monete, le quali sono del peso di un Denario Rom. pareggiate di peso alle medaglie di argento, che hanno scolpite le teste de i Principe Romani, le ho ritrovate differenti non poco del peso, si che quelle medaglie pesano quasi tutte meno del Denario; & havendo ancora pesate quelle medaglie che hanno scolpita la effigie de i Cæsari, le ho sempre ritrovate differenti fra loro nel peso. *Erizzo.*

(b) Blondus l. 5. de Roma triumph.

ignotis

ignotis verbis sunt à majoribus tradita, sed quia omnis ferè ætas suam habuit cudendi varietatem & formam. Wherefore, for farther satisfaction of the reader, I shall relate some observations of mine own, especially those of the twelve first *Cæsars*, which I took, with many others, by an accurate balance, from some choice cabinets in *Italy*. And first I shall begin with the gold coins: for seeing the *aurei* under the former *Cæsars* were *in duplâ ratione* to the *denarii*, therefore the weight of those being known, we cannot be ignorant of the weight of the *denarii Cæsarei*. Besides, they are not subject to be consumed by time and rust, but only *ex intertrimento*, and therefore we may the safelier give credit to them. And lastly, because the difference, tho' but of a grain, is of some consideration in gold, the masters of the mint use to be the more circumspect about them: whereas in silver coins, since it is hardly worth the pains to stand precisely upon the excess or defect of every grain, therefore there are few of these so exact, but either exceed or want in the very mint one or two grains, and sometimes more.

The Weight of some Aurei *under the first Twelve Cæsars.*

	Eng. gr.
* C. CAES. COS. III.	$123\frac{7}{12}$
* A second, on the reverse, A. HIRTIVS. PR	$122\frac{1}{2}$
* A third	$124\frac{1}{2}$
AVGVSTVS. CAESAR. III. VIR.	$119\frac{1}{2}$
A second, on the reverse, OB CIVES SERVATOS	$119\frac{1}{3}$
* A third, on the reverse, DIVOS. AVG. DIVI. F	119
TIBERIVS	$118\frac{1}{4}$
* A second { On the forepart, TI. CAESAR. DIVI. AVG. F. AVGVSTVS — On the reverse, a Temple.	$117\frac{1}{8}$
CALIGVLA	
CLAVDIVS, on the reverse, S.P.Q.R. OB. CIVES. SERVATOS--	117
A second	$117\frac{3}{4}$
A third	$118\frac{1}{2}$
* NERO, on the reverse, SALVS—	116
* A second, on the reverse, JVPPITER. CVSTOS	$113\frac{1}{2}$
* A third, on the reverse, CONCORDIA. AVGVSTA	113

GALBA,

Of the DENARIUS.

	Eng. gr.
GALBA, *on the reverse*, CONCORDIA. PROVINCIARVM ——	115
OTHO, *on the reverse*, SECVRITAS S. P. Q. R. ——	108¾
VITELLIVS, *on the reverse*, LIBERTAS. RESTITVTA ——	112¼
VESPASIANVS, *on the reverse*, PACI AVGVSTI ——	111
* *A second, on the reverse*, COS. III. TR. POT. ——	114¼
A third, on the reverse, PONT. MAX. TR. P. COS. VI ——	111
* *A fourth, on the reverse*, PACI. AVGVSTI —— ——	108¾
A fifth, on the reverse, PACI. AVGVSTI —— ——	110
* T. VESPASIANVS, *on the reverse*, ANNONA. AVG ——	109¼
* DOMITIANVS. COS. II. ——	113
* *A second*, DOMITIANVS. COS. VI. CAESAR. AUG. F. *on the reverse*, IVVENTVTIS. PRINCEPS —— ——	112¼

These *aurei* were selected by me out of several others, as the fairest and entirest; and amongst these, to such as I have prefixed an asterisc, they are such as seemed so perfect, that I could make no just objections against them. By these it appears

that

that (c) *Pliny*, speaking of the gold coins, rightly informs us: *Paulatimque Principes imminuere pondus, imminuisse verò ad* XLVIII. *That by degrees the Emperors lessened the weight* [of the aurei] *to the forty-eighth part of the* Roman *pound*; that is, to the fourth part of the ounce. For this is the lowest weight that I find till *Heliogabalus*'s time, who coined new sorts of *aurei*, different from what had been the constant practise of the *Roman* state; some of which were the fiftieth part of the *libra Romana*, and others again so massy, that they were *centeni*, or *bilibres*; which not long after were altered, and abolished by *Alexander Severus*. The manner is expressed by (d) *Ælius Lampridius*, in the Life of *Alexander Severus*: *Formas binarias, ternarias, & quaternarias, & denarias etiam, atque amplius, usque ad bilibres quoque & centenas, quas Heliogabalus invenerat, resolvi præcepit, nec in usu cujusquam versari: atque ex eo his materiæ nomen inditum est, cùm diceret plus largiendi hanc esse Imperatori causam, si cum multos solidos minores dare posset, dans decem vel amplius unâ formâ, triginta, & quinquaginta, & centum dare cogeretur.* Under the same *Alexander Severus* began the *se-*

(c) Plin. l. 33. c. 3.
(d) Lampridius in Alex. Severo.

misses

miſſes aureorum, and *tremiſſes*, to be coined, which had not formerly been in uſe. The *ſemiſſes* were anſwerable in weight to the *denarii Cæſarei* when they were leaſt, that is, ninety-ſix in the *Roman* pound; tho' *Agricola, Villalpandus*, and others, upon a miſtake, equal them then to the *drachma Attica*. (e) *Ælius Lampridius*, writing of *Alexander Severus*, plainly expreſſes, that in his time they began: *Túmq; primum ſemiſſes aureorum formati ſunt, tunc etiam, cùm ad tertiam partem aurei vectigal decidiſſet, tremiſſes, dicente Alexandro etiam quartarios futuros, quòd minus non poſſet.* Afterwards *Conſtantine, Conſtantius, Julian*, and other ſucceeding Emperors, leſſened the weight of the *aurei*, whereby there came to be ſeventy-two in the *Roman* pound; ſo that each of them weighed the *ſextula*, or four *ſcrupula*. That the *aurei* of *Conſtantine*'s time were ſixty-two in the *Roman* pound, is moſt evident out of the *Codex Theodoſianus*, where they are alſo abſolutely called *ſolidi*, without the addition of *aurei*. (f) *L. SIQVIS. C. THEOD. DE. PONDERATORIBVS, ET AVRI INLATIONE. Siquis ſolidos appendere voluerit auri cocti, ſeptem ſolidos quaternorum ſcripu-*

(e) Lampridius in Alex. Severo.
(f) Codex Theodoſ. l. 1, de Ponderatoribus.

lorum,

lorum, nostris vultibus figuratos, adpendat pro singulis unciis; XIV. *verò pro duabus, juxta hanc formam omnem summam debiti inlaturus : eâdem ratione servandâ, etsi materiam quis inferat, ut solidos dedisse videatur.* (g) *Pancirollus*, in his *Thesaurus variarum lectionum utriusque juris*, reads VI. *solidos* instead of VII. and XII. instead of XIV. And that it must necessarily be so, besides that the *solidi* of *Constantine* now extant prove as much, may be collected out of the proportion of weight which is here assigned by *Constantine* himself to the *solidi*, and that is four *scruples*, or the *sextula*. For the *solidus* containing four *scruples*, and the ounce containing twenty-four *scruples*, there will therefore be six *solidi* in the ounce; again, the pound consisting of twelve ounces, and the ounce of six *solidi*, the whole pound therefore will consist of seventy-two *solidi*. These *aurei* by *Justinian* in like manner are termed *solidi*. L. *QVOTIESCVNQVE. C. DE SVSCEPTORIBVS, PRÆPOSITIS, ET ARCARIIS.* Where he also defines the same weight: (h) *Quotiescunque certa summa solidorum pro tituli qualitate debetur, & auri massa transmittitur,*

(g) Gui. Pancirolli Thesaur. var. lect. utr. juris.
(h) Cod. lib. 10. tit. 70. in rescrip. Valentin. & Valentis Impp.

Of the DENARIUS.

(i) *in* LXXII. *solidos libra feratur accepta.* The same thing is implicitly confirmed by *Isidorus* (*l.* 16. *Orig. c.* 24.) *Solidus alio nomine sextula dicitur; quod iis sex uncia compleatur. Hunc, ut diximus, vulgus aureum solidum vocat, cujus tertiam partem ideo dixerunt tremissem, quod solidum faciat ter missus.* Where (k) *Agricola*, I imagine, truly finds fault with him for calling the *solidus sextula*; though the proportion he assigns is right, that is, that the *solidus* was the sixth part of the *Roman* ounce, and contained ἓξάγιε ςαθμὸν, *the weight of the sextula,* as it is attested by (*l*) *Zonaras*; or, which is all one, that seventy two *solidi* were made out of a *Roman* pound, as *Justinian* before expresly assigned; and as infinite store of the *solidi*, or *aurei*, from *Constantine*

(i) This excellent place very hardly escaped *Haloander's* emendation, who had a great mind to have play'd the critick, and to have altered it. For he thus writes: *In vetusto codice in rasam membranam hæc ita reposita sunt, ut certum sit alteram, & fortasse genuinam lectionem sublatam, & legendum, duodequinquaginta, aut certe quinquaginta.* A goodly consequence! because the parchment was scraped, and the first writing altered, therefore the true reading must be expunged, and a false one put in: whereas he might with more candour and ingenuity have concluded the contrary, that the false one was expunged by the scribe, and the true one inserted. For who uses in copying of MSS. to scrape any thing out of the *apographum,* but only when by collating it he finds it to be different from the original?

(*k*) Agricola l. 2. de Pond. & Temperat. Monetarum.
(*l*) Zonar. l. 3.

to *Focas*, which I have weighed, manifestly prove.

In the same place of (*m*) *Isidorus* we may collect the reason why the *aureus* was called *solidus*. After that the *semisses* and *trimisses aurei* were coined, the *aureus* was called *solidus*, because nothing was wanting to it: *Solidum enim antiqui integrum dicebant, & totum.* In which sense the *solidus* was also taken for the *libra* or *assis*; that is, as the *assis* is taken for the whole, according to that usual phrase of Civilians, *ex asse hæres*, when one is heir to the whole inheritance; so the *solidus* was taken for the whole *assis*. (*n*) *Volusius Metianus: Prima divisio solidi, id est libræ, quod as vocatur, in duas partes dimidias deducitur.* From hence (saith (*o*) *Salmasius*) the Romans called that the *solidus aureus*, *when it had the same weight in gold, which the* solidus, *that is, the* assis *had in respect of brass, that is, two* drachmes. Though I rather suppose, that the *aureus* was called *solidus* first of all in *Severus*'s time, not for containing two *denarii* in weight (which *Salmasius* calls *drachmes*) for so it always did under the later Consuls

---

(*m*) Isidorus l. 16. Orig. c. 24.
(*n*) Vol. Metianus de Assis distrib.
(*o*) Hinc & solidum aureum dixere Romani, ubi idem pondus habere cœpit in auro quod solidus, id est, as, haberet in ære, duarum nempe drachmarum. *Salmas. de modo Usur.* c. vi. p. 258.

Of the DENARIUS. 327

and first Emperors; but because the *aureus* was then first divided into two parts, that is, into the *semisses* and *tremisses*, and so relatively to these the whole *aureus* was rightly called *solidus*. Of the same opinion is *(p) Agricola*: *Quos aureos, cùm respectum ad semisses & tremisses haberent, tunc primò dixerunt solidos, quòd semisses ex dimidiâ eorum parte, tremisses ex tertiâ constarent.*

The *semisses* and *tremisses* of the other Emperors, at some distance after *Severus*, came to be less in the same proportion as the *aurei* were lessened. For the *aurei* of *Severus* were double to the *denarii Cæsarei*, and therefore but forty-eight in the pound, and not fifty, as *Heliogabalus* made, whose error *Severus* corrected. But when the later Emperors made seventy-two *aurei* out of the *Roman* pound, the *semisses* came also to be diminished, and were half of these new *aurei*, and not of the former, and the *tremisses* the third part. And here the *aurei* lost that proportion which they kept before, of being double to the *denarii*. Of these *tremisses* is *Justinian* to be understood, *L. FORTISS. MILITIBVS. COD. DE MILITARI VESTE*: *Fortissimis militibus nostris per Illyricum non binos tremisses pro singulis clamydibus, sed singulos solidos dari*

(p) Agricola h 2. de Pond. & Temp. Monetarum.

præ-

præcipimus. And this may be farther proved by a fair (*q*) *tremiſſis* in gold of mine own of *Juſtinian*, with the infcription D. N. JUSTINIANUS, weighing twenty-one grains *Engliſh*, and therefore wanting only three grains and one third, which it may have loſt by time; otherwiſe it would be exactly the 216th part of the *Roman* pound, that is, the third part of the *aureus* or *ſolidus* of thoſe times: whereas if it had been coined to the proportion of the *aureus* when there were 48 in the pound, it ſhould have weighed 36 grains and an half; ſo that it muſt have loſt 15 and an half, a difference ſo great in a piece of gold ſo fair, and withall of ſo ſmall a quantity, altogether improbable. And therefore this coin alone, if no more were extant, would confute their opinion, who maintain that the *tremiſſis* of *Juſtinian* differed not from the *tremiſſis* of *Severus*, and conſequently the *aurei* of them both, better than the reaſons produced by (*r*) *Covarruvias* to the contrary have done.

(*q*) I have ſince peruſed another *tremiſſis* in gold, a very fair one, with this inſcription, D. N. JUSTINUS. P. F. AUG. weighing twenty-two grains, and better, which formerly belonged to the learned Geographer *Ortelius*; beſides a third of *Majorianus*, with CONOB. ſuperſcribed (which ſignifies *Conſtantinopolitanum obrixum*, or *Conſtantinopoli obſignatum*) weighing likewiſe twenty-two grains; and a fourth, of *Juſtinian*, weighing twenty-three.

(*r*) *Covarruvias* tom. 1. c. 3. paragr. 1. & 2. de vet. aureis & argenteis nummis.

Of the DENARIUS.

The Weight of some of the fairest Aurei *of the* Roman *Emperors, from* Nerva *to* Heraclius.

On the fore part of the Aurei are these characters.	On the reverse these.	Engl. gra.
IMP. NERVA. CAES. AVG. P. M. TR. P. II. Cos. IIII. P. P.	FIDES. EXERCITVS	111½
IMP. TRAIANVS. AVG. GER. DAC. P. M. TR. P. COS. VI. P. P.	DIVVS. PATER. TRAIANI	110½
IMP. CAESAR. TRAIAN. HADRIANVS. AVG.	COS. II. P. M. TR. P. P. AVG	121¼
ANTONINVS. AVG. PIVS. P. P. TR. P. XII.	COS. IIII	119¾
ANTONINVS. AVG. ARMENIACVS	P. M. TR. P XVIII. IMP. II. COS. III. *In scuto Victoriæ.* VIC. AVG	118⅞
IMP. CAES. L. AVREL. VERVS. AVG	CONCORDIÆ. AVGVSTOR TR. P. II. COS. II	117¼
L. VERVS. AVG. ARM. PARTHI. MAX	TR. P. V. IMP. III. COS II	113¼
M. COMM. ANT. P. FEL. AVG. P. P	IOVI. VLTORI	114
SEVER. P. AVG. P. M. TR. P. X. COS. III	FELICITAS. SAECVLI	11⅛
IMP. M. ANT. GORDIANVS. AFR. AVG	CAESAR. M. ANT. GORDIANVS. AFR. AVG	114
* *Trebonianus Gallus*	P. M. TR. P. IIII. COS. II. P. P	75¼
* *Gallienus*	P. M. TR. P. III. COS. P. P	74½
IMP. PROBVS. P. F. AVG	VICTORIOSO. SEMPER	106
IMP. C. CARINVS. P. F. AVG	SPES. AVGG	72½

aa 3   DIO-

DIOCLETIANVS. P. F. AVG	IOVI. CONSERVAT. AVGG—	77$\frac{1}{2}$
------ MAXIMIANVS.	VIRTVS. MILITVM. T —	74$\frac{3}{4}$
CONSTANTINVS. MAX. AVG.	SECVRITAS. REIPVBLICAE— *infra*, TR	70$\frac{1}{2}$
CONSTANTINVS. P. F. AVG.	VIRTVS. AVGVSTI. N — —	68
CONSTANTIVS	GLORIA. REIPVBLICAE. VOT. XXX. MVLTIS. XXXX. *infr.* SNNS	70
IM. CAE. MAGNENTIVS. AVG	VICTORIA. AVG. LIB. ROMANOR. *infra*, TR	70$\frac{3}{4}$
FL. CL. IVLIANVS. P. F. AVG	VOT. X. MVLT. XX. *infra*, ANT.-	68$\frac{1}{4}$
D. N. IOVIANVS. P. F. PERP. AVG.	SECVRITAS. REIPVBLICAE — VOT. V. MVLT. X. *infra*, COS. P	68
D. N. VALENS. P. F. AVG	RESTITVTOR. REIP. *infra*, ANTO—	68$\frac{3}{4}$
D. N. VALENTINIANVS. P. F. AVG	RESTITVTOR. REIPVBLICAE —	69$\frac{1}{4}$
A second — —	—	69
D. N. GRATIANVS. P. F. AVG	VICTORIA. AVGG. *infra*, TROES—	69
A second — —	—	68$\frac{3}{4}$
D. N. THEODOSIVS. P. F. AVG	VICTORIA. AVGG. *infra*, CON —	68
A second — —	—	69$\frac{3}{4}$
D. N. ARCADIVS. P. F. AVG	NOVA. SPES. REIPVBLICAE— *intra corollam*. XX. XXX. *infra*, CONOB	67$\frac{1}{2}$
A second — —	—	68
D. N. HONORIVS. P. F. AVG	VICTORIA. AVGGG. *statua, cui inscript* R.V. *infra*, CONOB	69$\frac{1}{4}$
A second — —	—	69$\frac{3}{4}$
A third, D. N. HONORIVS. P. F. AVG	VICTORIA. AVGG. N. D. *infra*, CONOB	68$\frac{3}{4}$

D. N.

Of the DENARIUS. 331

D. N. THEODOSIVS. P. F. AVG	IMP. XXXXII. COS. XVII. P. F. *infra*, CONOB ———	69¼
D. N. PLA. VALENTINIANVS	VICTORIA. Avggg. *infra*, CONOB. —	68
D. N. VALENTINIANVS. AVG	VICTORIA Avgga. *infra*, CONOB ———	69¼
D. N. VALENTINIANVS. P. F. AVG	VICTORIA. AVGG. *infra*, TROES. ———	68
D. N. IVL. NEPOS. P. F. AVG	VICTORIA Avggg. A. *infra*, CONOB--	69¼
D. N. ANASTASIVS. P. F. AVG	VICTORIA. Avggg. *infra*, CONOB ——	68½
D. N. IVSTINIANVS. P. F. AVG	VICTORIA. AVGG, A. *infra*, CONOB--	69
D. N. FOCAS. PERP. AVG	VICTORIA. AVGG. *infra*, CONOB ———	68
D. N. FOCAS. PERP. AVG	VICTORIA. AVG. *infra*, CONOB ———	69¼
——— HERACLIVS ———	———	69¼
A second ———		69¼

And thus much of the *aurei* under the former and later Emperors, as they serve to illustrate and prove the weight of the *denarii Cæsarei*, which is our next, and principal enquiry.

The *denarii* under the *Cæsars*, were almost as various and unconstant as the *aurei*, sometimes more, sometimes less; and if they had not been so, they could not have kept that proportion to the *aurei* of the former Emperors which we assigned. From *Augustus*'s time to *Vespasian*, as I find by examining many of them, they continually almost decreased, till from being the seventh part of the *Roman* ounce, they came now to be the eighth part; and therefore ninety-six were coined out of the *Roman libra*; whereas before, under the Confuls, eighty-four. From *Vespasian* to *Alexander Severus*, as far as I have observed, the silver continued at a kind of stay in respect of weight, excepting only such coins as upon some extraordinary occasion, both then and in the first Emperors time, were stamped either in honour of the prince, or of the empress and *Augusta familia*, or else in memory of some eminent action. These last most usually were equal to the *denarii Consulares*, and many of them had these characters EX. S. C. or else S. P. Q. R. Under *Severus* and *Gordianus* the *denarii* began to recover their primitive weight, and came to be equal to the *denarii Consulares*, the half of which also were exactly the *quinarii*, and so continued during the succeeding emperors till *Justinian*, with little diminution, but most commonly with a notable abasement, and mixture of allay. After *Justinian*, there happened such a deluge of barbarous nations, which overflowed the greatest part of *Europe*, that not only the coins, but even the liberal arts and sciences, began with the majesty of the empire to decline from their first lustre and perfection.

Where-

Of the DENARIUS.

Wherefore I shall not speak of the μιλιαρήσιον, or μιλιαρίσιον, a sort of silver coin in use before and after *Justinian*, which some collect out of (*s*) *Cedrenus* to have been the eighth part of the ounce, and therefore equal to the *denarius* in the lowest valuation; though (*t*) *Suidas* renders μιλιαρήσιον τὸ τῦ νομίσματος δέκατον, and the *Scholiastes Basilic.* Eclog. 23. δωδέκατον, and to contain twenty-four φόλλεις. But I shall not positively determine either the weight of this, or of the κεράτιον, or *siliqua* in silver, both coined when the imperial seat was translated to *Byzantium*, unless I had examined some of the fairest of them. And for the same reason I shall not define the *Hebrew denarius*, mentioned by *Elias* in *Thisbite*, in the word דינר, and by (*u*) *Moses Gerundensis* upon *Exodus*, and by the *Chaldy Paraphrase*, 2 *Reg.* 5. 5. which I imagine to have been no other than the *Roman denarius* used by the *Jews*: neither shall I determine the *Arabian* دينار *dinar*, and درهم *derham*; the former of which the *Rabbins* call דינרא ערבאי, used by *Rhasis*, *Avicen*, *Mesue*, and by several other *Arabians*, both Physicians and Historians.

(*s*) Cedrenus in Histor. Compend.
(*t*) Suidas in voce Μιλιαρήσιον.
(*u*) p. 72. col. 4.

in medio spicæ, & 20 denarii faciunt unciam, & 12 unciæ faciunt libram. Under (*a*) *Edward* III. it came first to be diminished to the twenty-fixth part of the *Troy* ounce; and under (*b*) *Henry* VI. it fell to be the two and thirtieth. In (*c*) *Edward* IV's time it came to be the fortieth. Under (*d*) *Henry* VIII. at first it was the fortieth, then the forty-fifth. Afterward sixty pence were coined out of the ounce, in the second year of (*e*) Queen *Elizabeth*, and during her reign, sixty-two; which proportion is observed in these times. So that it is evident that *Ethelred*'s penny was bigger than three of ours. And after-times may see this of ours, as well as the *Roman denarius*, to be quite diminished, and brought to nothing. For if either our own exigencies, or the exigencies of foreign states, with whom we have commerce, cause us or them (as occasions will never be wanting) to alter the proportions of the gold and silver coins, either in respect of weight, or in respect of purity, or lastly, in respect of the valuation the gold bears to silver; by all, or some of these causes, there will inevitably happen such a diminution of the penny (and proportionably of our other coins)

(*a*) Stat. 9. Edw. 3. (*b*) Stat. 2. Hen. 6. (*c*) Stat. 5. Edw. 4. (*d*) Stat. 36. Hen. 8. (*e*) Stat. 2. Eliz.

that

Of the DENARIUS. 337

that at length it will not be worth the coining. But I leave this speculation to such, whom it doth more nearly concern. And certainly it is a consideration not of the least importance; money being as the sinews and strength of a state, so the life and soul of commerce; and if those advantages which one country may make upon another, in the mystery of exchanges and valuation of coins, be not throughly discovered and prevented by such as sit at the helm of the state, it may fare with them after much commerce, as with some bodies after much food, that instead of growing full and fat, they may pine away, and fall into an irrecoverable consumption. But I return to the *Roman denarius*, which we have brought so low, that there is nothing now left of it, but only the name, and that also suffered an (*f*) alteration. For the later *Greeks* instead of the δηνάριον, called it the δηνέριον; and both *Greeks* and *Latins*, and sometimes the *Arabians*, took it not in the same sense as it passed for in the first institution, that is, a silver coin, worth in valuation

---

(*f*) In the same manner the *solidus* or *aureus*, as it lost its valuation, so suffered an alteration in the *Greek* name. For instead of χρυσῦς, we find the Glosses to render it χρύσιν⊙. Glossæ. χρύσιν⊙ *solidus*; and in the same Glosses we read δηνδεια interpreted *biniones*, and δηνάριον *sestertium*, and δηνάριον λδικὸν *asprum*.

ten

ten or fixteen *asses*, but for any sort of coin whatsoever. And therefore (g) *Meursius*'s observation, in his *Glossarium Græco-Barbarum*, is worth our consideration: *Postea δηνέριον dixerunt ævo corruptiore, & generaliter pro quâvis pecuniâ. Sicut Itali* denaro, *Galli* denier, *Hispani* dinero. *Anonymus de Bello sacro*:

Δωσεια ἔχετε πολλά, δότε τῷ ταβερνάρῃ.
Ἐνδεετε πολὺν χρσὶ ᾗ πίνετε μετ' ἀυτες.

Whence the learned (g) *Joseph Scaliger* rightly observes, that *ultimis temporibus denarii pro exiguâ stipe usurpati sunt, ut hodie in Gallia. Imperator Aurelianus: Philippeos minutulos quinquagenos, æris denarios centum. Eos Vopiscus in Bonoso sestertios æris vocat. Macrobius de nummo ratito loquens, qui erat æreus:* Ita fuisse signatum hodieq; intelligitur in aleæ lusu, cùm pueri denarios in sublime jactantes, capita aut navia lusu teste vetustatis exclamant. *In Evangelio secundum Marcum* 12. λεπτὰ δύο ὅ ἐςι κοδράντης· *Hilarius duos denarios viduæ inopis Deo acceptiores. Luc.* 10. ἐκβαλὼν δύο δηνάρια· *Ambrosius, duo æra. Vetustissimus est igitur denarii usus* ἀντὶ τε χαλκισμε, *vel stipe.* Thus far *Scaliger*.

(g) Meursii Glossarium Græco-Barbar. in voce δηνέριον.
(h) Scalig. de re Numm.

Of the DENARIUS. 339

Such an uncertainty being then, as we have mentioned, both of the *aurei* and *denarii* under the firſt *Cæſars*, in whoſe times the pureſt coins and the beſt wits moſt flouriſhed, and ſuch an abaſement and impureneſs of the ſilver under the later Emperors, no reaſonable man can imagine, that either the ancient Grammarians, Poets, Orators, Hiſtorians, or eſpecially Phyſicians, whom it did moſt concern to be preciſe, and moſt of which lived under the former Emperors, did ever allude to the weight of the *denarius Cæſareus*, but rather to the *Conſularis*. And to this only, and to no other, did the *Attick drachme*, mentioned by *Dioſcorides, Cleopatra, Galen, Julius Pollux, Oribaſius*, and the reſt of the *Greek* authors correſpond. And thus have we finiſhed our diſcourſe concerning the *denarius*, in the notion and acception of the ancients, both *Greeks* and *Latins*.

Our next labour ſhould be to compare it with the ſtandards for weights of divers nations, uſed in theſe times. For which I had recourſe to the publick *zygoſtatæ* and *ponderatores* in my travels abroad; and for my obſervations I muſt refer the reader to this enſuing table.

A Table

340 Of the DENARIUS.

A Table of the Gold and Silver (i) Weights of several Nations, taken from their Standards, and compared with the Denarius.

	Eng. grains.
Such parts, or grains, of the *English* standard for gold and silver (or of the *Troy* weight) as the *denarius Consularis* containeth 62, according to the weight of the best coins, or according to the weight of the *congius* of *Vespasian*	62 4/7
The ancient, and modern *Roman* ounce containeth	438
The ancient, and modern *Roman* pound, consisting of twelve ounces, containeth	5256
The *Troy* pound, or *English* standard of gold and silver, consisting of twelve ounces, containeth	5760

(i) These weights (excepting the *rotulo* of *Damascus*) were diligently compared with the originals and standards; in like manner as I examined the measures above described. In both which, if any shall find some little difference from some originals, as five or six grains in the *English* pound, and it may be one or two parts of a thousand in the *English* foot different from the standards in the Exchequer, or the Tower, or at *Winchester*, or some other place, it is not much to be wonder'd. For I have found as great differences in collating the *English* standards themselves; and have heard *Gasparo Berti* (one of the exactest men in this kind that I have known) to complain of the same diversity at *Rome*. And though

Of the DENARIUS.

	Eng. grains.
The *Troy*, or *English* ounce (to which, five shillings two-pence of our money in these times are equal) containeth	480
The *Paris* pound, or standard for gold and silver, of sixteen ounces	7560
The *Paris* ounce	$472\frac{1}{2}$
The *Spanish* pound, or standard for gold and silver, of sixteen ounces, taken by me at *Gibraltar*	7090
Another weigh'd by me at *Gibraltar*	7085
The Spanish *pound in* Villalpandus *is (I know not by what error) but*	7035
The *Spanish* ounce at *Gibraltar* (the pound consisting of 7090 grains *English*)	$443\frac{1}{2}$

though it be a shame, that in any well-governed kingdom or common-wealth, the standards, which are the rules of commutative justice, should be unequal, and therefore unjust; yet unless more art and circumspection be used, than hitherto hath been put in practise, it is impossible but such inequalities will creep in.

But this observation of mine, by some may be thought too nice and curious. That which follows, I am certain is as necessary, as the preservation of the life of many a man. And that is, that some Physicians erroneously imagine the *granum auri* to be alike in all nations. And therefore *Fernelius*, a very able man (who, I think, was the first author of that opinion) writes thus: (*Fern. l.* 4. *c.* 6. *Method. Medendi*) *Granum, cui tanquam basi reliqua innituntur pondera, ratum constansque esse decet; neque id granum esse hordei, neque tritici, neque ciceris, neque frugis ullius, aut leguminis, quod nullius par sit ubique gentium pondus. At vero nummarium minutum, quod aurifabri granum appellant, & Latinè momentum dici*

Of the DENARIUS.

	Eng. grains.
The *Venetian* pound, or standard for gold and silver, of twelve ounces	5528
The *Venetian* ounce	460 $\frac{1}{3}$
The *Neapolitan* pound, or standard for gold and silver, of 12 ounces	4950
The *Neapolitan* ounce	412 $\frac{1}{2}$
The pound, or standard for gold and silver, of twelve ounces, at *Florence*, *Pisa*, and *Ligorn*	5286
The ounce at *Florence*, *Pisa*, and *Ligorn*	440 $\frac{1}{2}$
The pound, or standard at *Siena* for gold and silver, of twelve ounces	5178

dici potest, omnibus mundi nationibus unum idemque est, & stabile, quod auri sacra fames, & opum furiosa libido, inviolatè & incorruptè servat, idque signis & exemplaribus undique identidem collatis. Indeed it was an useful fancy of his to think of some common measure, in which all nations might concur; tho' it is more to be wished for, than ever to be expected. But that asseveration of his, *inviolatè & incorruptè servat, idq; signis & exemplaribus undiq; identidem collatis*, from a man of such rare-abilities, I cannot but extreamly wonder at. For if we shall go no farther to confute his assertion, than to compare our *grana auri* with those of *Paris*, which *Fernelius* used, we shall find ours much bigger; twenty-nine *English* grains almost equalling thirty-six of *Paris*. Or if we shall compare the *Spanish grana auri* with his, we shall find those much less, thirty-six *Spanish* grains weighing but twenty-eight and a half of his at *Paris*. The like could I demonstrate in those of other countries. By which dangerous and notable error, for want either of due care, or an exact balance, we may conceive, that whatsoever also is delivered by the ancients in the like nature, is not presently without due examination to be credited.

Of the DENARIUS.

	Eng. grains.
The ounce at *Siena*	431¼
The ounce at *Genoa* for gold and silver	405⅔
The *Turkish Okeh*, or *Oke*, at *Constantinople*, consisting of four hundred silver drams	19128
The silver dram generally used in the Great *Turk*'s dominions; as also in *Persia*, and in the *Mogul*'s countries, if I be not misinformed	47 $\frac{43}{50}$
The *Turkish sultani*, or *Ægyptian sherif*, being a gold coin, with which the *Barbary* and *Venetian chequeen*, and *Norimberg ducat*, within a grain, more or less agree	53⅔
The *ratel* or *rotulo* for gold and silver, of 144 drams, at *Cairo*	6886 $\frac{2}{25}$
The *ratel* or *rotulo* for silk, of 720 drams, at *Damascus* (with which I suppose they there formerly weighed their gold and silver; because most countries use the same weights for silks, gold, and silver)	34430⅖

In this table I judg'd it much fitter to compare the *denarius* with the standards for gold and silver of several nations, than with their gold and silver coins now current.

rent. Becaufe the pounds and ounces of the ftandard continue alway the fame; whereas the gold and filver coins being cut in feveral proportions, according to the exigencies of the ftate, admit of feveral alterations and diminutions.

The CONCLUSION.

IT was my intention from the *Pes Romanus* and *Denarius*, together with the *Congius* of *Vefpafian*, to have deduced the other weights and meafures ufed by the *Romans*; and from thofe of the *Romans*, by fuch teftimonies as are upon record in the writings of the ancients, to have inferred thofe of the *Hebrews, Babylonians, Ægyptians, Grecians,* and of other nations. A work I confefs intricate, and full of difficulties; wherein I could expect neither to give myfelf, nor others fatisfaction, without firft laying fome fure and folid principles for the bafis and foundation. Therefore that occafioned me to infift the more largely in the profecution of the *pes Romanus* and *denarius*, and to examine all the ways I could poffibly imagine for the evident proof and confirmation of them. What in this kind I have done, and with how much truth and diligence, I leave to the impartial teft of after times; the reft at more leifure may
be

The Conclusion.

be perfected. Yet these following observations, as a *coronis* to the whole work, I thought would not be unacceptable, if by way of anticipation I communicated them to the world: and those are, how the originals and standards of weights and measures, notwithstanding the revolutions and vicissitudes of Empires, may be perpetuated to posterity. Amongst several ways which I have thought of, I know none more certain and unquestionable, than to compare them with some remarkable and lasting monuments in remote countries, that have stood unimpaired for many hundred years, and are likely to continue as many more. In which kind I made choice of the first and most easterly of the three great Pyramids in *Ægypt*; of the basis of that admirable *Corinthian* pillar, erected (as I suppose) by one of the *Ptolomies*, a quarter of a mile distant to the south from *Alexandria*, being one vast and entire marble stone; of the rock at *Tarracina*, or *Anxur*, where it adjoins to the *via Appia*, and almost touches the *Tyrrhene* sea; of the gate or entrance into the *Pantheon*, or Temple of *Agrippa*, dedicated by him to all the Gods, and by the Christians to all Saints; of the *Porta sancta*, in that new and exquisite structure of St. *Peter's* church in *Rome*.

If the like had been attempted by some of the ancient Mathematicians, our times would have been freed from much uncertainty in discovering the weights and measures of the *Greeks* and *Latins*.

The first and most easterly of the three great Pyramids in *Ægypt*, hath on the north side a square descent; when you are entered a little past the mouth of it, there is a joint, or line, made by the meeting of two smooth and polish'd stones over your head, which are parallel to those under your feet; the breadth at that joint or line is three feet, and $\frac{463}{1000}$ of the *English* foot.

Within the Pyramid, and about the midst of it, there is a fair room or chamber, the top of which is flat, and covered with nine massy stones; in it there stands a hollow tomb, of one entire marble stone; the length of the south side of this room, at the joint or line where the first and second rows of stone meet, is thirty-four feet, $\frac{380}{1000}$.

The breadth of the west side of the same room, at the joint or line where the first and second row of stones meet, is 17 feet, $\frac{290}{1000}$.

The hollow or inner part of the marble tomb near the top, on the west side of it, is in length six feet, $\frac{488}{1000}$.

The hollow or inner part of the marble tomb near the top of it, on the north side, is in breadth two feet, $\frac{818}{1000}$.

The Conclusion. 347

The basis of the vast *Corinthian* pillar, about a quarter of a mile from *Alexandria* to the south, on the west side of the pillar, at *a b*, is in breadth 12 feet, $\frac{539}{1000}$; at *c d* it is fourteen feet, $\frac{417}{1000}$.

The rock at *Tarracina*, or *Anxur*, near the *via Appia*, close by the *Tyrrhene* sea, hath these figures, besides several others in the same perpendicular, very deeply engraven.

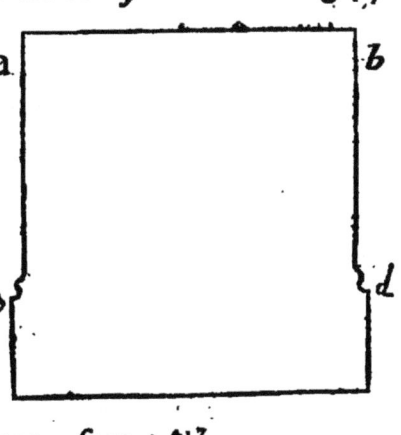

The uppermost line *b c* over the figures CXX, in the innermost and deepest part of the engraving, is in length four *English* feet, and $\frac{702}{1000}$. The lowermost line *d a*, in the innermost and deepest part of the engraving, is in length four feet, $\frac{692}{1000}$.

b b 4   The

The ſtately gate or entrance into the *Pantheon*, or Temple built by *Agrippa* in *Rome*, the jambs, and top and bottom of it, being all of one entire marble ſtone, is in breadth between the jambs or ſides, ſome three inches above the bottom, and ſome nine inches within, nineteen feet, $\frac{622}{1000}$.

The *Porta ſancta*, on the right hand of the frontiſpiece of St. *Peter's* church in *Rome*, is in breadth on the pavement or threſhold, between the jambs or ſides of the entrance, eleven feet, $\frac{928}{1000}$.

The great gate or entrance, which is the middlemoſt of the five in the frontiſpiece of St. *Peter's* church in *Rome*, the doors of which are cover'd with leaves of braſs, with very fair and exquiſite figures, is in breadth on the pavement or threſhold between the jambs or ſides of it, eleven feet, $\frac{948}{1000}$.

The meaſures being fixed, we may likewiſe fix the weights in this manner; by making a veſſel of a cubical figure, anſwerable to the proportion of any one of theſe feet, or palms, or braces, which are deſcribed in the table at the end of the firſt treatiſe. This cubical veſſel being filled with clear fountain water, we are to weigh it with an exact balance, and to expreſs the weight of it by ſome one of thoſe weights, which we have plac'd in a table at the
end

end of the second treatise. The side of this cube being known, and the weight of it in water defined, the rest of the weights in the second table, by way of consequence, by those proportions which we have assigned, may be discovered. Thus for example; the *Roman* foot described by *Villalpandus* is nine hundred eighty-six parts, such as the *English* foot contains a thousand: this being cubed (saith he) weighs of fountain water eighty *Roman* pounds. If therefore there be given nine hundred eighty-six parts of a thousand of the *English* foot, the cube of this will give us eighty *Roman* pounds in fountain water; and consequently the other weights will be discover'd by those proportions we have assigned to them in respect of the *Roman* pound. Again, eighty *Roman* pounds of water being given, if we reduce this into a cubical body, the side of it will give the *Roman* foot described by *Villalpandus*; and consequently the other measures may be deduced by those proportions we have given them in a peculiar table. Whereby it appears, that as by *measures* weights may be preserved, so on the contrary, by *weights* measures may be restored.

Some Directions to be observ'd in comparing the Valuations of COINS.

IN comparing the valuations either of ancient coins with modern, or of modern one with another, we are to consider, first, the *intrinseck* of them, and then the *extrinseck*. The intrinseck is either the *fineness* of the coin in respect of metal, or the *gravity* in respect of weight. The extrinseck I term, first, the *character* imprinted on the coin; and, secondly, the *valuation* injoined by the Prince or State: by which character and valuation, what *originally* and *materially* was but common metal or plate, comes now *legally* and *formally* to be current money. With these limitations if we shall compare ancient coins with modern, and modern one with another, it will be no difficult matter to proportion out their several respective valuations; and withal, to reconcile the seeming repugnancies either of ancient coins now found, differing from the traditions of ancient authors, or the traditions of ancient authors differing amongst themselves.

I shall

I shall first give an instance of modern coins compared with modern, in our *English* money compared with that of *Spain*, as being most familiar to us; the application of which will by analogy serve for all other distinct states and times, using distinct coins.

In comparing therefore *English* money with *Spanish* money in *England*, or *Spanish* money with *English* in *Spain*, we are thus to proceed: First, we are to examine whether they be of a like fineness for the *intrinseck*; if they be, then an ounce of *English* money and an ounce of *Spanish* (supposing the weight of the ounce to be alike) will be of like value in any other country out of *England* and *Spain*, where neither are current, but only considered as so much metal or plate. Secondly, we are to consider the *extrinseck*, that is, the form and stamp of the coin, with the valuation of it by the injunction of the prince of either state; and here that which before was *equal*, comes now to be *unequal*. For an ounce of *English* money in *England* comes to be more worth, than an ounce of *Spanish* money in *England*; because this wants the character, stamp, and valuation of our princes, whereby it is current: and for the same reason will an ounce of *English* money be less in valuation, than an ounce of *Spanish* money in *Spain*, suppoſing (as I ſaid) the ounce in both countries to be exactly one and the ſame.

The ſame analogy will be, if we compare ancient coins, as thoſe of the *Hebrews*, *Greeks*, and *Romans*, with our modern coins. We are firſt to conſider the *intrinſeck* of them, whether they be of a like weight and fineneſs for the metal with ours; and this is the *natural* or *phyſical conſideration*. From whence we may conclude, that if, for example, ſo many *Attick tetradrachmes* do equal in pureneſs and weight ſo many of our *Engliſh ſhillings* newly brought from the mint, or ſo many of our *Troy* or *ſilver ounces* taken from the ſtandard, then are they to be balanced with theſe in the acception of them as plate; and a ſilver-ſmith, abſtracting from the *extrinſeck*, that were to melt them both, would give a like value for them both. But if we, ſecondly, look upon them with the image and character of the ſtate, and in the notion of money, which is the *politick conſideration*; then that which before in the *trutina* and ſcale was equal, in the *foro* and in commerce comes to be unequal; and an ounce of *Engliſh* money ſhall paſs for more than an ounce in *Attick tetradrachmes*, with reference to the expenſes of the mint and to the civil valuation,

depend-

depending upon a mandate or law enacted by the prince.

In like manner it will be, if we compare ancient coins with ancient made in different states, as it is in comparing ancient with modern.

Upon these grounds of reason it will follow, that whereas the *Roman* authors make the *denarius Consularis* to be equal to the *drachma Attica*, and the *Greeks* equal the *drachma Attica* to the *denarius Consularis*, that both say true; and yet both of them, if we speak strictly and exactly, may be deceived. For the *denarius Consularis* examined by the *balance*, which is the best judge of the *intrinseck* (I speak of the *intrinseck in respect of weight*, and not of the *intrinseck in respect of fineness*, that being best discover'd by the *scale*, and this by the *test*; which last, for the more clearness of my discourse, I suppose in all these coins to be alike): I say, the *denarius Consularis* is found by me, contrary to the opinion of all modern writers, to be lighter than the *drachma Attica*, and therefore, to speak strictly and precisely, cannot be equal to it in the *intrinseck*. But again, if we look upon the *extrinseck* of the *drachma Attica* and *denarius Consularis*, that having the stamp of *Athens*, and this of *Rome*, here reason must be our balance, and not

not the *trutina*. For the *Athenian* coin being a foreigner, and not current in *Italy*, in the way of exchange and commerce will lose of its primitive valuation it had at *Athens*, and, for want of the *extrinseck* of the *Roman* stamp, necessarily rebate in the *intrinseck*. And therefore both *Greeks* and *Romans*, writing in *Italy*, might truly say, that the *denarius Consularis* and *drachma Attica* were equal, that is, speaking in *civil commerce* and *popular estimation*; although they were unequal in the *intrinseck* and *natural valuation*.

But if we shall change the scene, and carry the *denarius Consularis* to *Athens*, the case will be quite altered. For the *denarius* being a stranger, and the *drachma Attica* a denizon, that cannot have the same privileges with this. And therefore the *extrinseck* of the *denarius* being there of no use, and the *intrinseck* in respect of weight falling short of the *drachma*, it must necessarily be much less in valuation at *Athens* than the *drachma*: and I think no advised *Athenian*, writing in *Attica*, would make them equal; I am certain, no *nummularius* would.

The same may be said of the *Hebrew shekel* and *Attick tetradrachme*, and of all other coins of distinct states, mentioned in
classical

the Valuations of COINS.

classical authors. Thus *Philo* and *Josephus*, in *Judea*, both truly equal the *shekel* to the *Attick tetradrachme*, that is, in way of commerce; though the *shekel* be unequal, and less than the *tetradrachme* (as I have found by examining many of them) in a just notion of weight. The reason is evident by what hath been expressed before: for in *Judea* the *extrinseck* makes amends for what the *shekel* wants in the *intrinseck*; and on the contrary, what the *tetradrachme* exceeds in the *intrinseck* is diminished for want of the *extrinseck*, till at length in a popular estimation they come to be equal. But the quite contrary would happen in the transportation of the *shekels* from *Jerusalem* to *Athens*. Here the *shekel* would necessarily fall from its primitive valuation; and the *tetradrachme* being considered now no longer as a foreigner, would recover what it lost in *Judæa*, and consequently rise above the *Hebrew shekel*, as having a double advantage, in the *extrinseck* from the state, and in the *intrinseck* from its weight.

But what need we go so far for examples, when, as we instanced before, we have them nearer home? The *Spanish* quarters of the *dollar*, or *double rials*, pass ordinarily in our sea-towns but for *shillings*, (whereas they are worth in the *intrinseck* thirteen pence farthing) and our *shillings* pass in *Spain* scarce for a *rial* and an half. For theirs wanting in *England* our *extrinseck*, and ours in *Spain* wanting their *extrinseck*, must respectively rise and fall in their valuation.

The END *of this Discourse.*

www.ingramcontent.com/pod-product-compliance
Ingram Content Group UK Ltd.
Pitfield, Milton Keynes, MK11 3LW, UK
UKHW022322190325
456501UK00006B/53

DIOCLETIANVS. P. F. AVG	IOVI. CONSERVAT. AVGG ——	77½
—— MAXIMIANVS.	VIRTVS. MILITVM. T ——	74¼
CONSTANTINVS. MAX. AVG.	SECVRITAS. REIPVBLICAE —— *infra,* TR	70½
CONSTANTINVS. P. F. AVG.	VIRTVS. AVGVSTI. N ——	68
CONSTANTIVS	GLORIA. REIPVBLICAE. VOT. XXX. MVLTIS. XXXX. *infr.* SNNS	70
IM. CAE. MAGNENTIVS. AVG	VICTORIA. AVG. LIB. ROMANOR. *infra,* TR	70¾
FL. CL. IVLIANVS. P. F. AVG	VOT. X. MVLT. XX. *infra,* ANT. ——	68¼
D. N. IOVIANVS. P. F. PERP. AVG.	SECVRITAS. REIPVBLICAE —— VOT. V. MVLT. X. *infra,* COS. P	68
D. N. VALENS. P. F. AVG	RESTITVTOR. REIP. *infra,* ANTO ——	68¼
D. N. VALENTINIANVS. P. F. AVG	RESTITVTOR. REIPVBLICAE ——	69½
A second —— ——		69
D. N. GRATIANVS. P. F. AVG	VICTORIA. AVGG. *infra,* TROES.	69
A second ——		68¾
D. N. THEODOSIVS. P. F. AVG	VICTORIA. AVGG. *infra,* CON ——	68
A second ——		69¼
D. N. ARCADIVS. P. F. AVG	NOVA. SPES. REIPVBLICAE —— *intra corollam.* XX. XXX. *infra,* CONOB	67½
A second ——		68
D. N. HONORIVS. P. F. AVG	VICTORIA. AVGGG. *statua, cui inscript* R. V. *infra,* CONOB	69¼
A second —— *A third,* D. N. HONORIVS. P. F. AVG	VICTORIA. AVGG. N. D. *infra,* CONOB D. N.	69¾ 68¾

Of the Denarius.

The Weight of some of the fairest Aurei *of the* Roman *Emperors, from* Nerva *to* Heraclius.

On the fore part of the Aurei are these characters.	On the reverse these.	Engl. gra.
IMP. NERVA. CAES. AVG. P. M. TR. P. II. Cos. IIII. P. P.	FIDES. EXERCITVS ———	111½
IMP. TRAIANVS. AVG. GER. DAC. P. M. TR. P. COS. VI. P.P.	DIVVS. PATER. TRAIANI ———	110½
IMP. CAESAR. TRAIAN. HADRIANVS. AVG.	COS. II. P. M. TR. P. P. AVG ———	121¼
ANTONINVS. AVG. PIVS. P.P. TR. P. XII.	COS. IIII ———	119⅝
ANTONINVS. AVG. ARMENIACVS	P. M. TR. P XVIII. IMP. II. COS. III. *In scuto Victoriæ.* VIC. AVG ———	118⅞
IMP. CAES. L. AVREL. VERVS. AVG	CONCORDIÆ. AVGVSTOR —— TR. P. II. COS. II	117¼
L. VERVS. AVG. ARM. PARTHI. MAX	TR. P. V. IMP. III. COS II ———	113¼
M. COMM. ANT. P. FEL. AVG. P. P	IOVI. VLTORI ———	114
SEVER. P. AVG. P. M. TR. P. X. COS. III	FELICITAS. SAECVLI ———	11 ⅞
IMP. M. ANT. GORDIANVS. AFR. AVG	CAESAR. M. ANT. GORDIANVS. AFR. AVG ———	114
* *Trebonianus Gallus*	P. M. TR. P. IIII. COS. II. P.P ———	75¼
* *Gallienus*	P. M. TR. P. III. COS. P. P ———	74¼
IMP. PROBVS. P. F. AVG	VICTORIOSO. SEMPER ———	106
IMP. C. CARINVS. P. F. AVG	SPES. AVGG ———	72¾

Of the DENARIUS. 325

(*i*) *in* LXXII. *solidos libra feratur accepta.* The same thing is implicitly confirmed by *Isidorus (l. 16. Orig. c. 24.) Solidus alio nomine sextula dicitur; quod iis sex uncia compleatur. Hunc, ut diximus, vulgus aureum solidum vocat; cujus tertiam partem ideo dixerunt tremissem, quod solidum faciat ter missus.* Where (*k*) *Agricola*, I imagine, truly finds fault with him for calling the *solidus sextula*; though the proportion he assigns is right, that is, that the *solidus* was the sixth part of the *Roman* ounce, and contained ἑξαγίȣ ςαθμὸν, *the weight of the sextula*, as it is attested by (*l*) *Zonaras*; or, which is all one, that seventy two *solidi* were made out of a *Roman* pound, as *Justinian* before expressly assigned; and as infinite store of the *solidi*, or *aurei*, from *Constantine*

(*i*) This excellent place very hardly escaped *Haloander*'s emendation, who had a great mind to have play'd the critick, and to have altered it. For he thus writes: *In vetusto codice in rasam membranam hæc ita reposita sunt, ut certum sit alteram, & fortasse genuinam lectionem sublatam, & legendum, duodequinquaginta, aut certe quinquaginta.* A goodly consequence! because the parchment was scraped, and the first writing altered, therefore the true reading must be expunged, and a false one put in: whereas he might with more candour and ingenuity have concluded the contrary, that the false one was expunged by the scribe, and the true one inserted. For who uses in copying of MSS. to scrape any thing out of the *apographum*, but only when by collating it he finds it to be different from the original?

(*k*) Agricola l. 2. de Pond. & Temperat. Monetarum.
(*l*) Zonar. l. 3.

to *Focas*, which I have weighed, manifestly prove.

In the same place of (*m*) *Isidorus* we may collect the reason why the *aureus* was called *solidus*. After that the *semisses* and *trimisses aurei* were coined, the *aureus* was called *solidus*, because nothing was wanting to it: *Solidum enim antiqui integrum dicebant, & totum.* In which sense the *solidus* was also taken for the *libra* or *assis*; that is, as the *assis* is taken for the whole, according to that usual phrase of Civilians, *ex asse hæres*, when one is heir to the whole inheritance; so the *solidus* was taken for the whole *assis*. (*n*) *Volusius Metianus: Prima divisio solidi, id est libræ, quod as vocatur, in duas partes dimidias deducitur.* From hence (saith (*o*) *Salmasius*) the Romans called that the solidus aureus, *when it had the same weight in gold, which the* solidus, *that is, the* assis *had in respect of brass, that is, two* drachmes. Though I rather suppose, that the *aureus* was called *solidus* first of all in *Severus*'s time, not for containing two *denarii* in weight (which *Salmasius* calls *drachmes*) for so it always did under the later Consuls

---

(*m*) Isidorus l. 16. Orig. c. 24.
(*n*) Vol. Metianus de Assis distrib.
(*o*) Hinc & solidum aureum dixere Romani, ubi idem pondus habere cœpit in auro quod solidus, id est, as, haberet in ære, duarum nempe drachmarum. *Salmas. de modo Usur.* c. vi. p. 258.

Of the DENARIUS. 327

and first Emperors; but because the *aureus* was then first divided into two parts, that is, into the *semisses* and *tremisses*, and so relatively to these the whole *aureus* was rightly called *solidus*. Of the same opinion is *(p) Agricola: Quos aureos, cùm respectum ad semisses & tremisses haberent, tunc primò dixerunt solidos, quòd semisses ex dimidiâ eorum parte, tremisses ex tertiâ constarent.*

The *semisses* and *tremisses* of the other Emperors, at some distance after *Severus*, came to be less in the same proportion as the *aurei* were lessened. For the *aurei* of *Severus* were double to the *denarii Cæsarei*, and therefore but forty-eight in the pound, and not fifty, as *Heliogabalus* made, whose error *Severus* corrected. But when the later Emperors made seventy-two *aurei* out of the *Roman* pound, the *semisses* came also to be diminished, and were half of these new *aurei*, and not of the former, and the *tremisses* the third part. And here the *aurei* lost that proportion which they kept before, of being double to the *denarii*. Of these *tremisses* is *Justinian* to be understood, *L. FORTISS. MILITIBVS. COD. DE MILITARI VESTE: Fortissimis militibus nostris per Illyricum non binos tremisses pro singulis clamydibus, sed singulos solidos dari*

(p) Agricola l. 2. de Pond. & Temp. Monetarum.

præcipimus. And this may be farther proved by a fair (*q*) *tremissis* in gold of mine own of *Justinian*, with the inscription D. N. JUSTINIANUS, weighing twenty-one grains *English*, and therefore wanting only three grains and one third, which it may have lost by time; otherwise it would be exactly the 216th part of the *Roman* pound, that is, the third part of the *aureus* or *solidus* of those times: whereas if it had been coined to the proportion of the *aureus* when there were 48 in the pound, it should have weighed 36 grains and an half; so that it must have lost 15 and an half, a difference so great in a piece of gold so fair, and withall of so small a quantity, altogether improbable. And therefore this coin alone, if no more were extant, would confute their opinion, who maintain that the *tremissis* of *Justinian* differed not from the *tremissis* of *Severus*, and consequently the *aurei* of them both, better than the reasons produced by (*r*) *Covarruvias* to the contrary have done.

(*q*) I have since perused another *tremissis* in gold, a very fair one, with this inscription, D. N. JUSTINUS. P. F. AUG. weighing twenty-two grains, and better, which formerly belonged to the learned Geographer *Ortelius*; besides a third of *Majorianus*, with CONOB. superscribed (which signifies *Constantinopolitanum obrixum*, or *Constantinopoli obsignatum*) weighing likewise twenty-two grains; and a fourth, of *Justinian*, weighing twenty-three.

(*r*) *Covarruvias* tom. 1. c. 3. paragr. 1. & 2. de vet. aureis & argenteis nummis.